CHARLES LEOCHA AND WILLIAM WALKER

SKI
EUROPE

WINTER 1990

A comprehensive guide to
skiing Europe's best resorts

World-Leisure Corporation

Boston, Ma   Hampstead, NH

Send mail to:
World-Leisure Corporation
P.O. Box 160
Hampstead, NH 03841

Cover design by Jackie Schuman, New York

Illustrated country maps by Charles Kaufman

Printed in the United States of America

Distributed to the trade in USA, by
National Book Netwook, Lanham, MD
Tel. (212) 727-0190 for NY sales office or (301) 459-8696 in Maryland.

Distributed to the trade in Canada by Book Center, Inc., Montreal, Quebec,
Canada; tel. (514) 332-4154.

Distributed to the trade in Europe by
Roger Lascelles, 47 York Road, Brentford, Middlesex TW8 0QP
Tel. 01-847 0935.

Distributed to U.S. Military, Stars & Stripes Bookstores, Mail Order and
Special Sales by
World Leisure Corporation, 177 Paris Street, Boston, MA 02128
Tel. (617) 569-1966.

Library of Congress Card Catalog Number: 87-050899

ISBN: 0-915009-9-11-0 Ski Europe

CONTENTS

Ski Europe

New powder, a packed piste, moguls and bumps, a steep and narrow run, lunch at a tiny mountain restaurant amid the sun, the clouds, the sudden shadows . . .

Then, a soothing sauna, a dip in the pool, a leisurely meal with a fine wine, a moonlight sleigh ride, a fireside interlude in a cozy lodge, or dancing at a disco . . .

Or, a full day of strolling, shopping and sightseeing as you wander through Venice, Milan, Zurich, Munich or Salzburg . . .

This is not a dream. This is the reality of a ski vacation in Europe, one that can actually be less expensive than a similar vacation to U. S. resorts. That's because there are two major factors to be considered in the cost of a ski vacation: getting there and back, and staying alive in the manner to which you've become accustomed. More on this later.

Why Europe?

Until now, skiing in Europe has been considered a dream vacation—extremely expensive and difficult to arrange. That is all changing. Airfares, which have been dropping, are at their lowest during the winter months. European ski resorts have also benefited from the same tourist realities that make Italy and France great inexpensive summer vacation destinations, as well as some of the least expensive summer vacation destinations, as well as some of the least expensive winter destinations. Austria and Switzerland, which may seem like expensive destinations, have organized their respective skiing industries in order to transform their resorts into vacation bargains.

Time factors

One of the major obstacles to skiing in Europe you'll hear about during any discussion is time: "I don't want to spend all my vacation time traveling. I want to ski." In fact, though, it takes only slightly more time to reach a European ski resort than to reach many resorts closer to home.

Consider the average urban skier, who needs about seven hours or more to reach a major ski resort. If you take a closer look, the air and land transporation to a ski resort in the western United States from the East Coast can add up to seven hours. Even a drive from Philadelphia or New York to prime New England resorts can take seven hours or more. Traveling to Europe takes about the same time and, normally, it takes only another two hours or so to reach its skiing areas.

Cost factors

As was mentioned, there are two major factors that affect the overall cost of a ski vacation. The first is transportation, the cost of getting to the slopes from where you live. Second are the costs of getting onto the slopes and of keeping yourself alive in whatever manner you're used to. These include hotels, meals, lift tickets and other goodies.

Minor costs are those related to child-care services, buying ski fashions, evening entertainment and so on.

For a European ski vacation, the transportation cost factor will be the largest. And, while it normally costs more to travel to a European ski area than to a U. S. destination, once you have arrived at the European resort the second cost factor becomes much more important. The differences in hotel, meal and lift pass prices are phenomenal. Cheaper by far than U. S. prices, they more than make up for the increased transportation costs. Even the minor costs are much less in Europe than in the U. S.

A skier traveling to Europe from an East Coast city in the U. S. will actually save money on a one-week vacation. Similarly, a skier traveling to Europe from the West Coast will save money on any European ski vacation lasting two weeks or more.

Ski Europe

This book will help you get the best value for your money while skiing in Europe. Explained are the best times to ski in Europe, and which months guarantee the lowest hotel prices and smallest crowds on the slopes. Also provided are tips based on certain institutional facts that color the European skiing scene, which can be taken advantage of in order to get more for your money. What we mean by "more" is more time on the slopes, more time with instructors, a more spacious hotel room, better meals at restaurants and bargains in getting to Europe and getting around in the mountains.

What's new with this edition

This edition has been expanded to include the best hotels in each resort—or at least what we consider the best, middle of the road accommodations and the budget pensions. We also have listed the best restaurants—both high-priced and high-cuisine, as well as restaurants with those very affordable, traditional good-value meals. If you are going to ski in Europe and plan to shoot the works, take this book along. It will show you just where to aim your spending. Or, if you are traveling with a family and looking for ways to stretch your budget, this book will tell you when to travel for the maximum savings and includes information on apartments which allow real savings and on daycare facilities which allow real freedom to ski.

A disclaimer on pricing

The prices in this book were, to the best of our abilities, accurate as of press time; however, this means that, in most cases, the actual prices you will be reading are from the 1988/1989 ski season. The intention is to provide the best possible information for your planning purposes. At the beginning of each country section a price increase factor based on late reports from Europe will be included to let you know approximately how much the prices have increased during the past year. In general Switzerland and Austria's prices are expected to either remain the same or increase by only three to five percent. Italy

No hotel, restaurant or ski resort has paid to be included in this book. The recommendations have been made based on personal visits to each of the resorts mentioned and discussions with year-long residents in the resorts.

Help us do a better job

The research for this book has been ongoing for the past decade. We both spent every available weekend and vacation exploring new resorts or returned repeatedly to our favorites. Each ski season we return to update material, plus we visit new resorts in order to continue to expand the resort coverage.

If you find a new restaurant, hotel, bar, or disco, please write to us. Or if you find something in the book which is inaccurate, misleading, or has changed, please let us know. If we use your suggestion, we will include your name as the source and will send you a copy of the new Ski Europe. Send suggestions to: World-Leisure Corporation, Attn: Ski Europe, PO Box 160, Hampstead, NH 03841, U.S.A.

High vs. Low Season

The ski season in Europe seems to follow the relatively institutionalized vacation cycles of the Europeans more closely than the cycle of snow conditions. There are normally three seasons in the lexicon of resort operators: the super-high season (holiday period) during Christmas, New Year and Easter; the normal high season, which falls between the first weekend in February and the end of March; and the low season, which includes December, until the weekend before Christmas, the period between the weekend after New Year's Day and the first weekend of February and April.

While the reason for having a category of super-high holiday prices is obvious, increased rates for the February/March high season seem less obviously justifiable. This "high season" was developed to coincide with the school spring vacation breaks, which normally occur in February. This is the month when families can take a vacation together. It also means that the slopes are covered with more children than usual, even changing in character to become open ski classrooms as thousands of budding downhill racers zip fearlessly down every run.

Do everything possible to avoid planning your ski vacation around the holiday and high-season periods.

Low season, on the other hand, teems with bargains. Low season means nearly empty slopes during midweek, short lift lines with almost no waiting and hotel and restaurant services at their best. And low season, especially in high-altitude centers during January, offers some of the best snow conditions. In addition, in mid-March through April, beautiful, mild spring skiing is possible. Early December is often a period of good skiing, and prices are normally their low-season lowest, but snow conditions can be spotty. You should check with the resorts for the latest snow conditions before you go. High-altitude resorts, which offer summer skiing, are always guaranteed to have snow, especially those with glaciers.

How different are the prices?

Low-season discounts are not just promotional hype; prices really are different. In most areas, for example, ski school prices are 20 percent lower during low season. Lift ticket prices decrease by almost 20 percent as well.

In contrast, hotels and pensiones levy dramatic increases when they swing into high season. For example, a hotel package that costs 420 Swiss francs (SFR) may cost SFR 469 in February and SFR 560 during the holiday season. That amounts to a 33 percent increase in price between low and super-high season. One Swiss hotel we looked at had prices that differed by 44 percent between low and high season. It's the same story in Italy, France, Austria and Germany; the bottom line is you'll save a lot by planning your ski vacation during low season.

"White-week" packages

Every resort offers some form of "white week." This is a specially priced ski package that includes full or half pension based on a one-week stay. The costs of lift tickets and ski school are often included in the package price. If not, special prices are typically in effect, and these can be combined with the hotel's white-week package. At some resorts, these packages may also include free entrance to a public pool, sauna and ice skating rink.

White weeks are called *semaines blanches* in French; in German, they are *Weisse Wochen*; and in Italy they are referred to as *settimani bianchi*.

We've used white-week prices throughout this book, since they represent the least expensive way to ski. In addition, we've outlined exactly what is included in the prices given for each resort.

An example of the savings available during a white week in Switzerland is a program offered by the Hotel Schweizerhof, a four-star hotel in St. Moritz. There, the normal weekly low-season rate is SFR 980 (about $650). That rate is for a room with half pension only. With ski lessons and lift tickets added, the weekly price is SFR 1,332 ($888). The rate for the special white-week package—including a ski pass, lessons, races and torchlight skiing—is only SFR 885 (about $590) during December before Christmas; and only SFR 1,070 (about $713) in January. This represents a bargain that is repeated regularly throughout the European ski resorts.

At France's famous resort, Val D'Isère, the white week is organized into a series of formulas based on the package desired, hotel classification and meal plan. These plans are only available during the low seasons. Accommodations at a three-star hotel with bath, including half pension, ski pass, pool entrance, plus a special ski insurance package, will cost only 2,790 French francs (FFR) (about $465).

The same package but with bed-and-breakfast will cost FFR 2,190 (about $365) in the same hotel. A two-star hotel offers a similar package, including half pension, for FFR 2,415 ($402). The same three-star hotel arrangements if purchased separately could cost well over FFR 3,575 ($595), again showing that by advantage of the *semaines blanches* you can save more than 20 percent.

Tignes, a resort just down the valley from Val D'Isère, shares the same lift system and slopes. One white-week package in Tignes requires staying in an apartment. No meals are included, but a six-day ski pass is part of the package, which starts at FFR 1,230 ($205) just before Christmas. That comes to about $30 a day.

Thanks to the concept of low season and white-week packages, Europe can still be a skier's bargain paradise.

Getting To and Around Europe

As we mentioned earlier, the most expensive part of a European ski vacation is transportion. Getting across the Atlantic, then getting to the resort is simple enough, but doing your homework so you'll get the best deal can be a bit complicated. A travel agent can help out with the specifics, but if you are a do-it-yourselfer, remember that there are tradeoffs between cost and convenience. In short, you want to go to Europe to ski and see as much as possible; you don't want to spend seemingly endless hours in bus and train stations waiting for connections to remote mountain valleys.

Obviously, the major cost to be borne is in getting yourself from the United Stares to Europe. Indeed, while the trip to Aspen, Colorado, from New York City constitutes about 37 percent of a week's ski vacation budget, the transportation segment of a typical European ski vacation to Austria represents almost 60 percent of your total costs.

Trans-Atlantic air travel is also where a clever traveler can save the most money and an unwary sojourner can end up spending far more than necessary. Even the transfer from the airport to the resort can add up to significant costs in both time and money if you don't plan ahead.

Across the Atlantic

Airfares charged for crossing the Atlantic have been at all-time lows for several years. There is more capacity and more service from almost every area of the country, which makes getting to Europe more convenient, easier and less expensive than ever. And, of course, winter air travel works to a skier's advantage, because prices are often between 40 percent and 50 percent lower than during the peak summer months.

A travel agent can be extremely helpful during this phase. But supplement his information by doing some investigating on your own. Airline fare structures are complicated and seemingly change daily—even with scheduled airlines. And when charters and group tour flights are included, the options can become phenomenally complex.

Tell the travel agent exactly what you are looking for and explain what you think you should have to pay based on ads in papers and brochures you have read. The agent will either confirm your opinions or let you know what has changed since you last received information. Try to find an agent who will guarantee the lowest possible fare. These agents often will let you know exactly what is available and you can make a decision, even if it's to take a more expensive flight based on convenience or better connections. There is no additional cost for using a travel agent; you can only save both time and money by working through a good one.

You have three basic choices available for trans-Atlantic air travel:

Scheduled airlines —There are many advantages in taking a scheduled airline. For one, the airline must adhere to its general schedule. If there is a problem with the aircraft, passengers are normally transferred to a flight on another airline. In emergencies, a scheduled airline offers flexibility with additional flights and interline connections.

Another aspect of the flexibility offered by scheduled airlines is the ability to land in one city and leave from another. Called "open jaw" in travel jargon, this type of ticket allows you to land in Milan, ski the Italian side of the Matterhorn for a week, then head to Austria for the second week and fly home from Munich. You can also arrange limited stopovers for an additional charge, depending on your ticket, making it easy to squeeze in a few days in Paris or London on your way to the slopes or back home.

It helps to plan your trip as far in advance as possible. You may have to book—and pay—in advance by as much as a month in order to get special air fares that approach the lowest charter airline fares. Arrival and departure dates must be set in advance and any changes may result in additional charges.

Charter flights —These flights are money-savers and in some cases offer excellent connections for skiers. Special flights organized for ski vacations often land at airports much closer to the slopes than any scheduled airline. For example, the charters for many of the French resorts land in Lyons or Geneva, both of which are much closer to the mountains than Paris. This eliminates a significant amount of transfer time. These special ski charters are often sold with transfers to the slopes, which can also help avoid delays and hassles.

There are some problems with charters. Often you are only guaranteed the flight date rather than a time. The charters also reserve the right to reschedule your flight, cancel it and add fuel charges.

Your best protection is to fly with a charter airline that has been in business for some time, one with which your travel agent is familiar.

Try to get some form of flight cancellation insurance, in case you don't leave on the date requested, and also get additional medical insurance to cover the cost of an emergency trip home in case of an accident.

Package Tours —Package tours combine air travel, ground transfers and hotels. Make sure you understand exactly what you are getting in the package. The rates are normally very competitive; however, be sure to compare different programs. Seemingly identical packages, offering the same hotels, transfers, meals and dates can sometimes differ by more than 40 percent in price. One tour we checked out cost $468, while an identical tour offered by another operator cost only $325.

Depending on currency fluctuations, package tours can either be big bargains or end up costing you more than do-it-yourself arrangements. Since many tour operators guarantee their rates for the entire season, they gamble on the currency rate changes. If European currencies continue to drop against the U. S. dollar, the package tours, which are priced in dollars, will be less of a bargain as the ski season progresses. In this case, you would do better flying to Europe and making your arrangements directly at the resort. On the other hand, if European currencies strengthen against the dollar, the package tour could become a better bargain for the skier. Prices in this book are given in European currencies, so it should be relatively easy to judge whether the package is a better bargain than doing it yourself.

Dealing with jet lag

The most unwelcome traveling companion on an overseas ski vacation is jet lag. While there are no cures, following the time-tested suggestions below may help ease you into the European time zone.

—Go to bed early and wake up earlier for three or four days before traveling to Europe. This will allow your body to get a gradual head start in adjusting to European time. At 9 p.m. on the U. S. East Coast, it is 3 a.m. in Western Europe. If you can go to bed between 9 p.m. and 10 p.m. for a few days before your trip, you will only have to overcome about three hours of jet lag rather than six all at once.

—Try to sleep as much as possible on the plane. Many people take sleep aids and ask flight attendants not to disturb them for meals or drinks. If you have a sleep mask, use it.

—Drink as little alcohol and eat as little as possible during the flight; drink plenty of water, however, because the air in the cabin is very dry.

—When you arrive at the resort, take about a two-hour nap during the afternoon or early evening. Make sure to get yourself up, then go out and explore the town, returning to sleep at about 11 p.m. or midnight.

Car rental

For the independent skier who wants to get the most out of a European ski vacation, a rental car offers the most flexibility and is a bargain—especially when two skiers share expenses. Rental cars can be picked up directly at the airport upon arrival in Europe. Aside from making getting to the ski resort a breeze, a rental car gives you the freedom to explore the area around the resort or take a short side trip when ski conditions aren't perfect or when you just want a break from skiing.

The driver of the car usually must be 21 years old and must have a valid driver's license that has been in effect for at least one year. It is not necessary to have an international driving license; your home state license is acceptable.

If you make reservations seven days in advance of your arrival with any of the major car rental companies, you will qualify for special European vacation rates. These rates normally run about $200 a week, excluding taxes. This means that two people sharing a car can expect to pay a little more than $100 apiece for transfers to the resort and more freedom during their stay.

Depending on where you pick up the car, you will have to pay an additional value-added tax (VAT), which is significant. Current VATS are:

Germany	14 percent
Italy	19 percent
France	28 percent
Austria	21 percent
Spain	12 percent
Switzerland	none

As an example of how VAT can affect the total rental cost, consider a car that lists for $200 a week. Renting it will end up costing:

in Germany	$228
in Italy	$238

in France	$256
in Austria	$242
in Switzerland	$200

Of course, actual rental rates in all these countries will be different. The point is that to rent your car in the most advantageous country, you must consider the VAT and drop-off charges if you plan on picking the car up in one country and dropping it off in another. Generally, there are no drop-off charges if the car is returned in the country where it was picked up. The best rental car deals in the Alps are in Germany.

We called Avis, which has locations near almost all the ski areas of Europe. The prices for a category B car, including taxes and based on the exchange rate in June 1989, the time of our conversation were: in Germany—$214; in Italy—$240; in France—$277; in Austria—$305; in Switzerland—$191; and in Spain—$187.

When you make reservations, be sure to tell the reservation agent that you will require a ski rack and chains. Both are usually provided free when ordered in advance. When you pick up the car, the ski rack will be easy to see, but you'll have to check closer for the the chains. Make sure also that they are the correct size chains for your car. You are the one who will be putting the blasted things on, so you should have a great interest in making sure they are the right size. Check the number on the box carefully against the size of the tires. There is nothing more disconcerting than finding out that the chains are one size too small when you are stuck only a few hundred meters from the top of a pass.

Taking the train

There are good train transfers from Munich to Garmisch and to Austrian resorts; from Zurich and Geneva to most of the Swiss resorts; and from Milan to some of the Italian resorts. The major problem with rail travel is the hassle of dragging equipment on and off the train, compounded by the usual need to change trains at least once during a trip to an out-of-the-way resort. The Swiss rail system is the only one that has established a workable luggage transportation system. Baggage can be checked in at the train station at Geneva or Zurich airport and then delivered to your resort. The system works in reverse with the luggage actually checked through to your final destination—New York, London or anywhere. Cost for the service is SFR 9 per piece of luggage.

We recommend to avoid taking trains. Four people sharing a

car always save money over taking a train and, in many cases, two people can save money, or they will find the difference to be so small that car rental is the way to go.

The Eurailpass and other national train passes are not much good for a ski vacation. It is better to merely purchase a second-class ticket to the resort; remember, since you are going in order to ski, you will not be traveling by train enough to justify buying a long-term pass.

By bus

For many resorts, taking a bus is the only way to arrive if you choose not to rent a car. The bus system in the mountains is excellent. Most scheduled trans-Atlantic carriers offer connecting services with the major resorts as well. The carrier will inform you of the departure time and the travel time to reach the resort. Charter flights for ski tours are normally tied in with transportation to the resorts. Check before you go.

Accommodation and meals

Where you sleep, live and eat constitute the most expensive parts of your stay at a European ski resort. While the slopes are a common denominator, lodging and meals vary widely, not only with the type of hotel or restaurant but with the season as well.

Choosing a hotel

If you arrive in a resort without reservations, plan ample time to select a hotel. This means arriving a little earlier and taking about a half hour to check out what the room situation is like.

The local tourist office will steer you in the right direction and will tell you which hotels have rooms available. Ask for three or four recommendations, then check out the rooms in person. When traveling during low season—January or April—do not let yourself be pressured into taking a room you don't want; in most cases, there are plenty available.

Many times rates at hotels and pensiones vary significantly even within the same categories. When you have decided where you want to stay, there are several other factors that will affect the price of your room. You'll have to decide whether to take full or half board or only breakfast (see below). Make sure to ask if any reductions are available. You may get a special rate by staying a full week or by staying through Friday night and leaving on Saturday, the day most ski weeks turn over.

Ask for half pension or breakfast only and compare prices; make sure that you understand exactly what the room rate includes. Are the listed prices for the room or are they per person? If you insist on getting clear information in the beginning, it will make your trip much more pleasant.

Country by country

Hotels in different European countries are organized and run by different standards. These standards affect how the hotels are listed and what amenities you can expect within their various categories.

Accommodation in Italy and France is controlled by a government rating system which is too difficult to explain and often seems gory with similar room rates often vary greatly in reality. Some regulations produce confusion, such as a requirement in Italy that in order to be classified as first-class a hotel must have 40 rooms. Thus, some 36-room hotels with fabulous rooms and perfect service are listed as second-class.

Hotels and other accommodations in the mountains are usually far cleaner and the service far superior to what you normally find in the rest of France and Italy.

Switzerland, Austria and Germany are basically no-nonsense countries. The hotels are clean and neat. The visible rating system is based on stars, with the highest rating being a five-star hotel, which means luxury class. The hotels tend to be accurately rated based on price and category.

Yugoslavian and Bulgarian hotels are functional and uninspired, but provide mountains of food and are kept clean.

In general, almost any hotel room with bath is acceptable. Even the two- and three-star hotels are well maintained. Prices, however, are significantly higher in Switzerland, Austria and Germany when compared category by category with Italy or France.

One fact of life in the mountains during the winter season is the requirement to take at least two meals, or half pension (see below), in the hotel where you are staying. During high season this requirement is firm, and some hotels may even insist on full pension. The price is worth it in most cases. In your hotel search, however, ask several locals which hotels or pensiones have the best food. This research should also enter into your decision on where to spend your week in the resort. We will discuss alternatives below.

Season by season

The best season to stay in any resort hotel—and to eat at any restaurant—is low season. This is normally from December 1 through the weekend before Christmas, then again from the weekend after New Year's through the first weekend in February, and again from approximately mid-March through the month of April. The exact dates vary. Be sure to check with your destination resort to see when the low season starts and finishes.

Low season is when the hotels and the resorts are not packed to capacity, so the kitchen and hotel staff have time to provide exceptional service. In addition, the on-site facilities, such as sauna, steam room, pool or exercise room tend to be less crowded.

The realities of low season also allow you to bargain for the room you really want. Let's say you have visited four hotels and you have chosen one you feel offers the best services. You can speak discreetly with the manager and inform him that you would like to stay at his hotel but that the hotel down the road offers a room that is almost the same quality but costs less. Caution: This ploy does not work if you're not telling the truth! In many cases, the manager will offer a special rate on the spot that will match the rate of the other hotel, especially if you plan to stay for a week and he has an empty room.

You win in two ways: you get the hotel room you want and its price is a better bargain.

Such bargaining should only be attempted if you've arrived with no reservations. Be pleasant and smile—it's magic everywhere in the world. During the bargaining session you have a chance to get to know the manager a bit and he will not mind your haggling in the least.

If you have held the room for some time, you are committed to the agreed-upon price. Haggling over a reserved room is considered bad form and will not enhance your stay at the hotel.

Pensiones

Pensiones are usually smaller, family-run affairs that cost significantly less than hotels. The pensione guest is in many cases made to feel a part of the family during his stay.

Some lodgings have a bath and toilet in the room, others have the bath and toilet down the hall or just outside your door. The pensiones recommended in this book have rooms available with private bath and toilet. If you do not mind a semi-private arrangement, you can request that type of room and save even more.

Many pensiones, especially in the mountains, offer full restaurant service and will include all three meals in the price during the ski season. Many require that you take at least half pension (see below) when you stay for a week. It usually is well worth the price.

Bed-and-breakfast (Garni)

These are what the name implies: accommodations that offer room with breakfast only. Normally, you cannot take lunch or dinner there. This means heading out to discover local restaurants.

The bed-and-breakfast arrangement is often the least expensive in a mountain town, other than staying in private homes or apartments. Do not let yourself be fooled by the low price, though. Remember, you will have to pay for your meals in restaurants, which will add significantly to your costs. Although pensiones and hotels may appear to cost more, when meal prices are taken into consideration they may really be a bargain.

Garnis and bed-and-breakfasts do offer several advantages. First, you have a chance to try several different restaurants and different styles of cooking during your stay. Second, you can often save money by eating less. Hotel menus include a full meal with all the trimmings and each is priced expecting you to eat everything on the daily menu. You may only want to eat a plate of spaghetti and be on your way. In other words, you pay only for what you eat.

Full pension, half pension

What exactly do these terms mean?

Full pension means that your hotel will provide breakfast, lunch and dinner during every day of your stay. Many refer to it as full board. For example, if arrive Saturday at noon you will be able to eat lunch (perhaps served at 1 p.m.), then have dinner in the evening. On the last day of your stay you will be able to eat breakfast. Or if you arrived later in the afternoon, say, around 5 p.m., you would have dinner and would be allowed both breakfast and lunch on the day of your departure.

The meals are served during set times in most hotels and pensiones. If you miss the mealtime, the establishment is not required to offer an alternative meal. Some of the better hotels will offer you a meal in a smaller grill restaurant.

When you agree to full pension, ask whether the hotel will offer either a box lunch to take to the slopes or whether they have a coupon arrangement with a restaurant on the slopes. If the hotel does not have such an arrangement, you will be required to return to the hotel for every meal. This can really cut into your skiing time. Or you will have to forgo the meal even though you are paying for it. This could be an important consideration when deciding between hotels.

Half pension means that the hotel will offer breakfast, plus one additional meal, normally dinner, every day of your stay. Often referred to as half board, this is often the best arrangement. You are free to eat what you want and where you want during the day while on the slopes. If you plan to go out on the town to eat at a special restaurant, you will be able to arrange to have lunch at the hotel and leave yourself free to enjoy dinner elsewhere. Basically, you can easily eat every meal for which you are paying.

During high season many hotels require you to take full pension. But during low season you can often get the room at half pension only and, in many cases, with breakfast only.

The basic meal is all that is included in the full- or half-pension price. Any wine, water, extras, changes from the menu, coffee or liqueurs are billed as extra charges. Make sure to ask about them and that you know for what you are paying. If you ask only for a "wine from the region," you may be surprised when you see the price on your bill.

What is breakfast?

Since there is a big difference in what constitutes breakfast in Europe, here is a primer.

In Switzerland, Austria, Germany and Italy's Val Gardena region, breakfast means yogurt, cold cuts, cheese, jams and jellies, butter, rolls and endless coffee or tea. In some hotels, you get boiled eggs and juice—all included in the breakfast with the room.

In France and in most of Italy, breakfast means a basket of rolls, sometimes a few sweetrolls, butter, jam and jelly with coffee and tea. Juice and eggs are almost always extras. Cold cuts, yogurt, cereal and cheese are rarely available.

Staying in apartments or chalets

An alternative to staying in a hotel, pensione or bed-and-breakfast is to choose an apartment or chalet. These are often scattered through the town and offer reasonably priced accommodations.

Apartments are most popular in Switzerland and France. The Italians are now beginning to get their apartment rental arrangements organized, and some resorts, such as Courmayeur and Val Gardena, have several apartment choices.

Apartments come in all sizes. You can rent a studio apartment, which is perfect for a couple, or an apartment for four, five, six or eight persons. The price per person drops considerably as the size of the apartment increases. These are fantastic bargains. The daily price can be as low as $10 to $12 (£6-8) per person if two or more couples share an apartment.

The apartments are normally rented with a fully equipped kitchen, all utensils and a dishwasher. Sheets and pillowcases and a clean-up are sometimes included; other apartments may be rented with the bedding and cleaning services as extra charges. Check also for a utility fee. In some cases it is included; in others, you pay at the end of the stay based on the amount of oil or electricity used.

You can cook your own breakfast and as many meals as you want, which will also save a lot of money. A supermarket is usually nearby or on the ground floor of the apartment building where you are staying. Grocery prices are just about the same as those in any large European city.

If you decide that you would like to stay in an apartment or chalet, contact the tourist office and ask for a listing of the apartments available during the period you plan to visit. The tourist office will send you a list of the apartments. Make your choice and return the material to the tourist office. Some tourist offices will send an apartment listing and you will be required to direct subsequent correspondance to the owners.

If you arrive with no arrangements, the procedure goes like this: the tourist office will make several calls and send you off to see several apartments and to speak with the owners.

As with hotels and pensiones, you can bargain and you should look at a few places to get an idea of what is available. Note the distance to the nearest supermarket, sauna and swimming pool. Check out the distance to the lifts. It is a joy to be able to step outside your door in the morning and immediately start skiing.

The leading apartment/chalet rental firm in the world is Interhome. In some resorts this company virtually controls the apartment rentals. Interhome has offices in Britain as well as representatives in the United States. In the U.K., contact: Interhome Ltd., 383 Richmond Road, Twickenham TW1-2EF; tel. 01-8911294; telex 928539. In the U.S., contact Interhome at 36 Carlos Drive, Fairfield, NJ 07006, Tel. (201) 882-6864; fax. (201) 808-1742.

Staying in a private home

Private homes at many resorts will rent out rooms. These rooms are normally very inexpensive, with prices ranging between those of a bed-and-breakfast and an apartment. If you are traveling alone, a private home is often the best bargain you can get.

Staying in a private home can give you a better feel for the local scene, you pick up hints on the best places to go on the slopes and in town, and, in many cases, you will find yourself treated like a friend of the family.

Once again, start at the local tourist office. It has addresses and phone numbers of the families who rent out rooms. The tourist office often will call and make arrangements. Ask to see several rooms and then make your choice.

In some cases, the room price includes breakfast but the arrangements vary from house to house. Expect to pay between $10 and $20 (£7-14) a night, depending on the resort and time of the season.

Make sure that baths or showers are included in the price; if not, ask for the price and the best time of day to take a bath or shower. Hot water can be at a premium, especially just after the slopes close for the day.

The European ski scene

What should a skier expect when arriving at a European resort? Culture shock aside, there shouldn't be too many surprises because the U. S. ski industry has been modeled to a great extent on the long-established European resorts. But there are some notable differences; this chapter will deal with some of them and offer some tips on how to get more from your ski vacation in Europe.

The weather

A friend had just arrived in Switzerland from New England the week before Christmas and we were getting ready to go skiing. Her preparations for the day amazed me. She began by putting on lots of bulky clothing: sweaters, a jacket and other arctic-expedition-like paraphernalia.

"Whoa," I said. "What are you doing? You want to be able to move on the mountain, don't you?"

"I don't want to be cold," she replied.

"Well, you'll melt if you insist on dressing like that," I said.

After this argument she reluctantly agreed to take off half of the clothing (it wasn't enough) and risked taking my advice to wear only a turtleneck, a sweater and a windbreaker.

The point is this: Skiing in Europe is not a freezing proposition. The weather is very mild in its mountain areas. Even in the coldest sections of the Alps, the winter daytime temperatures hover at around 20 degrees Fahrenheit. Windy days, few and far between, usually herald a coming snowstorm.

What to wear

Try to dress in layers, and because temperatures are relatively mild, you will rarely need more than a ski jacket over a turtleneck shirt. On most days, a turtleneck worn under a light sweater and a windbreaker will be more than enough. Don't underestimate the temperatures, though; they seem to drop rapidly whenever you are sitting in the wind on a long chairlift ride. Europe's heavy use of T-bar and poma lifts will help keep you warmer, although American skiers may swear at having to stay on their feet during the trip up.

Protection from the sun

Europe's resorts are no different than any others when it comes to sun, especially in spring. Sunburn or snow blindness can ruin any vacation, so use sun screen, lip protection, and always wear glasses or goggles. The glasses do not have to be tinted; the glass itself stops harmful ultraviolet rays.

General snow conditions

Snow in Europe is not as dry as snow in Utah or Colorado, due to lower elevations and milder climate. Nor is it as icy as New England snow, thanks to more constant temperatures.

Generally, the slopes are not as carefully groomed as those in the U. S. and relatively consistent snowfall obviates the need for extensive snow-making equipment.

The best snowfall seems to take place in January, making both January and February good months in which to ski. Plan to go in January if you can, though, because February and March are also the most expensive times to ski, except for the Christmas, New Year's and Easter holiday periods. The week before Christmas is normally a pretty good time to go, but chancy.

Spring skiing sees the Alps at their finest and prices are again at low-season levels. An instructor is invaluable during spring skiing, for in his company you will learn the best times to ski different areas as the day progresses and the sun warms the snow. The secret is to get onto the run just before you begin breaking through the crust and then move to the next section of the mountain.

Lift lines

One major difference between skiing in Europe and the United States can be seen in lift-line etiquette. In the U. S., lift lines are relatively orderly: A line for singles is maintained along the far right or left, and most everyone takes pains to avoid stepping on or skiing over another skier's equipment. The result is that you almost never end up jammed together during the move through the lift line.

Not so in Europe. Although the lift lines in various countries on the Continent differ as to the degree of aggressive behavior, in general, they are a free-for-all. Until you reach the point where barriers have been set up to funnel skiers into the lift, there are no controls. He who moves the fastest and shuffles forward the most aggressively is usually the first to get up the lift. While there is a general effort not to blatantly trample over each other's skis, be resigned to the fact that your equipment will be stepped on no matter what you do or how angry you appear to be. Here are some tips to handling lift lines:

—Before you enter the line, see whether it turns to the right; if so, go to the far outside left of the line. If the line turns to the left, go to the extreme right. If you have ever tried to turn a sharp corner with skis on, you will begin to understand the wisdom of this suggestion. There is no mercy shown inside the lift line. Once you are stuck on the inside of a sharp right or left turn within the barriers you are in trouble.

—If the line is relatively straight, make sure to get on its outside edge. You will quickly see that the mass of skiers funnel down the narrow barriers on either side. Those who get caught in the middle get squeezed from both sides and move about half as fast as those on the outside edges of the crowd.

—When faced with a choice between a T-bar or poma lift and a chair or cablecar, pick the faster T-bar or poma. If the distance is great, however, the cablecar or chairlift will get you to the top of the run more quickly, even if getting onto it may mean more waiting time.

—Maintain a sense of humor. You can be sure that it will be tested, especially on weekends.

—The best time to ski and avoid the crowds is during lunchtime. You'll experience clear slopes, shorter lift lines and fewer frustrations. In Italy and France, the lines all but disappear as everyone heads back to the hotels for a big lunch. In Switzerland and Austria the noon-hour difference is not as great.

Etiquette on the slopes

The Austrian Tourist Office lists 10 rules for the slopes, which, although not especially profound, should be followed when skiing in Europe.

1. Keep equipment in good condition.
2. Do not endanger others or destroy property.
3. Ski in control, keeping weather and terrain in mind.
4. It's the uphill skier's responsibility to avoid the skier below him. Give other skiers a good safe margin.
5. After stopping, look around you before starting again.
6. Get up quickly after a fall and do not stop in blind spots on the trails.
7. If you must walk up a slope, keep to the edge of the run.
8. Obey all signs and markers.

9. You are obliged to help injured skiers. Protect them from further risk and get first aid.

10. If you are in a skiing accident, you are required to furnish identification.

Before you go

You really do not need to bring any special documents other than a passport for traveling in Europe. Before you go, take a close look at your health insurance to be certain that you will be covered in case of an accident. Most policies provide worldwide coverage, some are limited in the case of skiing accidents, while others group skiing accidents under the broad category of "accidental injury," which may mean that your deductible will be waived. Know what coverage you have. If you do not have coverage, arrange to buy special ski insurance. Your agent should be able to point you in the right direction.

Several companies, such as Europ Assistance, (tel. 800-821-2828) offer this insurance. In addition, you can purchase ski insurance once you arrive at the resort. Carte Neige in France is easy to purchase at most resorts. Check with the local tourist office for details.

Make a photocopy of your passport pages with your photo and personal information, and write down your passport number. Also, have a photocopy made of your airline tickets and the credit cards you will be taking with you. Make two copies: Keep one with you, separate from your passport, tickets and credit cards, and leave the second copy with a friend or relative.

In case you somehow lose everything, these backup records will be invaluable. The passport copy will help in getting a replacement at an overseas consulate or embassy. The ticket copy may help in getting a replacement and alerts the airline to look for a stolen ticket with that number. The credit card numbers will make reporting stolen cards and limiting your liability much easier.

Credit cards and travelers checks

Most large resorts and full-fledged hotels accept major credit cards, but don't expect the smaller pensiones and hotels to accept them. The normally accepted cards are American Express, Diners Club, Carte Blanche, Visa and MasterCharge (called "Eurocard" in Europe). Some resorts even allow skiers to pay for lift tickets with credit cards but they are few and far between. It is best to come prepared with adequate cash or travelers checks to cover your expenses during your trip. American Express offers the best-known travelers checks, but in this area of Europe almost all are easily exchanged.

The basic rule of changing money at a bank applies at ski resorts—even more so than in most places. The hotels and restaurants that accept travelers checks almost never give you a rate of exchange equal to the one you can get from a bank just around the corner. Plan ahead and save yourself the difference. If you want to change a small amount of money, it is often better to exchange it at your hotel because you normally will not have to pay a minimum exchange fee.

Taking your own equipment

Most airlines will allow you to check your ski equipment onto your flight for no additional charge. However, upon your arrival in Europe, check with personnel in the baggage-arrival area to find out where your equipment can be picked up. Skis are often delivered to a separate area of the baggage section.

Renting equipment

You can also rent all the equipment you'll need at your destination resort. Ski rentals—depending on the quality ski you want—range from about $6 to $15, with discounts for periods of three days or more and weekly rentals running about $33 to $75. It's best to bring your own boots, however, because these are extremely important to your comfort, and rental boots that are consistently comfortable have yet to be found. If you do rent boots, expect to pay between $3 and $8 a day, or about $16 to $37 a week, depending on the quality of the boot.

Buying equipment in Europe

One of the biggest bargains of your trip may be investing in new equipment. Ski equipment in Europe often costs less than identical equipment in the U. S. Depending on what and where you buy, you can recover some of your trip's expenses. Most of the world's ski boots, for example, are manufactured in Montebelluna in northern Italy. Prices for these boots are higher in the U. S. to cover shipping and higher retail overhead. If you plan to ski in the Dolomites, near Cortina d'Ampezzo, Montebelluna is only a short drive away. The expert skier may want to go directly to the factory and have the boots custom-fitted. Brands made in Montebelluna include Dolomite, San Marco, Nordica, Caber, Technica and Munari.

The roster of quality skis manufactured in Austria, Switzerland, Germany, Italy, Yugoslavia and France includes Rossignol, Atomic, Kneissel, Fischer, Vokl, Dynastar, Dynamic, Elan and Maxell.

Italy is a world leader in ski fashion, with designer labels such as Anzi Besson, Belfe and Fila, all available at prices well below those in the U. S.

One quirk worth noting is that unlike retailers in the United States, who place a premium on equipment sold at ski resorts, European resort retailers often find themselves in competition with stores in the bigger cities and are often forced to limit their markups. If you plan to buy ski equipment and clothing in January, or in the spring, keep in mind that at those times much of the equipment is offered at sale prices.

It often pays to make a purchase, such as ski boots, at the resort where you will be skiing. The small premium you pay there is well worth it. The shop owner, for example, can mold the boot to your foot if there is a problem with the fit. This can be done overnight, but if it is going to take longer, the owner will make sure that you have a rental boot for the next day.

Remember, whenever paying for your equipment, always ask how much of a discount is being offered for payment by cash. Frequently the shop owner will discount merchandise by as much as 10 percent. If you wave an American Express card around, the shop owner will almost always make a discount in order to get cash. This is because American Express requires a larger percentage from the retailers than other bank cards, which makes merchants very willing to deal.

Taking photos in the snow

The best souvenirs of any vacation are the pictures you take and bring home to share with friends. What's more, photos help you to remember the good times you had, the places you visited and the people you met.

Standard and automatic cameras, however, do not make it easy to take good photographs on ski slopes. The overall brightness of the snow and bright sky often confuses light meters and automatic exposure systems. Many travelers have returned home with pictures that are washed out and underexposed, or in which the snow looks like a dirty sheet rather than the sparkling whiteness they remembered and hoped to catch on film. Follow these tips in order to get the best results when shooting photographs in the snow.

—Always make sure that the sun is somewhere in front of you

when you take any picture in the snow. This allows you to capture the glistening sunlight and the texture of the snow.

—If shooting into the sun with a manual camera, close down the camera's f-stop to its smallest aperture (highest number). This will cause the sun to appear with a star-like effect.

—With a manual camera, remember that light is being reflected off the snow. In order to make allowances for that, set the camera's f-stop down about two numbers. The best solution is to meter directly off the subject, then take the picture.

—With an automatic camera, either override the automatic feature or select a plus-two f-stop setting if your camera will permit.

—Snow heightens the effects of ultraviolet UV rays. A UV filter helps insure accurate colors. If you are taking black-and-white photos, use a yellow, orange or red filter to heighten contrast.

—Your camera gets cold and so does the film. This means slower speeds unless you keep the camera warm. Try to keep it inside your jacket until ready to shoot.

Meeting the Europeans

Take along a small notebook in which to jot down names and addresses of people you meet at the resorts, or special things that you enjoyed and want to pass on to other friends. Don't be afraid to follow up some of the contacts you make on the slopes or at the resorts. Europeans are usually sincere when they invite you to come and see them. They tend to make the invitation out of sincerity rather than an assumed obligation. If you plan to spend some time in Europe or plan to return there, the people you meet can enhance any trip if you stay in touch. Remember, you add a difference to their lives and are as interesting to them as they are to you. Good friendships often result from such sharing.

Resort locals can also add to your knowledge of the country by recommending special ski runs that may be obscure, by suggesting a good wine or hot drink to enjoy after a day of skiing and by explaining which local specialties you should order in a restaurant or at your hotel.

If you remain open to everyone, you will enjoy your vacation and return far richer than when you left.

Cross-country

All European resorts are not equal as far as cross-country skiing is concerned. Although this book concentrates on the best-known downhill resorts, most have developed good cross-country facilities. Others are adjacent to some of the best cross-country skiing areas in the world.

In this section we have highlighted the cross-country possibilities for most of the resorts we cover in this book. We have also mentioned some other top cross-country areas not listed in the book and provided addresses and phone numbers for more information. Otherwise, use the resort section for hotel, restaurant and other information.

Switzerland

Arosa—The cross-country trails are modest (about 20 miles of prepared trails) but well maintained, and from the beginning of December into April you can count on a variety of trails through the countryside.

Champery—Very limited.

Crans-Montana—There are three main trails with a total of about 24 miles. Your best cross-country adventures will probably be on the nearly seven-mile loop on Plaine-Morte glacier.

Davos—Excellent cross-country trails in classic Alpine scenery. Altogether there are nearly 45 miles of prepared trails with seven main loops kept in top condition. Good choice for the cross-country enthusiast.

Engelberg—Low-rated for the cross-country enthusiast with less than 15 miles of prepared trails. Auto-free Melchsee-Frutt has an additional nine miles of trails.

Flims/Laax—Good cross-country area with a total of nearly 45 miles of double-tracked trails in Flims, Laax and Falera areas. Cross-country adventure treks with guides are offered in this region.

Gstaad—When considered with Saanen and other areas of the Weisse Hochland, cross-country is excellent with nearly 50 miles of trails, guided adventure treks and excellent instruction.

Jungfrau Region—Grindelwald, with about 20 miles of trails is the best in the area. Good instruction is available. Wengen and

Mürren are both very limited. The most beautiful trail is a seven-mile circuit in the Lauterbach valley near Lauterbrunnen.

Klosters—Moderately interesting with nearly 40 miles of tracks split between four prepared trails. Combined with Davos the area is quite extensive and beautiful.

St. Moritz—One of Europe's greatest. A paradise for the true cross-country fan. No one talks long about cross-country skiing without bringing up St. Moritz. This elegant resort has a remarkable network of 75 miles of trails in the immediate area, and there are about 200 miles of cross-country ciruits on the valley floor and frozen lakes in the region. St. Moritz also has a one-mile-long lighted trail for night-skiing fans. The course of the famed Engadiner Ski Marathon race is nearby.

A great place to vacation for the skier who seeks cross-country only and demands great variety.

Saas-Fee—Extremely limited.

Verbier—Has 42 miles of prepared trails, but the connecting network is not exceptional.

Villars—Limited.

Zermatt—Cross-country is only a side pursuit with limited trails totaling only 15 miles.

France

Chamonix—Moderately interesting trails total about 25 miles in the valley. Best if combined with downhill skiing, but not a good cross-country resort on its own.

Megève—Surprisingly good network of trails totaling nearly 45 miles in the Megève-Combloux area. Good variety and some good challenges on endurance.

Flaine—Moderate to mediocre quality network totaling about 20 miles. Go elsewhere if cross-country is first on your mind.

Tignes/Val d'Isere—Poor choice for real cross-country skiers. Only short trails with a total of nine miles of prepared track.

Les Deux Alpes—Below-average offerings with only 12 miles of prepared loops split between 10 trails.

Les Trois Vallées—Above-average network of trails by French resort standards. A total of nearly 50 miles of prepared loops spread over the rolling valley countryside.

The Jura—Europe's greatest cross-country ski adventure is a 120-mile trek across the highlands of the French Jura region, which stretches from Belfort along the Swiss border toward Geneva. Nearly 40 percent of this mountain region is wooded, and the connecting trail, called the GTJ (Grand Traverse du Jura) is a superb run. The trail sections are difficult, ranging from three to 29 kilometers each, as you make your way from Maise, near Belfort, nearly 120 miles to La Pesse, south of St. Claude. There are inns all along the trail.

For details on the Jura trek, write GTJ: Office de Tourisme Regional, Place de la 1e. Armée Française, F-25000 Besancon, France.

For general information on cross-country all-inclusive trips in the Jura, write Accueil Montagnard-Chapelle-de-Bois, F-25240 Mouthe, France; or A.G.A.D.-La Pesse, F-39370 Les Bouchoux, France.

Austria

The Arlberg—If you are only looking for occasional cross-country skiing, this will provide limited alternatives to the downhill religion in this region. The St. Anton/St. Christoph side of the mountain offers the best cross-country. Lech and Zürs are extremely limited.

Badgastein—There's more than enough variety in the Gasteiner valley for cross-country enthusiasts. A total of 55 miles of trails are divided among the resorts. The six trails from Bad Hofgastein offer the most variety. There's an added incentive for cross-country here because anyone who completes 75 kilometers (45 miles) earns a bronze medal. The gold is awarded for 1,000 kilometers (620 miles), but clearly is beyond the reach of one-time vacationers.

Innsbruck—Perhaps the second or third greatest cross-country area in all Europe with over 60 miles of trails in the immediate area of the city. Instruction is excellent. And as an added bonus, the marvelous resort of Seefeld is only a short bus ride away.

Seefeld—Our top choice for all of Europe is Seefeld, which hosted the 1964 and 1976 Olympic cross-country competitions. Nearly 100 miles of cross-country trails are maintained and most of the circuits lead from the Olympic Sport and Convention Center. Accommodations are outstanding and reasonably priced. In addition, an international atmosphere makes foreign visitors feel welcome.

There's a challenging 18-mile circuit, plus 15- and six-mile loops making up the heart of the trails here.

For more information contact—Verkehrsbüro, A-6100 Seefeld; tel. 05212-2313.

Ischgl—Less-than-average network totaling only 12 miles.

Kaiserwinkl—This is a cross-country skiers' paradise in the Austrian Tirol a few miles off the autobahn between Munich and

Innsbruck. The towns of Schwedt, Kössen and Walchsee have combined their trails for nearly 85 miles of Nordic runs. Each town has its own cross-country center and the interconnected circuits branch out from the centers. For information—Fremdenverkehrsverband, Postfach 127, A-6345 Kössen; tel. 05375-6287.

Kitzbühel/Kirchberg—Some of the best cross-country trails in Austria. Great variety and many miles of trails.

Montafon—When all 11 main resorts in the Montafon valley are considered, this is an excellent cross-country area. But you'll need a car to drive to the various areas. No single resort has enough variety for a vacation. Over a dozen trails total about 45 miles.

Schladming—Excellent cross-country trails especially on the Ramsau side of the valley where a wide-open plateau just below the Dachstein glacier offers perfect terrain. Plan to stay in Ramsau, because the other towns are a long trek away from the best cross-country areas.

St. Johann in Tirol—Excellent choice for cross-country vacation. Not as much variety as Innsbruck-Seefeld, but the nearly 74 miles of trails are maintained for the serious skier. Changing rooms, first aid and restaurant facilities are excellent on the loops. Also an excellent choice for the skier who wants to mix downhill with cross-country.

Oetztal—Meager offerings. Less than 10 miles of trails.

Kaprun/Zell am See—One of the best-kept secrets among cross-country devotees. A great network of nearly 72 miles of trails in the area, plus a connection to an additional 40 miles of trails in the neighboring valley. The ski school also has good courses.

Zillertal—Good variety with over 40 miles of track.

Germany

Allgäu—The most challenging network of cross-country trails in Germany is found in this region. The trails branch off from the ski towns of Oberstaufen and Immenstadt. Part of the network includes a great marathon-length, 26.2-mile loop. This area is not covered in this book. Contact the German tourist office for further information.

Garmisch—You'll discover long, exceptionally scenic trails with nearly 37 miles of loops in the Garmisch-Partenkirchen area. Above Garmisch, in the Graswang Valley, there is beautiful cross-country skiing that takes you near Linderhof, perhaps the most beautiful of Ludwig's Bavarian castles.

The Black Forest—Germany's best-known cross-country area. The best circuits are around Titisee and up to the slopes of the

Feldberg, the highest mountain in the region. Altogether there are about 600 miles of trails in the Black Forest with nearly 75 miles of loops near Feldberg. Perhaps the most challenging runs are from Neustadt, where organized cross-country groups kick and glide for nearly 60 miles with planned stops at hotels and guest houses along the way. This region is not covered in detail in this book—contact the tourist board for more information.

Italy

Italy has not developed an extensive cross-country system except in the Madonna di Campiglio area and in parts of the Dolomites.

Pinzolo—Only a few kilometers, or a 20-minute drive, from **Madonna di Campiglio**, Pinzolo is the site of one of cross-country's major 24-mile endurance races. The area near Campo Carlo Magno, in the Madonna di Campiglio area, has an expert cross-country course.

Cortina d'Ampezzo—Good cross-country area with more than 45 miles of prepared trails. A good place to mix downhill with cross-country if you wish. This resort was once the site of the Olympics.

Kronplatz—Few resorts mix the pleasures of cross-country and downhill better than those in Italy's Pustertal. Here in the south Tyrolean region, Kronplatz resorts boast nearly 90 miles of cross-country trails branching out from the central town of Bruneck (*Brunico*, in Italian) below the Kronplatz plateau.

If you come in January, you can take part in the 35-mile-long cross-country race, which begins in Innichen (*San Candido*, in Italian) and ends in Antholz. The shorter 24-mile race course ends at Olang.

Downhill skiers can try out the slopes from the 2,275-meter (7,462-foot) Kronplatz summit.

Not in this book; for more information, contact: Crontour, I-39031, Bruneck; tel. 0474-84544.

Gateways to the Alps

Amsterdam

Amsterdam makes a perfect hub from which to head for any alpine resort. KLM flights connect all the ski resort areas of Europe. In addition, special programs, such as Rhine cruises and rail passes through the Rhine Country, offer alternative travel possibilities to the mountains.

Amsterdam itself has easy connections from the airport to the city and provides sightseeing opportunities to travelers with as little as a four-hour layover. If you have more time, the city is rich with museums, nightlife and charm. A tourist information bureau is located just outside the railway station, and the city is easily explored by tram, bus, metro, tour boats, bicycles and foot.

The "Top 10" of Amsterdam for those on a quick swing through the city are: 1. A canal tour—it's full of great historical background and will provide a good orientation to the city. 2. The Rijksmuseum—packed with Rembrandts and plenty more. 3. Van Gogh Museum—just down the road from the Rijksmuseum and full of, you guessed it, Van Goghs. 4. The Begijnhof—this tiny, hidden courtyard preserves Amsterdam as it used to be. Calm in the center of the bustling city. 5. Anne Frank's House—the house with hidden rooms where Anne Frank lived with her family before being taken to the concentration camp. 6. The Red Light District—once upon a time a "must" for anyone in Amsterdam. It's still interesting, but stick to the main streets and don't do your wandering during the wee hours. 7. Leidseplein and Rembrandtsplein—the open-air café centers of Amsterdam and the heart of the pulsing nightlife. 8. Kalverstraat—the main shopping street and one of the best people-museums in Amsterdam. 9. The Albert Cuyp Market and the Flea Market—great street markets; open every day except Sunday. 10. The Heineken Brewery—take a tour of the most popular brewery in Europe and stop for a sample of the brew after the tour.

Zurich, Switzerland

Skiers striking out for virtually any Swiss ski resort or for resorts in the western part of Austria may find themselves in Zurich for a night or two. You might well expect the Swiss banking capital to present a stuffy commercial face to the world. But the real Zurich is a city that has managed to marry prosperity and progress with old-world tradition.

A good place to start is the **Bahnhofstrasse**, where you'll see a few of those famous Swiss banks and also some of the most exclusive shops—with some of the highest price tags in the country. This is the city's main street, often called the "picture window" of Switzerland.

If you walk the Bahnhofstrasse you'll eventually come to Bürkliplatz and Lake Zurich. Where the Limmat River flows out from the lake, boat tours offer the best views of the city.

On foot, you'll find the most scenic sections of the old town between Bahnhofstrasse and the Limmat. One of the city's major attractions is the **Swiss National Museum**, on the shore of the Limmat adjacent to the main train station. The museum chronicles Swiss civilization from prehistoric times to the present. The collection from the Roman era is particularly good.

The most-visited churches are also within walking distance of the central area. Across the Limmat, the **Grossmünster** 11th-century cathedral is distinguished by its twin towers. The Münster bridge from the cathedral leads to the 12th-century **Frauenmünster Church** with the famed stained-glass windows created this century by Chagall.

A few minutes' walk from the cathedral is Zurich's **Lunsthaus,** a beautiful art museum with an excellent collection of Swiss masters, as well as works by Van Gogh, Cezanne, Renoir, Manet, Degas and Picasso.

If you spend the night in Zurich, head for the **Niederdorf** section of town that stretches along the Limmat, across from the train station. This is where Zurich's citizens ease the stress of world financial responsibilities. Along crowded streets the old-town section of Zurich pulsates with live jazz, smoky bars, packed discos and scores of restaurants. For a more subdued outing, plan to have an elegant dinner in an old guild house.

Geneva, Switzerland

If your skiing plans are in the area of the Valais in Switzerland, any of the French Alps or in the Val d'Aosta in Italy, Geneva is an excellent gateway to Europe.

Geneva is one of Europe's most beautiful lakeside cities, and any tour should begin with a few moments on the **Pont du Mont Blanc,** the Mont Blanc bridge, for a panoramic view of the Alps; in clear weather the outline of Mont Blanc crests on the horizon.

Then a climb up the north tower of St. **Pierre Cathedral** offers a superb view of the city, which is built around the contours of a small section of Lac Leman (Lake Geneva). The interior of the cathedral, built over a period of 300 years beginning in the 10th century, offers a stained-glass illumination of Swiss religious art and architecture.

The attractions in Geneva are spread out, a bus tour may help to get an overall orientation of the city. Later, catch a city bus or a taxi to the places you want to revisit.

The ill-fated League of Nations, founded after World War I, had its headquarters here in the **Palais des Nations**. Today this building serves as the European headquarters for the United Nations. Tours of the building are offered throughout the year.

Geneva's greatest park runs along the lake and combines the Mon Repos, Perle du Lac and Villa Barton—all landscaped park areas that form a beautiful walking range.

The city's best-known museum is the **Art and History Museum,** which features distinguished collections in archeology and decorative arts.

For an offbeat fling, check the **flea market** held on the city's Plaine de Palais Wednesdays and Saturdays.

Frankfurt, West Germany

Although Frankfurt certainly is not in the heart of the Alps, skiers occasionally spend a night or two in the business capital while heading for or returning from an Alpine vacation. That time need not be wasted, for this is a vibrant city with attractions enough to keep anyone entertained.

Frankfurt's accessibility is outstanding—only 15 minutes by train or taxi from the airport. Trains leave approximately every 20 minutes and whisk passengers to the central train station. From there, it's only a short walk or quick taxi ride to any of the tourist attractions. If your time is very limited, take a cab; it allows you to save time waiting for the train. The fare to any of the main tourist sites should be no more than $12-$15.

The **Hauptbahnhof,** or railway station, is an adventure in itself, a genuine slice of pre-war Europe with soaring girders supporting a massive skylight roof that towers above nearly two dozen tracks. Here, stop in and visit the tourist information center where hostesses will orient you to the city and provide maps and brochures.

From the train station the first destination is the **Römerberg,** a square near the Main (pronounced *mine*) River that has been the focus of extensive city renovation efforts in recent years. The gabled facades of the three burghers' houses on the Römer square have come to serve as the symbol of the city and mark the core of the old quarter. Here the Kaisersack, or Imperial Hall, was site of many celebrations when Holy Roman Emperors were crowned in Frankfurt.

This is the district of the **Altstadt,** or old city; although the aerial bombings in World War II destroyed nearly 80 percent of the city, many of the oldest buildings have been restored, including historic St. Bartholomew cathedral, the Nikolai church on the Römerberg and the unique, oval Paul's church across the street.

Close by, for a visitor who wants to do last-minute (or first day) shopping, is the **Zeil,** Frankfurt's most fashionable pedestrian shopping street. The Hauptwache, a square where the main shopping streets Zeil and Rossmarkt meet, reigns as the commercial heart of Frankfurt. Further down the Zeil stands the recontructed **Alte Oper,** the old opera house, which rivals the beauty of pre-war Dresden buildings. In the same area is the **Goethe House** and museum honoring Germany's most famous writer.

For nightlife **Sachsenhausen** is lively and loud. The district across a footbridge on the opposite side of the Main River from the Römerberg area, bustles with pubs and restaurants, and all pour *Applewoi,* a distinctive apple cider.

Munich, Germany

The Bavarian capital is southern Germany's crown jewel, not only lovely but the country's greatest art center. Munich's greatest attraction, however, is that it rivals any other city in Europe for sheer merrymaking, much of it inspired by the formidable one-liter mugs of beer served morning, noon and night. Spend at least an evening in one of the city's great beer halls.

Every visitor should check out **Marienplatz,** the main square. At 11 a.m. daily the dancing figures in the town hall Glockenspiel perform. Nearby is the **Frauenkirche,** or Church of Our Lady. Its 450-year-old, onion-shaped domes topping the church's towers have come to symbolize Munich. The best view of the city is from the 332-foot-high north tower, where on clear days the Bavarian Alps nearly 50 miles away can be seen. For an even higher view, though a bit out of the center of the town, visit the 1972 **Olympic grounds** for an elevator trip up the television tower, which is almost three times higher than the church viewing tower downtown.

Munich's collection of art museums is too extensive to list, but suffice it to say that whatever your interest—paintings, ceramics, sculpture, ethnology—there should be a collection for you. Of special interest is the **Alte Pinakothek**, which houses one of the world's greatest art collections, including rooms full of Rubens and excellent Dürer paintings.

The **Deutsches Museum** features a great technical collection rivaling the Smithsonian and shouldn't be missed. This museum is a fantasy world of pushbutton fun with machines to crawl through and explore, including a WWI submarine. It's a place children never want to leave.

One excursion you may want to take is to **Dachau,** site of the German concentration camp, now preserved as a memorial. It's approximately a 40-minute drive from the center of the city.

If you have an extra day or two in Munich, consider a bus tour to the castles of Ludwig II, the Dream King—some called him mad—of Bavaria. A particularly good tour is called the "Royal Castles Tour," promoted by the Bavarian Tourist Board. The luxury bus trip visits **Neuschwanstein** (inspiration for Disneyland's castle), **Linderhof** and **Herrenchiemsee**, three great castles built by Ludwig, as well as some other residences of the Wittelsbachs, Ludwig's royal family.

Innsbruck, Austria

Innsbruck is the easiest arrival city to visit during a ski vacation because it's already in the Alps. Great skiing is only minutes away and that means you can take time at the end of a day or before you head out in the morning to tour.

Innsbruck—in German, the bridge over the Inn River—has twice hosted the Winter Olympics in the last 25 years (1964 and 1976). The city shares with Grenoble, France, the distinction of being the only two cities in the Alps with more than 100,000 population.

A nice thing about visiting Innsbruck in winter is that skiers are welcome everywhere. In some museums and public buildings in Europe you might get a second glance or feel uncomfortable visiting in your ski outfit. Not in Innsbruck. Innsbruck residents know that many visitors like to ski half of the day and sightsee the rest.

First-time visitors should head for the heart of the old town along the Maria-Theresienstrasse for the most breathtaking view of the Karwendel Mountain range in the distance beyond the famed city street. A two-hour walk through the old town takes in the oldest buildings, including the **Goldenes Dachl,** a former royal 16th-century building with gold-plated copper shingles on the roof.

Visit also the **Hofburg**, or palace, and **St. Jakob's cathedral**. Popular among visitors is the **Tirolean Folklore museum**, which has an outstanding display of traditional costumes and exhibits from the entire Tirol region. It's open every day (except Sunday afternoon) from 9 a.m. until noon and from 2 until 5 p.m.

Milan, Italy

Most skiers heading for the Italian slopes will land in Milan, the commercial and fashion heart of Italy. The city is only about an hour-and-a-half drive from the main Val d'Aosta resorts of Courmayeur and Cervinia. This surprising city deserves exploration either upon arrival or departure from Italy.

One of the jewels of Milan is the majestic white-marble **Duomo**, or cathedral. The facade, finished in the early 19th century by order of Napoleon, is breathtaking, and tours are organized to allow a walk on the roof where no less than 135 pinnacles and scores of marble statues adorn the cathedral.

Walk through the **Gallaria**, one of the first covered shopping malls, to the **La Scala**, the most famous opera house in the world. Here you can take a tour of the opera house and see the gilded splendor of one of the world's great theaters. If you are in Milan for an evening, check into seeing an opera here. The season lasts most of the winter.

The **Sforzas castle**, built in the mid-1300s, and the park that surrounds it are both fun to explore. The **Bera Palace** houses an art collection with works by most of the Italian Renaissance masters, as well as El Greco, Rembrandt and Rubens. Perhaps the jewel of Milan's art treasures is the painting of **The Last Supper** by Leonardo da Vinci. It can be seen in the Church of Santa Maria delle Grazia.

If you have additional time, a visit to the **Leonardo da Vinci museum**, filled with models of Leonardo's wild inventions, is fascinating. The museum also houses Milan's science and technology collections.

Lyons, France

Recently, Lyons has become one of the air gateways for skiers heading to the French Alps. While most French ski resorts can be reached by direct bus from the airport, Lyons deserves a visit of at least a day or two. This city is one of the commercial, artistic and gastronomic capitals of France.

The city's **Fine Arts Museum** houses the most impressive French collection of art outside the Grande Louvre in Paris. Other museums packed into the city include the **Museum of Textiles** with one of the best tapestry collections in the world.

The major attraction for tourists is the **old town**, which is the most extensive grouping of 15th-century and Renaissance buildings in France. A visit to the **St. Jean Cathedral** and a walk through the narrow streets past artisans' workshops in old gothic doorways and medieval courtyards yield a new discovery every few yards. This area is crisscrossed with covered passageways, called *traboules*, which give access from one street to another and pass through courtyards and old buildings. The old town has over 100 of these unique passages.

Take the cablecars to the top of the hill dominating the old town. Here enjoy the basilica, and a fabulous view over Lyons. The **Greco-Roman Museum** houses antiquities, such as inscribed old Roman tablets, a Gaulish calender and beautiful mosaics. Outside, the former Roman theater is restored, and new ruins of some of the most important Roman temples have been excavated.

The marionette, or string-controlled puppet, was created in Lyons. Today, *Guignol and Madelon*—the French equivalent to Punch and Judy—still perform and poke fun at national and local politics.

Lyons is one of the gourmet centers of France. A meal in one of the city's leading restaurants will be an experience you will savor for some time.

Annecy, France

This is the hub of the *Haute Savoie*. The lakeside city offers the old and the new in stark contrast to one another. Even along the lake, modernistic buildings around the Place de la Libèration tower over the hidden old town. But, down the Thiou canal, the city's most ancient waterway, the medieval town huddles between the modern buildings. The old town is built on a series of picturesque canals and is a sister to Venice and Bruges in that regard.

This is a tour to the Middle Ages. Visit the church of **Saint-Francois**, the **Palais de L'Isle** and **Old Prisons**. The **Castle of Annecy** dominating the town has been restored and offers a different view of the red roofs of old Annecy, the lake and the mountains in the distance.

If you have time, a trip around the lake by car is a joy. Take either the shorter coast road, or take the *col de la Forclaz* road for more spectacular views.

Austria

Austria is a country where sincere hospitality is deemed as important as great skiing. Austrians seem to go out of their way in order to make visitors feel at home. From the ski instructors to the hotel managers to the restaurant owners, they seem to take genuine pleasure in knowing that you have enjoyed yourself in their country. Their word for this spirit, *Gemütlichkeit*, encompasses everything a good host should be.

Although Austria is one of the skiing capitals of the world, it is very affordable—a factor that, when added to the warmth and hospitality you'll encounter, will engender one more fond memory to take home with you.

A note on prices

Most of the prices in this section reflect 1988/1989 winter season rates and should be used as a guide only. Expect them to increase approximately 1 to 3 percent during the 1989/1990 winter season. Where 1989/1990 prices were available they have been clearly identified.

All prices are given in Austrian schillings (Sch), and at the time the book was researched, the schilling was at an exchange rate of Sch. 12 to U.S. $1. Any subsequent change in the exchange rate will be the biggest factor affecting the prices.

When is high season?

High season—Christmas, New Year's, 20 December to 6 January and 4 February through 31 March.

Low season—until 19 December, 7 January to 3 February and after 1 April.

Use these dates for planning purposes. If you are planning to travel during the borderline weeks, check with the individual resorts because their dates may vary by a week due to local school holidays.

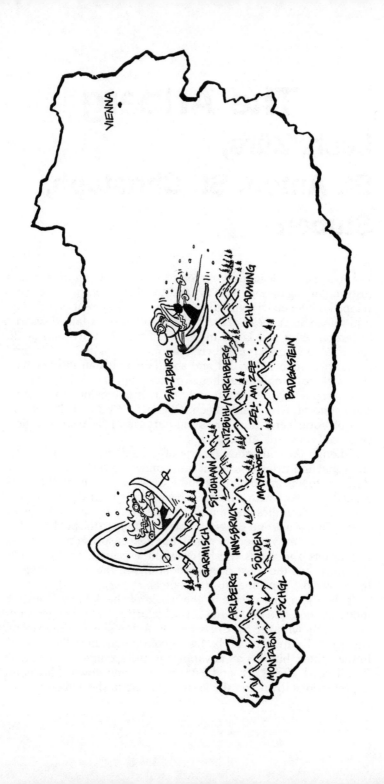

The Arlberg
Lech, Zürs, St. Anton, St. Christoph, Stuben

The Arlberg is a legendary region in Austrian skiing history. Ski instruction began here in 1907, and the techniques that were developed influenced a generation of teachers who went to America. And yet we don't speak of the Arlberg, rather of its famed resorts: St. Anton, Zürs and Lech, maybe even tiny St. Christoph or St. Jakob. All belong to the Arlberg Pass region, a skiing wonderland of resorts connected by lift and shuttle bus. It's an intermediate skier's paradise only three hours by car from Zurich airport.

Geographically, St. Anton and St. Christoph belong to the Austrian state of Tirol, while Lech, Oberlech, Zürs and Stuben are part of Vorarlberg. But, for skiing purposes, it's easier to collectively call them the Arlberg slopes.

Although the individual resorts of the Arlberg share the same snow and an intricate series of interconnected runs, they are very different towns in which to spend a week's vacation. **St. Anton** is a bustling resort with extremely easy access by train, bus or car because it straddles the main rail line and the major highway linking Innsbruck and Bregenz. This proximity to the public makes St. Anton an easy resort to reach, but also ensures that lift lines, restaurants and shops will be crowded, especially on weekends. The town has the most accommodations in the region, ranging from low-cost pensiones to ritzy hotels.

Stuben is a tiny village at the fringe of the Arlberg featuring moderate hotels. The Albona lift, which rises in two stages, connects easily with the St. Christoph/St. Anton side of the Arlberg. Due to its location it can be much colder than the other resorts in the winter, but has an advantage in the spring when its snow is still good after Lech and Zürs are winding down. This is an unpretentious town and the least expensive in the Arlberg.

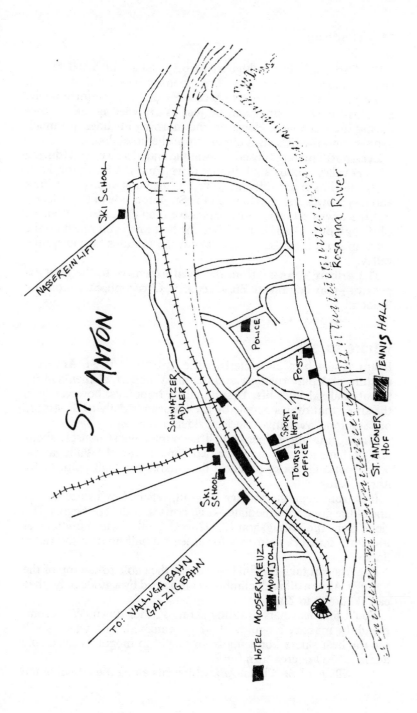

St. Christoph is the highest Arlberg village at 5,400 feet, a smaller, more exclusive and more expensive version of St. Anton. It is a good setting in which to get away from it all. Unfortunately, St. Christoph's lift lines can be just as crowded as St. Anton's during the weekends. However, the morning lift lines are much shorter, and the lifts start almost from the hotel doors.

Lech and Zürs are tucked away at the end of a dead-end (during winter) valley, about a 20-minute drive from the St. Anton Pass. They are thus more difficult to reach, meaning shorter lift lines and less crowded slopes than on the St. Anton side of the Arlberg. But the towns are also more expensive than either St. Anton, St. Christoph or Stuben. Zürs will be the first town you reach on the road up from the pass; Lech is about ten minutes farther up the valley.

The Arlberg resorts—from the most expensive to the least expensive—may be ranked: Zürs, Lech, St. Christoph, St. Anton and Stuben.

Where to ski

If any resort best characterizes the Arlberg, it is **St. Anton**, a mixture of Alpine rusticity and the most modern elements of international ski high life. Despite all its trappings, however, it is the snow that draws people by the thousands daily to St. Anton, or "Stanton," as many American skiers refer to it.

Throughout the Arlberg you'll encounter guest houses, shops and perhaps a *wurst* stand or two named after the Valluga, the 9,220-foot-high rocky pinnacle that marks the high point in St. Anton skiing.

It is from near the Valluga summit, reached by cablecar, that one of the great intermediate skiing cruises in Europe begins. The slope from the Vallugagrat (8,692 feet) is filled with hundreds of turns as you work your way for at least a half hour to the valley floor.

Experts can take the final section of the cable to the top of the Valluga. After a difficult climb--accompanied by a guide only--they can ski down to Zürs.

You'll find less nerve-rattling skiing farther down. We recommend the massive mogul field off the Tanzboden lift where you'll see the best skiers bouncing from mogul to mogul, occasionally adding a 360-degree turn for flair.

The village of **St. Christoph**, which sits along the crown of the

Arlberg Pass at 5,904 feet, is the other ground station for skiing this side of St. Anton.

The blue and red runs are cruises that offer great enjoyment. And there's good skiing for beginners from the base at St. Christoph.

The other ski area on this side of St. Anton is the Kampall, a 7,629-foot-high summit where you'll enjoy the two blue runs to the Gampen mid-station at 6,068 feet. From Gampen, continue through the trees into town, or drop over the ridge into the Steissbachtal and take the last half of the Valluga run. We prefer continuing along the blue run from the Gampen into town.

St. Anton's third ski area is the Rendl (6,888 feet) on the opposite side of town. The best intermediate run is from the Gampberg summit (7,872 feet) back into town.

Zürs and Lech can be skied together but there is no real connection between St. Anton and Zürs (as mentioned, guides take experienced skiers from the Valluga to the Zürs side) and between Stuben and Zürs. You have to depend on your car or a Post Bus, costing about Sch. 15.

In themselves, both Lech and Zürs qualify for resort status, even if their lift passes don't cover the entire Arlberg. In Lech, skiing centers on the Oberlech region, which is reached by a T-bar and chairlift from the center of the town. A system of 16 lifts takes skiers up to 7,799 feet. This area will keep an intermediate busy for two days, and off-slope skiing will challenge experts. Opposite Oberlech is the Rüfikopf area. From here experts, *real experts*, can drop down the face to Lech, or intermediates and beginners can comfortably cruise on to Zürs.

Zürs is a tougher area as far as marked trails go. All the runs from the top of the Trittkopf (7,985 feet) are rated intermediate, but would rate a black diamond in the United States. Once again, experts can make their own trails straight into town. The Madloch side of the valley has six long intermediate runs and three long beginner runs. However, after the area has been well skied, skiers can venture almost anywhere on this side.

The run between Zürs and Lech is one you'll enjoy. Take the lifts to the 7,997-foot-high Madloch Joch and then ski the red Madloch run into Lech. To get back, take the cablecar to Rüfikopf above Lech and then ski down and across to the base of the Hexenboden lift and Zürs. For a variation you can ski into neighboring Zug from the Madloch and then come back up via the Zugerberg lifts. From there, it's a red-rated cruise back down into Oberlech.

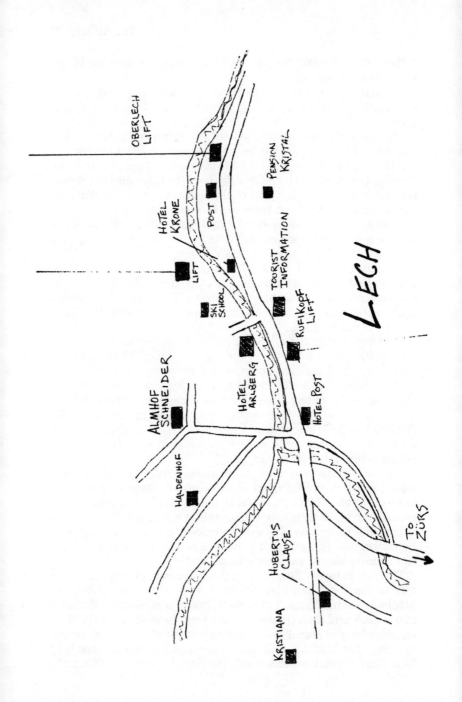

Stuben was our favorite bargain village in the region, tiny with only a few lifts. The best run was intermediate—from the Albona Grat (7,872 feet). Stuben is connected with St. Anton/St. Christoph by the blue-rated trail from the Albona mid-station to a crossover tow at Alpe Rauz. From there, take the chairlift to Pfannenkopf and work your way down into St. Christoph.

Mountain rating

Intermediates run the show in the Arlberg region. St. Anton is overwhelmingly red and blue on the ski map with some challenges that merit expert skills.

Lech and Zürs are beginner/intermediate areas by the color of the prepared runs. Experts can test their mettle by going off-trail, for the area has some of the best off-track powder skiing in Europe.

Beginners are not forgotten, for there is always a cluster of easy slopes at the bottom of each mountain.

Ski school

St. Anton advertises the "largest ski school in the world." However valid the claim, there are 300 teachers registered here and a total of nearly 700 in the area. The school classes form up in amazing numbers each morning at the base of the Kampall. Lech and Zürs also have 300 instructors, with classes forming at the base of the Schlegelkopf lift. Ski school prices are approximately the same throughout the region.

1989/90 Ski school prices for St. Anton/St. Christoph:

Individual lessons

for one day (four hours)   Sch. 1,550/1,700
                                                    H.S.
for two days   Sch. 2,900/3,200 H.S.
Sch. 150 additional for each additional person.

Group lessons

for one day	Sch. 360/380 H.S.
for three days	Sch. 850/870 H.S.
for six days	Sch. 1050/1150 H.S.

The cross-country ski school prices are the same as for alpine lessons.

Lift tickets

These are 1989/90 prices. The best bargain is the Arlberg area pass. There are discounts of approximately 40 percent for children and 20 percent for seniors (men 65 + and women 60 +). There is also approximately a 15 percent discount during the low season.

for one day	Sch. 335
for two days	Sch. 630
for six days	Sch. 1620
for seven days	Sch. 1880
for fourteen days	Sch. 2930

Accommodations

The local tourist offices maintain lists of area hotels, rental apartments and chalets *See addresses below. NOTE: If you are planning to be in the resort during Christmas or New Year's and are staying at a small hotel, plan to bring a jacket and tie. Guest houses and smaller hotels often organize a traditional dinner and small party. It is a beautiful tradition and makes the guests feel they are indeed there on a special day.*

The first price is for the special one-week package offered during January, sometimes called the *Pulverschneewochen*, which includes room, half board and lift tickets. The last price noted is the normal per-person price during high season for a double room. Expect to pay between 15 percent and 20 percent less during low season.

St. Anton

Hotel Schwarzer Adler (tel. 2244) Sch. 7,090-7,300—A great hotel if you want to splurge. Considered one of the best hotels in town. Great atmosphere in a place doing business since 1570. Normal daily rate: Sch. 1,150-2,500 (half pension).

St. Antoner Hof (tel. 2910) Sch. 8,980-9,120—Hotel is located away from the main downtown street but only about a three-minute walk away from the action and about five minutes to the lifts. Normal daily rate: Sch. 1,420-1,830 (half pension).

Hotel Mooserkreuz (tel.2730) Sch. 5,830-6,530—Sauna and indoor swimming pool, plus at the end of the day, ski back to the hotel. Normal daily rate: Sch. 980-1,180 (half pension).

Montjola (tel. 2302) Sch. 6,700—Small, cozy lodge of a hotel. About three minutes' walk from the center of town. Normal daily rate: 850-920 (half pension).

Berghaus Maria (tel. 2005) Sch. 6,950-7,950—Away from center of town and quiet. Excellent cooking; friendly service. Normal daily rate: Sch. 1,140 (half pension).

Hotel Mössmer (tel. 2727) Sch. 4,920—Normal daily rate: Sch. 500-600 (Bed-and-breakfast only).

Tannenhof (tel. 2364) Sch. 4,570. Normal daily rates: Sch. 450-600 (B&B only).

St. Christoph

Arlberg-Hospiz (tel. 2611) Sch. 15,500. The most exclusive spot on this side of the Arlberg. The restaurant is perhaps one of the best in Austria. Normal daily rate: Sch. 2,200 (half pension).

Maiensee (tel. 2804) Sch. 8,390-8,790—Right next to the lift with all the amenities. Normal daily rates: Sch. 1,190-1,320 (half pension).

Lech

Hotel Post (tel. 2206; telex: 52677) Sch. 13,000. Attracts a slightly older crowd with family money, but is a beautiful and cozy hotel in the alpine tradition. Normal daily rate: Sch. 1,450-3,200 (half pension).

Almhof Schneider (tel. 3500; telex: 52674) Together with the Post, considered the best in town. It is cozy, not as formal as the Post and more modern. Normal daily rate: Sch. 1,550-3,500 (full pension).

Arlberg (tel. 2134; telex: 52679) Sch. 14,765 (full pension). Old elegance, slightly worn. Normal daily rate: Sch. 1,480-3,280 (full pension).

Berghof (tel. 2635; fax. 26355) Sch. 9,550 (full pension). Top quality with sauna, whirlpool and tennis, but no pool. Normal daily rate: Sch. 1,370-1,780 (full pension).

Kristiania (tel. 2561; telex: 52183) Sch. 9865. A bit out of the mainstream of the town but very nice. Normal daily rate: Sch. 1,260-1,995 (half pension).

Sonnenburg (tel. 2147; telex: 52552) Sch. 8,920 (half pension). Located in the Oberlech section of Lech. Normal daily rates: Sch. 990-1,800 (half pension).

Haldenhof (tel. 2444; fax. 2444-21) Sch. 8,500 (half pension). A small family-owned hotel where the staff brings all the guests together each week. It is the perfect Austrian experience. Normal daily rate: Sch. 950-1,390 (half pension).

Hotel Lech (Tel.2289) Sch. 6,750 (half pension). Normal daily rate: Sch. 850-1,150 (half pension).

Kristall (tel. 2422) Sch. 6,890. Central location and friendly service. Normal daily rates: Sch.520-610 (B&B).

Hubertushof (tel. 2701) Rustic building; especially good bargain. Located out of the center of town in Zug. Make sure you specify that you want a room with private bath. Normal daily rate: Sch. 460-520.

Pension Sursilva (tel.2431) Sch. 7030 (half pension). New pensione in town. Good value and modern facilities. Normal daily rate: Sch. 790-830.

Zürs

Zürserhof (tel.2513; telex: 52673) Sch. 12,940-14,130 (full pension). This is one of the most luxurious hotels in the Alps in a class with the Palace in St. Moritz. Suites and mini-apartments are available for Sch. 18,010-19,130 during the ski weeks in low season. The normal room rates: Sch. 1,930-2,160 (full pension).

The other hotels in Zürs are all quite good. Try the **Arlberghaus** (tel. 2258) Sch. 7,580-9,680 for the ski week, or Sch. 870-1,150 normal daily rate. The **Schweiserhaus** (tel. 2463) is one of the least expensive at Sch. 6,030 for the ski week and Sch. 600 for the normal daily rate.

Stuben

Post Hotel (tel. 761) Sch. 6,450-6,975—A good choice for uncomplicated skiing with on-site ski rental, ski school and a bank. Ask about its all-inclusive plan. Normal daily rate: Sch. 695-820.

Haus Erzberg (tel. 729) Sch. 4,560—Small hotel(13 beds); includes breakfast only. Normal daily rate: Sch. 310-380

Hotel Mondschein (tel. 721) Sch. 6,675-6,975—Excellent hotel in historic building dating to 1739. Indoor pool and friendly atmosphere. Normal daily rate: Sch. 735-860.

Dining

Our tip in St. Anton is the dining room in the Hotel Berghaus Maria. If food plays a big part in your ski vacation plans, book a room here also.

The Schwarzer Adler (tel. 2244) sets a table that brims with Austrian specialties. Menu and à la carte prices start at Sch. 140.

To demolish your budget, we recommend the Arlberg Hospiz at St. Christoph where $40 is gone as quickly as the sumptuous noodles, creamed mushrooms, roast duck and so on. Don't expect to see Prince Charles on the day you've reserved, but he's numbered among its star-studded clientele.

All the way down to Earth, take a snack in the *Bahnhof* restaurant near St. Anton's famous Hotel Post. The food is good and inexpensive.

On the mountain, choose from several places, the most popular being the cafeteria at the Valluga cablecar's second station.

In Lech, try the restaurants in Hotel Montana (tel. 2460)—featuring the best wine celler in town,—and Hotel Salome (tel. 2306). Hotel Krone consistently gets good recommendations. For nouvelle *Austrian* cuisine, try the Goldener Berg (tel. 2205) or Brunnenhof (tel. 2349). The Hotel Post restaurant (tel. 2206) serves excellent traditional recipes, and the Schneider (tel. 3500) has excellent traditional Austrian food. Just outside Lech, in Zug, the restaurants Alphorn and Rotewand offer excellent food in the best of Austrian tradition. For cheaper eats, try Pizza Charlie for good Italian food and head up to Gasthof Omesberg for great traditional Austrian fare.

In Zürs the best restaurant is, naturally, in the Zürserhof. Try the Lorünser (tel. 2254), as well, for excellent meals.

Apartments

If you want to rent a vacation apartment, ask for the apartment listing brochure from each of the tourist offices in the Arlberg. They maintain a complete list of the several hundred apartments and chalets available in season.

In Lech, apartments can be rented with four beds for approximately Sch.1,500 a day, during high season. In Zürs, expect to pay around Sch. 1,750 a day during high season. In St. Anton, a four-bed apartment can be rented for about Sch. 1,400 a day. The prices are middle range.

Nightlife

In **St. Anton** for a one-stop nightspot, we recommend the Sporthotel near the center of town. Here you can arrange a week's lodging (half pension from Sch. 7,560), drink at the bar, dance in the nightclub and enjoy a good meal in the restaurant.

In St. Anton's central pedestrian zone you'll be able to find something that suits your night tastes by simply taking a stroll.

Our ski instructor recommended the Krazy Kanguruh, which has a reputation as the town's biggest après-ski watering hole, but we can't praise it wholeheartedly. Located away from the center of town, it was crowded when we visited.

We prefer the cozy Valluga Bar in town, a subterranean club with music.

In **Lech**, we were partial to the disco in the Hotel Almhof-Schneider, perhaps only because friends have stayed at the hotel. A more chic after-hours address is the bar and disco at the Tannenbergerhof, or head to the Hotel Krone where there is live music and a good local crowd. Expect to pay between Sch. 60 and Sch. 100 for a drink.

For a great evening of singing, yodeling and dancing, good food, wine from hanging decanters or beer, try the Hubertus Clause tucked away in Lech. The zither player, who has been playing here for more than 10 years, does a fantastic job on old rock'n'roll numbers and polkas. If you've been waiting to dance to "Hello Mary Lou" as played on a zither, here is your chance. Thursdays and Fridays are very crowded because the ski school classes descend *en masse*.

Child care

Ski courses for children are offered, as is a ski kindergarten for kids from age five, plus babysitting services (from three upwards). The ski school includes lunch with a drink and there are further reductions if the parents are also enrolled in the ski school.

Children's ski school

for one day	Sch. 480
for three days	Sch. 1,140
for six days	Sch. 1,570

The school is open from 9 a.m. until 4:30 p.m.

Kindergartens, for children two and older, are available in all the resorts. Prices in Lech and Oberlech are Sch. 350 a day and Sch. 1,020-1,100 for six days. Lunch is Sch. 70 extra. Opening hours are normally from 9 a.m. to 4 p.m. Expect to pay similar rates in the other Arlberg resorts.

Getting there

You'll probably fly into Zurich, although the trip is not any more difficult from Munich or Innsbruck.

From Zurich, it is a little over three hours by car, or you can take the train—the Arlberg Express—directly to St. Anton.

Getting to Lech and Zürs is slightly more difficult. One can get off the train in Langen and then take a bus up the hill, or get off the train in St. Anton and take another bus up to the villages. Swissair runs a special skibus from the Zurich airport direct to Lech at 12:30 p.m. On Saturdays the bus makes an additional run at 7 p.m. Fare is Sch. 400, one-way, and Sch. 700 round-trip. Reservations can be made at Tourist Office Lech (tel. 2161-15; telex: 052680).

Direct trains connect Langen with Cologne, Dortmund, Munich, Innsbruck, Salzburg, Zurich, Paris, Brussels and Calais.

Driving from Zurich, take the autobahn to St. Gallen and then to Feldkirche and to the Arlberg Pass. From Munich and Stuttgart it is easiest to travel to Bregenz, then head to Feldkirche and the Arlberg.

Other activities

Winter activities along the Arlberg Pass are centered around skiing, and you'll have to choose swimming, tennis or sightseeing for alternatives.

Day outings are offered to Innsbruck and Bregenz and the shores of Lake Constance.

Check with Heli Tyrol (tel. 2732) for information on express air trips to Innsbruck and Graz, Austria.

Tourist information

St. Anton: Fremdenverkehrsverband, A-6580 St. Anton a A.; tel. 05446-22690; telex: 058335; fax. 05446-253215
Stuben: Verkehrsverein, A-6752 Stuben; tel. 05582-761; telex: 52459.
Lech: Verkehrsamt, A-6764 Lech; tel. 05583-21610; telex: 052680; fax. 05583-3155.
Zürs: Verkehrsamt, A-6763 Zürs; tel. 05583-2245; telex 052670; fax. 05583-2982.

Badgastein

Skiing may be the number-one pastime in the Gasteiner valley, but the area's popularity as a meeting place for European vacationers keeps it lively year round. Austrians from all parts of the country head up the valley during the winter. The resort area is a grouping of four systems: Badgastein, Sportgastein, Bad Hofgastein and Dorfgastein.

Curiously, skiing may not even be the major reason for the arrival of tourists. Badgastein first gained fame as a thermal spa. The resort attracted the upper crust of society and a rather etiquette-conscious clientele. The formality that developed over the years, especially in the grand hotels—many of which still have private thermal pools—continues today. The winter coat of preference will probably be fur, and the lineup of shiny automobiles in front of the casino may look like a Mercedes dealership. Although spa visitors still cling to protocol, the modern skiing tourist has softened the formerly stiff rules of decorum.

Where to ski

The best skiing is from the top station on the Stubnerkogel at 7,373 feet, where an exceptional intermediate run streches nearly seven miles. This run, the Angertal, drops 4,264 feet. From the ground there is a lift connection to the Schlossalm area above Bad Hofgastein.

There's a challenging World Cup run from the Graukogel summit opposite the Stubner. The lift takes you up to 6,556 feet, and the black run takes you down; or a side trail accommodates intermediates.

Also try Sportgastein, about six miles away and easily accessible by bus. Best of the runs is from Schideck at 7,101 feet. From here an additional run—that from the 8,810-foot-high Kreuzkogel—is worth trying.

At the top, a choice of four different trails awaits you. Best of them is the north trail, which is left unprepared and provides great powder skiing with the right conditions. The nearly five-mile run covers a vertical drop of almost 4,950 feet.

Mountain rating

The valley, particularly Badgastein, is intermediate country, with the most notable exception the World Cup course. It is a good place to tune up your ski legs but leave some spring in them for partying later. If you are strictly expert, you'll enjoy the approximately dozen runs, but once finished with them you'll be ready to move on. Experts should check out an off-trail group or a guide for a morning. Both will offer little-known runs down unprepared sections of the resort and will provide most of the challenge you crave.

Ski school

Three ski schools with a total of 100 instructors provide courses in the valley. In Dorfgastein, call 06433-538; in Bad Hofgastein, call 06432-6339; and in Badgastein, call 06434-2260. Average instruction prices for one hour of **private lessons** are: Sch. 460 an hour. **Group lessons** will cost: One day—Sch. 420; three days—Sch. 1,050; and six days—Sch. 1,150. Three-day cross-country lessons are Sch. 450.

Lift tickets

The best choice is the Gastein *Super Ski Schein*, a combined ticket for the area resorts, linking 60 lifts and a network of buses and trains. These are 1989/90 prices.

for one day	Sch. 290
for two days	Sch. 560
for three days	Sch. 790
for six days	Sch. 1,400
for seven days	Sch. 1,580

Low-season prices are appproximately 14 percent lower

Accommodations

Choose from a great selection of hotels in Badgastein and Bad Hofgastein. There is less variety in Dorfgastein nearer the entrance to the valley. Of the three, Badgastein probably offers the most European ski atmosphere, including a healthy helping of nightlife.

There are four five-star hotels in Badgastein. Our favorites in town are the expensive **Bellevue** (tel. 06434-2571) and **Elisabethpark** (tel. 2551), while the four-star **Hoteldorf Grüner Baum** (tel. 06434-25160; telex: 067516), remains an excellent choice for resort accommodations outside the center of town. Rooms from Sch. 550 daily, with full pension from Sch. 710. The restaurant is one of the finest in the Gastein valley.

In town, consider **Das Weismayr**. This centrally located, 135-bed hotel (tel. 06434-2594; telex: 067531) offers traditional accommodations with sturdy old-style European furniture, thick carpets and tapestries. Daily rooms rates start at Sch. 650 with half pension.

Check out the 116-bed **Hotel Mozart** (tel. 06434-2686) with rooms from Sch. 215 a day; or Sch. 380 a day with half pension. Another budget choice is the **Hotel Stubnerhof** (tel. 06434-29910). Half-pension rates start at Sch. 360 a day, or rent just the room for Sch. 320.

Apartments

Most visitors stay in hotels and pensiones or a few private homes in the Gastein valley. But vacation chalets are also available, with the largest number in Bad Hofgastein. Details on chalet and apartment rentals are available through the tourist offices in any one of the three resorts.

Dining

We found a restaurant in Badgastein that is far above average. It's **Wörther** at the Hiss-Hotel, a palace of eating pleasure with prices to match. The menu runs from Sch. 300 to Sch. 880, but the dishes are outstanding. Fresh vegetables, perfectly prepared meat and, as might be expected from the name, a superior selection of wines. A great place to splurge. Most evenings reservations are recommended (tel. 06434-3828). For a traditional, inexpensive Austrian meal, try the **Orania Stuben**.

Nightlife

After a day on the slopes, the elite choose the tables at the Casino in Badgastein or retire immediately to the bar near the playing tables. After 11 p.m. the evening grows progressively wilder in Mühlhäusl disco club in Badgastein. The Glocknerkeller in Bad Hofgastein is a typical Austrian pub with live music and dancing each night.

Child care

Child care facilities are offered for children three years and above in Badgastein and Bad Hofgastein. The minimum age in Dorfgastein is four. Individual baby-sitting service is also offered. Details are available from the tourist office.

Getting there

The best international airport connections are through Salzburg. The best way to get to the resorts is by car, driving south, along the magnificent Tauernautobahn to Bischofshofen and on to the Gastein valley. Expect about an hour's drive.

Other activities

The three towns offer a wide variety of outdoor recreation. A day trip to Salzburg with a tour down the salt mines is one of the preferred outings. Badgastein and Bad Hofgastein are famed thermal spring resorts. Make sure to take time to enjoy the hot springs during your visit.

For the non-skier, the view from the Schlossalm at the 7,000-foot-high level is worth the lift ride up from Bad Hofgastein. In Badgastein, visit the Nikolauskirche and the local museum.

Tourist information

Kurverwaltung, A-5640 Badgastein, tel. 06434-25310; telex: 67520

Kurverwaltung, A-5630 Bad Hofgastein, tel. 06432-4290; telex: 67796

Verkehrsverein, A-5632 Dorfgastein, tel. 06433-277; telex: 67737

Innsbruck

Innsbruck, Austria's most famous ski resort, has twice hosted the Winter Olympic Games (1964 and 1976). This is the capital of Austrian Tyrol. Don't make the mistake of believing that if you sign up for a trip to Innsbruck you will be stepping into a quaint ski resort. Innsbruck is a bustling city that happens to be surrounded by a group of small resorts providing good skiing.

The city of 120,000 residents in the valley of the emerald-green Inn River has such a collection of cultural attractions that skiing is not the dominant factor as it is in most other resort towns and cities.

Fortunately, the skiers, although they will have to put up with the inconvenience of a relatively long bus ride to the lifts, will have a chance to ski up to five different areas in the immediate vicinity of Innsbruck, plus the opportunity to strike out for a day in St. Anton, Ischgl, Kitzbühel or the Stubaital. Europe's best cross-country resort, Seefeld, is also right next door. It is a good way to test a lot of Austria's skiing and have a better idea of where you may plan to spend more time next season.

Where to ski

There are five major ski areas ringing Innsbruck. They are—in descending order of difficulty—Hungerburg-Seegrube, Axamer-Lizum, Tulfes, Igls and Mutters. Altogether, nearly 65 miles of trails are prepared for downhill specialists and an equal length in cross-country circuits.

Experts should strike out for Hungerburg, across the Inn from the other slopes. This is the gateway to the great black trails of the Hafelkar. We recommend the mogul-studded, steep black run from the 7,657-foot-high summit as one of the most challenging we've skied in Austria. If you can't ski this one well, you're not an expert.

Of the Olympic slopes, the Axamer-Lizum is best known. The slopes of Axams, a village about six miles outside Innsbruck, start at the 5,249-foot level. There is nothing here but a parking lot and plenty of skiing for a day.

Heresy to say, but we liked three other runs better than the famous Olympic course, the Hoadl (7,677 feet). The first two, from the nearby 7,336-foot-high Pleisen and slightly lower Kögele, take you all the way back to the valley floor. The Kögele is best of the two with a great four miles of skiing. Hardest was the demanding

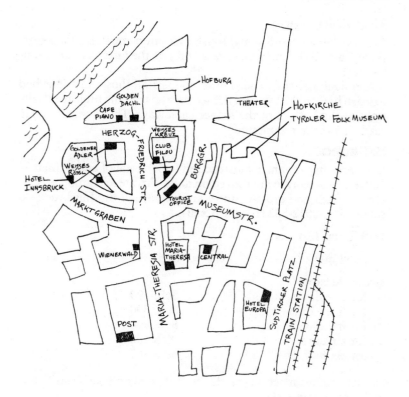

run down the Birgitzköpfl on the opposite side of the valley. The moguls pound your thighs and the steep slopes test an intermediate's courage.

Tulfes, nearly eight miles from Innsbruck, has skiing from the 8,783-foot level. For the powder and off-trail specialist, we highly recommend the area around the Glungezer summit. But you've got to climb half an hour or more on your own to enjoy the best off-trail variations.

Igls, at 2,952 feet is in the shadow of the Patscherkofel, the 7,372-foot-high summit station for the men's downhill run. You can ski the same 2.4-mile course traveled by Austrian Franz Klammer to win a gold medal at the 1976 games. The bobsleigh run is also at Igls and guests are allowed on the course. (Price: Sch.350/person).

The Mutters ski area, around the mountain from the Axamer-Lizum (or over the Birgitzköpfl and down the mountain), is good intermediate territory. The runs branch out from the Pfriemesköpfl (5,904 feet).

Mountain rating

As a two-time Olympic city, Innsbruck offers much for the expert skier. Each of the major ski areas will give the intermediate countless tests.

And beginner skiers need have no fear: All those Austrians had to learn how to ski, too, and the starter and training lifts are usually right at the bottom of the longer cableways. The moment you're ready, so is the mountain.

Ski school

Each area has organized instruction with a total of approximately 200 teachers working in the region daily. Private and group lessons for downhill and cross-country are given. Call the Innsbruck ski school (tel. 0512-582310) for details.

Individual lessons

one hour	Sch. 350

Group lessons

for one day	Sch. 390
for three days	Sch. 890
for five days	Sch. 990
for six days	Sch.1050
for six half days	Sch. 850

School courses meet on the slopes, but you can take a shuttlebus to the area you're skiing.

Lift tickets

Day tickets for the individual areas of the Innsbruck region cost from Sch. 160–250. The best bargain is the regional pass, which is good for a minimum of three days.

for three days	Sch. 655
for six days	Sch. 1,060
six of eight days	Sch. 1,170

Buses run daily from Innsbruck to the main slopes. For information, call 59850. In addition, buses also take skiers to the best cross-country circuits in the area.

Accommodations

While it may be more romantic to stay in one of the neighboring villages, the attraction of skiing Innsbruck is that you can enjoy the benefits of a major city—one of Europe's cultural capitals, in fact.

The city tourist office advertises accommodations ranging from a sleeping bag to a king's bed.

The best budget accommodations are offered through the tourist office-sponsored Club Innsbruck plan. Check with the tourist office for the plan's winter price list of accommodations, half pension included, unless noted, for a minimum of three nights. The half-pension, daily rate is given below unless otherwise noted.

Europa-Tyrol (tel. 0512-5931; telex 533424) Sch. 780—On Sudtiroler Platz, this is a quality choice for Innsbruck. It is only a short distance from the old city and near the top attractions.

Hotel Alpinpark (tel. 48600; telex 533509) Sch. 560.

Hotel Maria-Theresia (tel. 5933; telex 533300) Sch. 670 with breakfast only—a quality hotel in the center of town.

Hotel Goldener Adler (tel. 586334; telex 533415) Sch. 560—One of the old traditional and beautiful hotels in town.

Hotel Grauer Bär (tel. 5924; telex 533387) Sch. 560.

Hotel Weisses Kreuz (tel. 59479) Sch. 430—In the center of town; good location for city sightseeing.

Hotel-Pension Binder (tel. 42236; telex 534404) Sch. 330.

Gasthof Weisses Rössl (tel. 583057) Sch. 450 with breakfast—central location.

Gasthof Engl (tel. 83112) Sch. 330 (half-board).

In Igls—Igls, adjacent to Innsbruck, is the closest town to a mountain resort in the immediaate vicinity. In fact, it could make a very pleasant destination in itself with Innsbruck nearby for occasional forays.

The two best hotels in town are the **Schlosshotel** (tel. 512-77217; telex 533314) and the **Sporthotel** (tel. 512-77241; telex 533314). The first is formal and quiet, the second is right in the middle of the town and a bit bouncier. For middle-of-the-road hotels, try the **Astoria** or the **Bon-Alpina**. **Pension Gruberhof** and **Pension Oswald** are good low-priced establishments where you can get good half board for about Sch.350 per person a day. Two very nice bed-and-breakfast places to try are **Hotel-Garni Leitgebhof** and **Pension Tyrol**.

Apartments

Lodging in Innsbruck is primarily in hotels and pensiones. For information on chalet and apartment rentals nearer the slopes, contact the Innsbruck tourist office.

There are more apartments in Igls. Send your requirements to the tourist office and it will send back a list of available apartments.

Private rooms in Igls will end up costing, with bed and breakfast, about Sch.150-160 per person a night.

Dining

Restaurants listed below are in the heart of the city, where you'll also find the best lodging. In the individual towns there are countless dining establishments and mountain restaurants.

An excellent combination for eating and overnight lodging is **Weisses Rössl** (tel. 583057) at Kiebachgasse 8 in the old city. The menu ranges from Sch. 60 to Sch. 125. The staff prepares some of the best typical Tyrolean dishes.

Visit the **Goldener Adler** (tel. 586334) in the old city if you have a craving for good beef, especially grilled T-bone. The menu begins at Sch. 100. An excellent traditional restaurant. Expect to pay $40 for two. Another great Austrian restaurant is the **K&K Restaurant** in the Hotel Schwarzer Adler (tel. 587109).

We agree with a Tyrolean friend who took us to the **Altstadts-tüberl** (tel. 582347), promising that it was one of the most reasonably priced restaurants in the old city. The menu begins at Sch. 70.

Considered the best restaurant in town by many is the **Restaurant Kapeller** (tel. 43106).

Nightlife

We recommend you walk the Maria-Theresienstrasse and the central old city for just about all the nightlife atmosphere you could ever desire. The view is beautiful and small pubs and bars are hidden in alleys and under archways. Head to the "Cafe Piano" across from the Goldener Adler, and then try out the bustling "Club Filou" with a great disco and bar on Stiftsgasse.

If you want to find the section of town with students and more local discos, head for Riffi on Schöpfstrasse.

Check with the tourist office for a list of concerts taking place around town—tickets are also sold at the information office. You never know who's touring Europe while you're on vacation.

Child care

Child care and ski kindergarten courses (age four and up) are available in Innsbruck's ski areas. Contact the ski kindergarten (tel. 582310) for details.

In Igls, the kindergarten is in the Kurpark, tel. 777482. One hour costs Sch. 30, five hours is Sch. 130 and 10 hours costs Sch. 240.

Getting there

Innsbruck has its own airport with daily jet service from throughout Europe. Munich is the most frequently used international airport for travelers from the United States, but that is changing somewhat with the increased use of the Innsbruck airport. Tyrolean Airways, Innsbruck's hometown airline, is now flying scheduled service from Amsterdam, Frankfurt, Zurich, Vienna and Paris. Tyrolean Airways offers a perfect alternative to trains or a long drive by car or bus.

By car, the trip is from Munich via autobahn to the Inntal autobahn crossing, and then to Innsbruck—no more than three hours.

A more scenic auto trip is from Munich to Garmisch-Partenkirchen, scene of the 1932 and 1936 Winter Olympic Games, and then about a 70-minute drive over the mountains to Innsbruck. Add at least two hours for sightseeing in Garmisch.

Other activities

Innsbruck shares with Grenoble the distinction of being a town within the Alps that has more than 100,000 residents. It is the capital of the Austrian state of Tyrol and has a wealth of art and historical treasures. It is also on the way to the Brenner Pass, lowest route through the Alps to Italy.

Innsbruck is accustomed to visitors in ski outfits, whether inside a museum or at a fine restaurant. Visitors always head for the heart of town along the Maria-Theresienstrasse for the outstanding view of the Karwendel mountain range behind the classic old-city street.

The best way to see Innsbruck is to walk through the old town. Allow about two hours. The most photographed house in the old city is Goldenes Dachl, a former royal building from the 16th century, with gold-plated copper shingles on the roof.

Visit the Hofburg Palace, and St. Jakob's cathedral, plus the Tyrolean folklore museum. The city boasts dozens of other attractions listed for you by the tourist office.

Tourist information

Fremdenverkehrsverband Innsbruck-Igls und Umgebung, A-6021 Innsbruck; tel. 0512-59850; fax. 0512-598507; telex 533423.

Ischgl and the Paznaun Valley

Ischgl, hard to pronounce (say Ish'-gull) but easy to ski, became in a few short days one of our favorite Austrian resorts. High in the Alps (4,592 feet), hard on the border with Switzerland, this ski center in the Paznaun Valley is something of a secret to non-European skiers.

Ischgl is a resort that has it all, wide-open trails, cross-border skiing, extensive off-trail areas, small alpine village atmosphere and excellent après ski and nightlife.

Farther up the valley is Galtür, a much smaller and quieter resort with a correspondingly smaller ski area.

Where to ski

Ischgl's slopes are the best in the valley. In addition, neighboring See, Kappl and Galtür all have lifts. Across the range of mountains, in Switzerland, Samnaun is connected by lift with Ischgl.

Three gondola lifts connect Ischgl with the main skiing area 3,280 feet above the town. The Silvrettabahn and the Fimbabahn bring skiers from opposite ends of town to the Idalp area (7,582 feet). The Pardatschgratbahn takes skiers from the eastern section of town to Pardatschgrat at 8,609 feet. Although the lift lines at the Silvrettabahn look daunting, the wait, even on the busiest days is not excessive because the lift can move up to 2,400 skiers an hour.

From the Idalp sector, lifts fan out to all corners of the resort. In fact, even skiers choosing to go directly to the higher Pardatschgrat will have to pass through the Idalp area to reach the other sections of Ischgl's slopes. The immediate Idalp area serves as the nursery runs, offering a long, very easy swath with excellent lift support.

From Idalp, intermediates and experts take the chairlift up to Idjoch. Here, drop down into the Swiss Alp Trida section for long intermediate runs, or continue up to the Greitspitz for more challenging skiing in the Austrian section beneath the Palinkopf into the Hölltal or over another ridge to the Taja Alp.

At the end of the day, take one of the runs from the Idalp or down the Velilltal for beautiful, wide-open, intermediate cruising.

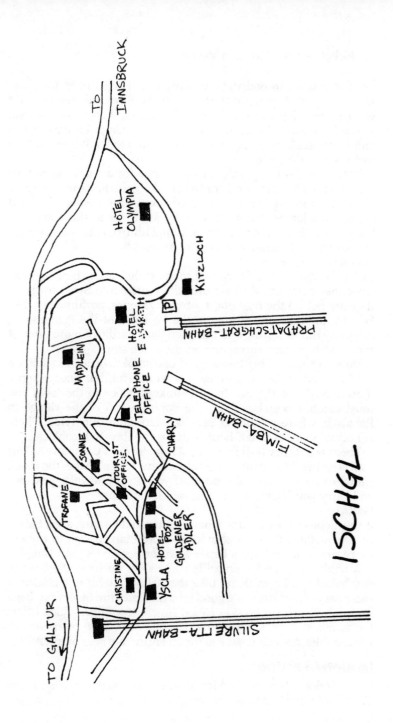

Or if you want to end the day with a challenge, drop from the Pardatschgrat. If you are staying near the Silvrettabahn, you will want to head left toward the middle station, then follow the No. 1 trail into town. For those closer to the Fimba or Pardatschgrat-bahn stations, keep going straight down into town. Where the trail forks, ski to the right.

Determined off-trail skiers can arrange for a snow cat to take them to the Piz Val Gronda or the Heidelbergerhütte with a guide for a day of skiing across untracked snow. This area is scheduled for lift development but it's a few years away at this time. The Swiss must first construct an additional lift from Samnaun before the Austrian lift-builders can raise a wrench.

Down to Samnaun

Swiss Samnaun is the target of many Ischgl skiers because they are either determined to ski over the border to a Swiss town, or they are hot on the trail of duty-free cigarettes, perfume or whiskey. In any case, the run from the backside of the Palinkopf is relatively uninteresting and the town itself hardly of more interest than a visit to the nearest airport duty-free store.

Duty-free here is big business. If one smokes or wants to fill up the hot toddy cabinet, Samnaun is wonderful, but once is more than enough for the run from Palinkopf. Once in the town you must catch a post bus from the opposite end of the village to Ravaisch, where a cablecar carries skiers up to Alp Trida. There is normally about a half-hour wait for the Ravaisch cablecar.

There is another trail from Alp Trida down to Compatsch. This trail is rather difficult and often closed due to avalanche (too much snow) or rocks (too little snow). If you do get down, a post bus will carry you back up to the Ravaisch cablecar.

Galtür

A shuttlebus runs from the village center to the skiing area. Skiing here is mellow. One day should be more than enough to explore every run. It is perhaps a better area for beginners than Ischgl.

A triple chair and a drag lift take skiers up from the base to Birkhahnkopf. From there, take the Ballunspitzlift to a choice of three easy expert runs or a good intermediate run. Skiers can head for a newly opened section called Innere Kopsalpe, which offers the toughest runs. On a sunny day this back bowl offers an advanced intermediate great fun for an entire morning or afternoon.

Mountain rating

Ischgl is not recommended for absolute beginners. English at the ski school is limited to technical ski jargon, and the nursery slopes are far above the town. Galtür would make more sense for a first-timer. The locals in Galtür also speak English more fluently than people in Ischgl.

Intermediates and experts will have a wonderful time in Ischgl. The area offers wide-ranging, well-prepared trails and 50 miles of off-trail challenges. Experts looking for super-steep terrain will be disappointed. The resort is perfect for a mixed intermediate/expert group.

Ski school

Ischgl has the largest ski school but probably only as many good English-speakers as Galtür. Although the instructors can teach in English, it is nice to have an instructor who can converse in English as well. Ask for a good English-speaker, especially if you are heading out for individual lessons.

Group lessons are aproximately 10 percent less expensive in middle season. For participants in the week-long January ski program there is an additional 10 percent discount.

Individual lessons (89/90 prices)

for two hours	Sch. 850
for each additional person	Sch. 150
for one day	Sch. 1,600

Group lessons

for one day	Sch. 380
for three days	Sch. 850
for five days	Sch 1000
for six days	Sch. 1,100
for five half days	Sch. 800

Lift tickets

All skiers except beginners should purchase the Silvretta ski pass, which is good for all area lifts (Ischgl, Galtür, Samnaun and the entire valley), plus shuttle bus transport. These are 1989/90 prices.

	high season	low season
for three days	Sch. 940	Sch. 815
for six days	Sch. 1,720	Sch. 1,440
for seven days	Sch. 1,960	Sch. 1,640
for thirteen days	Sch. 3,095	Sch. 2,610
for fourteen days	Sch. 3,210	Sch. 2,725

Individual area day tickets in Ischgl cost Sch. 350 during high season and Sch. 310 during middle season. In Galtür: Sch. 265 (high season) and Sch. 250 (low season).

Seniors over 60 and children from 6-15 years get approximately a 40 percent discount on lift tickets.

Accommodations

Prices noted are for half board. HS = high season; LS = low season. Special weekly package prices are listed at the end of each hotel description.

Ischgl

For the best in town, head for **Hotel Elisabeth** (tel. 5411; telex 58143) Sch. 1,550 HS; Sch. 1,300 LS. Located at the base stations of the Fimbabahn and the Pardatschgratbahn. A perfect location. Good English, pool, sauna and solarium. Special weekly price of Sch. 7,640 in early December, April and early May, including six-day skipass and seven days half board. In January, Sch.11,140.

Madlein (tel. 5226; telex 58143) Daily price is Sch. 1,350 HS; Sch. 1,150 LS. Centrally located. Features one of the best discos in town. Pool, sauna and solarium. Special weekly price of Sch. 7,290 in early December and late April and May, including six-day skipass and seven days half board. In January, Sch. 10,800.

The aging **Post** (tel. 5233, telex 58140) has all amenities, including a swimming pool. Staff at the **Sonne** (tel. 5302; telex 58258) and **Trofana** (tel. 5387) are good with English. Prices range between Sch. 900-1,200 HS and Sch. 700-850 LS. The Sonne is also an excellent après-ski location.

Gasthöfe Goldener Adler (tel. 5217) boasts one of the best kitchens in town, plus a sauna and steambath. Sch. 850-1,120 HS; Sch. 710-970 LS. Special weekly price, including skipass and seven days half board in early December and late April/May is Sch.5,190. In January, Sch.6,600.

Moderate

Olympia (tel. 5432; telex 58243) Sch. 940 HS; Sch. 720 LS. Located near the Fimba and Pardatschgrat lifts. Special week costs Sch. 6,390.

Yscla (tel.5275; telex 58261) Sch. 770-940 HS; Sch. 620-720 LS. Near the Silvretta lift. Convenient to everything with one of the best restaurants in town. Special Dec./April week costs Sch. 4,990 and January week is 6,950.

Charley (tel. 5434) Sch. 700 HS; Sch. 580 LS. Special week costs Sch. 5,900.

Bed and Breakfast

The best in town is **Christine** (tel.5346) Sch.600 HS; Sch.400 LS. Special weeks not available in January.

A moderate B&B is **Edi** (tel. 5351) Sch. 430-470 HS; Sch. 360-380 LS. A bit out of the way, but a good haven for English-speakers, and it has reasonable rates. Special Dec/April week costs Sch. 3,510 and the January week is Sch. 4,500.

The recommended lower-priced B&Bs are

Winkler (tel. 5350) Sch. 360 HS; Sch. 300 LS. Located across from the Silvrettabahn.

Palin (tel. 5268) Sch. 460-500 HS; Sch. 350-380 LS. Special week costs Sch. 4,710.

Engadin (tel. 5358) Sch. 420 HS; Sch. 360-390 LS. No special January weeks.

Galtür

Prices in Galtür are considerably lower than those in Ischgl. Be sure to ask about the guest card when you arrive. It confers several considerable discounts in the town. The hotel prices noted here are the HS-LS range with half board and bath. Telephone prefix is 05443.

The best lodging here may be **Alpenhotel Tirol** (tel. 206; telex 58262) near the center of town. Sch. 650-970.

Fluchthorn (tel. 202; telex 58271) Central village location with good disco. Sch. 630-790.

Post (tel. 422) In the village center with good disco. Sch. 670-770.

Zum Silbertaler (tel. 256) Near the tennis center and town pool. Sch. 590.

Postgasthöfe Rossle (tel. 232) Sch. 610-750.

Bergfried (tel. 208) Sch. 400-450.

Galtürhof (tel. 406) Sch. 450-550.

Luggl (tel. 386) Sch. 410-540.

Bed and Breakfast

Berta Lorenz (tel. 252) Sch. 250-260.

Dr. Köck (tel. 226) Sch. 270-290.

Garni Kurz (tel. 307) Sch. 250-300.

Hubertus (tel. 243) Sch. 250-330.

Apartments

The rental apartment business is well organized and bookings can be arranged through the tourist information office. When writing to the office, provide details about when you plan to arrive, how many people will be sharing the apartment and what facilities you desire. In return you will receive a listing with several apartment choices.

Make your selection and notify the tourist office or the individual owner, depending on the instructions you get from the tourist office.

Normally, linens and kitchen utensils are included in every apartment. Heat, taxes, electricity and cleaning services may be extra. Expect to pay between Sch. 100 and Sch. 200 per person a night, depending on how many are sharing the apartment, where it's located and its relative position on the luxury scale.

Dining

In Ischgl perhaps the best restaurant is the traditional kitchen of the **Goldener Adler**. Locals also recommend highly the **Trofana** for good international cooking. Try the **Kitzloch** for fondue and grilled steaks. **Yscla** has a good French and local menu.

In Galtür, be sure to eat once at the **Landle** and at **Zum Silbertaler**. The **Fluchthorn** also serves hearty fare at reasonable prices.

In Samnaun, try a meal at the **Hotel Post**. It's pricy but one of the best in town.

Nightlife

Here Ischgl shines. It has one of the best après-ski scenes from 3 p.m. until 7 p.m., then excellent nightlife from around 10 p.m. until about 2 a.m.

The best après-ski spots are **Christine**, just up from the Silvrettabahn and across the street from the Post and Goldener Adler, and the **Kitzloch** at the opposite end of town near Hotel Elisabeth and the Fimba and Pardatschgratbahn. Both spots rock from about 4 p.m. until 7 p.m., with a disk jockey spinning music, the bar serving half-liter beers and the crowd singing and dancing in ski suits and ski boots.

The Sonne also has a lively crowd, but no dancing.

The three major discos begin to crank between 10 and 11 p.m. The **Tenne** in the basement of Hotel Trofana offers the most crowded venue, with dancing and wild contests alternately competing for attention. The **Club Madlein** in Hotel Madlein and **La Not** in the basement of Hotel Post offer the best dancing, but you'll find yourself wanting to shift with the crowd, depending on which club has the best live band. Club Madlein has a Sch. 50 cover charge.

Galtür

Try **Almhof, Alpkogel** and **Wirlerhof** for après-ski at the bottom of the lifts. After dinner the action shifts into the village to discos in the **Fluchthorn** and at the **Post**. The Wirlerhof's disco is relatively quiet, good news if you're staying near the lifts. You might also enjoy the traditional zither evenings at Zum Silbertaler on Tuesdays and Thursdays and at the Hotel Almhof on Friday nights.

Child care

Child care services are available. Contact the Ischgl Tourist Office (tel. 05444-5266) for assistance in arranging care.

There is a guest kindergarten without ski school at Idalp. The price, including lunch, is Sch. 130 a day, and without lunch, Sch. 70 a day.

The Ischgl ski school (tel. 5257 or 5404) runs a children's program for kids four and up. Prices include a lunchtime snack. These are 1989/90 prices:

for one day	Sch. 445
for three days	Sch. 1,045
for five days	Sch. 1,325
for six days	Sch. 1,490
for twelve days	Sch. 2,680

In Galtür the ski school is open for children aged three years and up. It is located near the Birkhahn chairlift. Children attending ski school can get lunch and after-class supervision for an additional charge of Sch. 60 a day. Non-skiing kindergarten children must be picked up by their parents between 12 noon and 1:45 p.m.

Ski school prices in Galtür are: one day, Sch. 330; three days, Sch. 810; five days, Sch. 990; six days, Sch. 1,060. Non-skiing kindergarten costs Sch. 60 a day and Sch. 30 a half day for guests staying in Galtúr with a guest card. For others the cost is Sch. 60 a day and Sch. 35 a half day.

Getting there

The nearest international airport is in Munich. From there, the easiest highway route is Garmisch, Fern Pass to Landeck or Innsbruck and on to Ischgl. The train stops in Landeck, where there is regular bus service to Ischgl.

Other activities

Winter merely enhances rather than disguises the beauty of Galtür, a mountain village some 5,197 feet high. Galtür is the gateway to the Silvretta Alpine Highway, which is open during warm-weather months. If taking photographs of beautiful buildings is one of your hobbies, visit the parish church Maria Geburt in Galtür.

Landeck, an Alpine crossroads, around the corner from the valley opening is a regional shopping center, and is distinguished by the towering outline of Fortress Landeck.

As additional excursions from the Paznaun valley, you can travel to Innsbruck and Munich.

Tourist information

Fremdenverkehrsverband, A-6563 Galtür/Tirol; tel. 05443-204; telex: 58160 TIRGAL.

Fremdenverkehrsverband, Postfach 24, A-6561 Ischgl; tel. 05444-5266; telex: 58148 FVVSVRA; fax. 05444-5636.

Kitzbühel/Kirchberg

Kitzbühel has long held a reputation as one of the most beautiful alpine towns in Austria. It also is reputed to be one of the hot spots for après-ski and excellent intermediate skiing. In all cases it lives up to its reputation.

If possible, arrive before nightfall in Kitzbühel, when the wrought-iron entranceway lamps and flickering candles in the restaurant windows lend a special charm to the streets. You'll hear the jingle of bells on a horse-drawn sleigh, and somewhere in the distance, someone in a gasthaus will let out a hearty laugh that rises above the sounds of a piano or a zither. The exterior of Kitzbühel is old and lovely, quite romantic: The atmosphere inside is uniquely "Kitz"—light and bright, often boisterous and never dull. In Kitzbühel the skiing day is long enough to tire you out, and it is followed by a night that seems to last forever.

In January, when excitement is building for the famed Hahnenkamm World Cup competition, Kitzbühel vibrates with action. The streets are filled with people at midnight and the sounds of music and laughter ripple over the cobblestones and along the narrow alleyways of the scenic town center.

The Hahhenkamm Race festivities begin on 11 January 1990 with hot-air balloons, a film festival and ice show. The women's downhill takes place on 15 and 16 January and the Hahhenkamm men's downhill race is held on 20 and 21 January. Depending on your reasons for vacationing, this is either the perfect time to be in Kitzbühel or a time to avoid this resort.

Kirchberg, the resort that shares much of the same mountain, has become a major player in the area. Filled with a younger crowd and attracting more dedicated skiers and families, Kirchberg has a more limited nightlife and significantly lower prices than its glitzy neighbor. We will deal with Kirchberg in each section where the descriptions are not common.

Where to ski

The Ski Safari is a ski circuit through the Kitzbühel area that uses interconnecting lifts for more than 20 miles of runs. You can work your way from Kitzbühel to Pass Thurn, or reverse the direction and on the way tackle slopes that have about 19,000 feet in total vertical drop. For intermediates, it's quite an outing.

Kitzbühel—"Kitz" to insiders—centers on the famed Hahnen-

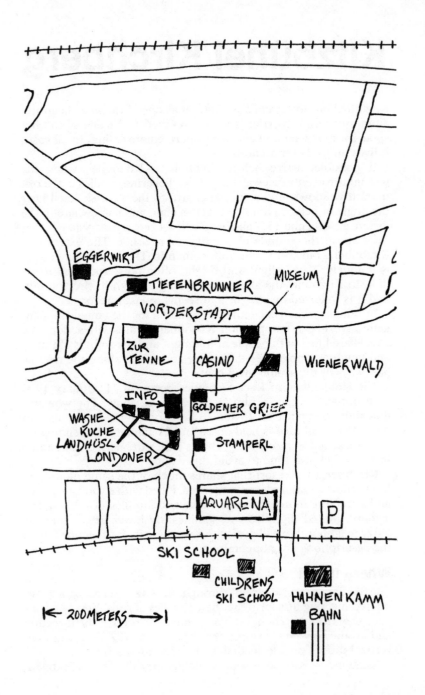

kamm, the primary slope above town where the World Cup circuit aces race each January.

Relatively low-lying slopes go from Kitzbühel at 2,560 feet up to approximately 6,561 feet. What this means is that before Christmas and after late February the slopes may not be completely covered.

To avoid long lift lines, a chronic problem, drive toward neighboring Kirchberg and take the new Fleckalmbahn to the Ehrenbachhöhe above the Hahnenkamm race circuit. On the way down, ski the "Streif run," site of last year's World Cup race, then begin working your way around the Ski Safari. It's marked by circular signs depicting an elephant on skis pointing the way. Don't pass up the red runs on either side of Pengelstein. The trail to Kirchberg off the top is the better of the two.

For runs in the sun, we prefer the gentle, seldom challenging slopes of the 6,549-foot-high Kitzbüheler Horn across town. We skied in January, and several local residents told us that the snow would melt in March. The best run is from the top station of the Hornköpfl lift all the way through the trees and into Kitzbühel.

The slopes on Pass Thurn, reached directly from lifts at the pass or by working your way up from nearby Jochberg, are more challenging. The runs are higher, up to 6,562 feet.

Mountain rating

The skiing in Kitzbühel and Kirchberg is strictly intermediate. There are enough blue runs available for the lower intermediate and beginner to keep harmony in any mixed-skill group of skiers vacationing here.

Experts, except those concentrating on their times along the Hahnenkamm run or the Gaiberg course above Kirchberg, should wedel on something more challenging than the prepared runs. Guides can take serious skiers on off-trail expeditions from Kitzbühel or Kirchberg that will delight even the most hardened experts.

For cross-country enthusiasts, there are 11 circuits with nearly 70 miles of prepared trails. Neighboring Jochberg sponsors evening skiing for cross-country fans.

Ski school

In Kitzbühel the "Rote Teufel" (Red Devil) ski school (tel. 2500) is led by Olympic triple-gold medalist Toni Sailer. Classes are also conducted in off-trail skiing. The Kirchberg ski school is located in the center of town (tel. 05357-2209).

Ski lesson prices are regulated throughout the Tirol. Full day group lesson—Sch. 340. Three days of group lessons—Sch. 740. Six days of group lessons—Sch. 950.

Private lessons are Sch. 1,750 for a full day per person and an additional Sch. 150 for each extra person. A half-day lesson with a private instructor costs Sch. 1,050 per person, with Sch. 150 due for each extra person.

Cross-country lessons are available: Half day—Sch. 300; three half days—Sch. 550; six half days—Sch. 770. Private instruction costs Sch. 1,050 for a half day, plus Sch. 150 for each additional person.

Check out the special ski weeks offered before Christmas and in March. For example, during the last three weeks in March an all-inclusive plan offers six days' accommodations, six days of instruction in classes with a maximum of nine skiers, plus a seven-day lift pass. The cost for this package starts at Sch. 3,245. Packages with breakfast only start at Sch. 2,780 in smaller pensiones.

Lift tickets (89/90 prices)

The best ticket is the Kitzbühel/Kirchberg area lift pass, which includes ski shuttle buses and swimming in Kitzbühel's Aquarena (even if you are staying in Kirchberg). These prices are for high season. Before Christmas, during January and from March 17 onward, prices are approximately 15 percent less.

for one day	Sch. 300
for two days	Sch. 570
for three days	Sch. 800
for six days	Sch. 1,450
for seven days	Sch. 1,570
for fourteen days	Sch. 2,600

Seniors (men 65 and over; women 60 and over) get approximately 15 percent discount. Children under 15 ski at half price.

Accommodations

Kitzbühel

An excellent variety of lodging can be found in the main part of Kitzbühel, close to the slopes and nightlife. The city's tourist information office in the center of town (look for the big "I") will assist you in making reservations.

We also recommend you ask the tourist office about reservations for rooms in private homes and farms in the area.

Because of the large number of restaurants, you may want to

choose bed-and-breakfast accommodations and try different restaurants during the week. Unless noted, prices are per person for double occupancy, high season, half pension.

Tiefenbrunner (tel. 2141) Sch. 1,080-1,300. One of the best hotels in town.

Zur Tenne (tel. 4444) Sch. 950 (bed and breakfast only). A top hotel in center of town with one of the best nightclubs on the second floor. It is a Best Western hotel.

Schloss Lebenberg (tel. 4301) Sch. 1,100-1,650. A converted castle just on the outskirts of the town. All the amenities you could ask for.

Am Lutzenberg (tel. 3279) Sch. 660-700. An excellent middle-range hotel.

Montana (tel. 2526) Sch. 800-900. Next to the Hahnenkamm lifts. Has swimming pool, sauna and a good kindergarten.

Bellevue (tel. 2766) Sch. 650-750. Middle budget hotel.

Klausner (tel. 2136) Sch. 740-820. Middle budget hotel.

Eggerwirt (tel. 2455) Sch. 600-680. A find. Our favorite, with a great restaurant. You'll love it.

Pension Foidl (tel. 2189) Sch. 400—Small pensione, 31 beds.

Kirchberg

The accommodations here are not as luxurious as those in Kitzbühel. There are no four-star hotels, but those listed below are excellent, providing good service. If traveling with your family, Kirchberg is a perfect place to stay.

Hotel Sonnalp (tel. 2741) Sch. 940-1030 (half pension). With sauna and pool. Great for families.

Parkhotel Kirchberg (tel. 2383) Sch. 840-930 (half pension). No pool.

Happy Kirchberg (tel. 2842) Sch. 840-930 (half pension). Excellent hotel with heated outdoor pool, sauna and a good kindergarten.

Hotel Seehof (tel. 2228) Sch. 520-560 (half pension). Beautifully redone rooms, great location with ice skating on the lake by the hotel. A real bargain.

Gasthof Kirchenwirt (tel. 2852) Sch. 380-470 (half pension). Newly renovated and in the center of town. Good food.

Apartments

Lodging in the Kitzbühel area is primarily in hotels, pensiones and private homes. The tourist office publishes a list of apartments, but it notes that the prices are set by the owners themselves. Expect to pay Sch. 225-275 per person a night for an apartment that will sleep between two and four people. For information on chalet and apartment rentals, contact the local tourist office.

In Kirchberg, expect to pay Sch. 200-230 per person a night for a two- to four-bed apartment. Again, the local tourist office will send information on available apartments.

Dining

In Kitzbühel, we were in the mood for a quiet meal and the **Schloss Lebenberg** (tel. 4301) outside town was a good choice, with a menu from Sch. 200. Try **Unterberg Stuben** for what may be one of the best meals of your vacation. The **Tennerhof** offers a delicious meal starting from Sch. 200, and if you win big at the Kitzbühel casino, take your friends to eat at **La Cave** (tel. 2555, for reservations). The menu there starts at Sch. 580. **Restaurant Reisch** and **Gasthof Eggerwirt** also have excellent kitchens.

In Kirchberg, most arrangements are for full pension. If you want to go out on the town, the best restaurant is the one attached to the **Sporthotel Alexander**. For excellent wild game, try the **Kirchenwirt**. On the slopes, head for the **Gasthof Schroll** for *Kaiser Schmarren aus der pfanne*.

Nightlife

In Kitzbühel, **Zur Tenne** hotel (tel. 4444) has some of the brightest live evening entertainment. The jet-set crowd often gathers here following après-ski tea at **Praxmair's** (tel. 2646), a café you should visit at least once during your stay.

Other good nightlife spots in Kitzbühel are the **Take Five** (after 10 p.m.), **Stamperl** (5-7 p.m.), **Washe Kuche** and the **Drop-in**. There is also a **Londoner Pub** in Kitzbühel, which is much tamer than the Londoner in Kirchberg.

Although we said earlier that Kirchberg is quieter than its glitzy neighbor, it does claim perhaps the wildest après-ski bar in Europe, The Londoner. The successful bar has been been copied in other towns, but none are as exciting as the original in Kirchberg. The action starts as skiers come off the slopes. It's "dance-'til-you-melt" time from about 4 p.m. until 8 p.m., when most head off to eat in their hotels. This is the wild après-ski party every skier has dreamed of.

Later in the evening, head to the **Pferdestalle, Fuchslöchl** or **Rauchkichl** for dancing. The party seems to shift locations each night, but Kirchberg is not so big that you can't check out the action and then head back to where everyone's hanging out.

Child care

Information on child care services is available through the local tourist office.

In Kitzbühel, the kindergarten for children from one to three years of age is called "Krabbelstubbe Max and Moritz" (tel. 2786). It costs Sch. 350 a day.

In addition, the local ski school (tel. 2500) offers ski kindergarten for children from ages two-and-a-half to five.

In Kirchberg there is a kindergarten (tel. 2406) open Monday through Friday from 8 a.m. until 4 p.m. (except Wednesday, closes at noon); and "Happy Kinderland" in Hotel Happy Kirchberg (tel. 2842) open daily, except Saturdays, from 8:30 a.m. until 5 p.m. The rates is Sch. 150 a day, which includes lunch.

The ski school in Kirchberg also has special children's programs; rates are the same as for the normal ski school, plus Sch. 75 for lunch.

Getting there

The best international airport connections are into Munich (although flights into Salzburg and Innsbruck bring you to the same area). From there, travel to Kitzbühel or Kirchberg by train.

By car, the trip is on the Inntal autobahn; take the Kufstein-Sud exit, then continue via St. Johann.

Other activities

Kitzbühel and Kirchberg have good train connections and are thus ideally suited for excursion trips to Munich, Innsbruck and Salzburg. Day-trips by automobile are also not difficult because travel in and out is rarely hindered by icy roads.

Kitzbühel has two very beautiful churches. The centuries-old Pfarrkirche (parish church) and the adjacent Liebfrauenkirche (Church of Our Lady) give Kitzbühel a distinctive old-world feel.

In Kitzbühel, also visit the Jochbergtor, the only remaining gate of the old fortified city.

The Traidkasten at Hinterstadt 32 was once a mill but now houses the local folk museum and a ski museum.

Kitzbühel is lively at Christmas, although expensive. The annual Christmas market, religious observances and holiday festivities attract thousands.

The last half of January usually includes the World Cup race, and in early February there's an international cross-country race.

Kirchberg has one of the best organized horse-drawn sleigh ride programs. Costs for a sleigh for up to five people is Sch 300-600, depending on the time of day and the operator.

Tourist information

Fremdenverkehrsverband, Hinterstadt 18, A-6370 Kitzbühel; tel. 05356-2155; telex 51-18413 FVVLA.

Fremdenverkehrsverband, Postfach 28, A-6365 Kirchberg; tel. 05357-2309; telex 51-371.

Fremdenverkehrsverband, A-6370 Aurach; tel. 05356-4622.

Fremdenverkehrsverband Jochberg, A-6373 Jochberg; tel. 05355-5229.

Mayrhofen, Zillertal and Tuxertal

The Ziller Valley has somehow avoided great fanfare despite its being one of the best and most accessible places to ski in all of Austria. The chief resort of this region and most visited by English-speaking skiers is Mayrhofen. It is typically Austrian with narrow streets, beautiful old buildings and cozy, timbered restaurants, cafés and hotels. Life revolves around the large square and the long, narrow main street. The cablecar station in the center of town is almost always crowded and the spillover of skiers and shoppers combines to keep the main street alive with visitors during the day.

Mayrhofen reminds us a bit of Söll, another small Austrian resort, although the former is larger and has more interesting skiing.

A smaller town that makes resort noises is Zell am Ziller and at the head of the Tuxertal, Hintertux is at the base of one of the best glaciers for summer skiing. Hintertux makes no pretensions about being anything other than a glacier ski resort. If it had sidewalks, they would be rolled up at lift closing time.

Where to ski
Mayrhofen and Zillertal

Wherever you look in the Zillertal there are lifts, and most of them open up good intermediate skiing.

The best skiing is at Mayrhofen. Here, from the 6,872-foot-high Penkenjoch, a network of trails for all levels of skiers branches out. Avoid the older cablecar from town and instead take the gondola from nearby Schwendau or the chairlift from Finkenberg on the other side of town.

At the top of the gondola from Schwendau, a chair takes you to the Horberg summit (8,331 feet). The two mountains are connected, and the runs here offer challenges for all levels, including expert.

Mayrhofen's second area, on the opposite side of the valley, is the Filzenalm. Take the long Ahornbahn cablecar to the Filzenalm at 6,284 feet. There were too many T-bar lifts and too little good skiing to hold us there for long.

In the Mayrhofen area, nine cross-country trails with a total of about 12 miles are prepared daily. Two of the trails are lighted for night skiing. Overall, cross-country opportunities are not interesting for the Nordic enthusiast.

Elsewhere in the valley, we recommend Hochfügen, only a short distance from the autobahn exit. Drive to the town from Fügen along an eight-mile mountain highway. From there, lifts ascend to 7,226 feet.

Take the Spieljoch cablecar directly to the 6,562-foot level above Fügen. From the top, at the Onkeljoch, there is a four-mile run back into the valley, the Zillertal's longest downhill run.

Zell am Ziller is a beautiful town, the most important in the lower part of the valley, but the skiing was too far from town to suit us. You can drive the 2.5-mile steep road up to the Gerlosstein lifts, but if you are not accustomed to driving with chains, take the bus or try another resort.

Hintertux and the Tuxertal

The glacier opens at the end of the valley, and from the ground station you can see most of the nearly 50 miles of trails above. The best run is the trail from the Grosse Kaserer (10,700 feet) down over a great, steep field of bumps to the gondola. A nice intermediate run leads from the top of the Gefrorene Wand to the Spannagel house, a cozy alpine hut serving excellent food.

Opposite the glacier is the Sommerbergalm, with skiing from the 7,544-foot level.

Mountain rating

Overall, Mayrhofen is known as an excellent area for beginners. The ski school—especially for children—is world-famous. The professionalism of the novices' ski instruction organization is even more important because the nursery slopes are not particularly convenient to hotel accommodations.

Attaching a rating to more than a dozen resorts in the valley is difficult. The majority of slopes are intermediate and lower-intermediate with very few exceptions where experts are challenged. In the Tuxertal it is more of the same, but with a few more thrills for an advanced skier.

Ski school

Mayrhofen has a large ski school (tel. 2795) numbering 130 instructors, many of them English-speaking. Lessons here are comparable in price to schools in other parts of the valley.

The Hintertux ski school (tel. 363) has 20 instructors.

Individual lessons (88/89 prices)

for one hour	Sch. 320
for each additional person	Sch. 110

Group lessons

for one day (four hours)	Sch. 300
for three days	Sch. 580
for five days	Sch. 730
for six days	Sch. 790

Lessons are also available for cross-country. Contact the ski school for registration.

Lift tickets

Tickets for the individual resorts are available, as well as for the regional Zillertaler-Superpass. We recommend buying the superpass. (88/89 prices)

	middle season	high season
for a half day	Sch. 155	Sch. 155
for one day	Sch. 230	Sch. 230
for two days	Sch. 440	Sch. 440
for three days	Sch. 650	Sch. 650
Zillertaler-Superpass		
for four days	Sch. 700	Sch. 840
for five days	Sch. 830	Sch. 1,010
for six days	Sch. 950	Sch. 1,160
for seven days	Sch. 1,070	Sch. 1,310

Accommodations

Finding rooms along the length of the Ziller Valley has been made easy with the help of the local tourist offices, which supply the usual brochures listing available housing and act as intermediaries in case you do not want to book your own reservation for an all-inclusive plan.

In Mayrhofen, the tourist office (tel. 05285-2305) also provides a listing of local hotels that are particularly good for families with small children. These hotels, marked by the sign of the Zillertal mountain fairy, provide discounts for children, children's games, coloring books, special menus for children and so on.

Elizabeth Hotel (tel. 2929) The most luxurious hotel in the region, with excellent food.

Hotel Neue Post (tel. 2131) On the market square near the train station.

Hotel Neuhaus (tel. 2203) Also centrally located, closer to railway station than the Neue Post. One of the recommended hotels for families with children.

Sporthotel Strass (tel. 2205) Provides good lodging close to the Penken cablecar. Excellent location for those who rate skiing as top priority.

Hotel Alpenhof Kristal (tel. 2428) medium-priced hotel on the main square. Popular with many English tour groups.

Hotel Kramerwirt (tel. 2216) Inquire at the nearby Hotel Bergland for more details on the Kramerwirt's half- and full-pension plans. Central location, short driving distance from the cablecar.

Hintertux has several hotels right at the base of the glacier. If you're intent on skiing and little else, they make a good choice.

Hotel Rindererhof (tel. 05287-501; telex 053990) Excellent location right at the gondola going up to the glacier. Superb for the enthusiastic skier.

Hotel Neu Hintertux (tel. 05287-318; telex 054643) Almost as close to the lifts as the Rindererhof.

Badhotel Kirchler (tel. 05287-312; telex 053990) Large hotel, a beautiful, expensive and comfortable place to stay.

Hotel Kirchlerhof (tel. 05287-431) A comfortable, medium-priced hotel in Lanersbach catering to families. Excellent breakfast buffet.

Apartments

The tourist office booklet, "Hotels-Pensions-Apartments," has a complete section on apartment and chalet rentals in and around town. To find the place that suits your needs, write first for the booklet, choose a place and the tourist office will assist with reservations.

Child care

Mayrhofen's tourist association provides a babysitting referral service (evenings only). Call the tourist office at 2635.

The ski school provides day care and ski instruction for children. It was Austria's first children's ski school, its organizers told us, and its program provides instruction, meals and entertainment for the children during non-skiing time.

for one cay	Sch. 415
for two days	Sch. 750
for three days	Sch. 965
for six days	Sch. 1,400

Ski school without lunch will cost:

for one cay	Sch. 340
for two days	Sch. 600
for three days	Sch. 740
for six days	Sch. 950

Dining

At Mayrhofen, the 400-year-old farmhouse restaurant, **Wirtshaus zum Griena** (tel. 2778) caught our fancy and was kind to our wallet. The food was excellent, the atmosphere marvelous. Duck your head to avoid the old and low ceiling beams. On the Penkenjoch, the **Vronis** restaurant served excellent lunchtime meals, and the service from the owner, Martin Huber, and his family was friendly.

In Lanersbach, try the restaurant in the Kirchlerhof and in Hintertux test slightly fancier offerings at the Badhotel Kirchler.

Nightlife

The evenings after skiing are cozy in the town's many hotel bars, but Mayrhofen will never be mistaken for St. Anton after dark.

There is life, however, in the **Schlussel** disco in the Brucke hotel. While it seems to draw mostly 18 to 25 year olds, a slightly older crowd will be found at the **Andreas Keller** in the Neue Post. Check out the **Tiroler Stuben** in the Neuhaus, one of our recommended hotels. We enjoyed "five o'clock tea" with a visiting English friend in the hotel. He stayed on for drinks and dancing at the après-ski bar and recommended it highly.

This town does get rocking immediately after the slopes close with serious drinking and dancing. In general, make for the area around the marketplace and choose your own spot for the evening.

In Hintertux, try the **Batzenkeller** disco and the **Almbar**.

Getting there

Travelers visiting the Zillertal fly into Munich. The valley lies along an autobahn exit (Achensee) between Munich and Innsbruck. The drive up the valley is easy and fairly short, only about 20 miles. There are both trains and buses offering service in the valley.

Other activities

One reason we based our visit to the Zillertal in Mayrhofen was the enthusiasm of its tourist office, which promotes a regular series of events to entertain guests. These include tea dances, chess competitions, color-slide lectures and other entertainment.

Each week a puppet show is staged for children, and on another evening games are scheduled for the kids.

An outing to Innsbruck for a museum and sightseeing visit is a must.

For the outdoor-minded who want to do more than ski, we recommend the Alpineschule Zillertal (tel. 2829), run by Peter Habeler, for mountain training and excursions into the region's rugged Alps.

Tourist information

Fremdenverkehrsverband A-6290 Mayrhofen; tel. 05285-2305; telex: 53850.
Fremdenverkehrsverband A-6280 Zell am Ziller; tel. 05282-2281.

Montafon Valley

The Montafon Valley, like neighboring Paznaun, offers good skiing and glorious scenery in the high country above the shores of Lake Constance. The two valleys are connected from June through November by one of the most beautiful Alpine roadways, the Silvretta highway.

The Montafon Valley, which branches off from the road to the Arlberg Pass at Bludenz, is made up of 11 resorts running along the valley: St. Anton i. Montafon, Bartholomäberg, Vandans, Silbertal, Schruns, Tschagguns, St. Gallenkirch, Gargellen, Gortipohl and Gaschurn, with Partenen, at the other end, the gateway to the Silvretta highway. The major towns are Schruns, Tschagguns and Gaschurn.

Where to ski

With nearly a dozen places to ski, it was difficult to do more than take a few runs along the best slopes in each area. However, settling on a favorite was easy. That is the six-mile run from the Sennigrat summit (7,544 feet) above Bartholomäberg, a few miles up the valley. You'll sing the praises of this intermediate cruise after skiing the valley's shorter runs. One piece of advice: Everyone wants to get up the mountain in the morning, so avoid the lines in Schruns and take the Lapellbahn chair from neighboring Silbertal. You can easily work your way up the mountain from that side.

For ski variety, we had two favorites. The Golm, at 6,232 feet above Tschagguns, offered moguls, trails through the trees on the lower slopes and even deep powder. The run from the top is nearly five miles long.

Second, we enjoyed the Silvretta Nova area, which is actually a circuit of lifts connecting nearly 50 miles of trails above the towns of Gaschurn, St. Gallenkirch, Gortipohl and Partenen.

We liked one other slightly isolated resort area. It is Gargellen, a 4,667-foot-high village, tucked into a side valley above St. Gallenkirch. Try the black run directly down the lift on the Schafberg.

For cross-country, the best circuit is the 12-mile loop connecting St. Gallenkirch, Gortipohl, Gaschurn and Partenen. There is also a nine-mile trail prepared on the snow-packed surface of the lake at The Bielerhoehe above Partenen.

Mountain rating

The runs here are intermediate for the most part with a few black trails to challenge the expert skier.

Beginner lifts abound at the foot of the mountains. The region is particularly good for advanced beginners just starting to perfect their skills on the red runs.

While the Montafon is not known as a cross-country region, the circuits are good and the mountain panorama is remarkable.

For those who like ski touring, there is a marvelous area with many trails along the Montafon's highest ridges and slopes. Even experienced skiers travel with a guide on these touring excursions.

Ski school

There are eight ski schools in the valley. The most popular and expensive are those of Schruns and Gaschurn. The school in Tschagguns has 40 teachers, several of them English-speaking, and in neighboring Schruns about 30 instructors are available. Lessons are offered, from beginner to advanced, with races for the guests each week.

Cross-country skiers can choose from several trails, including a new one on the Schrunser Feld. It's called the "Zelfen" circuit. Check with the ski school for information on cross-country lessons.

Individual lessons

for one hour (noon–2 p.m.)	Sch. 260-320
for one day	Sch. 1,600
for each additional person	Sch. 100

Group lessons

for one-half day (two hours)	Sch. 250
for one day	Sch. 400
for three days	Sch. 900
for five days	Sch. 1,100

Lift tickets

If you plan a variety of skiing, only the Montafon area ski pass should be considered. (1988/89 prices)

	adults	children
for three days	Sch. 790	Sch. 490
for six days	Sch. 1,410	Sch. 870
for seven days	Sch. 1,590	Sch. 990

Accommodations

We recommend the all-inclusive weeks sponsored by the Tschag-guns tourist office. Different packages cater to the beginner and intermediate skier, the advanced skier who wants to improve his technique and the experienced skier who wants to ski hard. All three packages include seven days at half pension. The beginner package includes six days of lessons, two hours a day. Prices begin at Sch. 2,850 a week (breakfast only, with bath) and run to Sch. 6,210 for the nicest accommodations.

We recommend signing up for one of the plans because, with 11 different towns offering hotels, choosing a place may take too much of your time. Fill out the accommodation card from the Tschagguns tourist office and its staff will find a hotel that fits your price and requirements. Specify whether you prefer to be in the center of town, want extra-quiet accommodations, want a room with a balcony or one near the lifts and so on.

If you choose to make your own arrangements, we found three hotels that offer special comfort, value and the extras most va-cationers expect.

Hotel Cresta (tel. 2557) Good service with a heated pool and sauna.

Sporthotel Sonne (tel. 2333) Good food, plus traditional moun-tain music and singing during folklore evenings.

Alpenparkhotel (tel. 2557) One of the best hotels in town.

Apartments

Check with the tourist office for information on apartment and chalet rentals in the area. Tschagguns, with about 2,500 year-round residents, has some 3,000 beds for tourists. Most are in hotels, guest houses and private homes. An apartment for four will cost between Sch. 350-600 a night.

Child care

The St. Gallenkirch ski school offers a ski kindergarten for children from age four. The school runs Monday through Friday, from 9:30 a.m. until 4 p.m. Prices include a lunchtime snack.

for five days	Sch. 1,190
for six days	Sch. 1,290

The ski school accepts children from three years for its babysitting service. A lunchtime snack is provided, and the service is offered

Monday through Saturday, from 9:30 a.m. until 4 p.m. Cost per day is Sch. 340.

Dining

The best restaurants in the valley are the **Romantik Hotel Heim-spitze** in Gargellan, the **Löwen Hotel** in Schruns and the **Montanella Stuble** in St. Gallenkirch.

For a good traditional meal, visit the **Gasthof Löwe** in Tschaggguns, the **Gasthof Krone** in Schruns and the **Gasthof Adler** in St. Gallenkirch. We have also had good reports about the **Alt-Montafon** restaurant (tel. 05558-232) at Gaschurn.

Nightlife

The nightlife in this valley is very limited. The main center is in Schruns, which has four pubs and four discos. For what après-ski activity there is, head to **Otto's Kuhstall** in St. Gallenkirch.

Getting there

The Montafon Valley is about 90 miles from the Zurich airport, where most international arrivals enter Switzerland for this Austrian excursion.

From Bregenz on Lake Constance, it's about one hour by automobile, or take the train to Bludenz near the entrance to the valley, where there's regular bus service.

Other activities

The center of adjacent, larger Schruns is only a 15-minute walk away. Both towns are set in the great natural beauty of the Montafon at the 2,000-foot level, with the surrounding peaks reaching nearly 10,000 feet.

Day excursions to Lake Constance, about an hour away, and Zurich are popular.

Until the snow closes the Silvretta highway (normally in November), the drive from Partenen over the Bielerhoehe to Galtür in the Paznaun valley is superb.

Tourist information

Verkehrsamt A-6780 Schruns; tel. 05556-2166.
Verkehrsamt A-6774 Tschagguns; tel. 05556-2457.

Oetztal Arena

Sölden, Hochsölden, Obergurgl, Hochgurgl

An excursion to Austria's Oetztal is part skiing and part sightseeing adventure. Good slopes and the glaciers guarantee year-round skiing. But it's the beauty of the Alpine backdrop that will leave a lasting impression. The valley follows the line of the Oetztaler Alpen, a range with 90 peaks over 3000 meters (9,843 feet) high and 86 different glaciers coming down from the summits.

The main resorts in the valley are Sölden and Obergurgl. Hochsölden is a suburb of Sölden huddled above the larger town, and Hochgurgl is merly a cluster of six hotels up the mountain from Obergurgl. Sölden is stretched along the main road that traverses the valley. If only the road had a way to go around the town, this would be a beautiful resort. As it is, Sölden is still beautiful but with constant traffic. Hochsölden, at the end of a mountain road does not have the same traffic problem. Obergurgl and Hochgurgl are both a farther half-hour drive back into the mountains from Sölden. Obergurgl is as picture-perfect as any alpine town tucked into the mountains on three sides, complete with old church steeple and picturesque hotels.

Where to ski

The top ski areas of the inner Oetztal are Sölden, Obergurgl, Hochsölden and Hochgurgl. In addition, Zwieselstein, Vent and Untergurgl have skiing areas. Unfortunately the areas are not interconnected, nor do they share a common ski pass. It seems that geography makes the lift interconnections difficult and lift-operator politics complicate the shared ski pass. A ski pass acceptable in the entire valley would be better for tourism.

We look first at the interconnected area above Sölden. It is split into two areas—the Haimbachjoch/Rotkoglhütte sector and the Gaislachkogl. The skiing overall is wide-open. Though there are trails marked on the map, with good snow, skiers can ski virtually anywhere, which makes Sölden a favorite of powder hounds and means plenty of skiing for a week above the treeline. The skiing is basically intermediate and beginner with some expert off-piste runs thrown in for good measure. In fact, an adventurous expert will have no trouble keeping busy above Sölden and in the Obergurgl/Hochgurgl areas.

Access to the slopes is either by cablecar starting from the upper end of Sölden or by gondola from the lower section of the town. I suggest the gondola because it moves many more skiers per hour. The gondola drops skiers in the middle of the Haimbachjoch/ Rotkoglhütte sector. Either take the chair or drag lift up to Rotkoglhütte, or traverse over to the restaurant and take the chair up to Haimbachjoch. The Haimbachjoch side of the mountain is by far the more difficult of these two sectors.

Connection with the Gaislachkogl sector requires skiing down to the bottom of the Langegg I lift, taking the Stabelebahn and then crossing the mountain to the middle station of the Gletscherbahn, which will bring you to Gaislachkogl. From here real experts can drop off to the right and take a steep unmarked Wasserkar trail. Tamer skiers (most of us) can head left and take the steep-enough red run back to the middle station. The Wasserkar triple-chair just below the cablecar mid-station opens a group of expert runs. To end the day, lower intermediates can head to the bottom of the Heidebahn lift and then take the trail back into town. Better skiers can drop down the lower sections of the Wasserkar and end up in Innerwald.

The skiing above Obergurgl and Hochgurgl is even more extensive but served by fewer lifts. That combination means plenty of off-piste action. There are no interconnecting lifts between Obergurgl and Hochgurgl. The slopes are not particularly difficult, but more challenging than those in Sölden. Above Obergurgl the Festkogl lift opens a wide face with unlimited intermediate skiing. Experts can drop to the right hand side of the lift and take the unprepared run through the Ferwaltal back to the lower lift station. This area is high (1,930 to 3,035 meters) with good, crisp snow. For a change, traverse over to the Hohe Mut area which has a good unprepared run from the Hohe Mut restaurant and a group of shorter lifts and runs.

Hochgurgl is reached by bus if you aren't staying there. This town has developed into a relatively upscale community anchored by one of the best luxury alpine hotels in Europe, the Hotel Hochgurgl. Lifts peak out at 3,082 meters where a mountain restaurant provides spectacular views. The skiing for experts is down the Königstal, for beginners in the center of the area and for intermediates under the Kirchenkarlift. Again, like Obergurgl, this area is perfect for continuous off-piste cruising.

Hochgurgl, Obergurgl and Vent, all above 1,900 meters, have some of Austria's best summer skiing. We have not skied the glaciers when flowers were blooming in the valley, but fellow skiers assure us it's an adventure not be be missed.

If you want to concentrate on cross-country skiing, choose another area. There are trails, but not the network you'll need to ensure variety.

Mountain rating

With a few exceptions, particularly from the Gaislachkogl, the area's runs are for intermediates.

There are enough training areas at the bottom for ski schools. The beginner has plenty of terrain, especially in the center of the Haimbachjoch/Rotkoglhütte sector, on which to keep busy practicing.

Experts looking for wild steeps will find the Oetztal only moderately interesting. Those searching unlimited off-piste will find a dream come true. In summer, when skiing is a real luxury, this is one of Europe's finest areas.

Ski school

The Sölden and Hochsölden ski schools have a total of 150 instructors. Obergurgl and Hochgurgl ski schools have more English-speaking instructors. Lessons are given daily, Monday to Saturday from 10 a.m. until noon and from 1:30 until 3:30 p.m. Private lessons are available through the local ski school (tel. 2364 or 2546) for about Sch. 300 an hour.

Group lessons (1989/90 prices)

for one day	Sch. 350
for two days	Sch. 610
for three days	Sch. 790
for five days	Sch. 920
for six days	Sch. 1070

Lift tickets

Tickets are good for all lifts in the **Sölden, Hochsölden, Gaislachkogel** area and for the ski shuttle bus. (1989/90 prices).

	adults	children (6-14)
for a half day	Sch. 250	Sch. 150
for one day	Sch. 330	Sch. 210
for two days	Sch. 630	Sch. 390

for three days	Sch. 89	Sch. 550
for four days	Sch. 1170	Sch. 710
for five days	Sch. 1380	Sch. 830
for six days	Sch. 1590	Sch. 950
for seven days	Sch. 1770	Sch. 1020

Lift tickets for the Obergurgl/Hochgurgl area are slightly higher

Accommodations

Sölden lives from its summer and winter tourist trade and has a complete range of accommodations. Unless indicated, prices are for half pension. HS: high season; LS: low season.

Hotel Central (tel. 05254-2260, telex 0533353) Sch. 1,350-1,550 HS. Sch; 1,150-1,350 LS. Includes whirlpool, sauna and Turkish bath.

Hotel Alphof (tel. 05254-2559) Sch. 740-840 HS; Sch. 540-640 LS. Includes many extras, such as pool, solarium and steam bath.

Hotel Hubertus (tel. 05254-2489) Sch. 650-820 HS. Sch. 500-650 LS. One of the best hotels in Sölden with great food. Mid-distance from both main lifts and very close to the final lift back from Fillip's and après-ski.

Hotel Regina (tel. 05254-2486) Sch. 840-1,350 HS. Sch. 580-700 LS. Near the main lift. Also offers apartments. The Austrian women's ski team usually stays here when training. Write early because this hotel is normally fully booked!

Hotel Sonne (tel. 05254-2203) Sch. 700 HS; Sch. 600 LS. Near the lifts. Friendly, competent service.

Hotel Tyrol (and Tyrolerhof) (tel. 05254-2288) Sch. 590-650 HS; Sch. 470-520 LS. In center of town within walking distance to chairlift.

Hotel Edelweiss (tel. 05254-2298) Sch. 850-990. Good hotel in Hochsölden.

Obergurgl and Hochgurgl
The first price is the January package price which includes seven days half pension and six days of lifts.

Hotel Edelweis and Gurgl (tel. 05256-223) Special week: Sch. 6,150. Perhaps the most convenient hotel to the lifts. A bit pretentious. Normal daily rates (full pension): Sch.850-900.

Hotel Romantik (tel. 05256-354) Special week: Sch. 5,660. Normal rates: Sch.810-910.

Pensione Wiesental (tel. 05256-263) Very convenient to the lifts in the old town. Special week: Sch.4330. Normal daily rate: Sch.620-650.

Pension Gamper (tel. 05256-238) In the center of the old town with an excellent kitchen. Weekly rate: Sch. 3,900-4,500. Normal daily rate: Sch. 650-690.

Hotel Hochgurgl (tel. 05256-265) Perhaps one of the best hotels in the Alps by any measure. This hotel is in the same company as the Zürserhof in Zürs and The Palace in St. Moritz. No special week. Normal daily rate: Sch. 1,190-1,590.

Hotel Ideal (tel. 05256-290) The bargain of Hochgurgl with all the right amenities—sauna, fitness room, TV's and garage. No special week. Normal daily rate: Sch. 600-750.
The Hotel and Wurmkogel and the Hotel Laurin in Hochgurgl are also recommended.
If you want a less expensive private home or apartment, try the following names: Carmen, Kristiana, Mina, Sepp Santer, Andre Arnold and Hans Seppl.

Apartments

The tourist office in Sölden maintains a list of rental apartments and chalets in the area. The Inner Oetztal Travel Office (tel. 2366) will arrange booking for you. Also check with the Hotel Alphof for their apartment prices.

Dining

Like its room prices, the Hotel **Central restaurant** (for reservations, call 2260) is expensive with a menu from Sch. 195, but it offers the best meal in town. The kitchen in the **Hubertushof** is considered exceptional for local fare.

The **Regina** offers traditional cooking at considerably lower prices. Try the **Alpenhof** for fondue and grill evenings, the **Sunny** for fish, and **Tyrolerhof** and **Sonne** for fondue. The **Nudeltopf** is the best Italian restaurant in town. **Höfle** has a traditional Öztal buffet once a week.

In Hochsölden, we recommend taking a room and meals at the **Edelweiss**.

On Obergurgl head to the **Romantik** for Italian food. Try the **Hochfirst** and then the **Grüner** for good Tyrolean cooking. The **Josl** is known for its wild game dishes.

Nightlife

Sölden is one of Austria's après-ski capitals. That is more due to the clientele than the variety of bars. In fact, there are only two spots for après ski from 3-7 p.m. Most skiers stop at **Filip's** (I'm not even sure it's spelled that way) across from the ski school. The dancing then continues at the ""**Après Ski**" on the main street of town. These bars are packed shoulder-to-shoulder with skiers in ski suits and ski boots singing and dancing up a storm. This goes on until about 8 p.m. when most head back to hotels to change for dinner.

The late-night disco and party action takes place again in the "Après Ski" but also in the **Almbar** in the basement of Hotel Tyrol.

In Obergurgl, try the **Skihaserlkeller,** the **Rendevous Bar** in the Hochfirst, the **Josl** and **Edelweissbar**. The town is small enough that with a little scouting the best spots can be easily found.

Child care

Child-care services are offered. For information, contact the Sölden tourist office (tel. 2212).

In Obergurgl the ski school runs a special course and a special non-skiing course for children, but parents must fetch children for lunch.

The ski kindergarten in Sölden (tel. 2364) accepts children from three to eight years and is open Monday through Saturday from 9 a.m. until 4:30 p.m.

for a half day (without meal)	Sch. 220
for one day (with meal)	Sch. 330
for three days (with meal)	Sch. 800
for six days (with meal)	Sch. 1300

Getting there

Sölden and Hochsölden are in the Oetz Valley, a side valley of the Inn. The easiest route is from Munich via Innsbruck and then up the Oetztal. More scenic is via Garmisch and over the Fernpass to the valley entrance. There is regular bus service from the train station at Landeck.

Other activities

The Oetztal is another of those destinations you choose primarily for skiing. Innsbruck is the closest large city and day tours are offered. Call the Oetztaler Tourist Office (tel. 05254-8105) for details on excursions.

There are horsedrawn sleigh rides for about Sch 400 an hour per group of four or five.

A new leisure center opened last winter with two indoor tennis courts, swimming pool, bowling, fitness room, sauna, steam bath and massage. (tel. 05254-2514).

There are also regular Rodelparties or tobogganing parties, where a bus takes a group to a mountain hut where there is beer and schnapps and dozens of toboggans. After drinking, eating and dancing everyone slides home on a long toboggan course. This is especially enjoyable during full moon.

Tourist information

Fremdenverkehrsverband Inneroetztal, A-6450 Sölden, tel. 05254-2212; telex 533247.

Fremdenverkehrsverband, A-6456 Obergurgl; tel. 05256-258; telex: 534557;

Fremdenverkehrsverband, A-6458 Vent; tel. 05254-8193.

Saalbach-Hinterglemm

You may have heard Saalbach's reputation as an après-ski "Animal House," but there's nothing that can prepare you for the reality of this: You have stopped to enter the dark, woodsy "Hinterhagalm" tea bar on the last run down, having worked up a thirst on the nearly two-mile "Asterabfahrt" trail into Saalbach. By the time the first beer arrives, the waitress has to swing her tray to adjust to the unspoken rhythm of the overflow crowd, the clumping of ski boots keeping time to the beat of traditional Austrian folksongs from the live band.

Even before the T-bar lift just outside the door officially closes for the day, the entire chalet becomes transformed into a dance floor. Legs dangling over the upstairs balcony jig to the two-step. By the time you're ready to locate your skis for the final 300-yard glide into the village, the way out is blocked by a swaying mass of bodies. You'll have to literally get down on your hands knees and make a crawl for it. No one seems to notice. Then just before you make it between the last set of legs separating you from the door outside, you hit your head on something. Looking up, you realize you've bumped heads with someone crawling in the other way. Welcome to the Saalbach-Hinterglemm "Ski Circus," Austria's season-long version of Mardi Gras.

Theories abound as to why some of the select ski resorts of Austria are touted by veteran skiers as the most friendly and fun in the Alps, and the simplest probably strikes closest to the truth—the locals are comparatively unspoiled by success. The chances are better in Austria than in any other Alpine country that your ski instructor or the bed-and-breakfast hostess works on a farm in the summer, or did until recent years. Switzerland is more efficient, France is more sophisticated and Italy has a greater flair for food, but Austria is down-home friendly and fun.

The fact that the rather expensive prices in Saalbach are beginning to distance it from smaller surrounding ski areas may be a warning sign that it's about to shake off its mantle of modesty.

Still, it's one of the premier areas in Austria, strictly on the strength of its ski slopes and extensive lift circuit. There's no denying that the Saalbach-Hinterglemm "Ski Circus" attracts more than its share of the fun-loving.

The village of Saalbach forms the epicenter of the area. Nestled in the narrow throat of the valley, with mountains crowding in as a backdrop for the chalet-style hotels and their carved-wood balconies, the village is as quaint as any you could hope for in the Alps. The custard-yellow steeple of an old church dominates the packed rooftops, and a mountain stream rushes noisily through the center of town.

The valley floor broadens considerably just a mile up the road at Hinterglemm, and the Sallach river runs the length of the valley, dividing the town in two. Here hotels are larger and the village fans out over a wider area. While it is as central to the main ski crossroads of the valley as Saalbach and has more mid- to upper-level hotels with full amenities, Hinterglemm loses some of the coziness that you'll find along the compact main street of Saalbach. While Hinterglemm has the look and feel of a resort, everything about Saalbach says that it was an Alpine village in its own right long before the ski rush began.

Where to ski

The rap on Austria has long been that while it offers some of the world's finest skiing, it lacks the all-in-one-pass ski circuits that make some of France's super resorts so mind-boggling. Nor can it compete, critics say, with the blood-curdling black runs so prominent in many Swiss ski areas. While there is some truth to those assessments, the Saalbach-Hinterglemm "Ski Circus" goes a long way toward proving itself the exception to the rule.

Indeed, the area offers what may be the best interconnected lift system in Austria. Even an expert skier determined to put as many miles under his skis as possible would find himself hard pressed to cover the area from one end to the other in a single day—never mind stopping along the way to enjoy the skiing. Because resorts seem to use different measurements for charting how many miles of prepared ski runs they have, it's almost useless to compare numbers. Suffice it to say that there are 60 separate ski lifts in this area, as well as Austria's largest cablecar. Alas, Saalbach also confirms that the Austrians remain more fond of the tush-tugging T-bar lift than any other country in the Alps.

The linear layout of the resort, with lifts covering both sides of the slopes along a single, lengthy valley, also argues for staying in its most central spot—Saalbach. That way you can head up the valley for a day's ski excursion and down the next. Anyone staying in Leogang at the far end of the valley, for instance, will find it hard to even reach the area above Hinterglemm without having to immediately turn around to catch the last lift home. (While there's excellent bus service up and down the length of the valley serving both Saalbach and Hinterglemm, Leogang actually rest in another valley.)

Experts should head directly for Austria's largest cableway, the 100-person-capacity Schattberg. The black run directly beneath the cablecar is a good example of why U.S. expert skiers keep coming back. It has good grade, it's bumpy, it's long and there's a single ride back up for those with enough stamina to do it again.

For another uniquely European experiece, head left at the top of the Schattberg cablecar down the "Limberg-Hochalm" trail. Although a relatively easy intermediate run, this is the longest trail in the area and is worth taking just for the sake of adventure. Vorderglemm at the bottom of this run represents the southern boundary of the area, and you can cross up to the other side of the valley on the Schoenleiten cablecar.

Experts who turn right at the top of Schattberg (Schattberg-East) and up the short Westgipfel DSB III lift to Schattberg-West can enjoy a whole mountainside of advanced intermediate trails leading down into Hinterglemm. There's plenty of tree skiing on this broad swath of mountain, and the run all the way down is worthy indeed. The only drawback is having to take two chairlifts to reach the top again. Advanced skiers will say that's OK, however, because it allows them advance up the valley and spend a lot of time in the "Zwoelfer" area, which rises above Hinterglemm on the valley's southwest side.

The runs down to the midstation from the top (6,509 feet) are nice and very bumpy, and there are lots of fine cutovers into untouched sugar for powder monkeys (snow permitting, of course). From the top you can also cut over to the Seekar T-bar, which has nice advanced intermediate runs from the top and an excellent powder bowl off to the right. The truly adventurous can skirt the ridge heading left off the top of Seekar, and after rounding the corner of the mountain head through generally untouched tree skiing.

Intermediate and advanced intermediate skiers will discover that they truly have the ringside seats for the Saalbach-Hinterglemm "Ski Circus." The entire northside of the valley is one intermediate run after another down an open mountainside. Spend a day in the "Hasenauer Koepfl" and "Reiterkogel" area just above Hinterglemm. If you head farther to the left up the valley toward "Spieleckkogel," you will stand about as high as you can in the valley (6,522 feet). Not only is the advanced-intermediate run all the way down to the valley floor long and excellent, but it's a single chairlift back up.

Advanced intermediates will also enjoy taking the long "Kohlmaiskopf" chairlift, which begins in Saalbach near the old church. From the top, there's a long three-kilometer advanced run down into Saalbach. This is one of the nicest sections of mountain in the entire area. Because of the relatively low height (5,886 feet from the top) of this area, all the runs seem to skirt or cut through beautiful forests. And at every juncture, there's the obligatory hut where you can enjoy a drink and a spectacular view from a balcony.

For a top-to-bottom basher, cut over to the "Bergeralm" chairlift, and from the top enjoy the challenging seven-kilometer "Bergeralm"-""Schoenleiten" run (Nos. 57 and 67 on the trail map) down to the valley floor to the Schoenleiten cablecar. The eight-person, standup cablecars will whisk you all the way to the top of Schonleiten, where from the restaurant you can enjoy the most spectacular view in the entire valley, and one of the truly memorable panoramas in the Alps. If you care to digest your lunch over some bumps, round the ridge toward Leogang and ski the three T-bar lifts. They're short, but sweet.

Beginners should take the "Bernkogelalm" chairlift from Saalbach and change chairlifts to make it all the way to the top of Bernkogel. The run from the top to the midstation is gentle, wide and very confidence-inspiring. In fact, this is where the Austrian ski instructors take their classes of first-timers. Those feeling a little more adventurous will find lots of manageable, broad runs down from the top of both the "Kohlmaiskopf" and "Bruendkopf" lifts.

Mountain rating

There are only a few runs that are strictly for experts, but there's plenty of challenging terrain in the "Ski Circus" to keep excellent skiers occupied. The fact that the area occupies so much of a broad valley means there always seems to be a tree glade beckoning somewhere.

Intermediates have discovered Nirvana. The whole north side of the valley is a canvas of intermediate runs waiting only for the intermediate skier to choose his or her favorite brushstroke. The fact that there is really no part of the "Ski Circus" that is totally off-limits to the intermediate skier (with the exception of the run under the Schattberg cablecar) means that you can enjoy all the pleasures of exploring the entire circuit without hitting a dead end.

Beginners and advanced beginners will also find Saalbach-Hinterglemm much to their liking. There are plenty of broad slopes even from the top that lead skiers on a gentle curve miles down into the valley.

Ski school

There are major ski schools in both Saalback and Hinterglemm. In Saalbach (tel. 065 41 246), the school is located just behind the church. Hinterglemm's ski and racing school (tel. 065 41 7511) is next to the large open area just behind the Zwoelfer chairlift. Combined, there are over 200 instructors in the area.

Group lessons (four hours, 10 a.m.-12 p.m. and 2 p.m.-4 p.m.)

one day	Sch. 350
three days	Sch. 900
six days	Sch. 1,150

Special children's classes begin at 10 a.m. and run through the day until 4 p.m. A full week (including lunch) costs Sch. 1,150. Cross-country ski lessons are also available, and there are 18 kilometers of cross-country ski trails in the area. Both ski schools also offer special off-trail ski adventures for expert skiers.

Lift tickets

Saalbach-Hinterglemm Ski Circus (high season is from December 23-January 6 and January 28-March 24). High season/Low season—H.S./L.S.

for half day		Sch. 200
for one day		Sch. 290
for three days	Sch. 819 (H.S.)	Sch. 655 (L.S.)
for six days	Sch. 1,480 (H.S.)	Sch. 1,180 (L.S.)
for 12 days	Sch. 2,290 (H.S.)	Sch. 1,945 (L.S.)

There are reduced lift prices for children under 15 years and further reductions for those under 10 years. Children also get 15 percent reductions during Christmas week, and after March 25th children ski free if they are accompanied by an adult holding a pass for six days or more. There are also special reductions for "Family Weeks" on the second and third weeks of January.

Accommodations

As befitting the Austrian's reputation for not standing on ceremony, the tourist office declines to rate local hotels by "stars." It feels the system is too arbitrary. Prices listed are per person, including half board (breakfast and dinner).

The Best

Alpenhotel (tel. 065 41 666 0)—Sch. 565. Every resort has its flagship hotel, and this is Saalbach's. The big red arch dominates the entrance of the village, and it announces that the Alpenhotel caters to all whims—sauna, solarium, massage, exercise room, indoor swimming pool, whirlpool and so on. There's also on-the-premises babysitting. The hotel also benefits from the fact that it houses the most most exclusive disco in Saalbach, the **Arena**.

Haider (tel. 065 41 228)—Sch. 390. Although not as fancy or as large as the Alpenhotel, the Haider is a personal favorite. It's quaint in the traditional Austrian mold, with carved wood bedboards and shutters. There's a sauna, solarium and a hot whirlpool, as well a hideaway lounge with fireplace. Besides an excellent restaurant serving traditional Austrian fare, there's also an informal pizzeria on the premises—always a plus for carbo-hungry skiers.

Spothotel Ellmau (tel. 065 41 7226 0) and **Glemmtalerhof** (tel. 065 41 7135)—Sch. 550. Both of these hotels in Hinterglemm are excellent and offer full amenities, such as sauna, solarium and indoor swimming pool. There's also babysitting on the premises.

Moderate

Mitterer (tel. 065 41 219)—Sch. 400. This inn in Saalbach is a good choice for those who want most of the trappings of a top hotel (including sauna and whirlpool), but in a quaint and more personable package.

Zwoelfer (tel. 065 41 317)—Sch. 294. Count this inn in Hinterglemm as good value. It's strategically located near the Zwoelfer chairlift.

Bed and Breakfast

Scharnagl (tel. 065 41 284)—Sch. 200. While it's too new to rate as quaint, this pensione scores high because of it's strategic location next to the old church and across the street from both the Kohlmais chairlift and the "Schi-Alm," perhaps the best après-ski bar in town. The rooms are clean and airy, and the proprietress, Frau Brudermann, is always willing to help. There's also a ski shop in the basement.

Other recommended pensiones in Saalbach are the **Montana** (tel. 065 41 283) Sch. 160-200; and the **Berger** (tel. 065 41 7140) Sch. 160-180. In Hinterglemm, try the **Flora** (tel. 065 41 7100) Sch. 190.

Dining

Austrian cooking mirrors the country and its people—hearty, simple and unpretentious. Few sights are more welcome after a full day's skiing than a generous pork filet with mushroom gravy and a heaping portion of "spaetzle," Austria's unbeatable doughy noodles. For a sweet treat on the mountain, try "Germknodel," a doughy sweetbread filled with jam and covered with warm vanilla sauce.

The **Hinterhagalm** just at the top of the Turm T-bar is something of a local legend. Its 5 p.m. "tea bar" is one the most notable après-ski events in the valley, yet at night this beautiful old lodge serves up traditional Austrian dishes with atmosphere galore. That atmosphere has even made it to the big screen, as the Hinterhagalm served as the backdrop for the Julie Andrews' movie, "Sound of Music."

Nearly all the major hotels in both Saalbach and Hinterglemm feature good restaurants, and you'll find menus with prices conveniently posted outside. Those with man-sized appetites should try the restaurant in the **Hotel Sonne** (tel. 065 41 7202), which features more than 20 different steak dinners. Also highly recommended is the Chateaubriand for two served at the **Hotel Reiterhof** (tel. 065 41 682). No ski resort is complete without an informal pizzeria with good food and reasonable prices, and in Saalbach that requirement is nicely fulfilled by the pizzeria in the **Hotel Haider** (tel. 065 41 228).

Nowhere in the world is eating on the slopes more convenient than in this area. There are no less than 40 mountain chalets serving food, and each lift seems to have one of these either at the top or bottom—or both. As well as the aforementioned "Germknodel," try the thick and meaty goulasch soup. Two mountainside chalets deserve special mention. The **Weidenkarkogel** at the top of the Schoenleiten cablecar for its spectacular panoramic view and the rustic **Thurneralm** (on the trail midway up the Reiteralm T-bar) for its hunting lodge flavor and ski-up bar.

Nightlife

Saalbach-Hinterglemm's reputation for excellent nightlife has more to do with the atmosphere and attitude of the area than its number of discos (officially only five). Along with the wild-and-crazy Austrians you're bound to meet tripping the light fantastic at night, there's also a healthy contingent of Scandinavians (especially Swedes) and British.

The **Arena** disco in the Alpenhotel is the most upscale nightspot in the valley. The action inside doesn't start until after 11 p.m. Expect to pay a cover (the cost varies depending on the entertainment) and about Sch. 110 for a mixed drink. There are two bars inside, a live band and plenty of overstuffed couches and secluded alcoves from which to take a break from the action on the dance floor.

It's a more casual crowd at the disco in the **Sporthotel** just up the main street from the centrally located Alpenhotel. This small nightspot is where the young and adventurous let their collective hair down. There's a circular balcony that overlooks the dance floor, and you need only pick out the partner of your choice from this strategic vantage point and then leap merrily into the crowded fray.

More off the beaten path, cross the stream just off the main street and walk uphill to the **Backstatt Stall**. The upstairs disco is on two levels, with another balcony for scoping the action on the dance floor. Prices are fairly reasonable by local, high-season standards (mixed drinks for Sch. 68, or around $5; beers for Sch. 23, about $1.75). The atmosphere is a little more woodsy and mellower than the spots mentioned above, and it's easier to find room on the dance floor.

As for après-ski, suffice it to say that it has to be witnessed to be understood. Where else, except inside the **Schi-Alm** at the bottom of the Turm T-bar (across from the old church), can you see Austrians dancing the can-can to "New York, New York," stacked three on top of one another and swaying like demented totem poles? The bedlam at the tea bar at the Hinterhagalm just up the slope is a close rival for honors as après-ski madhouse of the mountain.

Child care

There are two hotels that offer all-day nursery services and kindergarten for children one year and older. You have to call ahead, however, and make reservations to be sure they have enough help on hand. Call the Hotel Theresia in Hinterglemm (065 41 7414), or the Aparthotel-Adler in Saalbach (065 41 73 310).

Getting there

By train: There are direct trains to nearby Zell am See from both Munich and Salzburg. You can either take a cab the remaining

18 kilometers to Saalbach or wait for the regularly scheduled bus, which makes the trip to Saalbach nine times a day from the train station.

By car: The drive from the Munich airport to Saalbach takes about two and a half hours. Take the Salzburg autobahn and exit, following signs to Siegsdorf. From there, follow signs to Lofer-Maishofen, then you'll see signs to Saalbach-Hinterglemm.

Some hotels offer parking, or you can park in the large multideck parking garage just on the outskirts of town. Once in Saalbach you won't need a car, and a policeman is posted at the entrance to the main street to discourage all but commercial traffic.

Other activities

Try an afternoon excursion by horse-drawn sleigh. Lindlingalm offers tours that include a stop for a traditional Austrian lunch (tel. 065 41 7190). Sleigh rides are also offered by Taxi Schmidhofel (tel. 065 41 7163) and Lengauerwirt (tel. 065 41 7255).

On December 21, 1989 Saalbach will also host the World Cup ski circuit, sponsoring the men's downhill. That is in prepartion for January 1991, when the area will host the prestigious World Championships last held in Vail, Colorado.

Tourist information

Contact the Informationscenter, A-5753 Saalbach, tel. 065 41 74 44; telefax 065 41 79 00; telex 66507 vvsa.

Schladming
with Dachstein-Tauern Region

If you are up to the challenge of the fastest World Cup downhill run, looking for wide and long beginner and intermediate runs through thick pine forests; if you seek the excitement of glacier skiing on the Dachstein Glacier or the peacefulness of one of the most extensive cross-country areas in Austria, Schladming and the area around will deliver.

Although relatively unknown to Americans, Schladming, which is located in the center of Austria, hosts thousands of Austrian, German, Swedish, Danish, British and Dutch tourists. Already one of the leading vacation centers for the Austrians, the region has completed an extensive series of developments that have turned the valley into a world-class resort.

Schladming, the main hub of the area is nestled around a traditional town center, which offers good shopping, nightlife and restaurants—all within a five-minute walk from the main lift system.

Rohrmoos, about a five-minute drive up the mountain from Schladming, features more hotel rooms than Schladming, and guests can step out their door, put on their skis and set off down the mountain. But Rohrmoos is spread out and a long walk from the town center.

Ramsau lies on the opposite side of the valley, settled on a long plateau that features some of the most interesting cross-country skiing in Austria. Once again, accommodations are extensive but dispersed.

Haus im Ennstal, a short drive along the valley from Schladming, still appears to be a typical small mountain village. Perhaps the most picturesque of the main villages in the region, Haus has not succumbed to either modern hotels or pulsating tourist trade. It remains traditional, anchoring the Hauser Kaibling ski area, scene of one of the most exciting women's downhill courses. The town is interconnected with the other villages by ski buses that run frequently.

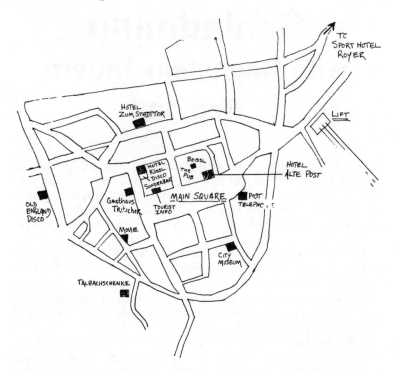

Where to ski

The *Skiparadies ski pass* opens more than 75 miles of prepared runs on seven mountains along the Dachstein-Tauern valley. The major areas are Planai (6,214 feet) above Schladming; Hauser Kaibling (6,610 feet) above Haus; Hochwurzen (6,069 feet) above Rohrmoos; and the Reiteralm (6,102 feet) above Pichl. Currently, only the Planai and Hochwurzen areas are interconnected by lifts, but plans to eventually connect the entire series of valleys are in the works. All other areas are connected by ski buses that ply the valley route continuously during the day. Each area mentioned above offers plenty of skiing for a day. That will mean having to take only one bus to an outlying area in the morning and one back home in the evening.

The Planai is served by one of the fastest cablecar systems in existence—waiting time in the valley is minimal even on Sundays. T-bars open the back bowls of the Planai area; the valley face of the mountain is crisscrossed by beginning and intermediate runs. The No. 1 run from the top of the Planai cablecar to the bottom station is the longest on the mountain and an absolutely joyful experience. Intermediates have a chance to cruise, and beginners can handle the entire run—the short steep sections sections are wide for an easy traverse.

The **Hochwurzen** area is reached through a series of T-bars and chairlifts. The lifts can take almost an hour if starting from the connecting chair with the Planai area. For people staying in Rohrmoos or skiers coming by ski bus, a single chairlift takes skiers to the top of the mountain. The upper areas are intermediate and the lower areas around Rohrmoos are a beginner's paradise.

Hauser Kaibling, rising above Haus, is normally not as crowded as Schladming. At times you'll find yourself alone on a beautiful mountain with some of the best intermediate slopes under your skis. The mountain offers a mix of intermediate and beginner trails, but intermediate is the main focus. The Knapplhof Descent, for example, is marked as a beginner trail, but it borders on intermediate. The trails are wide enough, however, for easy traversing. Take the bus or park at the base of the Hauser Kaibling cablecar just outside the town. The other cablecar rising directly from the upper reaches of the town looks great on the ski map but should be avoided unless your hotel happens to be located nearby. It only carries eight skiers about every 15 minutes.

Reiteralm, above the towns of Pichl and Gleiming, provides a good day's worth of skiing for intermediates. Beginners have too limited an area to make the half-hour series of lifts worthwhile unless they are staying in one of the base towns.

Overall, the area uses up a week of skiing without repeating a section twice. Even good skiers will be hard pressed to cover every trail on just the four main mountains in six days of hard skiing.

Mountain rating

The area is an intermediate skier's paradise. Beginners should center their efforts on the Rohrmoos area, although each section has beginner runs. After three days of lessons beginners are even brought all the way down each of the mountains by their ski instructors.

Experts should keep their eye out for good powder and test themselves high up on Hauser Kaibling or on the lower sections of the World Cup downhill runs both in Haus and Schladming. The *real* experts should look into hiring a guide to take them off trail for a great day or week of skiing.

Ski school

Individual lessons (1989/90 prices)

one day (five hours)	Sch. 1,300
one hour	Sch. 350
additional person	Sch. 100

Group lessons
Note: one lesson equals two hours of instruction

three days	Sch. 700
five days	Sch. 880

Rather than sign up for a ski course, you may want to be part of a more informal group of skiers and get a chance to explore the valleys with expert mountain guides. Sepp Schweiger and Herbert Thaller have organized a **Ski Safari** program in Schladming. They will take experts in small groups to find powder, moguls and hidden tracks; intermediate skiers will have a chance to really explore the mountain with someone who knows every trail and mountain watering hole. The groups allow skiers to easily meet others of the same level, and provide picnics and evening ventures into the bars and discos in town. Your guide will be a fully certified mountain guide and/or ski instructor. This is a perfect way for good skiers arriving alone to hook up with a new group of friends. Contact Sepp and Herbert through the tourist office, or call direct: Sepp—03687-22537; Herbert—03687-61148. Prices will range from Sch.420 a day to Sch. 1,050 for five days.

Lift tickets

The regional lift tickets cover four cable cars and 53 chairlifts and T-bars over seven mountains. Although it seems inconceivable that anyone would want a two-and-a-half hour "try-out ticket," the region offers adults such a ticket for Sch. 170, plus a Sch. 250 deposit; children get a pass for Sch. 105, plus a Sch. 195 deposit. If the tickets are returned within the two-and-a-half-hour time limit, the deposit, plus Sch. 100 for each adult and Sch. 70 for each child are refunded. It could be a good way to ride the gondola up for lunch.

The other one-day and half-day fares offer the opportunity to limit the areas, but the differences are minimal. The following fares are for the entire seven-mountain area: (Children get an approximate 35 percent discount.)

one day	Sch. 260
two days	Sch. 500
three days	Sch. 710
six days	Sch. 1,300
fourteen days	Sch. 2,350

Accommodations

These are our selections for the best the resort has to offer.

Sporthotel Royer (tel. 03687-23240; telex 38227) Located in Schladming. The only five-star hotel in the area. This is a modern hotel with pool, indoor tennis and squash courts, sauna, jacuzzi and pony rides. Daily room rate, including half pension: Sch. 1,200.

Romantik-Hotel Alte Post (tel. 03687-22571; telex 38282) In Schladming. The oldest, most traditional hotel in town, located on the main square. Daily rate, half pension: Sch. 750.

Hotel Zum Stadttor (tel. 03687-24525; telex 38287) In Schladming. Has whirlpool and sauna. Daily rate, half pension: Sch. 750

Hotel Pichlmayrgut (tel. 06454-305) Located in Pichl. If you want to stay in an old Austrian estate, this fits the bill, with pool, sauna and steambath. Pichl lifts start at about a five-minute walk from the hotel, or catch the ski bus to Haus or Schladming. Daily rate, half pension: Sch. 640

Moderate to Budget

There are many hotels and pensiones for between Sch. 430-500 a day, including half pension. One recommendation in the center of Schladming is **Gasthof Tritscher** (tel. 03687-22435).

In the center of Haus, the **Hotel Hauser Kaibling** (tel. 03686-2378) offers pool and sauna, plus a location in the center of the charming town for Sch. 580 a day, half pension.

The adventurous can stay near the top of the Hauser Kaibling in the **Krummholzhütte**, where you have to share a bathroom and shower, for Sch. 280 a day, half pension. You get a room at the top of the mountain and about a 10-minute schuss down the mountain when you step out the door.

Contact the tourist office and describe what you want how much you will pay. The office maintains a centralized computer system that tracks all bookings in the Schladming area.

Dining

The best restaurants in town are the **Alte Post, Sporthotel Royer** and the restaurant in the **Stadttor.**

Restaurant Tritscher is recommended as the best place to spend the least money and still eat well.

The Kalkschmiede has perhaps the best local traditional meals. It is located on the northern side of the valley on the road to Ramsau.

For great ski slope meals on the Planai, stop in at **Onkel Willi's Hütte** (yes, that's Uncle Willi's Hut), only a few ski glides from the top of the main Planai lift. On the Hauser Kaibling, the **Krummholzhütte** at the top and the **Stöklhütte** where the three lifts meet both have good skiers' food.

The **Bürgerstube** at the Hotel Hauserkaibling in Haus/Ennstal has also been recommended.

Nightlife

For wine and quiet talk, try the **Talbachschenke** in three small rooms, each built around a toasty ceramic stove. The best dancing is at the **Sonderbar** under the Hotel Rössl. For the younger disco dancers, try the **Old England Disco.** Other cozy meeting places include **The Pub** and **The Beissl**, both just off the main square. The Beissl is in the passageway at 12 Main Square and is a good place to meet people. Stop in and check out La Porta, a newly opened bar near the town's old gateway.

The two main discos outside town, and also the two best spots for meeting European tourists, are the **Sport Alm** in Ramsau and the **Taverna** in Rohrmoos. If you are in Haus/Ennstal, stop into the new **Pub** in the old castle.

Child care

There are no organized child care services for children under four years. Those four and over can sign up for ski school at the same prices as adults. The ski school will take the children for the entire day. Add Sch. 70 a day for lunches.

Getting there

There are good train connections from Munich and Salzburg, both of which have international airports. If driving, the autobahn going south from Salzburg passes within 20 minutes of Schladming. Take the Ennstal exit.

Other activities

Visit Salzburg or the salt mines near Salzburg.

The Loden fabric factory gives tours if arranged in advance by calling 06454-203. The factory and a factory outlet are located in Mandling, only about 10 minutes from Schladming.

Some of the most famous caves in Austria are in the Dachstein region. The Ice Cave, Mammoth Cave and the Kappenbrullenhöhle are open for visits. Call 06134-362 for information.

Horse-drawn sleigh rides are available; ice skating rinks are open in Rohrmoos and Haus/Ennstal; and there are public swimming pools in Schladming and Ramsau.

Tourist information

The central tourist office for the region is Gebietsverband Dachstein-Tauern, Coburgstr. 52, A-8970 Schladming; tel. 03687-23310; telex 38286. It handles reservation requests for any town in the area. There are additional local tourist offices in Schladming, Pichl, Haus, Rohrmoos and Ramsau.

St. Johann in Tirol

St. Johann in winter is a Tyrolean resort town just far enough from the lifts to keep locals aware of the need to welcome visitors with a smile. At that time the town is afloat in a sea of snow, lending a special atmosphere to a place that can't decide whether it is a resort village or a valley town.

Although St. Johann is only 2,297 feet above sea level, the snowfall here is certain and heavy from Christmas until March. That one fact should please serious skiers. The setting is picturesque, with the familiar outline of the Kitzbühlerhorn forming part of the valley panorama. Kitzbühel, which also shares the mountain, is about 12 miles away.

The old Tyrolean hotels are large and have a deserved reputation for hospitality sometimes missing in bigger, better known resorts. At night you'll know immediately from the lower decibel levels that this is not Kitzbühel. The streets don't exactly fold up at 8 p.m., but the nightlife is quieter. During the cross-country races in February the tempo picks up a bit.

Where to ski

The trails run along the flanks of the Kitzbüheler Horn. You can reach them from neighboring Oberndorf by chairlift or by cablecar from St. Johann. The top station is Harschbichl at 5,577 feet. At the top you have a choice of blue and red runs and one black trail.

We liked the black run, which really begins from Penzing at 4,799 feet and swings down through mogul fields to the parking lot above Oberndorf.

Intermediates take the run to the Eichenhof lift on the far side of St. Johann for a good downhill cruise. From the Jodlalm, just below the Harschbichl, you can follow the lines of a dozen different trails cut into the mountain.

There are easier slopes with beginners' lifts at the bottom of the mountain.

One of the year's biggest events is the Koasalauf, an international cross-country championship staged each February. It begins at the Koasa Stadium and cross-country center on the edge of town. St. Johann offers more than 40 miles of cross-country runs and is one of the best locations in the country for combining Alpine and Nordic skiing.

Mountain rating

St. Johann is for intermediates and primarily for lower intermediates. The slopes are rarely challenging, and only beginners and advanced beginners will find the skiing interesting enough for a week. However, with the regional ski pass you can try a number of challenging slopes in the area, in particular those on the Steinplatte, above Waidring about 15 miles from St. Johann.

Ski school

St. Johann and its neighbor towns have approximately 130 instructors available for the winter season. Many instructors are unable to teach in English, and the number of courses for English-speaking students is limited, so inquire beforehand.

A price reduction is offered on six-day group lesson cards for early and late season instruction. Call the ski school at 2515.

Individual lessons

for one half-day	Sch. 900
for one day	Sch.1,500
(additional person)	Sch. 200-300)

Group lessons

for one day	Sch. 400
for three days	Sch. 850
for five days	Sch. 980
for six days	Sch. 1,050

Cross-country lessons

for one half-days	Sch. 300
for three half-days	Sch. 650
for six half-days	Sch. 790

Lift tickets

The St. Johann pass includes 19 lifts serving about 27 miles of prepared trails. These are high-season prices. There is a small discount during low season, and children pay approximately 30 percent less. These are 1989/90 prices.

for a half day	Sch. 180
for one day	Sch. 260
for two days	Sch. 480
for three days	Sch. 670
for four days	Sch. 850

for five days	Sch. 1,020
for six days	Sch. 1,180
for seven days	Sch. 1,320
for thirteen days	Sch. 1,010

A combination ski and pool pass for seven days during high season costs Sch. 1,420; for 14 days, Sch. 2,300.

Accommodations

St. Johann has one of the best organized accommodation services in Austria. In fact, using the St. Johann hotel-apartment list with an accompanying reservation form, available free from the tourist office, you can arrange for any type of accommodation—from simple bed-and-breakfast to apartment rentals.

We recommend that you come in early March when the snow is still good and the maximum price reductions are offered. The all-inclusive package is outstanding: for seven days at half pension in a top-ranked hotel, including a six-day ski pass for St. Johann, six days of free swimming and six days of ski school, the price is Sch. 5,690. Our favorite deluxe hotels are the Hotel Crystal (tel. 05362-2630) and Gasthof Dorfschmiede (tel. 05362-2323). The price for a middle-class hotel or guesthouse is Sch. 4,710, about the price you'd pay for accommodations only at some resorts.

If you want the least expensive accommodations, consider the budget all-inclusive bed-and-breakfast plan, which includes the other extras mentioned above for only Sch. 3,240.

Eleven hotels and guesthouses offer the mid-range all-inclusive package for Sch. 4,710. Of the eleven, we recommend four:

Hotel Kaiserhof (tel. 2545) On the edge of town. Good for cross-country with a six-kilometer loop near the hotel and other trails close by.

Hotel Schöne Aussicht (tel. 2270) Excellent location on the slopes near the Angereralm lift ground station.

Gasthof Hinterkaiser (tel. 3325) A cross-country skier's paradise in the heart of the trail circuit, but isolated for alpine skiing.

Apartments

Apartment rental is as easy as finding hotel or pensione lodging in St. Johann. Five hotels—the Fischer, Crystal, Brückenwirt, Europa and Sporthotel Austria—also offer rental apartments. Apartments that sleep four range in price from Sch. 500-700 a night.

Dining

Our favorite restaurant in town is in the **Hotel Europa** (tel. 2285). It is very traditional and has only recently been open for other than hotel guests. Also try out the **Fischer** restaurant, with Austrian specialties, and the **Speckbacher Stuben**.

Nightlife

We liked the **Café Rainer** where the après-ski atmosphere was excellent from tea at five onwards.

For a change of pace, visit the **Café Klausner's** traditional Tyrolean evenings with dancers and music. For a basic funtime bar, try **Bunny's-Pub**.

Child care

Ski instruction for children and a ski kindergarten are offered (tel. 2515). The ski instruction prices are the same as for adults.

For details on babysitting services, call the St. Johann tourist office (tel. 2218).

Getting there

St. Johann is about 55 miles from Munich and Innsbruck; most visitors arrive from Munich. Take the Inntal autobahn and exit at Felbertauern/St. Johann in Tirol. Regular train service connects St. Johann with Innsbruck.

Other activities

In recent years St. Johann has pushed hard to expand its recreational activities. Bowling (tel. 3377), horseback riding (tel. 2484) and tennis (tel. 3377) are now popular activities. Horse-drawn sleigh rides cost Sch. 150 for 2 1/2 hours (tel. 38333 or 2207).

The town is beautiful in winter, with one Tyrolean house after another presenting traditional Austrian scenes that are painted on their exterior walls.

For outings, visitors travel most often to Munich, Innsbruck or Salzburg.

Tourist information

Fremdenverkehrsverband St. Johann, A-6380 St. Johann in Tirol; tel. 05352-2218/3335; telex 51606; snow info: 05352-4358; fax. 05352-5200.

Söll

The village of Söll in the Skigrosssraum/Wilderkaiser area of Austria is a tremendous favorite with English skiers and young people in general. The wide expanse of slopes with the backdrop of the rocky Wild Kaiser boasts 86 lifts spread above 7 villages, earning the title of the largest connected ski area in Austria.

The entire ski area is perhaps the most accessible in Austria to skiers coming in from Germany, situated as it is only 20 minutes from the Kufstein border crossing about an hour from Munich.

Söll carefully cultivates its small town image with little shops and stores whose operators are overwhelmingly friendly and usually strike up a conversation in English at the first opportunity. The main street, which leads past several hotels and most of the shops, is full of visitors at almost any hour of the day or night. While traffic is heavy, pedestrians have taken priority, causing motorists to wait, sometimes impatiently, as they crisscross the roadway to browse in shops.

It's quite clear from the heavy shopping in the local grocery stores that not everyone takes full pension. Full shopping bags mean a lot of picnic lunches and homemade breakfasts are prepared back in the room. Everywhere you encounter young couples strolling hand in hand, quite a change from the more elegant and expensive European resorts where the crowd is older and not always so affectionate.

Where to ski

The best skiing is concentrated in the valley headed by Soll, pronounced Zull. Up the valley is Sheffau, Ellmau and finally Going. Around the mountains in another valley are Itter, Hopfgarten, Westendorf and Brixen i Thale. Each has lifts. And all but Westendorf are on an interconnected circuit. Free bus service is provided from Westerndorf, providing skiers with a two-valley network of about 80 lifts and more trails than you'll be able to manage in one week.

The most convenient access is from Söll where a new eight-passenger gondola went into service for winter 1988-89 replacing the antiquated single chair which has been a bottleneck in years past.

From the top of the Hohe Salve (1829 meters) at Söll you can appreciate the massive dimensions of the Wild Kaiser area which the English and Austrians know better as the SkiGrossraum, lit-

erally the Big Ski area. You view includes the 1650-meter Brandstadl summit at Sheffau, the 1555-meter Hartkaiser at Ellmau-
Going and further to your right the town of Kirchberg, gateway
to Kitzbühl.

On the skyline you can see ski slopes as far as Pass Thurn and
the famed Grossglockner is on the distant skyline.

Good parallel skiers should do the Grossraum tour which begins
and ends in Söll. Skiers work their way up and down the ridges,
visiting Itter, Hopfgarten, the outskirts of Brixen, then back up to
Zinsberg, down and finally back to Brandstadl and over to Hartkaiser, stopping along the way in Sheffau, Ellmau and perhaps
Going although it's a short hike all the way into Going from the
lifts at the bottom.

The black run from the summit of Hohe Salve above Söll will
challenge a good skier. It's a 4,000 meter-long trail with a vertical
drop of about 700 meters. The best intermediate run is the Rigi
along the backside and then around the Hohe Salve, all the way
down to the Gasthof Kraftalm where they serve a Jägextee (Hunter's Tea) which will blast your ski boots off. The recipe, according
to the gasthof owner is tea, some rum, some more red wine, plenty
of schnapps, a goodly amount of sugar and some herbs for aroma.
He adds, don't light a match near the mixture while hot.

Mountain rating

The Wilder Kaiser is intermediate country with a capital I. You
can head down any slope without hesitation and enjoy moderately
challenging, well-groomed runs. A fine place to hone your skiing
skills. Not recommended for the demanding skier craving black
trails and thrills.

Ski school

Each town has a ski school. The largest of them, Schischule Söll,
run by Sepp Embacher, has 90 instructors. Both valleys are noted
for the high percentage of English-speaking instructors, a definite
strong point for the Wilderkaiser region.

Lessons are offered daily beginning on Sunday and Monday.
Instruction is from 10-12 and 2-4 p.m. Private lessons are also
offered through the ski school office for approximately 320 schillings per hour with another 110 schillings for each additional stu-
dent. The telephone information number is 05333-5454 or 5484.
Beginners lessons are given directly across from the ski center on
the beginner slope. Advanced and experts are taken up the mountain immediately. Even beginners go up after a couple of days at
the bottom.

Group lessons

for one day	Sch. 340
for two days	Sch. 680
for three days	Sch. 740
for five days	Sch. 900
for six days	Sch. 950
for ten days	Sch. 1450
5 half day course 2-4 p.m.	Sch. 690

Lift tickets

The individual towns sell tickets good only for the local lifts, but the regional ticket is a better bargain and makes sense for the active skier. For those who anticipate limited skiing the point cards are best.

	Adults	Children
For half day (noon)	Sch 180	115
For one day	Sch 240	150
For two days	Sch 460	280
For three days	Sch 660	410
For four days	Sch 820	480
For five days	Sch 1000	585
For six days	Sch 1140	665
For seven days	Sch 1280	750

Check also the special ticket which allows some variation on ski days. A choice of 5 ski days in 7 days is 1140 schillings for adults and 665 for children. A choice of 7 ski days in 10 days is 1400 for adults and 830 for children. A choice of 10 ski days in 14 days is 1750 for adults and 1030 for children.

Note: A photo is required for all ski passes of 8 days or longer.

Accommodations

Söll is the most convenient because it's the first of the seven towns you come to in the Wilder Kaiser and the one we liked best. Especially quiet is Gasthof Greil, a ten-minute walk from the center of town. The hotel is quiet, the food tasty and filling and the staff friendly. About 400 schillings per person daily half pension. This hotel has a cooperating arrangement with larger British tour agencies and there are substantial room savings when guests use the tour agency rather than booking privately. Telephone 5333-5289.

The best hotel in town is Postwirt, a renovated, beautiful building right in the center of action, near the local tourist office. A room and breakfast is 590 schillings daily, half pension stay is 790 schillings. Low season rates are slightly reduced. The local phone is 5333-5221.

Equally attractive and historic is Feldwebel, just down the street. This 85-bed hotel has rooms from 340 schillings in high season (420 half pension). Telephone 5333-5224. Hotel Tyrol, about half-way between the Greil and the center of town, is Sch. 480 daily in high season with breakfast and about Sch. 580 half pension. Telephone 5333-5273.

On the mountain we liked the Salvenmoos where bed and breakfast was 250 schillings and half pension was Sch. 350. This is for skiers who want to hit the slopes immediately and those who don't need to go into town every few hours. Telephone 5333-5351.

There are over two dozen hotels in the Söll area proper. And private room and bed and breakfast houses are numerous. The local tourist office, beside the Postwirt Hotel, will find you a room in almost any price range almost immediately. For reservation information call 5333-5216.

Dining

The best meal we had was in the Greil, but we dined there several times so the chances were better that one would suit us. Good Austrian specialties.

The Stube of the Postwirt has the most atmosphere, given the group of old timers at the big front table who puff on their pipes and argue loudly about everything from Austrian politics to the merits of retired Formula One driver Niki Lauda and current ace Gerhard Berger (both Austrian, naturally). The food is good and filling. The Stube came in second for best apple strudel in town. It was good but not quite as fine as cafe Meribel, up the street past the local office for Thomson Tours.

Nightlife

The ski instructors and longtime visitors gather after skiing in the small bar of the Postbierstuhe. Just keep going past the Stube and you'll find the bar tucked away on the left. For laughter, some sing along action and live entertainment the Pub 15, an Italian place despite the name, is the place to visit. When we dropped in, the singer was American and the songs were English and American favorites. A good place to meet new friends is the Dorfstadl in the cellar of the Hotel Tyrol. There's a younger crowd and louder music at the Whiskey Muhle and at Disco Klaus.

Even though Söll is realtively small, with about 2,000 residents, the town has considerable experience with hosting visitors and there's a wide variety of entertainment to suit the taste of nearly all age groups.

Child care

The ski kindergarten is across the street from the ski school building. There is a price reduction for children from 5 to 15 who have at least one parent in the adult ski school.

Five day kindergarten	Sch 765
Six day	Sch 810

For an additional 80 schillings daily the ski kindergarten includes care and instruction for the whole day from 9:30 a.m. until 4:15 p.m. For information telephone the ski school at 5333-5454.

Getting there

The main arrival airport is Munich, about 70 minutes by bus from Söll and other towns in the area. If you're driving you take the Salzburg autobahn out of Munich and then the Rosenheim cutoff (called Inntal autobahn). You cross the border near Kufstein and take the second exit, Kufstein Sud. Söll will be marked on the autobahn exit sign. From the turnoff, it's about 15 minutes on a two-lane highway over one slight uphill grade to Söll. Altogether, the trip is one of the most convenient for the motorist or bus driver.

Other activities

Söll has a well-developed recreation complex with an extensive network of cross country trails. The recreation center has a beautiful indoor pool with a heated outdoor extension.

One advantage Söll has is its nearness to the Inntal autobahn. You are only about an hour's drive from either Salzburg or Innsbruck. Both cities are superb visiting points at any season of the year with a wide range of museums and scenic outdoor attractions. In addition, it is not unusual for the visitor with a car to visit Innsbruck and then venture down the Brenner motorway for a short excursion into Italy. The same is true for a visit to Munich when visitors arrive via Innsbruck or Milan without first visiting Germany.

Tourist Information

You'll find the tourist office in all the villages of the Wilder Kaiser helpful, particularly so in Söll where the staff of Christian Becker puts out the welcome mat for thousands yearly. For assistance and free brochures call 0043-5333-5216.

Zell am See-Kaprun

Once you've seen beautiful Zell am See and skied its runs, as well as those on the neighboring Kaprun glacier, the area will number among your favorite European winter resorts. The "Europa-Sportregion," as the area calls itself, is a popular destination for travelers from across Europe and the U.S.

Where to ski

There are two major areas: Zell am See's Schmittenhöhe lifts take skiers to the 2000-meter level, while Kaprun is famed as a year-round ski area with runs on the glacier beneath the summit of the 3203-meter (10,506-foot) Kitzsteinhorn.

To ski the Schmittenhöhe, avoid the main cablecar from town and opt instead for either the Sonnenalmbahn or, better still, the Areit chairlift from neighboring Schüttdorf and work your way up the mountain with the series of lifts.

The runs are good for intermediates and there are some expert challenges, too, particularly the two runs used in World Cup and regional downhill races. Our favorite is the trail from the Kapellenlift summit to Breiteckalm and then down a wonderful turning slope parallel to the woods. From there, it's black to the bottom. Locals call this run the "Trass." A trail intermediates may enjoy more is called the "Standard"; it drops from the top to Breiteck but then breaks back to the right over the Hirschkögel trail.

Kaprun is about six miles from Zell am See and it's another three and a half miles to the base of the area's lifts. Take the older cable car up to the glacier, or take the *Standseilbahn* that climbs the mountain inside a tunnel. Both go to the Alpin center, while the aerial cable continues on up to the top station at 3029 meters (9935 feet).

The skiing is intermediate with a couple of notable exceptions. One is the final part of the run from the top to the Breitriesenalpe cable car mid-station, and the other, if you have a guide and if you really are an expert, is through the rocks from the Salzburger Hütte.

Mountain rating

Zell am See is outstanding for intermediates; its network of trails and connecting lifts make skiing interesting.

For the beginner there are training slopes and plenty of room to take a fall or two without serious suffering.

Experts will head for the glacier at Kaprun where there are also plenty of challenging intermediate runs.

Ski school

Instruction in the Zell am See-Kaprun classes is conducted by approximately 150 teachers. Courses ranging from beginning through competition racing techniques are offered. Beginners classes start at 9:30 a.m. and advanced classes begin at 10 a.m. Information is available through the ski school office in the valley station of the Sonnenalmbahn (tel. 3207). Private instruction costs Sch. 1520 for one day (four hours) or Sch. 380 per hour.

Group lessons

for one day (four hours)	Sch. 340
for three days	Sch. 750
for six days	Sch. 950

Lift tickets

Tickets for the Europa Sports Region Pass (88/89 rates):

	high season	**middle season**
for three days	Sch. 790	Sch. 660
for four days	Sch. 1000	Sch. 840
for five days	Sch. 1240	Sch. 1010
for six days	Sch. 1400	Sch. 1180
for seven days	Sch. 1570	Sch. 1300

Daily rates at the separate sections of the Europe Sports Region are approximately Sch. 290.

Accommodations

Many of Zell's hotels and pensions are located near the lifts. In addition, for those who want to be nearer the Kaprun glacier there is accommodation in town and there's also a mountain hotel on the glacier.

Thumersbach, across the lake, is separated from the best skiing, but quite scenic. Check with the tourist office in Zell or in Kaprun for further information.

Zell also offers 24-hour service to individuals who come without reservations. Visitors can check an information board similar to those used at many U.S. airports at Zell and at the ground station of the Kaprun glacier cable car. By pushing a button next to the hotel's name, its location is illuminated on the map. You can then telephone the hotel directly and check on room availability.

The all-in package is good here. It's called "Schnee-Okay" and is available in low and middle season. First-class half-pension accommodation is available from about Sch. 4550 a week. Schnee-Okay includes seven days accommodations, a six-day regional pass, unlimited use of the ski shuttle bus and six days' admittance to swimming pools in Zell and Kaprun. At the other end of the price scale is simple bed and breakfast accommodation with all the other extras starting at Sch. 2535 a week.

The following hotels will arrange for the all-in plan for low budget accommodations:

Pension Bergkristall (tel. 8476)
Gasthaus Fischer (tel. 7114)
Pension Griesser (tel. 8403)
Pension Holzmeister (tel. 8513)
Pension Steiner (tel. 8415)
Hotel Tirolerhof (tel. 3721)
Hotel Waldhof (tel. 2853)

At the top end of the hotel scale, nine establishments in Zell and seven in Kaprun participate in the Winter Package Plan. Our top choices of the top category hotels were the Sporthotel Falkenstein (tel.7122), Hotel Sonnblick (tel. 8301) and the Sporthotel Kaprun (tel.8625). A top rated hotel is the Hotel St. Georg (tel. 3533 or through Best Western).

Apartments

The tourist office will provide a list of available apartments and chalets in the area. In addition, you can book directly through agencies in the area. For more information, call the Prodinger travel agency (tel. 2170), OAMTC travel office (tel. 2208), Schüttdorf (tel. 7216) and Apartmentservice (tel. 7539). Apartments large enough to sleep four will range in price from Sch. 500-600 per night.

Dining

We can highly recommend the Erlhof (tel. 3173) overlooking Zell as a good place to eat with traditional Salzburgerland atmosphere and typical Austrian dishes. The wild deer venison is excellent. We also liked the homemade specialties in the Hotel St. Georg restaurant (tel. 3533).

Nightlife

We fell behind in our nightlife outings in Zell after trying to squeeze both skiing on the Schmittenhöhe and the glacier into the same day. We did venture out to meet a lively early-evening crowd at Disco No. 1 Taverne in the Café Feinschmeck. Later, we settled into the quieter, beautiful panorama bar on the roof of the Grand Hotel by the lake. Have at least one drink there during your stay.

Another alternative is to make the evening a sporting evening at the Kaprun Optimum, an indoor swimming pool and fitness center which is crowded through the evening with fitness-minded Europeans and is a great place to meet other skiers. Nightlife takes on a new meaning here.

Child care

The guest kindergarten in Zell is open Monday through Friday from 8 a.m. until 4 p.m. All-day care costs Sch. 80; until noon, Sch. 60.

Another kindergarten is the Schuttdorf-Areitalm (tel. 6020); Rates: Sch. 260 for full day, Sch. 700 for three days, and Sch. 1000 for six days.

Ursula Zink (tel. 76583) also sits for children from one year of age. Rates: One day—Sch. 260, three days—Sch. 650, and six days—Sch.1000.

The children's ski school is open daily from 10 a.m. until 4 p.m., except Sunday. A lunchtime snack is included and children from four to ten are accepted.

In Kaprun, call 8644 for information, and in Zell the number is 2600.

Getting there

Zell is about fifty miles from Salzburg, which has jet service from other European airports. The usual airport for international arrivals is Munich, about 115 miles away. Vienna is about 240 miles distant.

Zell has regular train service and offers a bus service to Kaprun.

By automobile from Munich, drive to Salzburg by autobahn, and head toward Bischofshofen. Rental cars are available in Salzburg or Munich.

Other activities

A visit to nearby Salzburg, made famous a generation ago by the movie, "The Sound of Music," attracts millions each year.

In Salzburg, visit Mozart's birthplace and the Hohensalzburg fortress; take time to shop in the old city.

Both Zell am See and Kaprun deserve exploration. The Zell skyline is distinguished by the outlines of the St. Hippolyt church and the Vogtturm, (city tower).

Even non-skiers will enjoy the Schmittenhöhe on a clear day when you can see at least thirty 3000-meter (9843-foot) or higher peaks in the region.

At Kaprun, visit the Gothic Pfarrkirche and the castle ruin. If you're skiing the Kaprun glacier in summer or early autumn, visit the Tauernkraftwerk, a massive power plant on the outskirts of Kaprun. It's open daily from 8 a.m. until 5 p.m., April to October. Roads to the dams and lakes built for the power project may not be open after the first snow.

The swimming pool os open from 10 a.m. to 10 p.m. Entrance is Sch. 60 for adults or Sch. 490 for ten tickets. The sauna located at the pool costs Sch. 100 per session or Sch. 850 for ten tickets.

Tourist information

Check with the Kurverwaltung, A-5700 Zell am See; tel. 06542-2600; and Verkehrsverein Kaprun, A-5710 Kaprun; tel. 06547-8643; telex: 66763.

Switzerland

For many, Switzerland *is* the Alps; *ergo*, Switzerland *is* skiing in Europe. Of course, Switzerland contains only a portion of the Alps and there are other places to ski in Europe. Still, as the heart of the Alps and the home of alpine skiing, Switzerland deserves the superlatives bestowed upon it: its skiing is excellent, its resorts efficient, its tourist offices more than competent, its lift systems well run and its hotels exceptional.

A note on prices

Most of the prices listed in this section are valid for the 1988/89 winter season. Where the 89/90 prices were available they have been clearly noted. While prices were carefully researched, they always seem to change, so use them as a guide only. Ask for the latest prices before buying anything or staying anywhere.

All prices are given in Swiss francs (SFR). As the book was being researched, the Swiss franc was at an exchange rate of SFR 1.5 to $1. Any subsequent change in the exchange rate will be the biggest factor affecting the prices.

When is high season?

In Switzerland the 1989/90 ski season will be broken out as follows (based on the Flims/Laax region):

High Season: 24 December 1989 to 6 January 1990 and 29 January through February 26.
Low Season: January 7-29 and February 27 to April 2
Pre-season: December 10-24

Switzerland's romantic mountain railways

The skier whose timetable is not completely filled with skiing adventures can take a scenic ride on one of the world's most advanced mountain railway systems in the world. The regional Swiss railroad lines and the post bus system have organized three spectacular trans-alpine routes: the Glacier Express runs from St. Moritz to Zermatt; the Bernina Express traverses the Alps from Chur to St. Moritz to Tirano and on to Milan; the Engadin Express connects St. Moritz with Austria's Landeck and Innsbruck.

The Glacier Express
Perhaps the most famous of the Swiss rail trips, the Glacier Express is advertised as the world's slowest train. Indeed, the trip lasts seven and a half hours—spanning more than 291 bridges as well as burrowing through 91 tunnels—on its way from St. Moritz in Switzerland's southeast corner to Zermatt. Passengers are awarded a special Glacier Express certificate upon the completion of the journey.

Trains run from Zermatt to St. Moritz and vice versa. Both leave in the early morning and arrive in the late afternoon. In their elegant dining cars a complete three-course lunch is served during the Chur-to-Andermat leg. The meal costs approximately $20, excluding beverages. Reservations are required for the meals on the trains. Wine glasses on the Glacier Express are tilted to prevent one's wine from spilling due to the route's many steep turns and gradients. The tilted glass does mean that you have to regularly turn it to keep it tilted in the right direction.

Bernina Express
The Bernina Express, which crosses into Italy over the Alps in Switzerland's southeast corner, is Europe's highest trans-alpine railway. While the train trip follows the same route as the Glacier Express from Chur to St. Moritz, it then strikes off for the Bernina Pass, Poschiavo and on to Tirano in Italy.

Along one short, eight-mile stretch, the track runs through five looping, or corkscrew, tunnels, passes through two straight tunnels and crosses eight viaducts. The train crosses the Bernina Pass at 7,405 feet and, in doing so, climbs the steepest gradient of any non-cogwheel train in the world.

The Engadin Express
This train and post bus route connects St. Moritz with Innsbruck, Salzburg and Vienna. The trip from St. Moritz to Landeck done mostly by post bus, lasts almost three hours and is considered by many to be one of Europe's most romantic trips.

After leaving St. Moritz, the train chuffs alongside a beautiful Swiss national park, through the village of Scuol; then the post bus takes travelers past the famous castle of Tarasp and on to Vulpera. This is the home of the fourth language of Switzerland, Ladin. The mountain folk here preserve the ancient language, but most still speak English as well as German or Italian. The express ends in Landeck, Austria, in the Tyrol district.

Making reservations
These train trips can be booked in the United States through the
Swiss National Tourist Office (tel. 1-800-223-0048; in NYC 1-212-
757-5944); in Britain through the Swiss National Tourist Office
(tel. 01-734-1921); in St. Moritz at the Rhaetic Railway station
(telex 693518); in Chur at the main train station (telex 693158);
and in Zermatt at Zermatt-Tours (telex 472104).

Arosa

A long-established Swiss ski resort, Arosa played a part in the development of skiing as a popular winter sport. Today, it is known for relatively easy, wide-open skiing and good off-slope activities. The town is tucked within a circle of mountains above Chur at the end of the Schanfigger valley.

Everything in Arosa is within easy walking distance. If you drive a car to the resort, park it in the public area and forget about it, unless you decide to escape to some other area later in the week.

Where to ski

At 5,900 feet, Arosa's lifts fan out to reach the two major peaks in the area, the 8,241-foot-high Hörnli and the Weisshorn at 8,704 feet. While there are only 16 lifts, their combined capacity exceeds 17,000 skiers an hour. Some 45 miles of runs are long and spread out, adding up to plenty of skiing. The entire resort is above the trees for wide-open skiing and perfect cruising. There are also nearly 20 miles of groomed cross-country trails.

Mountain rating

Arosa is Eden for beginners and intermediate skiers because of its wide and long runs. After several days without a snowfall, when skiers have broken new trails between the normally prepared runs, you can virtually ski across the entire mountain.

One run that does require an expert is the descent from the top of the Weisshorn to the Carmennahütte. This very steep run is wide enough to allow a gutsy intermediate to traverse widely and make his way down the slope, but it also offers expert-level practice on the steeps with plenty of room for error.

Ski school

The Swiss Ski School in Arosa (tel. 311996) has more than a hundred qualified instructors, most of whom speak English. Special courses for children, deep-snow, cross-country and other events are organized by the ski school, including torchlight descents accompanied by fireworks, descents by full moon and ski races. The tuition for the ski school is as follows:

Individual lessons

| for a half day
(two hours) | SFR 80 |
| for one day
(four hours) | SFR 160 |

Group lessons

for a half day (two hours)	SFR 21
for three half days	SFR 62
for six half days	SFR 110
for six full days (Mon.-Sat.)	SFR 150

NOTE: Reductions for children are available.

If you are ready for a ski touring experience, check in with a group that has organized the Radiant Orbit Program, a six-day program of skiing with a mountain guide. The skiing is hard but the area covered is fantastic and the experience excellent. The programs normally run from January through April. Cost for half pension and six days of a mountain guide's services is SFR 1,300 for a room with bath. For more information, contact Erwin Lamm at the Hotel Haus Lamm, Arosa (tel. 311366).

Cross-country courses are also available for SFR 22 a half day, SFR 42 for two half days and up to SFR 95for five half days. A half day is two hours. Private instruction is SFR 40 an hour for one to two persons.

Lift Tickets

All lift tickets issued for more than two days require a photograph.

	adults	children (to age 16)
for one day	SFR 38	SFR 19
for two days	SFR 72	SFR 36
for three days	SFR 102	SFR 51
for six days	SFR 158	SFR 79
for seven days	SFR 172	SFR 86

During the first three weeks of December, lift tickets are reduced an additional 15 percent. Senior citizens and one adult member of a family also will be given 15 percent reductions on lift passes.

Accommodations

Arosa has a hotel for everyone—from the most luxurious to the bargain one-star. The all-inclusive program, with prices ranging from SFR 525 for two-star to SFR 1089 for five-star properties, includes a special seven-day, half-pension, private bath or shower and toilet and lift-tickets. The low-season daily-prices for half pension with private bath are noted for the hotels listed below. Add between 15 percent and 25 percent during high season.

Our recommended five-star hotels are (ski week prices Sfr 875-1,089):

Kulm Hotel, tel. 310131. SFR 180.
Savoy Hotel, tel. 310211. SFR145.
Tschuggen Grand Hotel, tel. 310221. SFR 180 (no ski week).

Our recommended four-star hotels are (ski week prices are SFR 630-949):

Hohenfels, tel. 311651; telex 74538. SFR 101.
Posthotel, tel. 310121. Right in the center of the town near the train station. SFR 125.
Sporthotel Valsana, tel.310275; telex 74232. By the lake, this modern hotel features a good restaurant and child care facilities. SFR 117
Waldhotel National, tel. 312665. A bit back in the woods, this hotel nevertheless is considered to be excellent. SFR 115

The three-star hotels most convenient to the lifts are (ski week prices are SFR 560-897):

Anita, tel. 311109. SFR 90.
Astoria, tel. 311313. SFR 89.
Belvedere-Tanneck, tel. 311335. SFR 95.
Hohe Promenade, tel. 312651. SFR 95.
Obersee, tel. 311216. SFR 95.

Our recommended two-star hotels are (ski week prices are SFR 525-844):

Alpina, tel. 311658. Most of the hotel was recently restored and is beautiful. SFR 75.
Erzhorn, tel. 311526. SFR 85.

Apartments

Arosa is well organized to handle tourists who want to rent apartments during the ski season, normally for a minimum of one week, Saturday to Saturday. During the Christmas and Easter seasons, a minimum two-week rental is required.

The tourist office keeps track of which apartments are available. When writing, include the number of beds required, the preferred number of rooms and your planned vacation dates. You will receive a quick response that lists a selection of apartments and prices. Select the apartment you want and return the information. You'll receive confirmation in writing and be directed to contact the owner upon arrival.

Several hotels in Arosa also provide apartments that share common hotel amenities, such as pool, steam room, tennis courts and TV room. Perhaps the best of these "aparthotels" is the Savoy, followed by the Park Hotel, both with five-star hotel facilities. At Hotel Savoy, medium-priced apartments for four people cost SFR 1,200 in January, SFR 1,500 in February. There is a charge for final cleaning of SFR 90. Guests can also sign up for half pension with the hotel for an additional SFR 48. Similar apartments in the Park Hotel cost SFR 950 in January and SFR 1,540 in February. The Hotel Alpina (a two-star) also rents out apartments for families.

Normally, linen and kitchen utensils are provided. Other communal or private amenities, such as swimming pool, sauna, TV or room phone, all add to the costs. Standard apartments rent for between $12 and $20 a person a night. Prices vary significantly from low to high season.

Dining

The following restaurants come recommended by local Arosa residents:

Stuva, Hotel Alexandra Modern Art, Hotel Hof Maran Im Stubli, Hotel Central Arven-Restaurant Chez Andrè and Gspan. For something different, take the sleigh ride up to the Hotel Alpenblick above Arosa and enjoy a special meat platter that is grilled at your table.

Nightlife

Arosa is not the nightlife capital of Switzerland. The fun is where you make it, usually with groups that seem to form on their own during any ski trip. Arosa's après-ski activities center around the hotels in the evening. Here you'll find smaller bars with bands or piano players. There are approximately 20 such bars. Nuts is probably the hottest disco in town.

More organized after-ski activities include indoor tennis, squash, chess evenings, bridge and so on.

Child care

There are two public kindergartens for children from three to six years at the Park (tel. 310165) and Savoy (tel. 310211) hotels. The Park Hotel kindergarten is open Monday through Friday from 9 a.m. until 5 p.m. The rates are SFR 7 for a half day and SFR 20 for a full day with lunch.

The Savoy Hotel kindergarten opens at 9:30 a.m., closes at noon and reopens from 2 until 4 p.m. Prices are similar to those at the Park Hotel. There are reductions for child care on a weekly basis.

Another kindergarten is run by the Swiss Ski School in the Skihalle Kulm, Inner-Arosa. It is open daily, except Sunday, from 9:30 a.m. until noon and again from 2 until 4:30 p.m. Arrangements for lunch can be made at the school. This kindergarten does not include a ski school. The ski school (tel. 311996) can provide additional information on the children's ski course. Prices are approximately the same as for the kindergartens listed above.

Getting there

The closest airport is Zurich, nearly a three-hour train ride from Chur. There, catch a special train for Arosa just outside the main train station entrance. The train ride from Chur to Arosa takes about one hour.

Driving from Zurich to Arosa will take about two and a half hours in good weather. Follow the signs to Chur and after entering the city, follow the signs to Arosa. The road is steep and narrow and requires chains during most of the winter. Arosa has a car park for 460 cars.

Other activities

Arosa is known for its off-slope activities. There are indoor swimming pools; ice skating on three open-air rinks and one covered rink; more than 18 miles of walkways, which are maintained all winter; squash and tennis courts at the Park and Savoy hotels; and horse-drawn sleigh rides. The town is also active in arts and entertainment, scheduling concerts, lectures and exhibitions throughout the winter.

For horseback riding, contact E. Ritsch in Weierhof. Eight horses are available for hire, and the cost is SFR 17 an hour.

Want to learn about the strange game of curling? Arosa offers organized curling lessons every Tuesday starting in January for SFR 4 a lesson.

Ski racing fans can see the women's World Cup slalom races in January and February.

Make sure to ask about the special "sunrise brunch" served at the top of the Weisshorn several times during each month.

Don't miss late January's horse races held on ice.

If you want to get away from Arosa, you must make an effort and it does take time. The train ride down the mountain to Chur lasts about an hour. However, in good weather Arosa is only about an hour and a quarter away from Klosters or Davos by car and within easy reach of other resorts, such as Laax, Flims or Lenzerheide.

Chur is worth a visit. So is the deepest gorge in Switzerland, the Via Mala, which leads to the St. Bernard Pass and is about another half-hour's drive from Chur. Tiny Liechtenstein, one of the world's smallest countries, can be reached from Arosa in just over an hour. Visiting provides a chance to send postcards to everyone back home.

Tourist information

Contact Tourist Office Arosa, CH-7050 Arosa; tel. (081) 311621; telex 74271. Office hours are Monday through Saturday, from 8 a.m. until noon and from 2 until 6 p.m. (until 5 p.m. on Saturday).

Crans-Montana

These twin villages perched high on a plateau above the town of Sierre were the site of the 1987 Alpine Skiing World Championships. The new racing runs that were created and ski lift improvements that were made in preparation for the World Championships resulted in one of the most accessible skiing areas in the world. Indeed, for the intermediate skier, Crans-Montana may be heaven on the slopes. Long, challenging trails coupled with virtually no waiting at lifts make for a combination that most skiers will find hard to beat.

This area was already inscribed in skiing lore long before the 1987 Swiss medal sweep. In 1950, the first Swiss ski championships were held here. And even earlier, in January 1911, the founder of modern downhill racing, Sir Arnold Lunn, had the idea to organize a race from the highest point on the Plaine Morte glacier down to Montana. Unlike today's closely timed individual runs, in that race all contestants started together, and the first one to reach the town was declared the winner. The race eventually developed into today's famous "Kandahar" held in St. Anton, Mürren, Chamonix, Sestriere and Garmisch.

Crans-Montana has been recently connected with a budding purpose-built resort, Aminona. This Crans-Montana-Aminona area is served by 40 interconnected lifts, with almost one mile vertical drop and 100 miles of prepared trails.

Crans and Montana do have some distinctions, although both names are most often said in the same breath. Neither is a paragon of alpine architecture. It appears that an architects' convention was given free hand to erect as many different buildings as possible. Unappealing, square, concrete boxes stand beside massive triangular "Toblerone" shaped hotels, with a smattering of traditional chalets seemingly out of place amidst the concrete and glass.

Crans has a more concentrated city atmosphere, while Montana's inner city dissipates quickly. The shop signs in Montana read simply—Cheese, Fondue, Real Estate or Restaurant. In Crans, the signs read Gucci, Louis Vuitton, Piaget and Cartier. Crans is chic—Montana more for the family. Crans can be crowded with furs, while in Montana one is more at home in a ski outfit.

Be prepared to hike up and down hills, because both towns are built on the side of the mountain. But this slope, although many curse it by day, provides many hotels with spectacular views to the Alps in the south.

Where to ski

The Plaine Morte trail starts atop the 9,843-foot-high Plaine Morte glacier, which also serves as a summer ski area. Sometime during your stay take the gondola and then cablecar up from Violettes and measure your time against the Kandahar ski pioneers, whose best time was just over one hour for the run. The run is a long nine miles of intermediate terrain with expert tendencies due to the chance for frequent off-trail shortcuts. The trail down from Plaine Morte is closely controlled for avalanche danger. After even a relatively light snowfall the run from the glacier back to Violettes is often closed, but opens as soon as precautions are taken.

The area of Crans-Montana-Aminona is reached from four major lifts. From Crans, a gondola lift brings skiers to Chetzeron (6,825 feet), which was the starting point of the men's Super G. A gondola lift takes skiers to Cry d'Err (7,173 feet), which is the hub of the entire area. From Montana, a new six-passenger gondola lift whisks skiers to Cry d'Err. At Barzettes, a five-minute bus ride from Crans or Montana, another new and fast gondola brings you to Violettes (7,176 feet). Five minutes on the bus will bring you to Aminona, where a gondola takes skiers to Pt. Mont Bonvin (7,836 feet), where a wide-open, above-treeline area provides fantastic uncrowded conditions.

The most crowded lifts in the morning are from Crans and, especially, the lift from Montana. But a short, free bus ride to Barzettes and the Violettes or Aminona lifts will get you up the mountain faster.

The Cry d'Err sector of the mountain is the most crowded. Ten lifts bring skiers to Cry d'Err. After a long, flat traverse, the skier arrives in the Crans section of the mountain. From here the best bet is to take the Super G/Slalom run back into Crans, then catch the gondola back to Cry d'Err. The runs below Cry d'Err heading to Montana are intermediate playgrounds but suffer from a serious bottleneck near Pas du Loop as the four trails merge, and slip through a narrow gap before widening on the way to town. At the end of the day, realize that this bottleneck will be crowded—ski slowly and in control.

From Cry d'Err another trail traverses to the right, bringing you into the Violettes section. This area is separated from the Montana section by a sheer cliff whose edge is marked generally by the National run on the ski map. The Violettes area is the favorite of many intermediates, featuring twisting runs down through the trees to the gondola mid-station, plus four other lifts opening more great intermediate skiing.

Across the valley from Violettes is the Aminona area and the La Toula lifts, a favorite section of the resort. La Toula offers challenging expert runs, and Aminona boasts wide-open, uncrowded cruising. Take advantage of the great skiing before the area gets "discovered."

Mountain rating

Intermediates will rate Crans-Montana one of the greatest places they've ever skied. The variety is outstanding.

Beginners are extremely limited on this mountain. In Crans, absolute beginners start on the golf course, which is perfect, but the next step—directly onto the mountain—is a big one. Montana beginners start above the Signal restaurant. Instructors admit that the area is limited, and after a few days it is up to Cry d'Err where the blue runs are really very wide, lower intermediate slopes. Beginners manage through wide traverses and learn fast or crash. In Violettes there are no beginner slopes, and the beginner sections of Aminona are for those who have been on skis at least three or four days—even then the gentle slopes are isolated in a sea of red-rated trails.

Only experts need worry at all about whether there are enough challenges to keep things interesting. Experts will find no real steep sections, but there is plenty of off-trail and tree skiing. The championship runs are also a good test.

Ski school

The Crans-Montana area has more ski instructors (about 200) than some Swiss ski villages have permanent residents. There's a lesson being given somewhere on the slopes from Crans to Aminona nearly every hour of the day. For information on lessons, call 027-411320 or 411480.

The Montana ski school is by far the most international. It boasts qualified Swiss Ski Instructors from the United States, Australia and Britain. The Crans ski school is a relatively closed Swiss shop.

For private ski instruction, the cost is SFR 42 an hour for one or two students, and SFR 56 per hour for three to four people.

Group lessons 89/90 rates (three hours a day):

one half day	SFR 20
seven half days	SFR 95

Children pay SFR 18 for one day and SFR 75 for one week.

Cross-country lessons are offered, and four different trails with a total length of 25 miles are prepared during the season.

Lessons are offered for two one-week periods each December before Christmas by the Swiss Ski School Association as part of its certification of teachers. The one-week package includes lessons, hotel with half pension, plus bus and lift tickets. Prices start from SFR 725 weekly in a three-star hotel.

Lift tickets

The 1989/90 Crans-Montana area pass is available at the following rates: (Children between six and 15 enjoy a significant discount of approximately 40 percent.)

half day	SFR 23
one day	SFR 37
two days	SFR 72
four days	SFR 127
five days	SFR 150
seven days	SFR 186
fourteen days	SFR 286

Accommodations

Crans-Montana can be very upscale. It doesn't claim many movie stars or much of the old rich, but it is an oasis for the "corporate rich." The town boasts more five-star hotels than any other Swiss resort, except St. Moritz, and a dazzling selection of prize-winning, expensive restaurants. Finding the ritziest isn't difficult—digging for the good solid values for the middle-of-the-road crowd takes a bit more time.

Crans-Montana is an excellent resort to rent an apartment or chalet. Of the 30,000 people who may be staying during peak season, 25,000 of them can stay in vacation apartments or chalets. We'll list the traditional hotels first. The first price given is for the special ski week, which Crans-Montana organizes during January and late April. February and March packages are also available for about 15% more. It includes seven days at half pension, seven days of ski passes and seven half days of ski instruction. The last price noted is the normal high-season, non-holiday (Feb. & March) price for half pension. Expect to pay approximately 20 percent less during low season.

Grand-Hotel Rhodania (tel. 411025; telex 413754) SFR 1,015—Considered to be the most elegant hotel in the Crans side of town, the Rhodania has almost everything a hotel guest could look for—except a pool. Normal daily rate: SFR 165-200.

Crans Ambassador (tel. 415222; telex 473176) SFR 1,015—The best hotel on the Montana side of the town. It is next to the cablecars, has good nightlife and an indoor pool. Normal daily rate: SFR 187-233.

Le Quatre Canetons (tel. 411698; telex 473425) SFR 780—From the outside this box-like edifice looks like a converted hospital, but once inside the doors you enter a world of cozy, quiet elegance. The large rooms look out on one of the most spectacular mountain range views in the world. The food is gourmet quality. The lounge has a crackling fire after dinner and the service is excellent. There are no fancy extras like saunas or pools—just top-quality hospitality. Excellent English is spoken. Normal daily rate: SFR 88-102.

Etoile (tel. 411671; telex 473195) SFR 780—This hotel is directly at the bottom of the Crans/Cry d'Err lift. The two ladies who run the place are a big help and will make your stay memorable. Normal daily rate: SFR 91-105.

De la Foret (tel. 413608) SFR 780—A bit of a walk to the downtown area but close to the Violettes lift. Has a covered swimming pool. Normal daily rate: SFR 88-102.

National (tel. 412681) SFR 780—This lower-priced hotel is near the Crans lifts. It is used by British tour groups but the owner can be cantankerous. Normal daily rates: SFR 88-102.

Cisalpin (tel. 412425) SFR 595—Right next to the lifts. Normal daily rate: SFR 59-66.

Pensione Centrale (tel. 413767) SFR 595—Everything the name implies. Smack in the center of Crans. A family-run pensione. Normal daily rate: SFR 59-66.

Teleferique (tel. 413367) SFR 595—At the departure of the Cry d'Err lifts. If you want to take two steps and be on the lift, this is the place. Normal daily rate: SFR 56-63.

Vieux-Valais (tel. 412031) SFR 495—Small family-run hotel with only 15 beds. Normal daily rate: SFR 44 (B&B).

Olympic (tel. 412985) New hotel in the center of town. Normal daily rate: SFR 60.

Dining

This town, as noted above, has plenty of great eateries. These are some of our favorites—from expensive to moderate to inexpensive.

For top gourmet cuisine, head to **Le Chamois d'Or** (tel. 415553), where the chef works at Maxim's in Paris between seasons. The **Rostisserie de la Reina** (tel. 411885) is renowned for its fresh fish and shellfish, and **Le Sporting** (tel. 411177) has top French and Italian food.

For moderately priced meals, try **Le Trappe** in the Hotel Cisalpine (tel. 412425). Try their *Fondue la Trappe*. The **Hotel Aida** (tel. 412781) has a beautiful rustic dining room.

The budget crowd should indulge at **Le Bistro** and **Mamma Mia** in Montana, and at the **Ambassy Restaurant** at the Montana edge of Crans.

On the mountain, we liked the lunch menu at **Des Violettes** and **Bella-Lui**. Or if everything on the slopes is crowded, try the restaurant at the lower station of the Montana/Cry d'Err gondola. The scenery from **De la Plaine Morte** restaurant (tel. 413626) on the glacier is the stuff memories are made of.

Apartments

Rental apartment and chalet listings in Crans-Montana are overwhelming. Twelve major rental agencies in Crans and 17 in Montana maintain listings.

Expect to pay SFR 660-790 for a two-bed studio during high season (February and Easter); SFR 920-1060 for a four-bed, two-room apartment; SFR 1,720-1,900 for a four-room, six- to eight-bed apartment.

To book an apartment, write to the tourist office in either town with details of what you want and the price range. You'll get a prompt reply.

Nightlife

By U.S. and British standards, there isn't much. Immediately after the slopes close, the only bar with a crowd is in Montana—**Le Grange** . It's small and very smoky. The **Pub** in Crans is reportedly an après-ski spot, but we can't confirm it.

Discos really don't get going until between midnight and 1 a.m. If you're determined and well-heeled, head for **Le Sporting** and **Pacha** in Crans, but expect to pay a SFR 20 cover charge, which includes a drink. In Montana, the place to be seen is the **Number One**. There is no cover, but a beer costs SFR 15.

If you have the urge to go out between 9 p.m. and midnight, try some of the normally quiet piano bars. **Memphis Bar** in Crans sometimes has jazz.

Child care

The ski school for children (six to 12) runs only half days. The cost for a half day is SFR 19; seven days, SFR 80; all-day nursery, including lunch, is SFR 45. Call 411320 in Crans and, in Montana, 411480. A new kindergarten has opened for children from three to seven years. It is located near the station for the Grand-Signal lift. The kindergarten is open from 8:30 a.m. to 5 p.m. Rates are SFR 32 for full day with lunch, SFR 17 for half day and SFR 6 an hour. Call 412022.

Getting there

You'll most likely arrive at the Geneva airport. From here, it's an uncomplicated car or train ride around the lake and into the mountains. From Sierre, take the cablecar around the corner from the railway station, or the bus from directly in front of the railway station.

Other activities

Crans-Montana is a center for hot-air ballooning and hang-gliding, with instruction in hang-gliding available. Call 413041 for information about both. A winter meeting of hot-air balloon enthusiasts is held annually, usually in February. A balloon ride for two costs SFR 650; for three, SFR 800.

Sled-dog races are run several times during the season at courses in the area.

Tourist information

Check with the tourist office, Crans, CH-3963, Switzerland; tel. (027) 412132; telex 473173 TURCH CH. In Montana, the address is CH-3962, Switzerland; tel. (027) 413041; telex 473203 TURM CH.

The tourist offices provide an automatic phone information service that gives snow condition reports during the season. Call 41335.

Davos

Davos is a queen among winter resorts, one of the first to be developed and still considered to be one of the best in the world. Located in Switzerland's Grisons region, in the southeast corner of the country, the town is dwarfed by mountains rising on both sides of the valley. The mountains have been developed into five separate ski areas.

The town is not quaint by any stretch of the imagination. Where a dreamer might expect to find wooden chalets, reality showcases square, concrete hotels. But Davos maintains a sense of being comfortable. Traffic moves easily along the upper and lower main arteries without buildup. The hotels have a long and distinguished tradition for excellence, and practically every type of recreational activity is available. If you want to buy a Rolex, pick up the latest in Gucci accessories or the finest Atomic racing ski, you'll find all of them without any problem. Residents are politely correct in dealing with visitors, perhaps not as warm as in small Austrian towns totally dependent on the influx of tourists, but friendly nevertheless.

At night the mix of people has unusual variety, from teenagers in town for the good skiing to elderly couples enjoying the crisp, clear mountain air and the restorative powers of an Alpine vacation. Nightlife is adequate, if restrained. Everything seems to be done in moderation.

Davos will remind you of the best of Switzerland: beautiful, organized, tourist-oriented, enjoyable to visit at any time.

Where to ski

Best known is the Parsenn area, one of the major reasons why Davos has become a premier European resort. It is reached by the Parsennbahn, a cable railway that leaves every 15 to 20 minutes during the ski season. It peaks at the Weissfluhgipfel, at 9,331 feet, where it drops with two expert runs to the Parsenn. Here, runs are wide open and offer intermediate and beginning skiers a paradise for cruising. The Parsenn has 40 seemingly endless runs, including what was once Europe's longest—from Weissfluhjoch to Kublis.

The Jakobshorn area is the second major area in Davos, on the opposite side of the valley from the Parsenn. A cablecar rises from the town to the lower station of the Jakobshornbahn, which peaks at 8,497 feet. Here, 14 marked trails will keep a skier busy for at least a day. The area is more challenging than the Parsenn and often less crowded, but the runs are shorter and more limited. The other three areas are the Rinerhorn area at Glaris just up the valley from the main town, with 13 runs and several good advanced intermediate descents; the Pischa area, reached by a short bus ride from Davos and offering limited but uncrowded runs; and the Schatzalp/Strela area, which joins the Parsenn by way of a cablecar that runs from the Strelapass to the Weissfluhjoch. This last area has significantly more difficult runs and offers a change of pace for several afternoons after one has warmed up on the Parsenn.

All of the runs end in the valley and most are within walking distance of the hotels. Where runs end in Kublis, Saas, Klosters, Wolfgang or in Glaris, at the opposite end of the valley, frequent trains bring skiers back to the center of Davos. The train connection is included in the lift-pass price.

Mountain rating

Davos earns an A-plus when it comes to beginning and intermediate skiers. This is perhaps the ideal terrain for learning to ski and perfecting techniques. For experts, the Parsenn terrain can become somewhat boring, and they should ask the instructors where the most challenging skiing—normally off the Parsenn—can be found.

The best expert runs on the Parsenn are from the top of the Weissfluhgipfel. Otherwise, stick to the trails that drop into town alongside the Parsennbahn, or take the Drostobel-to-Klosters run, which is narrow and sometimes steep. The Strela area, Rinerhorn and Jakobshorn all have some good expert runs, but expect easy cruising for the most part. On days with good fresh powder, it pays to hire an instructor who will take you to the special spots for some thrills in the powder for the morning.

Ski school

The Davos ski school has more than 150 instructors. Almost every one of them speaks some English. There are some reductions for groups of senior citizens and for children. Inquire at the ski school to see whether such a group has been organized. Lesson rates are:

Individual lessons

one day (five hours)	SFR 200 a day
five consecutive days	SFR 185 a day
half day	SFR 110 a day

| one hour (for one or two persons) | SFR 44 a day |

Group lessons

one half-day	SFR 22
one day	SFR 40
five half-days	SFR 90
five full days	SFR 150

A discount is offered for lessons given during the first three weeks of December. Children from four to 12 years get a 25 percent discount, depending on the length of the course. Ask when signing up.

Lift tickets (89/90 prices)

Separate passes are sold for each of the five areas outlined above, although there is a combination pass for Strela and the Parsenn area.

The most convenient pass, especially if you plan to ski for a week or more, is the all-inclusive regional pass. This pass gives you use of all lifts, as well as the train through the valley from Glaris to Kublis. The only restriction is that it's sold only for more than two days.

three days	SFR 120
six days	SFR 200
seven days	SFR 224
fourteen days	SFR 360

NOTE: A single day ticket for the Parsenn area costs SFR 40. Children get a 25 percent discount.

Accommodations

Davos' hotels range from posh and plush to plain and priceworthy. The following hotels make our top recommendations in each category. The high-season 1989/90 normal daily rate for period 31 January through 25 March 1990 is the last price quoted for each hotel.

Our recommended five-star hotel is:

Steigenberger Belvedere , tel. 21281; telex 853110. Many consider this the best hotel in town. Normal daily rate: SFR 215.

Our recommended four-star hotels are:

Morosani Post Hotel, tel. 21161; telex 853150. Normal daily rate: SFR 185.

Sunstar Park Hotel, tel. 21241; telex 853192. Normal daily rate: SFR 175.

Sporthotel Central , tel. 21181; telex 853188. Normal daily rate: SFR 165.

Derby Hotel, tel. 61166; telex 853236. Normal daily rate: SFR 173.

Meierhof, tel. 61285; telex 853263. Normal daily rate: SFR 180.

Our recommended three-star hotels are:

Hotel Cristiana, tel. 51444. Normal daily rate: SFR 105.

Hotel Des Alpes, tel. 61261; telex 853241. Daily room rate: SFR 120.

Our recommended one-star hotel is:

Edelweiss , tel. 51033. (bed and breakfast). Normal daily rate: SFR 53.

Apartments

As at most Swiss resorts, the rental apartment business is well organized and bookings can be arranged through the tourist information office. Write to the office, and provide details about when you plan to arrive, how many people will be sharing the apartment and what facilities you desire. It will respond quickly with several apartment choices.

Keep in mind that you want to stay in Davos-Platz or Davos-Dorf. If you end up in Davos-Laret or Davos-Wolfgang, you will face a good walk to the lifts every day and may have to catch a shuttle bus. Make your selection and notify the tourist office or the individual owner, depending on the instructions you get from the tourist office.

Normally, linen and kitchen utensils are included in every apartment. Heat, taxes, electricity and cleaning services may be extra. Expect to pay between SFR 25 and SFR 42 per person a night, depending on how many are sharing the apartment, where it's located and its relative position on the luxury scale.

Dining

Davos has scores of restaurants. Try **Ammann's Steakhouse**, and the **Rössli**. **Bündnerstübli** at Dischmastrasse in Dorf is very local and very reasonable. **Palüda-Grill** is very rustic and located in the Derby Hotel in Dorf. In the Hotel Davoserhof, the **Bündnerstübli** is elegant with upper level prices and high-class cuisine.

Just outside of the town, try **Hubli's Landhaus** in Laret (tel. 52121) or the **Hotel Post** in Frauenkirch (tel. 36104); both are excellent and reservations are strongly recommended.

The best pizza in town is found at **El Padrino** in Platz. The best Italian restaurant is **Trattoria Toscana** in Hotel des Alpes in Dorf.

Nightlife

For nightlife, head to the **Postli Club**, open every evening from 8:30 p.m., the **Cabanna Club**, which gets started at 9 p.m., or the **Central**, which also opens its doors at 9 p.m. Don't expect many exciting things to happen before 11 p.m., though. Most discos stay open until 2 a.m.

Child care

Two organized kindergartens in Davos offer supervision for children between the ages of three and 10.

The Mickymaus Bolgen Kindergarten (tel: 34048) is in Davos-Platz, next to the Jakobshornbahn's lower station. It is open every day except Sunday from 9 a.m. until 5 p.m. The costs are:

for one hour	SFR 15
for one day	SFR 30
for six consecutive days	SFR 100

Lunch is served from 11:30 a.m. until 2 p.m. and babysitting service during lunch will cost SFR 20. The charge for lunch if the school feeds the child is SFR 7. Advanced booking is required. Contact Davos-Jakobshorn Cable Airways (tel. 37001) for more information.

The Pinocchio Kindergarten in Bünda, Davos-Dorf, is open every day except Sunday from 9 a.m. until 5 p.m.. Its prices are:

for one hour	SFR 15
for one day	SFR 30
for six consecutive days	SFR 100

Lunch is served from 11:30 a.m. until 2 p.m. and sitting during that time costs SFR 20. If the child is to have lunch there, the charge is SFR 7 extra. Reservations are required. Contact the Swiss Ski School of Davos, Promenade 83, 7270 Davos-Platz; tel. 37171.

Getting there

The closest airport is Zurich, nearly three hours away by train. You must change in Landquart if you decide to take the train.

If you opt for a rental car, follow the signs to Chur on an excellent superhighway until you get to the Landquart/Davos exit. The drive from Landquart to Davos is through the narrow valley and passes through Kublis and Klosters before arriving at Davos-Platz. The total distance from Zurich to Davos is about 150 kilometers, or just under 100 miles.

Other activities

Davos is a well-developed resort with a swimming pool, saunas and a solarium. The cost for the public pool and sauna is SFR 11 a visit; alternatively, buy a 10-visit book of coupons for SFR 90. If you just want to swim, pay only SFR 4.50 a session, or SFR 35 for 10 visits.

There is a tennis and squash center in Davos-Platz with four indoor tennis courts and two squash courts, tel. 083-33131.

Europe's largest natural ice skating rink is open, and skate rentals are available. Admission for adults is SFR 4 and for children, SFR 2.50. Tel. 37354.

Horseback riding can be arranged by calling Hans Lenz at (083) 53888 or 52368.

Hang-gliding courses are taught by Heini Heusser in Davos-Platz; tel. 36769.

Horse-drawn "sleigh rides to anywhere" can be arranged by calling 35135.

There is also a new toboggan run with banked turns and a total drop of over 750 feet. It is open from 10 am to 9 pm. There is no admission. Toboggans are available for rental at the base of the run. Tel. 35726 or 35590.

Both Zurich and Lucerne are only about a two-hour drive from Davos.

South, toward the San Bernadino pass, drive through the Via Mala, the deepest gorge in Switzerland, presided over by the recently restored castle of Hohen Rathien in Thusis. If the pass from Sils to Davos is open and you have tire chains, the drive that completes the loop around the mountains is beautiful.

Tourist information

The tourist information office is open daily from 8 a.m. until noon and from 1:45 to 6 p.m. On Saturday, it closes at 5 p.m. It is closed on Sunday. Write: Davos Tourist Office, 7270 Davos-Platz; tel. (083) 35135; telex 853130.

Engelberg

When you ski at Engelberg, in central Switzerland, just remember that the Gerschnialp is for beginners and the Titlis is for the advanced. It will save you a few difficult moments if you're wary of the ski school of hard knocks.

Skiing in Engelberg is done in two major areas. The Brunni is on one side of the valley, with slopes all the way up to the Schonegg at 6,691 feet. From Schonegg it's an intermediate cruise down to the village.

The finest beginner and lower intermediate skiing is on the opposite mountain below the Titlis glacier on Gerschnialp. Ski out the doorway of the six-person gondola station and down the mountain to the Gerschnialp lifts.

Because it is central Switzerland's major resort, Engelberg is crowded on weekends. During the week, things are far less hectic. Everyone but the rank beginner eventually makes it up to the 10,624-foot-high summit of Titlis. This is where the best skiers sharpen their skills. To join them, take the gondola from the valley floor to Trübsee and then the two-section cablecar the rest of the way up to Klein-Titlis at 9,908 feet. You've spent over 90 minutes geting to this point, so enjoy the view all the way to the Gotthard Pass in one direction and past Lucerne to the Bernese Oberland and Interlaken in the other.

From Titlis there is a memorable run all the way to Trübsee from what seems (on clear days) like the roof of the Europe. The run crosses the summer ski area and becomes a black trail as you begin the biggest part of the nearly more than 2,500-foot drop from Station Titlis to Stand. Take it easy the first time down. The glacial ice, sharp turns and the steepness of the slope can be treacherous. Follow the trail markers and don't let the nets, set out at the worst places, break your concentration.

After one run, some intermediates choose to stay on the wider red run from Stand down to Trübsee. If you make this decision, take the horizontal T-bar across the frozen lake to Alpstuebli where you can go up to the 8,474-foot-high Jochstock. The red run down to Jochpass and Alpstuebli is good before cruising down to the Kanonenrohr entrance.

The Kanonenrohr (cannon barrel) section is only a few hundred meters, but you'll turn enough to keep your thighs burning for a while. Lower intermediates should opt for the blue trail to the left of the toughest section. To repeat the best part of the run, stop at the Untertrübsee cablecar station and go back up. Jochstock down to the ground station is about six miles, while from the Titlis peak to the ground station is eight miles.

The best off-trail skiing is on the Laub above the Ritz restaurant and below Titlis. The 1,000-foot vertical drop is a challenge for even experienced skiers, and a guide (cost: about SFR 120) is recommended.

Mountain rating

For beginners, the slopes of the Gerschnialp and Untertrübsee are best.

Intermediates will be challenged on both sides of the valley, particularly up top on Titlis.

Experts will discover whether they really merit that classification after several runs from the glacier summit. In short, Engelberg is an excellent ski destination for the broadest range of skiers.

Ski school

Two ski schools (for information, call 941161) with a total of 65 instructors offer both group and private lessons.

Individual lessons

one hour	SFR 40
half day (3 hrs.)	SFR 140
all day (5 hrs.)	SFR 194

Group lessons

Group lessons are offered in five full-day blocks. The Schweizer school offers five and a half hours of instruction a day. A half-day costs SFR 45; a full day—SFR 54; two days—SFR 108; three days—SFR 162; five days—SFR 249.

Cross-country lessons are given for three hours per day. Rates are one day—SFR 25; two days—SFR 49; three days—SFR 73; four days—SFR 96; five days—SFR 106.

Lift tickets

The Engelberg ticket is good for all 24 lifts in the area, opening a total of about 32 miles of trails. There are discounts for children, senior citizens and families. Ask about "shoulder season" rates. In addition, for day tickets the price drops three francs per hour after 10 a.m. (88/89 prices)

| for one day | SFR 45 |
| for two days | SFR 70 |

for three days	SFR 93
for six days	SFR 162
for seven days	SFR 170

Accommodations

Engelberg is a relatively small town (pop. 3,100) with a major tourist capacity. Overall, there are nearly 10,000 beds available in hotels, guesthouses and pensiones, plus another 6,500 in private homes and apartments.

The all-inclusive plan should be your first choice. The plan offers a week's accommodation and half pension, six-day ski pass, bus transfers and other extras beginning at SFR 550 a week. Our choices:

Engelberg (tel. 941168, telex 866183) A pleasant hotel in the city center. The ski week package will cost SFR 650 H.S. and SFR 610 L.S. Normal high season rates are SFR140-160 for a double room.

Hotel Central (tel. 941239; telex 866269) Ideally located for all activities in town. Hotel has its own swimming pool and sauna. The ski week package costs are SFR 650 H.S. and SFR 610 L.S. Normal high season rates are SFR 120-140 for a double.

Hotel Europaischer Hof (tel. 941263) Normal high season rates are SFR 144-148 for a double.

Dorint Hotel (tel. 942828) One of our favorite hotels in town. Special weekly all-inclusive package available for SFR 830 H.S. or for SFR 680 L.S. Normal high season rates are SFR 186-226 for a double.

Hotel Hess (tel. 941366, telex 866270) Here you get friendly staff, traditional, nice rooms and, above all else, excellent food. Ski week packages are SFR 830 H.S. and 630 L.S. Normal high season rates are SFR 186-226 for a double.

Sporthotel Trübsee(tel.941371) Hotel has a great location halfway up the Titlis bahn. Weekly plan is approximately SFR 600 without half pension. The normal high season rates are SFR 135-160 for a double.

If the hotels in Engelberg are fully booked, as they often are in peak season, the lakeside city of Lucerne is a good alternative. It is only 30 minutes from the slopes by car. An excellent waterside hotel is **Bellevue et Balances**.

Dining

The Tudorstubli restaurant at Hotel Hess (tel. 941366) is the best restaurant in town and offers excellent lamb specialties.

Apartments

Engelberg has much to offer the person seeking apartment accommodations. Prices start at SFR 520 a week for a one-bedroom apartment.

The tourist office has a computerized listing of available apartments, and an inquiry will generate an answer mailed to you the same day.

Several agencies offer apartments in the city. Their names, total number of apartments offered by each and telephone numbers are listed below:

Interhome; 100 apartments, chalets; tel. 942340
Neuschwaendi organization; 30 apartments; tel. 942516
Sunnmatt; 100 aparftments; tel. 941461
Uto-ring; 35 apartments; tel. 01-2024310
Würsch; 40 apartments; tel. 943165

Nightlife

A pleasant place to meet is at the bar of the Bellevue Terminus Hotel opposite the railway station and ski school. Later in the evening you can drop into the **Spindle** in the cellar of the Alpenclub Hotel. It's crowded with the 18- to 25-year-old set, as is the nearby **Carmena** club. Our favorites were **Dream Life**, an English pub at the Central Hotel, and **Peter's Pub**, just up the street.

The **Casino**, close to the ski school office, has a slightly older crowd and a nightclub.

Child care

The local ski school operates a ski kindergarten program for children from three to six. For skiers rates are: half-day—SFR 7; full day—SFR 12; lunch—SFR 7.

For kids who ski the rates are: full day—SFR33; three days—SFR 99; five days—SFR 159; lunch—SFR 7.

Phone the ski school for more infomation at 941074 or 944240.

Getting there

The main international airport is Zurich, and transfers are by train or automobile. Driving time from Zurich is about one and a half hours. If possible, make a sightseeing stop in Lucerne along the way. Rental cars are available in Zurich, Lucerne and Engelberg.

Other activities

Engelberg is sunny most of the year. The biggest non-skiing pursuits are hiking and sightseeing.

Engelberg has a sports center with indoor and outdoor ice skating, plus indoor tennis courts, a fitness center and a curling competition area.

Horse-drawn sleigh rides are available throughout the winter, and on Friday from January through March nighttime sleigh rides are a tradition.

Visit the beautiful 12th-century Benedictine abbey at the edge of town. For more extensive touring, take the train for a tour of Lucerne and the four lakes area.

On Friday during ski season there is a visitors' ski race. In addition, there is a major ski jumping competition from the Titlis 90-meter tower each February.

For the advanced skier, courses in trick skiing are offered (tel. 941074).

The most scenic local excursion, other than the ride up the Titlis bahn, is the trip to Schwand, about five miles away, where from the vantage point above the church you get the best view of the ring of mountains in the Engelberg area.

Tourist information

Contact the Kur-und-Verkehrsverein, CH-6390 Engelberg, Switzerland; tel. 041-941161; telex 866246.

Flims/Laax

Flims/Laax is still one of the undiscovered ski areas in Switzerland, at least as far as American and British skiers are concerned even with excellent ski club patronage. Unlike the "best-known" Swiss ski resorts, which were patronized by English visitors during the early years of skiing's rise to popularity, Laax and Flims were discovered by the Swiss and the Germans, who know a good area when they find it.

Flims is a town in the traditional sense. The ski lifts start from the town center and the major hotels are spread throughout the town. Laax, as far as skiers are concerned, is limited to the new hotels and apartments that have been purpose-built at the base of the Crap Sogn Gion cablecar. Not only the major hotels are centered here but also the major nightlife. Flims is perhaps a more Swiss experience. Laax is perhaps a purer ski vacation experience.

It is hard to describe the incredible expanse of skiing that surrounds a skier as he gazes from the top of the Crap Sogn Gion cablecar station that rises from Laax. This is a wide-open area that cries out for all-day skiing.

Where to ski

Laax and Flims are at an altitude of about 3,609 feet. One major lift from each resort town carries skiers to the snowfields, which are in turn linked by a far-flung, 32-lift system. These lifts are not tightly packed but efficiently service the trails belonging to four major sections: Cassons Grat, La Siala, Crap Sogn Gion and Vorab.

After the lifts split above Flims, one continues to Cassons Grat, a spectacular snowfield set on the Flimserstein. Here, powder and off-trail skiers can have a field day. The other fork of the lift takes skiers to Grauberg, which is linked with other lifts under the La Siala peak.

Above Laax, the cablecar reaches the Crap Sogn Gion at 7,283 feet and a second continues to Crap Masegn, 650 feet higher. From here, skiers can shoot back into the valley toward Falera or to the lower cablecar station. Other runs drop into the opposite valley, where more lifts bring skiers up to the La Siala area above Flims. High-altitude buffs head to the Vorab area, which, at over 9,842 feet, presents a great panorama and beautiful skiing.

Mountain rating

The beginner will find the best areas under La Siala and on the Vorab and Flims-Foppa.

Intermediates will be overjoyed with the Crap Sogn Gion section and can find more than enough challenging runs anywhere in the resort area.

The expert skiers can stay busy when the mood strikes them, especially beneath the Crap Sogn Gion cablecar, the back side of the Vorab and through Cassons Grat's powder and trails.

Ski school

Ski school is available in both Flims and Laax. The prices are almost identical. Private instruction costs: SFR 100 for a morning lesson; SFR 95 for afternoon sessions; and SFR 175 for a full day

Group lessons for adults are: SFR 40 for a full day; SFR 100 for three full days; SFR 140 for five full days.

Group lessons for children are: SFR 18 for a half day; SFR 43 for three half days; SFR 74 for five half days; SFR 124 for ten half-full days.

A private instructor for powder work can be hired for SFR 115 for a half day.

Lift tickets

The lifts are run by separate companies, one from each resort. The Flims lifts operate in the Cassons Grat and La Siala areas. The Laax lifts cover the Vorab and Crap Sogn Gion areas. 1988/89 prices for a combination ticket that allows unlimited skiing in both areas are as follows:

	adults	children (6-16)
for one day	SFR 41	SFR 21
for two days	SFR 75	SFR 38
for six days	SFR 198	SFR 99
for eight days	SFR 248	SFR 124
for twelve days	SFR 324	SFR 162

NOTE: A photo is required for lift passes of four days or more, but the photo will be taken free of charge at the lift station.

Accommodations

These are our recommended hotels, each of which has been visted by a SKI EUROPE representative. The price given is the normal high-season price with half pension, based on double occupancy. Expect prices to be around 20 percent lower during low season.

All inclusive "white week" packages are also available. They include seven nights hotel, six days lift tickets and five days of lessons in January and late April.

NOTE: the local phone prefix is (081).

Park Hotel Waldhaus (tel. 390181; telex 851925) The best hotel in Flims/Laax. A beautiful hotel that is almost its own small village. The buildings are interconnected by covered paths and underground walkways. You can be elegant and formal or as casual as you please in this sprawling complex in the woods above Flims. Normal daily rate: SFR 175-215. White week rate: SFR 1223-1328.

Adula (tel. 390161; telex 851960) In Flims, this runs a close second to the Park Hotel. In fact, many people prefer it because it is much cozier and smaller. The Barga restaurant is considered to be one of the best in the entire region. It has an indoor pool, sauna and fitness room. Normal daily rate: SFR 130-180. White week rate: SFR 1083-1188.

Comfort Inn-Hotel National (tel. 391224; telex 851977) In Flims, this hotel is fun. The owner is a great cook and enjoys having a weekly ski barbecue in his mountain hut. The atmosphere is laid back, and the hotel is just across the street from the main lifts in Flims. The hotel is part of the Comfort Inn group. Normal daily rate: SFR 95-110. White week rates: SFR 838-908.

Arvenhotel Waldeck (tel. 391228) In Flims-Waldhaus, this hotel is known for a good restaurant. Rooms have been redone in knotty pine and the ambience is casual. Normal daily rate: SFR 86-104. White week rate: SFR 880.

Hotel Meiler-Prau da Monis (tel. 390171; telex 851901) In the center of Flims and close to everything. Normal daily rate: SFR 90-114. White week: SFR 978.

Hotel Crap Ner (tel. 392626; telex 851908) Its name means "black rock" in the local dialect. A sport hotel five minutes from the lift station in Flims-Dorf. Excellent menu in the Stiva Crap Ner restaurant, and cozy atmosphere in the cellar Tschuetta Bar. Normal daily rate: SFR 96-124. White week rate: SFR 929.

Happy Rancho Complex (tel. 086-30131)

This is a group of three hotels: Happy Rancho (four-star), Little Rancho and Old Rancho (both three-star). The Happy Rancho consists of similar-sized apartments, studios and hotel rooms. Ski Week here (with lifts and instruction) costs SFR 950. The Old Rancho and the Little Rancho are interconnected by underground passages and therefore share swimming pool and other facilities, all of which are first-class. We would rather stay in one of the smaller Ranchos, Old or Little. The normal room rates are: Happy, Old and Little Rancho—SFR 115-140.

Apartments

Flims and Laax are well organized to handle tourists who want to rent apartments during the ski season. Apartments are normally rented out for a minimum stay of one week, Saturday to Saturday; during the Christmas and Easter seasons, a minimum two-week rental is often required.

The tourist office keeps a computerized, constantly updated listing of available apartments. When writing, include the number of beds required, the preferred number of rooms and your planned vacation dates. You will receive a quick response that lists a selection of apartments and prices. Select the apartment you want and return the application.

Normally, linen and kitchen utensils are provided. Other communal or private amenities, such as swimming pool, sauna, TV or room phone all add to the costs. Standard apartments rent for between SFR 15 and SFR 20 per person a night. Prices vary significantly from low to high season.

Dining

Area restaurants are reasonably priced and most feature a good selection of international and regional specialties. The best in the region is the **Restarant Barga** (tel. 390161) in the Hotel Adula. In fact, Gault/Millau considers it one of the best in Switzerland. The other top restaurant is the **Segnes und Post** (tel. 391281). For good basic value and Swiss tradition in Flims, try the **Waldeck** (tel. 391228); the **National** is noted for its fish dishes. The **Cabana** is run by the Hotz family, which also operates the Barga. In Laax, both the **Capricorno** (tel. 086-35454) and **Posta Veglia** (tel. (086-34466) are highly recommended for traditional Swiss cooking.

Nightlife

The best discos in the area are the **Sardona** in Flims, which caters to a younger crowd earlier in the evening. The later crowd is older, which congregates for the special shows that start around midnight. In Laax, the **Camona** offers year-round action reminiscent of big city discos. A live band starts at about 11:30 p.m. The **Casa Veglia** in Laax has a somewhat older crowd and is appropriately more sedate. Cover charges for all discos are around SFR 10. Expect to pay about SFR 10 for a beer and SFR 15 for a mixed drink.

Child care

Kindergartens that are associated with the famous Swiss Ski School operate in the area. In Flims and Laax, the children's ski school and kindergarten is open from 9 a.m. until 5 p.m., and normally includes skiing lessons for children old enough to learn. Rates are SFR 16 for a half day; SFR 30 for a full day; SFR 43 for three half days; SFR 74 for five half days and SFR 100 for five full days, including lunch. Lunch with any program will cost an additional SFR 7, unless specifically included.

Ski nursery prices are the same, and children who do not wish to learn skiing can spend the day making handicrafts, tobogganing and playing.

The Hotel Happy Rancho has an in-house kindergarten for families staying in the complex. Non-guests may leave their children on a space-available basis.

Getting there

The closest airport is Zurich. From there you can take a train to Chur, where you must change for a post bus to Flims and Laax. The entire trip will take about three hours.

If driving, take the main road to Chur and continue until you see signs for Flims to the right. Driving time is about two hours. Do not make the mistake of trying to approach Laax and Flims from the west—the pass is closed during the winter.

Other activities

Consider a trip to Chur, only a half-hour drive down the mountain. The Via Mala, Switzerland's deepest gorge, is just 45 minutes from Flims, and the tiny country of Liechtenstein can be easily reached by car in about an hour.

There are horse-drawn sleigh rides for SFR 80 for one to three persons; SFR 100 for four to five; or SFR 120 for six to seven. Riding stables are open, with horse rentals for SFR 50 for 50 minutes or SFR 180 for a 10-hour ticket. Call 392435 or 392593.

Ice skating is available for SFR 4 a day. Skates are also available for hire for SFR 6 a day.

There are covered tennis courts for SFR 30 an hour in the Park Hotel in Flims and in the Hotel Signina in Laax.

Five heated hotel pools are open to the public—Park Hotel,

Schweitzerhof, Des Alpes, Adula and Crap Ner. The entrance is SFR 6 for adults and SFR 3 for children. The Park Hotel pool is a bit more expensive at SFR 18 for adults and SFR 6 for children.

A public swimming pool is open in Laax every afternoon from 1:30 p.m. to 9 p.m., except Saturday and Sunday when it closes at 6 p.m.. It is also open from 10 a.m. until noon on Sunday. Entrance is SFR 5 for adults and SFR 2.50 for children.

Tourist information

Flims

Tourist Office, CH-7018 Flims-Waldhaus, Switzerland; tel. (081) 391022; telex 851919.

Laax

Tourist Office, CH-7031 Laax, Switzerland; tel. (086) 34343; telex 856111

Gstaad and the White Highlands Region

Gstaad is linked with the jet-set more often than with good skiing, and that's a mistake because it has outstanding slopes for beginners and intermediates. This Alpine village tucked into a scenic valley, two hours from Geneva and 90 minutes from Interlaken, is part of a thriving ski circuit called *"Das Weisse Hochland,"* the White Highland. When you buy a lift ticket in Gstaad, or at one of the 10 smaller resorts in the area, you can use any of 69 lifts opening up about 150 miles of prepared trails. The other villages lay stretched along the railway line (from east to west): St. Stephan, Zweisimmen, Saanenmöser, Schönried, Gstaad, Saanen, Rougemont, Chateau d'Oex, Les Moulins—with Launen, Gsteig and Reusch accessible by bus up the valleys fanning from Gstaad.

Where to ski

The skiing in the immediate area of Gstaad is fragmented. The relatively low Eggli (1,672m/5,494 feet) is the largest area and interconnected with the peak of Videmanette and the towns of Saanen and Rougemont.

The Wasserngrat (1,940m/6,365 feet) and the Wisple (1,950m/6,397 feet) are the two other totally separated areas. The Wasserngrat is the most challenging of the three areas, but is limited to two lifts. However, the skiing is superb and there is hardly ever a line. If the Eggli is crowded, this area offers skiing with no waiting. Beginners and lower intermediates may be out of their league here.

The Wisple is not as difficult as the Wasserngrat and is closer to town as well. This is a good intermediate area with limited lifts but long, enjoyable runs. Wide stretches of the slopes are left unprepared for powder hounds. It also has short lines and is within walking distance of the Eggli lifts. The Swiss Ski School is located at its base and the two drag lifts are used mainly by the ski school.

The Eggli shows two black runs—however, an intermediate skier should seldom feel anxiety here. The run through the trees from

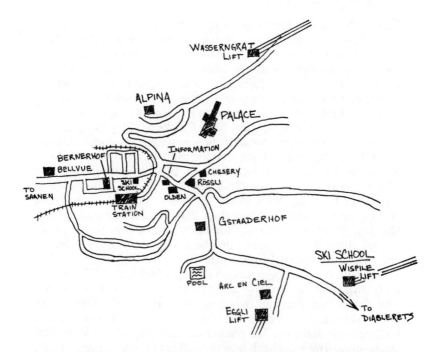

the chairlift at Eggli Stand to the ground T-bar station in neighboring Saanen has enough moguls and turns to hold your interest.

There is some genuine skiing adventure above Gstaad. The finest
is La Videmanette. Ski over the Eggli and down to the Pra Cluen
chairlift to reach the area above neighboring Rougemont, or drive
there. From Rougemont, four-passenger gondolas ascend past
rocky pinnacles to the La Videmanette summit at (2,156 m/7,071
feet). The run down through the rocks off the backside is strictly
for experts.

On the Videmanette front side, the first 300 meters straight over
the edge (skittish types can take the traverse around the rim of
the bowl) is also an eye-opener. There's a difficult mogul field to
negotiate before beginning the remainder of the 3.5-mile intermediate run to Rougemont. Alternatively, ski around the corner
to the top of the Pra Cluen chairlift and take the 3.5-mile *schuss*
to the valley floor.

There is summer glacier skiing at Les Diablerets (3,243 m/10,637
feet), which is reached via a three-stage cablecar from Reusch at
the end of the valley.

The Hornberg section is the largest interconnected grouping of lifts in the "White Highlands." It is not directly connected with Gstaad but is easily reached by bus or train (both included with your ski pass). Take either the Horneggli lift from Schönried or the Saanerslochgrat gondola from Sannenmöser. Both lifts are opposite the respective railway stations, making getting lost impossible. This area, a lower intermediate's paradise, is served by 14 lifts, which keep waiting time to less than five minutes.

For more challenging runs, head for the St. Stephan lifts connected with Hornberg. Take the Saanerslochgrat gondola and ski down to Chaltebrunne. Then take the chairlift up to the Gandlouenegrat, which sits at the top of the St. Stephan section. The face of the mountain from Gandlouenegrat down to Chaltebrunne is one of the best slopes I've skied. There is something for everyone from expert to advanced beginner. Playing here can take up half the day. If you time it right for lunch, make sure to eat at the Chemi Hütte at Lengebrand on the slopes above St. Stephan at the end of the chairlift from town.

Opposite the Hornberg section is the Rellerligrat (1,934m/6,285 feet) with what many claim is the most beautiful view of Gstaad. The slopes face the sun, meaning that they are the first to lose snow. Mornings can be icy and afternoons slushy, but skiing here on sunny days is a joy. The restaurant at the top is one of the best in the area. The runs back into the valley are long cruising trails, with a long black run under the gondola for experts and advanced intermediates.

Zweisimmen offers an unfortunately isolated ski area flanked on the left by St. Stephan and on the right by the Hornberg lifts. There is no lift connection with either. The gondola from town to the Rinderberg opens up seven prepared runs served by five lifts. It is pleasant for a day's skiing. Most of the people who stay in Zweisimmen take the train to ski the Hornberg section.

Chateau d'Oex is another small area included in the regional ski pass. Here the La Braye gondola lifts skiers over a ridge behind the town to a mellow intermediate area of about a dozen runs.

The last area on the lift pass is reached from Les Moulins and is served by two long lifts. This area offers two very long beginner runs and one good intermediate trail back to the town from the top of Monts Chevreuils.

Despite the relatively low-lying intermediate slopes, Gstaad enjoys good snow most years from mid-December until mid-April.

Mountain rating

If you are a beginner, Gstaad is an excellent destination. There are plenty of gentle inclines to practice snowplows and stem-christies. The finest beginner run is the 1,253-meter-long Skilift Schopfen slope from the gondola station on the Eggli.

Intermediate skiers will be overjoyed at the variety. Just when you think you've mastered everything, you can cut through the woods or go over the edge of a mogul field you've been bypassing and suddenly realize you haven't learned quite everything.

The expert can enjoy Gstaad if more emphasis is placed on technique than thrills. Plus there are many opportunities to break through trees and ski through powder.

Ski school

Gstaad, with more than 100 ski teachers, has an outstanding reputation for English-speaking ski instructors and for private lessons. It is open from 8:30 a.m. to noon and from 2:30 p.m. to 6 p.m.

Individual lesson rates: one hour (one to four persons)—SFR 45; half day—SFR 110; all day—SFR 200.

Group lesson rates: half day—SFR 19; full day—SFR 37; six consecutive days—SFR 140; six non-consecutive days—SFR 156.

Many ski classes meet directly on the Eggli slope or at the entrance to the Eggli gondola station. Call 41865 for information and bookings. Lessons are available for cross-country.

In Chateau d'Oex the ski school (tel. 029-46848) offers half-day group lessons from only SFR 15 a day; SFR 40 for three days; SFR 72 for six days. Private lessons are only about 10 percent less expensive than in Gstaad.

Lift tickets (89/90 prices)

These tickets are good for the entire "White Highlands" area covering 69 lifts and 250 kilometers of runs. They are good on the railroad, on buses and for entrance to the covered pool in Gstaad.

for a half day	SFR 27
(from 1:30 p.m.)	
for one day	SFR 35
for two days	SFR 72
for three days	SFR 104
for six days	SFR 188
for seven days	SFR 212
for 13 days	SFR 314

Children from ages six through 16 get approximately a 40 percent discount if accompanied by an adult paying the full price.

A Chateau d'Oex limited area lift ticket for Chateau d'Oex/Mt.

Chevreuils can be purchased for approximately 33 percent less than the "White Highlands" pass.

Accommodations

These hotels offer a special one-week ski program, which includes seven nights half pension and six days' lift passes, plus entrance to the indoor swimming pool and use of the public transport. Add another SFR 48 for six days of ski lessons. These weeks are available during January 8 to February 5, and from March 5 to April 9. The package for cross-country skiers without ski pass but with six days instruction is the price indicated, reduced by SFR 70. The final price is for the normal high-season (February) per person with half pension based on double occupancy. These are 88/89 prices.

Gstaad Palace (tel. 83131; telex 922222) SFR 1790—The best in town. A chance to rub shoulders with the best of the movie, fashion and jet-set world if you can afford the entrance. Normal daily rate: SFR 285-400.

Grand Hotel Alpina (tel. 45725; telex 922270) SFR 1050—Second best in luxury with excellent food, but no pool. Up the hill from town next to the Palace. Normal daily rate: SFR 140-190.

Hotel Bellevue (tel. 83171) SFR 980—Part of Best Western. One of the best hotels in town just below the luxury level. Normal daily rate: SFR 135-175.

Bernerhof (tel. 83366; telex 922262) SFR 980—Centrally located with swimming pool. Noted for spacious rooms, good service with excellent kindergarten. Many consider the hotel one of the best in town. Normal daily rate: SFR 129-141.

Hotel Arc-en-Ciel (tel. 83191; telex 922286) SFR 980—Best location for skiing the Eggli. Opposite the gondola station and near a ski rental shop. Quiet, with a good restaurant. Normal daily rate: SFR 110-165.

Hotel Gstaaderhof (tel. 83344; telex 922242) SFR 980—Good location relatively near lifts, station and downtown. Normal daily rate: SFR 95-120.

Hotel Alphorn (tel. 44545) SFR 980—Good location for skiers; near the lift for the Wispile. Across the highway from the Eggli gondola. Normal daily rate: SFR 95-120.

Posthotel Rössli (tel. 43412; telex 922299) SFR 875. This is one of the hotel prizes in Gstaad, but is small and booked very early. The restaurant is one of the best in town. Normal daily rate: SFR 90-130.

Sporthotel Victoria (tel. 41431; telex 922221) SFR 875—Excellent food; has two restaurants and a pizzeria. The most reasonable hotel in town. Normal daily rate: SFR 90-100.

Saanen

Hotel Steigenberger, in Gstaad-Saanen, (tel. 83388; telex 922252) This is, after the Palace, the most luxurious accommodation in the Gstaad/Saanen area. It has everything—pool, sauna, good disco and two restaurants. Normal daily rate: SFR 195-270.

Hotel Residence Cabana, in Gstaad-Saanen, (tel. 44855; telex 922255) SFR 735—includes seven days half board, six days ski pass, six days ski school, free entrance to fitness center. Normal daily rate: SFR 143-180.

Landhaus (tel. 44858) A good, middle-priced hotel in the center of town. Normal daily rate: SFR 70-80.

Krone (tel. 41449) A low-priced bed-and-breakfast alternative in Saanen. Normal daily rate: SFR 50.

Saanenmöser

Hotel Hornberg (tel. 44440) SFR 830—includes ski school. Everything a good ski hotel should be: Near the lifts, with pool and sauna and an owner who helps his clients. Normal daily rate: SFR 85-150.

Schönried

Hotel Alpenrose (tel. 41238) SFR 800—includes ski school. You don't stay here for the luxurious rooms—this small hotel's only a three-star with 12 beds—you come for the great food, believed by many to be the best in the area. Normal daily rate: SFR 130-145.

Hotel Bahnhof (tel. 44242) SFR 700—includes ski school. This is the lowest priced major hotel in town. Nice rooms and close to the railway station. Normal daily rate: SFR 65-85.

Chateau d'Oex
This town down the tracks toward Montreux from Gstaad is significantly less expensive than the Saanenmöser-Gstaad-Saanen area. The town is in the French part of Switzerland. It is not as charming nor as "alpine" as Gstaad. But for overall savings of about 25 percent, this might be the place to stay if you don't mind the half-hour train ride to the major slopes above Gstaad and Schönried.
These hotels have been doing good English-language business. The January week-long package is indicated first includes half-board, lift tickets for all area lifts, train and bus transportation and entrance into Gstaad's indoor pool. The last price is the normal high season, half-board based on double occupancy.

Hotel Beau-Sejour (tel. 029-47423) SFR 552—This hotel is very convenient, across from the train station and the cable car to the Chateau d'Oex area. Normal daily rate: SFR 72-93.

Hotel Ours (tel. 029-46337) SFR 552—Located in the center of town about three minutes from the lift and railway station. Normal daily rate: SFR 72-93.

Hotel Roc et Neige (tel. 029-45525; telex 940097) SFR 472—This brand-new, sparsely furnished giant hotel does brisk group business and is located just downhill from the main town. It is a short five-minute uphill walk to the lift and the train station. The restaurant is self-service, which keeps prices down. Normal daily rate: SFR 47-57.

Dining
Even with Gstaad's jet-set reputation, the best restaurants are just outside town. Naturally, the Palace has several world-class restaurants, but then again most of us are not up to Palace prices. The **Cave** in the Olden Hotel in the center of town provides excellent dining by anyone's standards. Expect to be paying top price and you'll never know with whom you can expect to rub shoulders. Still in town and considerably more reasonable is the **Rossli** across the main street from the Olden—this is typical Swiss cooking at its best. Behind the Rossli, try the **Chesery** which is good but not as exceptional as the Rossli. The **Arc-en-Ciel** opposite the Eggli gondola station has no atmosphere but serves excellent Italian food at low prices.

Out-of-Gstaad Places
Schönried has the Alpenrose (tel. 41238) with a Relais et Chateau gourmet restaurant. This small nouvelle cuisine restaurant is one of the tops in Switzerland. An exceptional traditional Swiss restaurant is the **Bären** (tel. 51033) in the town of Gsteig on the road from Gstaad to Les Diablerets. Down the road from Gsteig try the **Rossli** in Feutersoey (tel. 51012 and 51180). Tucked into another valley in the tiny town of Lauenen enjoy a meal at the **Wildhorn** (tel. 53012). Finally, don't miss the 17th-century **Restaurant Chlösterli** (tel. 51045) just outside town on the road to Les Diablerets.

On the slopes
The best mountain restaurants above Gstaad are at the Eggli and Kalberhöni. Above Schönried, try the **Hornberg** restaurants —one is slightly more upscale, the other has wonderful Rösti and plenty of pasta . . . both have great terraces to enjoy the sun. The **Rellerli Mountain Restaurant** on the opposite side of the valley from Hornberg enjoys a storybook view of Gstaad. The other mountain eatery worth heading for is the **Chemi Hütte** at Lengebrand above St. Stephan.

Apartments

Vacation apartment rentals are available in Gstaad and Saanen. Information on rentals is provided by the tourist offices. In middle season an apartment with one bedroom, living room and furnished kitchen costs approximately SFR 500-700 a week. Ample room for four people is typical.

Saanen and the other surrounding towns have apartments for about SFR 100 less.

Nightlife

The place for après-ski just off the slopes is the **Olden Bar**. It's normally packed. Otherwise, even on Friday night, this town snoozes until midnight. The **Chesery Bar** and the **Stockli Bar** in the Bernerhof were recommended as the best places to have a beer or drink, but both are very quiet. The **Taburi** in Hotel Victoria offers a live Swiss folk group, but the crowd when we visited was deadly. If you come with your own group, though, you're sure to have fun.

The well-heeled enjoy an après-ski drink in the **Palace Hotel** lounge above the city. Take along some money if you want to join them. For starters, the Palace disco cover is SFR 30.

After dark there's a lively crowd and live music at the **Chlösterli** disco outside town. Also try the **Greengo** at the Palace Hotel and the Steigenberger Hotel disco in Saanen for dancing.

Child care

Hotel Gstaaderhof (tel. 83344 or 41055) has a child care center for children from two to six years of age. It is open from 9:30 a.m. to 5 p.m. Expect to pay SFR 5.50 an hour or SFR 30, plus meal-costs per day. Mornings from 9:30 to noon cost SFR 13, and afternoons from noon to 5 p.m. are SFR 17. Weekly rate for six days is SFR 150.

In Chateau d'Oex contact, Mme. Blati at Les Clematites (tel. 029-473551). She takes children from two months old. The ski school also has children's lessons (tel. 029-46848).

Getting there

The most popular international airport is Geneva. From there, it is about two hours by train to Gstaad. Rental cars are available in Geneva.

Other activities

Gstaad has an excellent covered swimming pool.

Gstaad is in a good location for train or auto excursions to Montreux, Geneva, Lausanne, Interlaken and Bern, all within approximately two hours by train.

A local air service provides sightseeing flights in the area (tel. 44025).

Ballooning over the Alps provides a once-in-a-lifetime thrill. Balloon rides can be arranged through Hans Büker, tel. 43250, or through the reception of the Palace Hotel or the Steigenberger Hotel in Saanen. The average price is between SFR 350-400 per person for about two hours. This is based on SFR 1,400 per total trip with a minimum of four persons.

Ice skating and curling, with instruction for both, are available (tel. 44368).

Tourist information

Information on the White Highland region is available through the tourist office in the center of Gstaad. Write CH-3780 Gstaad, Switzerland; tel. (030) 41055; telex 922211.

Information on other towns in the area may also be obtained from the tourist office in Saanen, CH-3792 Saanen; tel. (030) 42597.

Tourist Office Chateau d'Oex: tel. (029) 47788; telex 940022.

Jungfrau Region–
Grindelwald, Wengen, Lauterbrunnen, Mürren

The Jungfrau region is near Interlaken and at the end of the Alpine rainbow for intermediate skiers. A network of 185 miles of trails is spread over a vast expanse of slopes, all set in two majestic valleys about an hour's drive from Bern, the Swiss capital.

The backdrop created by the Jungfrau, Mönch and Eiger mountains is one you'll see on travel posters the world over.

The Jungfrau region has three major ski areas accessible from its twin-valley towns. The best-known resort is Grindelwald, a picture-postcard settlement nestled at the foot of nearly 10,000-foot-high. peaks about 30 minutes by train or car from Interlaken. There is skiing at Grindelwald First, reached by chairlift (to your left as you enter town), and on the slopes beneath Kleine Scheidegg (on your right), reached by cog train or gondola.

The second area is just beneath the Eiger. Here, Wengen and Kleine Scheidegg offer car-free villages on the mountain and Lauterbrunnen is in the valley on the opposite side of the Lauberhorn. It is also a second starting point for the cog train up the mountain. The auto-free resort, Wengen, is halfway up the mountain along the train route overlooking the Lauterbach valley. Up on the ridge plateau is Kleine Scheidegg at the base of the Eiger, a settlement with railway station and hotels.

The third ski area, Mürren/Schilthorn, is across the Lauterbach Valley and is also reached by cog train or cablecar.

Where to ski

Mürren—For ski challenges in this region, savvy downhillers head for the Schilthorn. Take the cog train from Lauterbrunnen to Mürren and then go by cablecar the rest of the way; or take a direct cablecar from Stechelberg, outside Lauterbrunnen.

There is less good skiing but more challenges on the Schilthorn than at any of the other locations. Overall, there are 18 slopes with about 30 miles of runs. The eye-opener is the black run from the 2,971-meter (9,744-feet) Schilthorn. Start by quaffing an extra-strong cup of *espresso* in the Piz Gloria revolving restaurant atop the Schilthorn, then tackle the famed "Inferno," also called the "007 Run" in honor of the stunning ski scenes from the James Bond movie. The lower section, called the "Kanonenrohr," or cannon barrel, sends you hurtling down a narrow, steep, rutted and often icy chute.

If you visit in late January, watch at least a part of the "Inferno-Renne," the traditional (since 1928) Schilthorn race that pits nearly 1500 (as many as 4000 apply) would-be champion skiers against the clock and the 12-kilometer course. It takes a world-class skier almost 15 minutes to come down.

Adventurous skiers also tackle the black runs from the 2145-meter (7035-foot) Schiltgrat. Connecting lifts take you to the Winteregg and Almendhübel, the mountain's other two ski areas, where intermediate skiing—with an occasional black run—is the rule. The best intermediate run leads down to the base of the Winteregg chair where you can lunch at the excellent new restaurant. There is also a stop for the Mürren train here, so you can start your ski day skiing from the Winteregg chair.

Grindelwald First—The 2928-meter (9609-foot) Schwarzhorn on your left as you enter town is the backdrop for the Grindelwald First slopes. Intermediates, this is your territory with a few challenges and lots of cruising. The upper runs descend over an open, treeless slope from the Oberjoch T-bar at 2468 meters (8095 feet). The Schilt T-bar, in the shadow of the Schwarzhorn at 2250 meters (7381 feet), offers more of the same. Trails continue all the way into town.

The First is a place to work out those kinks before moving on to tackle the runs over on the Kleine Scheidegg side of the valley.

Grindelwald/Kleine Scheidegg/Wengen The cog train, takes about a half hour to reach Kleine Scheidegg. Across the parking lot from the Grindelwald Grund station is the Männlichenbahn, a gondola lift. In 25 minutes the gondola deposits you near the summit of the Männlichen at 2235 meters (7333 feet). Before you is a marvelous 15-minute run to Grindelwald or a series of trails and interconnecting lifts that take you around to Kleine Scheidegg. The Arvengarten chair is now a quadlift, which greatly cuts the waiting time to get back up to Kleine Scheidegg. Despite the increased lift capacity, the Arvengarten is still a bottleneck at the end of the day when skiers are transiting from the Männlichen side to Kleine-Scheiddeg and the reverse. The Männlichen T-bar run to the left of the top gondola station takes you down a challenging mogul field. And the wide runs off the Gummi chairlift between Männlichen and Kleine Scheidegg are challenging for most intermediates.

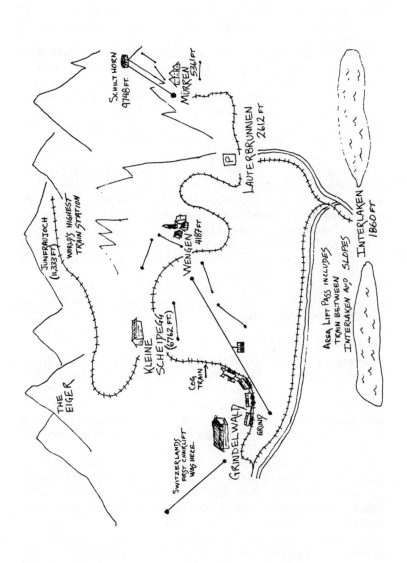

THE EIGER

JUNFRAUJOCH (11,333 FT)
WORLD'S HIGHEST TRAIN STATION

SCHILTHORN 9748 FT

MÜRREN 5361 FT

KLEINE SCHEIDEGG (6762 FT)

WENGEN 4187 FT

LAUTERBRUNNEN 2612 FT

SWITZERLANDS FIRST CHAIRLIFT WAS HERE

COG TRAIN

GRINDELWALD

GRUND

AREA LIFT PASS INCLUDES TRAIN BETWEEN INTERLAKEN AND SLOPES

INTERLAKEN 1860 FT

The finest intermediate run is reached by the Lauberhorn lift from the Kleine Scheidegg train station stop in the Eiger's shadow. The cog train continues through the Eiger north face to the highest slopes of the Jungfrau (a supplementary ticket is necessary for the final section).

Ski both outstanding runs from the 2,472-meter (8,110 feet) Lauberhorn above Kleine Scheidegg. One leads to Wengen along parts of the famed World Cup Lauberhorn run. It's a delightful ski experience with a seemingly endless variety of dips, turns, mogul fields and occasional ice patches—perfect territory for the advanced intermediate. Try the run from the Lauberhorn to the Wixi chairlift, picking your way through the mogul fields. When the snow is good, this run is exceptional.

The run down the opposite face of the Lauberhorn brings you down into Grindelwald passing Arvengarten before a network of intermediate trails which offer a touch of adventure—there is always an easier way around the tough places for the less advanced. This 30-minute run to the car park of the Männlichen gondola or to the cogwheel train station, may be the highlight of your stay in the Jungfrau region, unless you're counting the chills of Mürren's "007 Run" as a fun experience.

For variety, take the cog train to the Eiger glacier stop and ski from near the glacier's base at 2,320 meters (7,621 feet) all the way down into Grindelwald.

Mountain rating

Mürren—Don't plan to ski the Mürren area extensively if you're a beginner. There are some intermediate slopes that the absolute beginner may be able to handle after a few days, but just barely.

Grindelwald—First should present no difficulties for the lower intermediate. Beginners use the short Bodmi lifts above town with ease while everyone from advanced beginner and above goes right to the top.

Kleine Scheidegg/Wengen—The Männlichen side offers no surprises, and intermediates will handle everything but the toughest mogul fields with ease. Working one's way around the mountain toward Kleine Scheidegg from the Männlichen requires more skills but can be handled by most intermediates. The Wengen side with the Lauberhorn run is perhaps the most challenging. But Wengen, with its position on the slopes and good nursery slopes, may also be the best spot other than Grindelwald First for beginners.

Experts will find challenging runs in all three areas.

From May until September a 300-meter (984-foot) lift operates on a slope of the Jungfrau above Kleine Scheidegg. Expect "more sunshine than real skiing on this run."

Ski school

More than 70 ski instructors are assigned daily to individuals and groups seeking lessons on the Wengen and Grindelwald slopes.

The Mürren ski school has 25 instructors giving group and private lessons.

Prices are uniform in all three ski areas, with Mürren having the highest rates by a few francs a week. These prices are for the Wengen Ski School.(89/90 rates)

Individual lessons for a half-day (2.5 hrs)   SFR 100

Group lessons two hours of instruction each half-day.

for one-half day	SFR 19
for three half-days	SFR 53
for six half-days	SFR 92
for 12 half-days	SFR 168

Cross-country instruction is available. The best circuit is the seven-mile loop around the outskirts of Lauterbrunnen. Wengen does not have a cross-country run and Mürren has a simple half-mile circuit.

Check with the ski school for information on Alpine ski touring and powder skiing:

Grindelwald ski school, tel. 036-53202;
Wengen ski school, tel. 026-552022;
Mürren ski school, tel. 036-551247

Lift tickets (89/90 rates)

A special Jungfrau region ticket for a minimum of three days includes Mürren, Kleine Scheidegg and Grindelwald First. Individual tickets good only for one of the areas are also available.

Jungfrau region

for three days	SFR 114
for six days	SFR 198
for seven days	SFR 202

Grindelwald First
for one day	SFR 36
for three days	SFR 82
for six days	SFR 136
for seven days	SFR 142

Kleine Scheidegg/Männlichen
for one day	SFR 38
for three days	SFR 98
for six days	SFR 168
for seven days	SFR 172

Mürren
for one day	SFR 36
for three days	SFR 86
for six days	SFR 148
for seven days	SFR 152

Accommodations

These hotels and pensions are recommended for accommodation. Prices, unless otherwise noted, are for seven days at half pension (breakfast and one meal, normally dinner) plus seven days of lifts during January and free entrance to the respective sports center. The final price noted is per person based on double occupancy during February with half-board.

Grindelwald

Hotel Regina (tel. 545455; telex 923263) SFR 1145—Grindelwald's only five-star hotel with excellent location adjacent to the Jungfrau cog railway station. As luxurious as it gets in this town. Jacket and ties worn in the candlelit dining rooms. Old world elegance. Daily rooms cost SFR 195-215.

Hotel Schweitzerhof (tel. 532202; telex 923254) SFR 690—Large chalet-style hotel with downtown location across the street from the Jungfrau cog railway station. Daily rooms cost SFR 113-140.

Sunstar Hotel and Sunstar-Adler (tel. 545417; telex 923230) SFR 690—Across from the Grindelwald-Frist lifts. This is a modern hotel in chalet style. Daily rooms cost SFR 136-150.

Hotel Spinne, (tel. 532341; telex 923297) SFR 860—Includes seven days half pension, six-day ski pass, and entrance to the sport center and swimming pool. Ski School is an additional SFR 135. Normal daily rate: SFR 111-125.

Derby Bahnhof Hotel (tel. 545461; telex 923277) SFR 585—Excellent location adjacent to the Jungfrau cog railway station. Daily rooms cost SFR 95-115.

Scheidegg Hotels (tel. 551212; telex 923235) No Ski Week—the finest lodging in the area for the skier; overlooks Kleine Scheidegg station in the shadow of the Eiger. 30 minutes by train into the mountains from Grindelwald. Reserve well ahead.

Hotel Hirschen (tel. 532777; telex 923279) SFR 585. An affordable hotel in the center of town. Normal rates: SFR 82-94.

Bellevue Garni (B&B) (tel. 531234) No ski week.. A small 16-room B&B in the center of town. The rooms were recently renovated. Ask for a room with bath. Normal rates: SFR 44-55.

Wengen

Ski week prices not available at press time.
Sunstar Hotel (tel. 565111; telex 323266) The top choice hotel with an excellent location between the station and the lifts. All amenities necessary for a great vacation. Normal rate: SFR 89-168

Hotel Silberhorn (tel. 555131; telex 923232) One of the first hotels in Wengen located dierctly across the street from the station. Known for healthy portions at the dinner table. Normal daily rate: SFR 84-142.

Hotel am Waldrand (tel. 552855; telex 323240) Popular with ski racers, particularly during Lauberhorn race week, but a bit out of the center of town. Normal daily rates: SFR 90-130.

Hotel Eiger (tel. 551131; telex 923296) Located directly behind the station. This is a real locals place as well. Not as Alpine-looking on the inside as it seems from the outside. Normal daily rates: SFR 79-130.

Alpenrose (tel. 553216; telex 923293) A lift is directly outside this hotel. Noted for its quiet setting and traditional meals. Normal daily rate: SFR 74-135.

Hotel Eden (tel. 551634; fax. 553950) Loaded with charm, but short on rooms with bath. Make sure to ask for one of the few, or you'll be walking down the hall. The hospitality here is about as good as it gets in Switzerland. Normal daily rate: SFR 76-95.

Hotel Edelweiss (tel. 552388) A real bargain and only five minutes' walk from the town center. Make sure to ask for one of the few rooms with bath. Cooking is done without alcohol and the rooms are non-smoking. Normal daily rate: SFR 58-61.

Mürren

Hotel Mürren (tel. 552424; telex 923225) SFR 806—A renovated grand old hotel which has been throughly modernized. It is located next to the sports center with pool, squash and tennis courts. It "Inferno" disco is located here. Normal daily rates: SFR 120-150.

Hotel Alpenruhe (tel. 551361) SFR 764—Located as close to the lifts as you can get. This is a restored chalet with great views. The interior has exceptionally beautiful decor in the old Swiss style. Normal daily rates: SFR 105-120.

Hotel Alpina (tel. 551361) SFR 730—Good hotel with reductions offered for families. Excellent view of the valley and a quiet setting, but a long walk from the lifts. Normal daily rates: SFR 75-90.

Hotel Alpenblick (tel. 551327) SFR 730—Small hotel two minutes from the cog-train station.

Jungfrau (tel. 552824) SFR 817—Excellent location near both the slopes and the sports center and indoor pool.

Lauterbrunnen

Hotel Silberhorn (tel. 551471) SFR 587 (includes ski pass and ski school)—Ten minutes' walk from the cog trains to Kleine Scheidegg and Mürren.

Hotel Staubbach (tel. 551381; telex 923255) SFR 677 (includes ski pass and ski school)—Comfortable; eight minutes' walk from the cog-train station.

Hotel Alpenrose SFR 450—In Wilderswil at entrance to Lauterbach valley, 15 minutes by car from Lauterbrunnen. Family-run hotel three minutes from ski train to Lauterbrunnen or Grindelwald and two miles from Interlaken.

Staying in Interlaken

Interlaken has begun to emerge as a hotel center for skiers planning to ski the Jungfrau area. It is only a 30 minute bus ride from the lower lift stations and as a relatively large city it has nightlife and good dining. The reasons for staying in Interlaken fall into two categories. First reason—Interlaken hotels and ski packages are much less expensive than those of Wengen, Mürren and Grindelwald. Second reason—if you are traveling with a non-skier, Interlaken has more to offer than the liveliest Jungfrau resort, Grindelwald, and it is in a perfect position for day trips to many Swiss cities such as Bern, Lucerne, Zurich and even Zermatt. If one of these two reasons don't suit you then head into the mountains.

Dining

Hotel restaurants offer typical dishes with emphasis on meat, potatoes and cheese specialties. In Grindelwald you can choose from more than 30 restaurants.

For a special (and expensive meal), try the dining room in the **Grand Hotel Regina** (tel. 545455). The restaurant at the **Hotel Spinne** has good Swiss and international specialties, complemented by a full wine celler. The most crowded eatery in town is normally the **Gepsi Restaurant** (tel. 532121) which serves up grilled meats, spaghetti and fondues.

Near the slopes in Wengen we like the restaurant **La Cabane** in the Hotel Eiger (tel. 551131). The **Felsenkeller** (tel. 565131) in the Hotel Silberhorn has special dinners each night of the week. Check with them to get the listing of the program.

In Mürren, enjoy at least one midday meal inside the Piz Gloria, a revolving restaurant (tel. 552141) on the Schilthorn.

Apartments

There are many apartments, chalets and chalet apartments for rent in the Jungfrau region. The local tourist office has price and location info and will assist in a booking.

A typical rental apartment in Grindelwald with one-bedroom, living room (with sleeping space for two more people), kitchen and all utensils, costs about SFR 825 a week during high season; SFR 550 in midseason. Expect to spend another SFR 50 for electricity, cleaning service and linen fees.

Nightlife

Take a walk along Grindelwald's main street and choose the atmosphere you want to enjoy, from quiet pubs to raucous discos. The **Eiger Bar** seems to be the singles meat market. The **Spyder** disco in the celler of the Hotel Spinne is probably the hottest spot for nightlife and dancing, but very crowded.

In Wengen, check out the Eiger Hotel's Eiger Bar. Nightlife is more limited here since after dark only the group staying on the mountain will usually be around, although trains run until late evening.

At Lauterbrunnen, the Tiffany Disco in the scenic Hotel Silberhorn is lively, while on the mountain, in Mürren, the **Inferno** bar-disco in the Sporthotel Mürren is a good choice. If you want to meet new people each night, choose Grindelwald. Wengen and particularly Mürren tend to cater to sedate habitués.

Child care

Grindelwald and Wengen offer ski kindergarten for children from ages three to seven. The school begins at 9:30 a.m. and lasts until 4:30 p.m. Hourly rates are SFR 3. The cost for one day is SFR 22 with lunch and SFR 95 for a full week with five lunches.

Wengen with its no-traffic environment is one of the premier resorts for families with children. It also has good nursery slopes and plenty of easy tracks back to the town from all over the mountain.

Other activities

Interlaken is an international tourist center and starting point for excursions in the Bernese Oberland, one of Switzerland's most beautiful regions.

The smart shops in Bern and the rustic center of the old capital city merit a side trip.

Scenic Lucerne at the foot of Mount Pilatus is a little over an hour's train ride through the Alps.

The Jungfraubahn cog railway, which takes skiers up the mountain, is also a delightful outing for the non-skier. The train goes up through the Eiger's north face to the Jungfrau slopes. The stop inside the north face gives passengers a chance to look through protective glass windows at the treacherous mountain face. Special reductions are offered for non-skiers who use the train.

Grindelwald offers the widest range of non-skiing sports activities, including horseback riding, ice skating, curling, hang-gliding and hiking.

One of the most exciting excursions is a sightseeing tour of the area via plane or helicopter from the Männlichen summit. For more information, check at the Grindelwald tourist office.

Getting there

The most frequently used international airports are Geneva and Zurich. Rail connections are excellent to Interlaken and then on to Grindelwald, Lauterbrunnen, Wengen or Mürren.

Tourist information

Interlaken Tourist Office, 3800 Interlaken, Switzerland; tel. (036) 222121; telex 923111.

Verkehrsbüro Wengen, CH-3823 Wengen, Switzerland; tel. (036) 551414; telex 923271.

Verkehrsbüro Grindelwald, CH-3818, Switzerland; tel. (036) 531212; telex 923217.

Verkehrsbüro Mürren, CH-3825 Mürren, Switzerland; tel. (036) 551616; telex 923212.

Klosters

The English royal family, most notably Prince Charles, has chosen Klosters as its winter ski center for several years. They come for the excellent skiing and also for Klosters' relaxed, elegant atmosphere. Those are the same reasons you will probably choose the resort. The houses surrounding the town proper are a bit more elaborate than most other places you'll visit, giving an immediate tip-off that Klosters is a cut above. The small central town area is quaint but packed with specialty stores.

Think of Klosters as Davos' little sister resort. Smaller, quainter and not as modern (it could be called a small, chic resort that has been kept a secret), Klosters is little more than a suburb of Davos. Both resorts share the Manhattan-sized, wide-open snowfields of the Parsenn, but Klosters has more challenging runs into town than Davos. Klosters also has its own ski runs and lift system in the Madrisa area, which is on the opposite side of the valley from the Parsenn. The entire Klosters/Davos ski area offers 200 miles (320 kilometers) of ski runs served by more than 50 lifts.

Where to ski

From the 1200-meter-high village the lift system takes you to 2844 meters on the Parsenn side at the Weissfluhgipfel, and up to about 2400 meters on the upper lift of the Madrisa area.

The Parsenn is the best-known area and is reached by the Gotschna cable car, which leaves every 15 to 20 minutes during the ski season. The cable car lets you off at the Gotschnagrat, where skiers can either traverse over to the Parsenn or ski beneath the cable car to a T-bar and chairlift. The Parsenn peaks at the Weissfluhgipfel (2844 meters) where it drops with two expert runs. Here it is wide open, offering both intermediate and beginning skiers a paradise for cruising. The Parsenn has 40 seemingly endless runs, including what was once Europe's longest—from Weissfluhjoch to Kublis. If you like carefree cruising, you will love skiing the Parsenn above Klosters and Davos.

The Madrisa area is much smaller: approximately 30 miles (50 kilometers) of runs served by six ski lifts. The area is reached by cable car from Klosters-Dorf, which is a hike from the center of town. The area's runs are mostly of the intermediate and beginner level. When there is sun the Madrisa slopes are bathed with warming rays the entire day, something to remember when it's quite cold, but sunny. The longest and most scenic Madrisa run is from

St. Jaggem at (2542 m/8340 ft) down to the Schlappin overlook and down to the Madrisa cable car.

For the jaded, Madrisa is a springboard for an exciting ski mountaineering trek to Austria, which combines both skiing and climbing. The Swiss Ski School can line you up with a guide for this adventure if the snow quality is good.

Mountain rating

Klosters earns an A-plus from beginning and intermediate skiers. The Parsenn is perhaps the ideal terrain for learning to ski and perfecting technique.

Experts may find the Parsenn terrain somewhat boring and should ask instructors where the most challenging skiing can be found. The best expert runs on the Parsenn are from the top of the Weissfluhgipfel. Otherwise, stick to the trails that drop into town alongside the Parsennbahn, or take the Drostobel-to-Klosters run, which is narrow and sometimes steep. The Wang trail, which runs directly under the Gotschna cable car, is one of the toughest expert runs in Europe. Unfortunately, it seems it is closed more than it is open. If the trail is open and there is no avalanche danger, you're in for an experience. On a day after a good, fresh snowfall it pays to hire an instructor for the morning to find those special spots for some thrills in the powder.

The Madrisa area is strictly for intermediates, beginners and sunworshipers.

Ski school

The Klosters ski school is divided into six levels and in addition offers special children's courses and cross-country instruction. Depending the skiers' level, classes are held either on the Madrisa or on the Gotschna side of the valley. Check with the ski school (tel. 083-41380) in order to arrive at the proper area for your level.

Individual lessons—89/90 prices (one to four people)

one day (4½ hrs)	SFR 200
half day (2¼ hrs)	SFR 110
one hour	SFR 45

For each additional person there is a fee of SFR 10.

Group lessons (89/90 prices)

half day	SFR 25
three half days	SFR 60
six half days	SFR 100
six full days	SFR 150

Lift tickets

The most convenient lift pass to purchase is the Kloster/Davos all-inclusive pass. This pass includes the Madrisa side of the valley, plus use of the train that runs between Davos and Klosters and as far down the valley as Kublis. The tickets are only available for periods of three days or more.

three days	SFR 120
six days	SFR 200
seven days	SFR 224
14 days	SFR 360

There are discounts of about 20 percent for children and for lift passes purchased for the pre-season—before December 22, 1989.

Daily lift passes for the Gotschna and the Parsenn are SFR 40 and for the Madrisa, SFR 32.

Accommodations

The best time to ski Klosters is during one of its special organized "ski weeks." Contact the tourist office for the special rates which include lift tickets together with room and board. January ski week prices range from SFR 880-520.

For my money the **Hotel Alpina** (tel. 44121; telex: 74547); is the finest place to stay in Klosters. It has a great location, classy indoor pool, the people are nice and it is easy to make reservations. Double room costs with half pension are SFR 250-330 low season and SFR 360-400 during high season.

Perhaps the most traditional hotel is the **Chesa Grischuna** (tel. 42222; telex: 74248). It is a Romantic Hotel, but though it has ambiance and is cozy, the rooms are small and there is no pool. Expect to pay SFR 310-360 during low season and during high season for a double with half-board.

Also available at the upper end of the scale is the **Hotel Pardenn**, (tel. 083-41141; telex: 853364). A five-minute hike from the ski shuttlebus and 10 minutes from the center of town, but with plenty of 5-star comfort including pool, sauna, and fitness room. Rates: Low season—SFR 280-360; high season—SFR 320-420.

The **Hotel Vereina** (tel. 41161) is a large rambling old hotel which is popular with American tour groups. It's location is central and it has a beautiful pool. Rates: Low season—SFR. 210-270; high season—SFR. 280-360.

The less expensive hotels are located in Klosters-Dorf which is near the lifts for the Madrisa area but a long hike from the Parsenn lifts.

Apartments

Klosters has plenty of apartments for rent. The apartments are normally rented out for a minimum of one week, Saturday to Saturday; during the Christmas and Easter seasons a two-week minimum rental is required.

The tourist office keeps track of available apartments. If you write and supply all the information, including the number of beds required, the preferred number of rooms and the period for which you are planning your vacation, you'll get an immediate response with a choice of apartments and prices. Select the apartment you want and return the information.

Normally, linen and kitchen utensils are provided, while extras, such as swimming pool, sauna, TV or room phone all add to the cost. Standard units rent for between $16 and $28 per person a night. Prices vary significantly from low to high season.

When making reservations, make sure that your apartment is in Klosters or Klosters-Platz, *not* Klosters-Dorf. They are a good distance apart. Not only is Klosters-Dorf dead, it also requires a good hike to reach the Gotschna cable car, which serves the major skiing areas.

Dining

For restaurants featuring good local specialties, try "Hotel Alpina," "Hotel Rufinis" and "Restaurant Steinbock." Other restaurants recommended by Klosters natives are "Alte Post Aeuja" (for lamb specialties), "Casanna," "Madrisa" and "Porta." For pizza and a great lunch buffet head to the cellar Pizza in the Vereina Hotel. We recommend the Chicago-style thick crust deluxe. It's a meal in itself.

Nightlife

Klosters' nightlife centers around its major hotels. For discos, there are "Funny Place" and "Casa Antica." The Funny Place is a great place to meet people, but it charges a hefty SFR 10 cover charge, has overpriced drinks, even by Swiss standards, and the staff is not particularly pleasant, even with a guide from the tourist office there.

The bar in the Pardenn for a late evening visit is intimate and relaxing, but a bit stuffy. Save it for impressing a stuffy friend. Better still is the bar of the Chesa Grischuna where there is quiet piano entertainment.

Child care

A kindergarten for children from two to six years of age operates Monday through Friday in the Hotel Vereina from 9:15 a.m. until 4:30 p.m. Call 41161 for further information. A half day with lunch costs SFR 27 with lunch of SFR 15 without lunch. A full day with lunch will cost SFR 40.

Children in the ski school can have lunch included in their program for an additional SFR 12.

Babysitting service in town can be arranged for SFR 10 per hour by calling 41877.

Getting there

The closest airport is Zurich. Klosters is two-and-a-half-hours by train ride and you must change in Landquart.

If you decide to rent a car, follow the signs towards Chur until you get to the Landquart/Davos exit. The drive from Landquart to Klosters is through the narrow valley and passes through Kublis before arriving at Klosters-Dorf and then Klosters. The total distance from Zurich to Klosters is about 140 kilometers, just under 90 miles.

Other activities

Klosters is rather quiet. Visitors who are looking for other activities should take the train to Davos, which is only fifteen minutes away. Davos has a public heated outdoor swimming pool and an open-air skating rink. In addition, there are seven covered hotel pools in town and two heated outdoor pools; you will have to check with the hotel to get the rates for using their facilities. The hotels also have several squash and tennis courts, as well as saunas and solariums. Again, check with the concierge for the charges.

If you want to leave town, both Zurich and Lucerne are only about a two-hour drive away. Or drive to Landquart, then south towards the St. Bernard Pass, where you can drive through the Via Mala, Switzerland's deepest gorge, and see the recently restored castle of Hohen Rathien in Thusis. If the pass from Tiefencastle to Davos is open and you have chains, the drive that makes a loop around the mountains is beautiful.

Tourist information

Tourist Office, CH-7250 Klosters; tel. (083) 41877; telex: 74372. Normal hours are Monday through Saturday, from 9 a.m. until noon and from 2 until 6 p.m. (until 5 p.m. on Saturday).

Portes du Soleil
Champéry
Les Crosets
Champoussin

The Portes du Soleil ski area nestled just south of Lake Geneva and straddling Switzerland and France claims to be Europe's biggest ski area. Though the Trois Vallées region makes a similar claim, the skiing in Portes du Soleil is seemingly endless. Where a skier in the Trois Vallées may be able to easily transfer from valley to valley, transfers in the Portes du Soleil area take time and effort. Where the lift system in the Trois Vallées forms a tight web linking miles of prepared slopes, the lifts through the Portes du Soleil are more of a gossamer strand linking far-flung pistes. I remember, after a long morning of continuous skiing from Champéry in Switzerland to Chatel in France, having my guide point out a peak seemingly somewhere on the other side of Mont Blanc. When he announced to me that was where we had started, I was incredulous and forgot any notions about a relaxed afternoon cruising home.

The Portes du Soleil area is made up of more than a dozen different resorts. Four to six lie on the Swiss side of the border and the remaining eight or 10, depending on how one counts resorts, are in France. The key resorts are Champéry in Switzerland and Avoriaz in France. Les Crosets and Champoussin tucked high on the mountain between Champéry and Avoriaz also offer an excellent central location for exploring the Portes du Soleil.

Champéry is a mountain town that has not realized it is an international ski resort. The old chalets look lived-in, the odor of cow manure wafts across the main street, a plucky kid goat prances in the back of a station wagon, the discos look like a throwback to the 1950's and no tour buses are packing the center of town. Unfortunately, Champéry will probably be nudged into the mainstream of tourism in the next five years, but until then it is an unpretentious change of pace.

Les Crosets, set in the midst of the ski area, is a cluster of

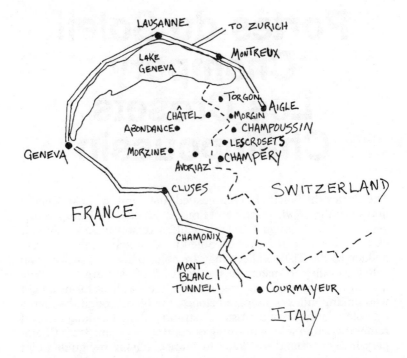

apartments providing easy access to the slopes and little else. But this enclave is also earmarked for growth. With plans for underground garages, new apartments and new lifts, it is the major topic of discussion among the local families that own the land and are planning the developments.

Champoussin has already started in the direction of a purpose-built resort but stopped recently due to a shortfall of capital. Champoussin, unlike Les Crosets, was developed by outsiders, which added to its problems, but the town has a good ski-in/ski-out location, controlled alpine chalet-style buildings with restaurants, discos and an indoor pool.

Where to ski

This is a real skier's area. But not only is skiing the slopes challenging, finding your way from resort to resort can test the skills of an Eagle Scout. The area does provide good lift maps with suggested itineraries to make crisscrossing the region less difficult. With such an expanse of skiing no one map allows sufficient detail for extensive skiing. When you arrive in a new section, stop and pick up a local lift map that details runs in the immediate area.

Note that the lift system does not perfectly interconnect. In Chatel there is a shuttle bus between the Linga and the Super-Chatel cablecar.

Experts can strike out in any direction but will find the biggest challenges dropping down runs in the World Cup section of Avoriaz, yoyoing through the Plaine Dranse and Linga and daring the "wall of death," or Chavanette. No expert will leave feeling complacent after any of those experiences.

Intermediates should be ready for an endurance challenge of the first order. Forget any attempts to ski every run during a week-long vacation. It is just not possible. There are plenty of intermediate circuits that will provide a very full day of skiing. Try from Champéry to Avoriaz and back, or vice versa. On another day, take intermediate runs from Avoriaz to Chatel and return.

Beginners will not have a chance to really enjoy the expansive skiing of Portes du Soleil. The best bets for beginners are Le Crosets, Champoussin, Avoriaz and Chatel.

Mountain rating

Score this one as a test of any expert, extensive enough for every intermediate on your list and more than any beginner can handle. Chavanette also known as the "wall of death" and the "Swiss wall," between Avoriaz and Les Crosets, has lured experts for decades. As you stand at the lip of the drop, due to the steepness, you cannot see the slope that falls under the tips of your skis. Once you gather the courage to drop off the rim, it's a wide-open, expert steep. As I stood above Chavanette I recalled reading that snow would not stay on a slope so steep. Those snow scientists obviously didn't study in the class I was about to attend. Don't be ashamed to take the path around the "wall" at this point—more skiers choose this option here than at any other place I've skied in Europe. If you are in shape you can get the most from this far-flung area. If you're not, get ready to suffer or limit your skiing.

Ski school

The Swiss Ski School in Champéry offers both downhill and cross-country lessons.

Downhill group courses cost: half day—SFR 30 (SFR 15 for children under 12); one week—SFR 100 (SFR 68 for children). Private one-hour lessons: SFR 40—for one person; SFR 50—for three or four. Half-day private lessons for groups of one to four cost SFR 130. Full-day lessons for groups of one to four cost SFR 230.

Cross-country lessons are a bit less expensive. Group lessons are given in one-and-a-half-hour segments. One lesson—SFR 14; two lessons—SFR 30; six lessons—SFR 65. Private cross-country lessons per hour are: one person—SFR 30; two people—SFR 36; three to four people—SFR 42. Half-day private lesson—SFR 90. Full-day private cross-country lesson—SFR 190.

A good way to get to know the area is through organized "Discover the Portes du Soleil" groups of five skiers on Saturdays and Sundays for SFR 40. The groups, organized by the Swiss Ski School in Champéry, normally make a loop through Les Crosets, Champoussin, Morgins, Avoriaz and return to Champéry.

A ski-safari across the Portes du Soleil is normally organized in late January and again in late March and April. These ski safaris are either seven-day or 14-day event. The seven-day price—SFR 940— includes four nights in Switzerland, three nights in France, six-day lift ticket, hotel with half-board, a guide, luggage transfers between hotels and swimming pool passes. The 14-day program—SFR 1,850—is similar with seven nights in Switzerland and seven nights in France. The ski-safari groups are for eight to 10 skiers and are open to good skiers only.

Lift tickets

The Portes du Soleil ski pass (for adults, 12 years and older) will cost: one day—SFR 36; six days—SFR 178; 14 days—SFR 309.

A pass for only the Champéry, Le Croset, and Champoussin lifts costs: half day—SFR 16; one day—SFR 27; two days—SFR 49.

Both passes are discounted for children under 12 years.

Accommodations

Champéry, Les Crosets and Champoussin have only a handful of hotels but plenty of apartments. There is also an excellent weekly program, which includes seven days half board, six-day lift tickets for the entire Portes du Soleil area, free entry to the covered pool, ice rink and the thermal baths in Val-d'Illiez. The special weekly price is noted and the normal high season half-board rate is also noted for each hotel.

Champéry

Hotel Suisse tel. (025) 791881, telex 456412. My choice as the best place in town. The Hotel Suisse was completely redone between the 85/86 winter and the 86/87 winter. Special week: SFR 780. Normal rate: SFR 84-174.

Hotel de Champéry tel. (025) 791071; telex 456285. Special week: SFR 820. Normal rates: SFR 93-172.

Beau-Séjour tel. (025) 791701, telex 456284. A nice hotel with good restaurant and reasonable prices. The change in the location of the lifts will have an impact on this hotel. Last year it was the closest place to the main lifts up to Planachaux, but with the new cablecar being located next to the sports center the Beau-Séjour will lose this advantage. Special week: SFR 695-750. Normal rates: SFR 81-101.

Hotel de la Paix tel. (025) 791551. An almost legendary hotel for young people. It's friendly, helpful and has great food and lots of it. The crowd is usually young and very international. It also used to be very close to the main lift, but will be about a five-minute walk away when the new cablecar is in place farther down in the valley. Special week: SFR 595-650. Normal daily rates: SFR 56-72.

Hotel des Alpes tel. (025) 791222. More upscale than the Paix with a fancy and expensive a la carte restaurant. This hotel could possibly creep to the next higher category with some planned renovations. Special week: SFR 595-650. Normal daily rates: SFR 75-85.

Les Crosets/Champoussin

Télécabine tel. (025) 791421. There aren't many other choices in Les Crosets but this fills the bill. Anglo/Swiss staff members are very helpful and speak excellent English. Special week: SFR 685. Normal daily rates: SFR 70-85.

Alpage tel. (025) 772711; telex 456254. This is the center of Champoussin and a great ski-in/ski-out location. If you are traveling by yourself I'd suggest somewhere in Champéry rather than up here, but with a group it can be a great time. Special week: SFR 685. Normal daily rate: SFR 79-112.

Apartments

Champéry has a special weekly rate including apartment, six-day lift ticket, free entrance to the pool, skating rink and thermal baths in Val-d'Illiez, as well as cleaning fees. This special offer is effective from 10-23 January and from 13 March to the end of the season.

Studio apartment will cost SFR 430 per person for two people and SFR 390 per person for four people sharing.

Two-room apartment (means one bedroom and two beds in the living room) will cost for three people sharing—SFR 410 per person; and for four people sharing—SFR 370 per person

Three-room apartment (means two bedrooms and two additional beds in the living room) costs for four people—SFR 410 per person; five people—SFR 370 per person; Six people—SFR 320 per person.

The normal January weekly rates for apartments: Studio—SFR 500; two-room—SFR 650; three-room—SFR 750; four-room (often an entire chalet)—SFR 900. In February prices jump: Studio—SFR 600; two-room—SFR 850; three-room—SFR 1,050; four-room—SFR 1,330. These prices are from one agency only. Other rental agencies may be more or less expensive depending on location and luxury.

To reserve apartments you may write to the tourist office; however, it will only send you a listing of the agencies in town. Try these:

In Champéry: Agence Immobilière de Champéry—tel. (025) 791444; or Agence Mendes de Leon—tel. (025) 791777. I found the people in Mendes de Leon much more helpful than in the Agence Immobilière de Champéry.

In Les Crosets, try Bureau Dents-du-Midi, V. Rey-Bellet—tel. (025) 791893; or Les Cimes—tel. (025) 791867.

In Champoussin: Location Services—tel. (025) 772681.

Child care

The ski school (tel. 791615) has a special "Mini-Club" for children from four to seven years. It is open from 9 a.m. to 5 p.m. daily. It includes ski lessons, games and lunch. Half-day cost—SFR 22; Full-day with lunch—SFR 43.

For younger children from three months to four years a nursery has been organized. It is open from 8:30 a.m. to 5:30 p.m. One day with lunch costs SFR 28. A half day with lunch from either 8:30 to noon or from 11 a.m. to 5:30 p.m. costs SFR 24. A full day without lunch is SFR 22. A half-day without lunch is SFR 18. The nursery school telephone is 791969, or contact the tourist office at 791141.

Dining

Champéry's cooking benefits from its proximity to France. For the best meals in town try the **Restaurant le Mazot** in the Hotel de Chapéry, the Restaurant Victor Hugo in the Hotel Suisse or the **Restaurant des Alps**. Slightly more reasonable, the **Vieux Chalet** was repeatedly recommended by locals and the **La Paix**, which also garnered many local recommendations. For Italian food and pizzas, head to **Cime de l'Est** or, if desperate, try the pasta in the **Pub**. For traditional food try **Restaurant le Centre** or the **Res-**

taurant Grand-Paradis. Chez Gabi, on the slopes above Champoussin, also had excellent food and makes a great midday stop or a good evening meal after a ride up the mountain on a snow cat.

Nightlife

Champéry, Les Crosets and Champoussin are not known for their nightlife or aprés-ski. After skiing the meeting place of choice seems to be **Le Pub** in the middle of Champéry. To me it is dingy and depressing but the place to be if you hope to find any action. Later, after 10 p.m., the disco opens and begins to fill up near midnight. The crowd is normally very British. The locals seem to congregate in **Dancing le Levant** after having the compulsory beer in "Le Pub."

In Champoussin, try the disco in the basement of the hotel or head for **Le Nid** for a quiet place to drink and meet other lost tourists. Expect to pay SFR 7 for a mixed drink and between SFR 3 and SFR 6 for bottled beer.

Other activities

Champéry is a bit out of the way to allow easy access to major cities, but if one doesn't mind the half-hour winding drive down the mountain Montreux and Lausanne are within an hour's drive. Monthey in the valley has a covered bridge and open-air market.

A visit to the thermal baths of Val-d'Illiez is a relaxing must, especially with free entrance included in most of the special packages that bring tourists to this area. Normal entrance is SFR 7. Buses run from Champéry to Val-d'Illiez twice a day—check with the tourist office for exact times.

For those interested in para-gliding, contact Catherine Crevoisier at (025) 772083 or the tourist office in Champoussin (025) 772727.

Tourist information

Champéry: Office du Tourisme, tel. (025) 791141; telex 456263.

Champoussin/Les Crosets/Val-d'Illiez: Sociète de Dévelopment, tel. (025) 772077; Val-d'Illiez/Champoussin, tel. (025) 772727; Les Crosets, tel. (025) 791423.

Saas-Fee

Saas-Fee is a village of very narrow streets, chalets and small hotels and year-round skiing. It's for serious skiers—those who place more importance on the number of black-rated runs on the mountain than on the number of discos in the village. Nestled in the neighboring valley to Zermatt, Saas-Fee allows no private cars in town; you park on the outskirts and take public transportation.

Saas-Fee has its own snow-making equipment on the lower beginner slopes. That, combined with the glacier runs above, means there's never a danger that poor snowfall will threaten your vacation. In fact, its tourist office guarantees snow for visitors.

The town occupies a magnificent site at 5,904 feet, ringed by 18 separate peaks of 13,000 feet or more. Snowcaps on these mountains are permanent, as is skiing on the 9,840-foot-hig Felskinn.

Where to ski

Saas-Fee's nearly 50 miles of downhill trails are superbly divided among beginning, intermediate and expert levels. Absolute beginners start on the Saas-Fee town lifts, where they will stay for about three days. The ski instructor then takes them up either the Plattjen lift or the Felskinn.

For all other levels of skiers, Saas-Fee offers four distinct areas. The Hannig area gets the first sun in the morning and normally has the smallest crowds. The lifts are very limited, but the gondola and the two drag lifts open long runs back into town.

The next section to get the morning sun is the Spielboden/Längfluh area. These runs are on good intermediate to expert terrain. The first section of the mountain under Längfluh down to the chairlift is intermediate terrain. If you ski past this middle station get ready for the steep and narrow.

From the top of the Längfluh cablecar the unique "Fee-Chatz" connects this area with the Felskinn and Mittelallalin areas. The "Fee-Chatz" is basically a bus on runners that is towed behind a snow cat. This creative lift system is a must because the 30-meter flow of glacial ice each year makes a fixed lift system an impossibility.

The Felskinn/Mittelallalin area is the most popular section of Saas-Fee's trails. Two small lifts tow skiers from town to the lower station of the Felskinn cablecar. Unfortunately, the wait here can be over an hour. Creative skiers can take the quickly moving, less-

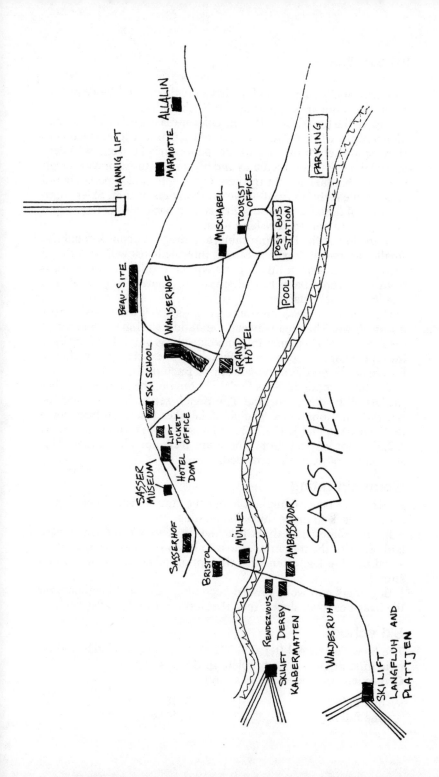

crowded Speilboden/Längfluh lifts and then the "Fee-Chatz" to reach the same area served by the Felskinn lift.

Once at the top of the Felskinn cablecar, Saas-Fee's underground Metro Alpin whisks skiers up another 1,600 feet to Mittelallalin. Here, stop to enjoy the magnificent panorama of dozens of 13,000-foot-high peaks. Intermediates and beginners (those brave enough to come this far) should traverse to the left, and experts should cross to the right, in front of the revolving restaurant. Skiers have a choice of doing several runs or heading back to the Metro Alpin underground and the Felskinn area.

To the left of the Felskinn cablecar a drag lift opens a delightful smaller area—the Egginer. Strong intermediates will be satisfied with the Egginerjoch lift. Experts will be thrilled with the drops from the Hinterallalin lift, which, unfortunately, is often closed due to avalanche danger.

The rest of the Felskinn runs crisscross under the cablecar back toward town. The area between the middle station and the top of the Felskinn is a beginner/intermediate playground. The drop back into the village steepens considerably, and experts have a chance for challenge on the Kanonenrohr or Bach trails.

The final section of Saas-Fee's ski domain, the Plattjen, catches the last of the day's sunshine. This area is served by only two lifts, but they are long ones. The gondola takes skiers up from town (5,850 feet) to Plattjen (8,342 feet), resulting in a run with almost a 2,500-foot vertical drop. There are trails for all abilities. This section is not normally crowded.

Mountain rating

Experts will never complain about the runs at Saas-Fee. There's enough black to make things interesting.

Intermediates may think that the lift network and trails were laid out with them in mind. Most trails above Saas-Fee start with a red or blue leg, often with the option of taking a black-rated stretch.

Beginners can work toward becoming advanced beginners on the Saas-Fee town slopes; then the slopes above the valley beckon.

Ski school

The Saas-Fee school (tel. 028-572348) has approximately 100 instructors. English is no problem in this resort.

Group lessons (three hours a day)

half day	SFR 20
one full day	SFR 36

| six days (full days of instruction) | SFR 145 |
| twelve half days | SFR 175 |

Lessons for children are SFR 17 a half day; SFR 30 for a full day; SFR 133 for 12 half days; and SFR 110 for the six-day ski course. When lunch and after-school supervision are included, the cost is an additional SFR 16 a day.

Private lessons cost SFR 40 an hour for one or two persons; SFR 50 an hour for three to four people; SFR 185 for a full day.

Cross-country lessons are also offered, but only a five-mile loop around Saas-Fee is prepared. Lessons cost SFR 70 for five half days.

Special ski-mountaineering off-trail adventures have been organized in the past for climbs to the top of the Alphubel and Allalin. These treks start with a two- to four-hour climb on skins and end with long, high-altitude powder cruises through virtually virgin snow. Tours are limited by both the weather and the availability of qualified instructors. From mid-February through the end of the season the treks depart approximately once a week.

""The Haute Route" is a classic ski adventure trek between Saas-Fee, Zermatt, Courmayeur and Chamonix. These treks are organized from mid-April until the end of May. For this tough physical trek participants should be in good shape and must be able to ski in deep snow. The mountain climbing school conducts the special tour from early May until the first week in June. Contact: Bergsteigerschule Saastal, CH-3906 Saas-Fee; tel. 028-572348, or the tourist office at 028-571457. The cost for the classic "Haute Route" tour is approximately SFR 750, which includes guides, accommodations in mountain huts, meals, hotel expenses during the tour, mountain railway and bus fares.

Lift tickets
Saas-Fee lifts (1989/90 prices)

for one day	SFR 42
for two days	SFR 80
for three days	SFR 110
for six days	SFR 190
for seven days	SFR 215

Beginners need only purchase tickets for the Saas-Fee town lifts at SFR 18 a day for adults and SFR 14 for children.

Children from six to 16 get approximately a 40 percent discount on the normal lift fees.

NOTE: The Fee-Chatz shuttle between the Längfluh and the Felskinn area is not included in the lift pass prices. If you decide to take the snow cats, the price per ride is SFR 4 for adults and SFR 1 for children. The Fee-Chatz is not included in the lift ticket because the snow cats may be needed on another section of the mountain during an emergency and their operation cannot be guaranteed.

Accommodations

The first prices listed are special ski week rates normally available in January. They include hotel, half pension, ski pass, ski lessons and pool fee. There is also an active entertainment program of ski racing, fashion shows, fondue and raclette parties and torchlight processions. The final price noted is the normal high-season, half-pension price based on double occupancy.

The Best
Walliserhof (tel. 028-572021; telex 472221) SFR 1,058—The best hotel in town. For a sensuous splurge, try the suite with living-room, round bed, white marble bath and private sauna. Normal daily rates: SFR 144-187.

Ambassador (tel. 028-571420) SFR 890—Renovated with new pine furniture. In town near the ski school assembly point. Has indoor swimming pool. Normal daily rates: SFR 107-139.

Allalin (tel. 028-571815; telex 472208) SFR 806—This beautiful three-star hotel is really four-star quality. It is located at the far end of town from the ski lifts, but with ski storage facilities at the lifts there is no need to drag equipment back and forth. Served is some of the best food in town. Normal daily rates: SFR 81-105.

Moderate
Mischabel (tel. 572118) SFR 806—At the entrance of the town, about a seven-minute walk to most lifts. Normal daily rates: SFR 81-105.

Hotel Marmotte (tel. 028-572852) SFR 806—The rooms could be bigger, the decor could be more traditional mountain Swiss and the location could be closer to the main lifts. But this hotel shines because of its mad owner, Karl Dreier, who makes everyone feel at home. Karl, who doubles as the chef, cooks some of the best hotel food we've eaten. There is a free ski storage arrangement with the Waldesruh Hotel opposite the Felskinn lift, plus a free babysitting arrangement with Hotel Alphubel, which has the reputation of being one of the best hotels for children in Switzerland. Normal daily rates: SFR 81-105.

Derby (tel. 572345; telex 472207) SFR 806—Family hotel, excellent location on the road to Felskinn and Plattjen lifts. Normal daily rates: SFR 81-105.

Hotel Europa (tel. 572791; telex 472229) SFR 785—A small hotel (55 beds) with good location for those planning to do most of their skiing on the Hannig. Normal daily rates: SFR 75-97.

Hotel Waldesruh (tel. 572295; telex 472214) SFR 806—Convenient to the Plattjen and Längfluh gondola ground stations. Caters to families. Normal daily rates: SFR 81-105.

Budget
Mühle (tel. 572676) SFR 708—Very small hotel offering basic accommodations. Normal daily rates: SFR 62-80.

Feehof (tel.572308) SFR 590 (bed and breakfast only). A bargain-basement garni. No telephone, no public restaurant and no credit cards accepted. Normal daily rates: SFR 35-44.

All of the hotels in Saas-Fee are good. We've picked out some exceptional ones we know. The best way to select a hotel if you're traveling with a group or tour package is to decide whether being close to the main lifts or being in the center of town (and its nightlife) is more to your liking. Perhaps you want to be near the Hannig lift and in the sunniest part of town.

Near Felskinn, Plattjen and Spielboden lifts: Waldesruh, Derby, Burgener, Bristol, Ambassador, Feehof, Mistral, Mühle, Rendezvous, Saaserhof.

Center of town: Beau-Site, Britannia, Christiana, Dom, Gletschergarten, Grand, Mischabel, Park, Walser, Walliserhof, Zurbriggen.

Near Hannig on the sunny side: Allalin, Alphubel, Domino, La Collina, Marmotte, Sporthotel, Tenne.

Dining
The best restaurant in the area is the **Fletschhorn** (028-572131), about a 30-minute walk out of town or a 10-minute taxi ride. This restaurant is considered to be one of the best in Switzerland and features nouvelle cuisine.

Perhaps the second-best eatery is the **Hohnegg** (028-572268), just about a 10-minute walk above the town, or call for its taxi service. Also nouvelle cuisine.

The Walliserhof **Le Gourmet** restaurant (028-572021) is also a top nouvelle cuisine restaurant.

For excellent traditional Walliser food, try the **Saaserhof** (028-571551) and the **Schäferstube**. For cheese and Swiss specialties, the top recommendations are the **Vieux Chalet** (572892) and the **Arvu-Stuba**.

For good, less expensive meals, try the **Hotel Allalin** (028-571815)—a rebuilt 300-year old room with wooden beams and hand-carved chairs make it magical by candlelight; **Hotel Dom** (591101) for great *röstle*; **La Gorge** (572641); the **Hotel du Glacier** (571244) also has excellent fondue and raclette.

For pizza, try the pizzeria/steakhouse under the **Hotel Beau-Site**; the **Boccalino**—in front of the Saaserhof—or the pizzeria in the Walliserhof. Pizza costs from SFR 8-12 and pasta about the same.

On the slopes, be sure to have at least one lunch in the revolving restaurant at the top of the **Metro Alpin** lift, the world's highest such restaurant. Amazingly, the prices are down-to-earth. The mountain restaurant **Berghaus Plattjen**, a third of the way down the National run from the top of the Plattjen lift, is great for a late lunch when the area catches the sun. On the opposite side along the Längfluh run, where it meets the Gletschergrotte trail cutting off from the Kanonenrohr, is the **Gletscher-Grotte**, which catches sun most of the day.

SFR 20 will cover a good lunch with beer and coffee.

Apartments

Apartments are the way to go if you really want to save money. Saas-Fee alone has about 1,500 chalets and apartments for rent. Write to the tourist office and ask for a list of apartments that will be available during the time you will be in Saas-Fee. Include in your requirements details on the number of people in your party. The office will send a list of available apartments in town, plus a map showing apartment locations. You then select the apartment you want and correspond either with the tourist board or directly with the apartment owner.

The apartments normally include linen and kitchen utensils. You will be charged a visitor's tax, and there may be an extra charge for the electricity and heat you use during your stay.

Expect to pay between SFR 25 and SFR 40 per person a night, depending on the number of people sharing the apartment and its location.

Nightlife

Saas-Fee is known as a town for young skiers and those who think young. You'll meet a lively crowd in the evening. The three main live-music places are within a stone's throw of one another. The Walliserhof's **Le Club** has a good band and an older clientele—25-45 years old. The **San Souci** across the street also provides good music but with a younger crowd (18-25). During the low season when there is no school break neither disco is overrun with teenagers. For slightly more traditional dancing, most locals go to the **Yetti** in the basement of the Hotel Dom. At discos expect to pay about SFR 7 for a beer or glass of wine. No disco in Saas-Fee charges a cover.

There is also a good group of bars: **Pic Pic** is a Swiss locals' spot; the **Fee Pub** across from the Yetti normally has a good crowd; **Walliser Stübli** under the Hotel du Glacier and the **Metro Bar** near the Hotel Beau Site are lively.

Après-ski as the slopes close is an early affair because the sun drops behind the mountains quickly. If you're off the mountain at around 3 p.m. the terrace bars at the Derby, Mühle, Rendezvous and Christiana do a great business. After four when the sun drops out of sight, the crowd evaporates. Most gather in bars like **Chemi Stube** in the Christiana, the **Saaserhof** or inside the **Rendezvous**, which have live music, but good dancing music and really wild après-ski merriment are not to be found here.

Child care

Saas-Fee's ski school (tel. 574348) is for children ages five to 12, with a half-day fee of SFR 16. The six-day course of all-day lessons is SFR 105. Lunch costs an additional SFR 15 a day.

Children from three to six will be taken care of by a nurse in the town kindergarten. Enroll children at the tourist office. Prices for guests with visitor's card: full day with lunch—SFR 16, without lunch—SFR 12; half day with lunch—SFR 11, without lunch—SFR 6; one week with lunch—SFR 80, without lunch—SFR 60; one week of half days with lunch—SFR 55, without lunch SFR 30.

Getting there

By train: From Zurich airport via Bern, Spiez, through the Lötschberg tunnel to Brig. At Brig you change to the Post Bus, which meets the train and leaves from the front of the railway station about 15 minutes later.

From Geneva, trains run directly to Brig.

By car: Travel via Montreux, then up the Valais pass through

Sion to Visp, where you turn south and follow the signs to Saas-Fee.

If you are driving from Zurich or Basel, you can choose to take the Lötschberg tunnel from Kandersteg to Goppenstein, above Brig and Visp. This tunnel requires that you load your car onto the railway. Trains transit the tunnel every half-hour from 5:35 a.m. to 11:05 p.m. The trip takes only 15 minutes. Cost per car (including 9-seat vans) is SFR 15. From Goppenstein, continue driving to Visp, then on to Saas-Fee.

Park in the public lot at the entrance to the town. Call your hotel from the phone at the tourist office, or take a taxi to your hotel. Taxis from parking/bus station to town cost SFR 13 for two people, SFR 16 for three and SFR 17 for four.

Other activities

Visit the Saaser Museum, packed with photographs of the old Saas valley, plus old tools, kitchen utensils and furniture of mountain people. Open from 2 p.m. to 6 p.m., the museum charges SFR 3 for adults, SFR 1 for children.

For exercise, the Bielen sports and leisure center offers an 80-foot, heated indoor swimming pool, children's pool, two tennis courts, exercise room, whirlpools, steambath and coed sauna. Entrance fee, with the visitor's card, is SFR 10.50 or SFR 15 (with sauna). Discounts are available for repeat visits. Tennis courts should be reserved and cost, with the visitor's card, SFR 22 an hour from 8 a.m. to 4 p.m. and SFR 28 an hour after 4 p.m. until 10 p.m.

Tourist information

Write Verkehrsbüro Saas-Fee, CH-3906 Saas-Fee, Switzerland; tel. 028-571457; telex 472230.

St. Moritz

When you have visited all the other great resorts, enjoyed the fine hotels elsewhere claiming to pamper guests to the extreme, when you've seen all the mountains said to be grand and great, then and only then journey to St. Moritz. You'll find that although there is elegance and alpine beauty everywhere in Switzerland, nowhere is it concentrated in such huge amounts as it is on the rooftop of Europe in St. Moritz, the original Swiss winter resort.

In winter the great expanses of snow-covered lake provide a massive, scenic foreground for the celebrated town whose name has become a synonym for quality and luxury. The most elegant aspect of St. Moritz, the great hotels, are expensive, almost prohibitively so, but everything else, restaurants included, is there for nearly everyone.

The central area of St. Moritz Dorf is compact, really only a mesh of two main streets with a few side streets and a single, small main square. Sports shops abound, and prices are surprisingly low. There are actually true bargains in February and March when sales are offered. Movies are up-to-date, nightlife superb, moonlight strolls on the lake wonderful. The range of entertainment fits every pocketbook and taste.

Where to ski

Until you have experienced St. Moritz, your education on alpine Switzerland is incomplete. Exclusive, expensive, exciting—that's the two-time winter Olympic site—1928 and 1948—which is home to some of the finest intermediate skiing anywhere.

Altogether there are 150 miles of groomed trails. The setting is stunning: 6,000 feet high in the southwestern corner of Switzerland, near its border with Italy in the twin shadows of the 9,270-foot-high Piz Nair and the 10,833-foot-high Piz Corvatsch.

The main runs are clustered around the summits of the two mountains. The Corviglia runs come downhill near St. Moritz-Dorf and the Corvatsch into St. Moritz-Bad (the Hahnensee run only) on the valley floor.

The finest run is the Hahnensee, a black trail that is intermediate for most of the five-mile length. The run boasts a vertical drop of more than 4,900 feet.

It's a five-minute walk from the end of the Hahnensee run to the Signalbahn cablecar, which takes you up to Corviglia.

On the second run down the Hahnensee, break off at the Mandras T-bar and climb to the Murtel cable midstation. Here, the run down the Surlej is peppered with moguls and dips, while the panorama includes the frozen lakes of Champfer and Silvaplana. The adventurous work their way along the slopes via the T-bars at Alp Margun to the 9,186-foot-high Culoz de las Furtschellas. From here, there is an interesting run to Sils-Maria on the Silvaplana lakeshore. Be sure to have the regional lift ticket or face paying a SFR 5 surcharge for the Sils-Maria lifts.

The longest and favorite run of many is from Piz Nair, either down the front side to St. Moritz or over the ridge at the 8,154-foot level at the cablecar station in Corviglia and down to Marguns. For the greatest length along an intermediate trail, climb to the top of the Fuorcia Glisha T-bar, behind Piz Nair, for the run to the valley floor.

The single most challenging run in the valley is "The Hang," a chilling drop from the top at Lagalb on the Bernina Pass. It's rated black-plus. On the other side of the pass approach is Diavolezza. The skiing there is average, but a stunning glacier ski trek awaits after a 25-minute walk on skis to the mountain bar run by Otto Rohner—and then on to the glacier. On full moon nights there is a unique alpine experience in glacier skiing.

There is also summer skiing on the summits at Corvatsch and Diavolezza.

Mountain rating

Eighty percent of the slopes in the St. Moritz area are for intermediates. Beginners will start to feel at home after several runs on one of the longer trails. When in doubt, tag behind the advanced beginners of a St. Moritz ski class for the best slope that day.

Experts will head for the toughest parts of the back side on the Piz Nair, as well as Corvatsch summit and the super challenge of the black run at Lagalb.

Ski schools

St. Moritz area ski schools employ more than 145 instructors. In 1927, the world's first ski school was established here. The main ski school (tel. 082-34980) is in the center of town adjacent to the tourist office.

Individual lessons (89/90 prices)

one hour	SFR 70
half day	SFR 110
all day	SFR 200

Group lessons
(normally three hours of lessons daily)

one day	SFR 48
three days	SFR 120
six days	SFR 182

Lessons are available for cross-country, which is extremely popular because of the nearly 75 miles of well-maintained trails in the valley. Cross-country buffs will probably want to participate in the Engadin Marathon course, a 26-mile cross-country circuit. Come in March and take part along with as many as 12,000 others in one of the world's great cross-country ski races.

Helicopter ski transport for off-trail skiing, powder skiing and deep-snow skiing instruction is available.

Lift tickets (89/90 prices)

The Engadin regional pass includes St. Moritz and Corviglia, Sils Maria, Silvaplana, Surlej, Champfer, Celerina, Samedan, Pontresina and Zuoz. The pass serves 59 lifts covering 350 kms. of prepared trails.

for one day	SFR 41
for two days	SFR 78
for three days	SFR 114
for six days	SFR 190
for seven days	SFR 211
for twelve days	SFR 285

Accommodations

Over half of the hotels in St. Moritz are four- and five-star, the highest concentration of quality hotels in Switzerland. Prices here are per person based on double occupancy with half-board during high season.

The Engadin region also organized special all-inclusive "Sunshine Ski Weeks"which include seven days half-board, six days of lifts and six days of instruction or ski guide. The off-peak prices for the ski week during January are given for each participating hotel. Contact the tourist ofice for details and the peak season prices.

The best of the best is the **Suvretta** in neighboring Champfer. This wonderful monument to Swiss hotel expertise is overshadowed in reputation by the **Palace** in St. Moritz-Dorf. The Suvretta (tel. 21121; telex 744910 is a model of understatement, a great hotel on the mountainside with its own lift connection to Corviglia.

Half-pension rates are SFR 215 to SFR 430 during high-season. Ski Week—SFR1,080.

Second in our ranking of the five five-star hotels in St. Moritz is the **Kulm** (tel. 21151; telex 74472), on the road to the bob and Cresta runs. Rooms cost between SFR 210 and SFR 420 with half pension. Ski Week—SFR 1,080.

Badrutt's Palace (tel. 21101; telex 74424) is still the place to stay if you want to be seen. It is one of the most famous and elegant hotels in the skiing world, where if you have to ask the price you should be staying somewhere else. Prices range between SFR 210 and SFR 270 a night with half pension during low season. Badrutt's has an exclusive ski-week package that includes breakfast, dinner at a different restaurant each night and a regional ski pass, with prices (per person, double occupancy) from SFR 1,600 for a small room facing the mountain to SFR 2,300 for a large room facing the lake. Come prepared with dark suit and tie or you will not be allowed to wander through the public areas after 7 p.m. For reservations, call Leading Hotels of the World in the U.S. at (800) 223-6800 or (212) 838-3110; and in Britain at (800) 181-123.

Hotel Albana, (tel. 33121, telex 74465) SFR 140-210. Excellent downtown location with superb staff and a very good kitchen. Ski Week—SFR 940.

Schweizerhof (tel. 22171; telex 74447) SFR 200-240. One of the most comfortable hotels in town. Ski Week—SFR 800.

Hotel Steinbock (tel. 36035) SFR 110-150. Small hotel (26 beds) with good restaurant and a reputation for making guests comfortable. Ski Week—SFR 800.

Hotel Nolda (tel. 082-35855) SFR 105-165. This family hotel with 70 beds has a good location at the end of the Corviglia run and adjacent to the Signal cablecar lift. Has its own sauna, swimming pool, solarium and whirlpool.

Neues Posthotel (tel. 22101; telex 74430) SFR 140-190. Within a short walk of main tourist office. Ski Week—SFR 940.

Steffani (tel. 22101; telex 74466) SFR 180-210. Comfortable midtown hotel around the corner from the parking garage. Ski Week—SFR 940.

National Hotel (tel. 33274) SFR 75-90. Ski Week—SFR 695.

Waldhaus am See (tel. 37676, telex 74759) SFR 110-150. Quiet location directly on the shore of St. Moritz lake; only three minutes' walk from the train station. Ski Week—SFR 800.

Sporthotel Bellaval (tel. 33245) A bed and breakfast only minutes from the center of St. Moritz-dorf. SFR 43-65.

Sporthotel Bären (tel. 33656) SFR 76-82. No Ski week program. Silvaplana offers two excellent hotels.

Chesa Guardalej (tel. 23121; telex 74781) SFR 175 (high-season price per person, double occupancy, including half pension)—One of the best hotels in the Swiss Alps. The hotel consists of a group of small buildings connected by underground passages. The rooms are excellent. There are several different dining areas and restaurants, plus the hotel is equipped with a full exercise room and swimming pool.

Albana (tel. 49292) High-season, half-board rate per person: SFR 100. The hotel has an award-winning restaurant.

Dining

One dining experience you should enjoy is the excursion to **Muottas Maragl**, a mountain hotel restaurant bear Pontresina at Samedan on the way to the Bernina Pass. You take a funicular up to the hotel, which has a truly spectacular location overlooking the valley. Go up on the funicular (runs every half hour from 7 a.m. until 11 p.m.) just before sunset and watch the lights come on in the valley. Reserve in advance (tel. 082-33943) and ask for a window seat.

The great hotels of St. Moritz, which incidentally charge between SFR 1,500 to SFR 2,000 and up a week for half pension, boast equally famous dining rooms with the same high prices. Opt instead for something down to earth, like the Italian specialties in the basement pizzeria at the **Chesa Veglia**. The full-service restaurant there is also superb, although considerably more expensive.

For wild-game specialties, such as deer steak, try **Talvo** (tel. 34455), a restaurant in nearby Champfer. (Take Highway 27 out of town.) The menu here ranges from SFR 28 to SFR 45.

Try also the restaurant at the Steinbock hotel for tasty, reasonably priced Swiss specialties.

To demolish your budget and add an unforgettable dining experience, lunch at **La Marmite** (reservations required), a gourmet restaurant atop Corviglia. It's in the funicular station near the self-service restaurant.

The **Stuvetta**, a cozy corner of the restaurant building at the Marguns lift station, is great for lunches, particularly pasta dishes. And the last stop of the day should be the **Alpina Hutte**. the St. Moritz ski club hut in the shadow of Piz Nair where you should order a *grischa*, a traditional hot wine-filled pot with drinking spouts for up to four. One of the most reasonably priced restaurants in the area is **Veltlinerkeller**, down the hill from Dorf toward Bad.

Apartments

Vacation apartment rentals are popular but expensive here. Altogether there are about 6,500 apartment beds, but only about 2,900 are available as rentals. In some cases you'll pay 25 percent more than you would in other Swiss resorts. A typical two-room rental apartment within walking distance of the lifts rents for approximately SFR 1,000 through one of the large rental firms maintaining a catalog for the area. Check first with the local tourist office. In addition, Interhome operates an office in the town opposite the Kulm hotel. You can arrange for an apartment there.

Nightlife

At 1 a.m. most evenings the streets are full of visitors sampling St. Moritz's great nightlife. The most famous address is the **King's Club** disco at the Palace where SRF 30 gets you in (men, bring a tie) and buys one drink. The most fun we had, by far, was at the **Stubli**, the typical Swiss wood-paneled bar in the lower level of the Schweizerhof. The ski instructors come early and stay late. There's usually so little room you are crowded, shoved and shuffled from one spot to another. You'll like it.

The **Cresta Bar** in the Steffani is a good meeting place after the walk down the hill from the Corviglia funicular, but from there you might move on after 10 p.m. to the nearby **Vivai**, a disco with a young following. Nearby also is **Cascade**, a sort of combination bar and pub you'll like almost as much as the Stubli. Another disco, the **Spotlight**, is near the tourist office. And there's not a cozier place than the bar/sitting room in the Albana after a day on Corviglia.

It's chic in the late afternoon to order a hot chocolate and whipped cream-covered slice of Black Forest cake at **Hanselmann**, the famed chocolate specialist adjacent to the Hotel Albana in the center of town.

Child care

The ski school for children from six to 12 runs half and full days. A half day without lunch costs SFR 24. Six half days cost SFR 122. The full-day price is SFR 38; SFR 98 for three days of instruction; and SFR 148 for a full week.

There are new supervised classes for children between three and six years of age at the Suvretta Ski School. Rates are: SFR 45 for a full day, SFR 125 for three full days and SFR 190 for six consecutive days. Lunch costs SFR 10 per day.

Child care programs are available at the Carlton, Parkhotel Kurhaus and the Schweizerhof (in ascending order of prices). At the Carlton (tel. 21141) full day costs are SFR 20, half-day costs SFR 12 and lunch will cost SFR 8. At the Park hotel (tel. 22111) and the Schweizerhof (tel. 22171) the full day costs with lunch included is SFR 30-34 or you can bring children by the hour for SFR 5 per hour.

Getting there

You'll most likely fly into Zurich and then catch a train to St. Moritz station. There is regular turboprop service from Zurich to St. Moritz and return for SFR 370 via Air Engiadina.

Train costs: Zurich to St. Moritz—SFR 116 (first class); SFR 74 (second class). Rental cars are available in Zurich and St. Moritz.

If you are driving, the easiest route is Zurich-Chur-Thusis, then a 30-mile stretch over the Julierpass (chains needed only in the worst weather) or through the Thusis-Samedan car-train tunnel when the pass is closed.

If you stay in St. Moritz and not in one of the outlying towns, you'll pay a stiff fee for parking, about SFR 14 a day unless you are staying for more than a week. In that case, there is a discount card available. The main garage is centrally located, however, two minutes down the hill from the Corviglia funicular. If you buy the regional ticket, the ride on the PTT Sports Bus to any of the slopes is free.

Other activities

If possible, ride the Glacier Express, a 150-mile crossing of the ice-covered landscape between St. Moritz and Zermatt. The train leaves St. Moritz shortly before 9 a.m. and crosses 292 bridges and goes through 91 tunnels before arriving at Zermatt at approximately 4:45 p.m. Going the other way, the train leaves Zermatt at 10:05 a.m. and reaches St. Moritz at 5:52 p.m.

It's possible to ride the famed Cresta Bob run without risking your life. Sign on as a guest rider on non-racing days. The fee for five rides as a passenger on the one-mile course is about SFR 400; each additional ride costs SFR 38. The ice track closes in early March. Horse-drawn sleigh rides range from a run down the lake (about SFR 80) to a romantic trip into the Rosegg Valley (about SFR 240).

The first "Skijoring" races, with horses pulling skiers on the frozen lake racetrack, were run in 1901. The competition continues. Try to see one of the events during the first three weekends in February.

For information on hang-gliding instruction, call 32416. You can take a Delta hang gliding taxi ride for SFR 190.

Excursions to Italy—over the Bernina Pass at one end of the valley and the Maloja at the other—are easy, and bus tours are available if you are not driving.

St. Moritz has two museums, the Engadine, with an emphasis on local history, and the Segantini, an art museum.

If you are looking for mountain hiking gear or climbing equipment, Testa Sport (down the hill toward St.Moritz-Bad) or Scheung Sport (just off the main square) are well stocked.

The local movie house, across from the Kulm hotel, shows current films in their original language.

Tourist information

Check with the Kur-und-Verkehrsverein, CH-7500 St. Moritz, Switzerland, tel. 082-33147; telex 74429.

In neighboring Pontresina, the address is Verkehrsverein, CH-7505 Pontresina, Switzerland; tel. 082-66488.

Verbier

This world-class resort is located in Switzerland's southwest corner, roughly between Zermatt to the east and Courmayeur and Chamonix to the west. Verbier itself is the major town in an area comprised of four valleys that have been interconnected by a spectacular lift system. The highest peak, Mont-Fort at 10,919 feet, is the nexus for lift systems that rise from Verbier and Super-Nendaz. Some 80 lifts within the network service more than 180 miles of runs.

Verbier, the town, is upscale, chic and very well known, but reasonable accommodations can be found. Super-Nendaz is connected with Verbier and offers considerably less expensive accommodations. The lower lodging costs are offset by a slow and arduous lift system, which starts at Super-Nendaz and brings you to the top of the Tortin, where you can connect with the rest of the Verbier lift system.

Mountain rating

Verbier is considered tops by expert skiers. The expert runs are steep and hair-raising. We don't recommend runs such as the Tortin from Col des Gentianes for non-experts or for skiers who are not at least advanced-intermediates; if you fall, there is no stopping for at least a hundred meters. Other expert steep runs are not as long.

Intermediate skiers will find challenging terrain and technique-perfecting runs.

Beginning skiers can glide down easy bunny slopes. However, they shouldn't expect the rest of the mountain to be conquered by week's end.

The lifts and the runs in the Nendaz area are shorter and easier than those in Verbier (except for the expert-level Tortin). This area will provide a nice break from Verbier's more crowded sections. During the week Verbier is no problem, and lift lines are relatively short. On the weekends crowds arrive from Montreux, Lausanne and Geneva.

Ski school

The ski school has 170 instructors and is located in the Chalet Orny (tel. 026-74825).

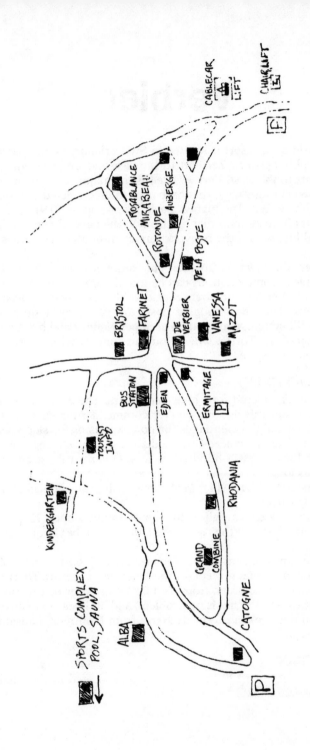

Individual lessons (89/90 prices)

for one or two persons (1 hr.)	SFR 42
for three or four persons (1 hr.)	SFR 56
for one or two persons (full day)	SFR 230
three or four persons (full day)	SFR 270

Group lessons

These are offered from 9:30 a.m. until 11:45 a.m.

for one day	SFR 19
for three days	SFR 52
for six days	SFR 92
for six days (consecutive)	SFR 84

"Special Wedel Course"

A week-long program consisting of six full-day lessons lets skiers tour the area's trails while honing their skills at the same time. The course is given during low-season periods in December, January and March. It runs from Sunday through Saturday.

Skiers are separated into classes according to skiing ability. Each class is assigned an instructor who stays with it all day for each of the six days (Sunday through Friday). The instructor takes the skiers over most of the mountain runs that are within their ability. It's a great way to spend a week, ski the entire mountain and leave a much better skier, no matter at what level you began. Cost: One week in January and March with half pension, lifts and lessons is around SFR 1096 in a four-star hotel; SFR 946 in a three-star hotel; and SFR 886 in a two-star hotel. The December weeks are less expensive.

Lift tickets

These 1989/90 lift ticket prices are for the entire four-valley area, without Mont-Fort. Skiers can purchase the Mont-Fort supplement on a daily basis for SFR 12. A half-day supplement for Mont-Fort is SFR 7.

for one day	SFR 44
for two days	SFR 84
for three days	SFR 120
for six days	SFR 220
for seven days	SFR 248
for fourteen days	SFR 420

Half-price tickets are available for skiers over 60 years and for children younger than 16 years. The lifts are also discounted during certain low-season periods.

Family vacationers should be sure to ask about discounts, because a formula is used to calculate a healthy discount for families. For example, if two parents bring two children between the ages of six and 16, they must only purchase two full tickets and the children's tickets are free. Or if two parents are traveling with two children between the ages of 16 and 25, they get all four tickets for the price of only two and a half tickets. Similar discounts apply to single parents.

Accommodations

The normal high-season rate with half pension, based on double occupancy, is noted after each hotel:

Four-star hotels:
Rosalp (tel. 76323; telex 473322) SFR 165-210.
Vanessa (tel. 70141; telex 473621) SFR 145-175.
Grand Combine (tel. 75515; telex 473795) SFR 115-150.

Three-star hotels:
Rhodania (tel. 70121; telex 473392) Normal daily rate: SFR 125-133.
Chamois (tel. 76402; telex 473247) SFR 85-114.
Mazot (tel. 76812; telex 473812) SFR 110-145.
de la Poste (tel. 75681; telex 473357) SFR 97-117.
Rotonde (tel. 76525; telex 473247) SFR 97-117
de Verbier (tel. 75346; telex 473846) SFR 97-117.
Vieux-Valaise (tel. 75955; telex 473247) SFR 97-117

Two-star hotels:
Auberge (tel. 75272; telex 473357) SFR 84-102.
Rosa Blanche (tel. 74472) SFR 68-80.
Crystal (tel. 75349) SFR 68-80.
NOTE: Rosa Blanche and Crystal can be reached by telex at 473247.

The following are bed-and-breakfasts.
Bristol (tel. 74022) SFR 60-75.
Ermitage (tel. 74977) SFR 77-100.
Farinet (tel. 76626) SFR 75-85.
Mirabeau (tel. 76335 SFR 65-84.

Apartments

Verbier is extremely well organized to handle apartment-seekers during the ski season. Minimum stays are normally one week, Saturday to Saturday. During the Christmas and Easter seasons, a minimum two-week rental is required.

The tourist office's computer keeps track of which apartments are available. Write and give details on the number of beds required, the preferred number of rooms and the dates you plan to be there. An immediate response with a selection of apartments and prices will follow. Select the apartment you want and return the information to the tourist office.

Bed linen and kitchen utensils are usually provided in each apartment. Other communal or private amenities, such as swimming pool, sauna, TV or room phone all add to the cost. Standard apartments rent for between $15 and $25 per person a night. Prices will also vary significantly from low to high season.

Dining

In Verbier's excellent restaurants prices vary depending on the establishment's relative position on the luxury scale and the quality of the food. But with the strong French influence here, it is difficult to find a poorly prepared meal. The following restaurants come recommended by locals: Rosalp and Vanessa for a splurge; also, Au Vieux Valais and Le Mazot. Head to the Refuge under the Hotel Rhodania for good spaghetti and other Italian food. They serve "spaghetti by the meter, " which guarantees a good time.

Nightlife

The most popular drinking spots are **The Pub**, which is very English, **Nelsons, Fer a Cheval**, with great hot wine, and **La Luge.**

The best discos in town are the **Tara Club** and the **Farm Club Disco**. The **Scotch Club** is not as popular. Expect to pay about SFR 20 to enter, which includes a drink.

Child care

A kindergarten, "Chez les Schtroumpfs" (""Smurfs' Place"), is located in Chalet Lesberty, just a short distance from the tourist office. Open daily from 8:30 a.m. until 5:30 p.m., its rates are SFR 35 a day, including lunch; SFR 30 for a half day with lunch; and SFR 20 for a half day without lunch. The kindergarten accepts infants as well. Call 77555 for details on the exact ages accepted.

The ski school also runs a ski nursery (tel. 74825 or 77469), which offers beginning ski lessons for children from three to 10 years. Rates are SFR 18 for a half day; SFR 43 for three half-days; and SFR 75 for six half-days. Its hours are from 8:30 a.m. until 5 p.m.; closed Sunday.

Getting there

The closest airport is Geneva. Train service runs from Martigny on the Simplon line to Le Chable, where you can either take the cablecar to Verbier or a direct bus from the station during the winter.

If your airline cannot arrange free or direct transfer from the airport to the resort, a rental car shared by several people makes the trip much easier; the car can also be used for side trips back to Montreux or Lausanne. The drive from Geneva should take about two hours. Follow the signs to the St. Bernard Pass (home of the famous St. Bernard dogs) until you reach Sembrancher. There, turn left and drive up the hill to Verbier.

Other activities

Verbier has recently built an extensive sports center, which features an indoor swimming pool, ice rink, curling rinks, squash courts, whirlpools, saunas, solariums and two indoor tennis courts. The resort is approximately an hour's drive from Montreux and Lausanne, two of the most beautiful and interesting Swiss cities.

On Lake Geneva, just before Montreux, visit the castle of Chillon. The town of Sion is very picturesque with a beautiful castle dominating the center of town. In the spring, a stop at the monastery at the St. Bernard Pass to visit the dogs makes for a pleasant tour.

For a change of pace, skiers may want to visit Villars, Leysin or Crans-Montana, all within an hour's drive from Verbier.

Tourist information

Tourist office, 1936 Verbier l; tel. (026) 76222 or 77181; telex 473247 TURVE CH.

Villars

Villars is a gentle postcard town huddled on the side of the mountains overlooking the Rhone Valley with spectacular views of Mont Blanc. The spectacular views across the Rhone Valley from the winding approach to the town, either along the road or on the train from Aigle, are a beautiful introduction to the resort. The quiet village still retains its alpine character with only a handful of square concrete buildings marring the harmony of chalet-style architecture. Villars is a town that for years has successfully balanced different generations—the older, upscale vacationer and teen-age students at private schools and colleges. Except for those looking for extremes—steeps that leave you breathless by day and wild parties that leave you exhausted by night—Villars is a resort for everyone. It has one of the largest sports centers in Europe with plenty of activities for the non-skier, as well as slopes for every level of skier.

Where to ski

The major ski area of Villars is reached by either the Roc d"Orsay gondola or by the cog train that leaves from the center of town and reaches the major mountain hub at Bretaye (5,905 feet). Either ascent will allow similar explorations of the ski area. For those starting at Roc D'Orsay (6,562 feet), the first run is a gentle warmup reaching Bretaye. From here three chairlifts and three drag lifts fan out to open the slopes surrounding Bretaye. Head up the Grand Chamossaire (6,955 feet) and the Petit Chamossaire (6,673 feet) for the morning hours. The runs down from the Grand Chamossaire are gentler and a bit longer than those from the Petit Chamossaire, but both can be handled by all but the absolute beginner. Petit Chamossaire offers significantly more challenging terrain, both on and off trail, for the expert. The opposite side of Bretaye topped by Chaux de Conches (6,650 feet) and Chaux Ronde is an intermediate joy, with virtually unlimited off-trail possibilities for both intermediates and experts. Once again, trails allow even beginners to enjoy the skiing. The trail map of the back side of Chaux Ronde and Chaux de Conches stretching down to La Rasse looks like a dozen blue threads streaming to one point, however the impression of only easy slopes is misleading. Here experts can find jumps and tree-skiing—especially directly beneath Chaux de

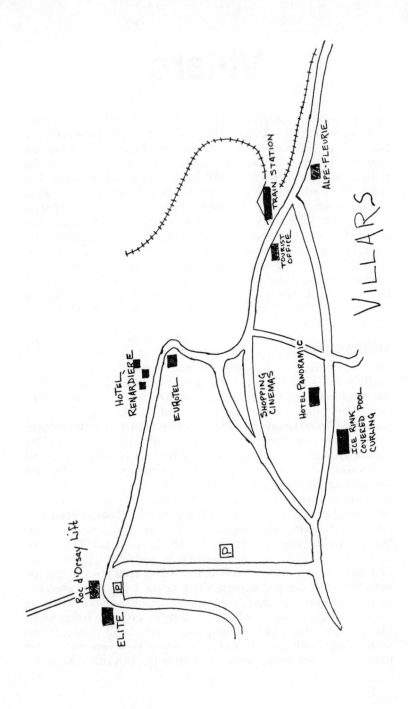

VILLARS

Roc d'Orsay Lift
ELITE
HOTEL RENARDIERE
EUROTEL
SHOPPING CINEMAS
HOTEL PANORAMIC
ICE RINK COVERED POOL CURLING
TOURIST OFFICE
TRAIN STATION
ALPE-FLEURIE

Conches—and intermediates can push themselves off-trail virtually anywhere in this area.

Reaching the Gryon area is an easy two-step process. From La Rasse a short lift brings skiers to Sodoleuvroz, where a long drag lift reaches Les Chaux (5,741 feet) and another stretches even higher to Croix des Chaux (6,627 feet). Here skiers of every level can enjoy the snow and the views, including very long off-trail runs down to the Gryon gondola.

The other major area of Villars is the connection with Les Diablerets. Dropping behind Meillerets and Les Mazots is a web of between-the-tree runs, which link up with a lift bringing skiers to Isenau and then another gondola reaching Pierres Pointes just beneath the glacier. Skiing under the Pierres Pointes gondola is some of the most challenging within miles. Two cablecars bring skiers up to Scex Rouge (9,744 feet), where the actual glacier skiing opens up. The required adventure is the long run around the Oldenhorn and down to the cablecar station at Oldenegg. Take the cablecar up to Cabane, then ski back down to Oldenegg beneath the lift. Note: This all-day adventure takes time—make sure to start early and head back by around two in the afternoon in order to make the series of lifts needed to reach Villars by late afternoon.

Mountain rating

Villars, although predominately a fantastic place for beginners to learn and for intermediates of all levels to frolic, is also a playful mountain for experts. There is adequate terrain to keep most adventurous skiers happy for an entire week. Although a dedicated expert skier might not keep busy in Villars for a week, the resort is wonderful for a mixed-level group of skiers and friends.

Ski school

Villars has two ski schools—the traditional Swiss Ski School and the more avant-garde "Ecole de ski moderne."

Swiss Ski School: For groups, a half day—SFR 18 (SFR 17 for children); three half days—SFR 50 (SFR 45 for children); six consecutive half days—SFR 80 (SFR 70 for children). Private lessons cost SFR 40 an hour per person, SFR 45 an hour for two and SFR 50 for three and four people. A private instructor for a full day costs SFR 200. Cross-country lessons are the same prices as downhill.

"Ecole de ski moderne" This school is very English-oriented. It uses the graduated length method of instruction, which has skiers starting on short skis and then using long skis within a week. There are also "hot dog" ski lessons, ski ballet, surf, telemark and off-trail opportunities. Group lessons cost: SFR 15 for adults and SFR 12 for children. Private lessons: SFR 35 for one person; SFR 40 for two; SFR 45 for three; and SFR 50 for four. A private instructor for a half day is SFR 120; for a full day, SFR 220.

Lift tickets

The lift tickets include Villars, Gryon, Meilleret and Isenau. Tickets for the Diablerets glacier cost extra.

1989/90 prices: Half day—SFR 23; Full day—SFR 32; Six days—SFR 155. Children get a 20 percent discount.

Accommodations

Villars does not have thousands of hotel rooms—that's part of its charm. The hotels in town are quality establishments. You can either correspond directly with the hotels or contact the tourist office (tel. (025) 353232) for reservations. The prices for hotels noted here are for half board, based on double occupancy.

There is also a special "White Week" program that links the lifts of the Lake Geneva region and includes seven days half board, free entrance to the pool, skating rink and fitness center, plus unlimited skiing in Villars, Chateau-d'Oex, Les Diablerets, Leysin, Les Mosses and La Lécherette. The low-season prices are noted for each hotel.

Grand Hotel du Parc, tel. (025) 352121; telex 456218. One of the leading hotels of the world. Very upscale and formal—requiring a jacket at dinner and in the public areas of the hotel after seven p.m. Swimming suits acceptable in the covered pool. Rates: SFR 135-235. White-week price: SFR 1,300.

Panoramic, tel. (025) 35211; telex 456228. This is the newest hotel in town. Beds fold into the wall to allow more room during the day. Although its restaurants are considered some of the best in Villars, the half-board menu quality varies greatly. Covered pool. Rates: SFR 78-175. Ski-a-Go-Go price: SFR 880.

Elite, tel. (025) 351341; telex 456203. A modern but soulless hotel at the bottom of the Roc d'Orsay gondola. This is Villars' ski-in/ski-out hotel. No pool. Rates: SFR 81-128. White-week price: SFR 780.

Eurotel, tel. (025) 353131; telex 456206. The bottom of the four-stars. This hotel seems to have been designed for groups. It has a pool, but we would try the other four-stars before bedding down here. Rates: SFR 81-141. White-week price: SFR 780.

Le Renardière, tel. (025) 352592; telex 456215. Considered by most as the best-kept secret in Villars, but as rooms are hard to come by, it may not be that well kept. Make reservations early. Tucked between trees, this hotel is actually a cluster of three chalet-style buildings. Rates: SFR 78-118. White-week price: SFR 780.

Alpe Fleurie, tel. (025) 352494. This hotel looks like the one on the postcards you send home to friends and family. Very family-oriented, it is located directly across from the train station and close to everything in town. Rates: SFR 90-115. White-week price: SFR 780.

Golf et Marie-Louise, tel. (025) 352477; telex 456212. Although there are plenty of rooms with private bath, this hotel also has less expensive rooms with bath down the hall. Rates (with private bath): SFR 83-130. White-week price: SFR 780.

Ecureuil, tel. (025) 352795. This very traditional bed-and-breakfast has some rooms with kitchenettes, allowing preparation of meals in the room. A good budget choice. Rates (with bath): (B&B) SFR 37-65. White-week program: SFR 670 (half board).

Villars-Palace, tel. 352241. One of the most prestigious Club Meds in Europe. French, as you might expect, is the language. Particulars from Club Med.

Apartments

Apartments are the best choice if you really want to save money. Apartment rentals are normally only available for stays of one week or longer. Villars alone has about 7,000 chalet and apartment beds for rent. Write to the tourist office and ask for a list of apartments that will be available during the time you will be in Villars. Also, include your requirements, such as the number of people in your party. The office will send a list of available apartments in town, plus a map showing apartment locations. You then select the apartment you want and correspond either with the tourist board or directly with the apartment owner.

The apartments normally include bed linen and kitchen utensils. You will be charged a visitor's tax and there may be an extra charge for electricity and heat.

Expect to pay between SFR 25 and SFR 40 per person a night, depending on the number of people sharing the apartment and its location.

Apartments are also available through rental agencies, such as **Interhome**, with representatives in the United States and offices in Britain, West Germany and throughout most of Europe.

Child care

The Swiss Ski School (tel. 025-353907) has a special children's program for kids from three to 10 years of age. Open Monday through Saturday from 9 a.m. to 4:30 p.m., it is located behind the train station in Villars. Prices (including lessons, lifts and lunch): one day—SFR 45; three days—SFR 120; six days—SFR 230.

Club Pré Fleuri (tel. 025-352348) takes care of skiers and non-skiing children from the ages of three to 11. Prices (including lunch): half day—SFR 33; full day—SFR 50; six days—SFR 280.

Le Nid (tel. 025-351518) takes children from two and a half through five years. Open Monday to Saturday from 8:30 a.m. to noon and from 2 p.m. to 5 p.m.

Nightlife

Most people bring their good time with them. But for those who insist on leading the disco-frenzied nightlife, Villars boasts one of the glitziest and best discos in the Alps, the **New Sam**. New Sam is built on many levels and claims one of the best light shows in Europe. As all French-influenced discos in Europe, New Sam doesn't start to roll until very late—after midnight.

A much smaller disco where prices are about the same but the crowd is younger is the **El Gringo**. It starts late and claims the smallest light show in Villars.

Depending on whether the crowd is lively, the **Bridge Pub** can be a nice hangout.

Other activities

Villars has some of the best developed non-ski activities in Switzerland. The Sports Center has six covered tennis courts, two squash courts, sauna and Turkish bath open from 8:30 a.m. to 10 p.m.

There is a covered pool, a covered skating rink, a special fitness club, bowling and horseback riding.

Geneva, Montreux and Lausanne are only a short drive away.

For hang-gliding or para-gliding lessons, call Denis Giraud or Pascal Balet in Gryon (025) 682683.

Tourist information

Office du Tourisme Villars, CH-1884 Villars, Switzerland; tel.(025) 353232; telex 456200.

Zermatt

Zermatt, Switzerland's best-known ski resort, was the base from which the famous assaults of the Matterhorn were launched. The killer mountain still casts its shadow over the storybook town, which has developed into one of Europe's premier winter playgrounds.

Fortunately, Zermatt is a destination resort, that is, the village is difficult enough for weekend skiers to reach to keep most of them away. The town has a total of about 17,000 beds and a lift capacity on the slopes of almost 29,000 people an hour, with more than 93 miles of marked ski trails. Even during the busiest seasons lift lines are not impossibly long and uncrowded slopes can be found.

The town itself is everything a quaint Swiss village is imagined to be: Tiny chalets line the roads, and the hotels in the center of town are picturesque. No cars are allowed; a train connection is the only way to arrive in Zermatt. All cars are parked in a large lot outside the village. Unfortunately, the horse-drawn sleighs that carry tourists and townsfolk alike through the town, along with bags of groceries or ski equipment, have been replaced for the most part with speeding electric trucks and carts. When you hear a ringing bell, get over to the side of the street.

Where to ski

Zermatt sits at the end of a long valley and is bounded by three major skiing areas. Each area will keep skiers busy for at least two days' worth of thrills.

The Sunnegga area (7,513 feet) is quickly reached by an underground cable railway and has ski lifts that reach the Unterrothhorn at 10,170 feet. This area is the least time-consuming to reach. It also gets the most sun in the valley and has recently been equipped with snow-making facilities that stretch from the top station down to Sunnegga. From the Unterrothorn, avoid the run returning to Blauherd if you only plan to return. The cablecar is the slowest lift on the Sunnegga area and normally has a wait. A better area to explore for intermediate skiers is the Kumme side, where a triple chair allows almost continuous skiing and long runs back down to Tuftern will keep experts and intermediates happy. The Fluhalp run down to the lower station of Gant offers good initial skiing but long runouts at the lower levels. For those planning to

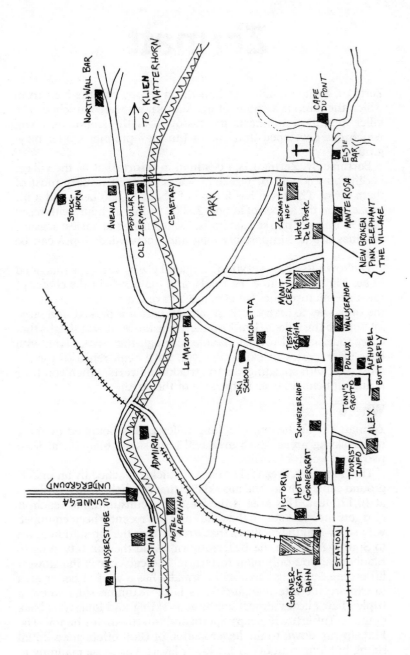

connect with Gornergrat it's the only connection, but not recommended for other than advanced intermediates.

The Gornergrat area is served by a cog railway, which is convenient to get to, but the ride takes nearly 45 minutes to reach the upper station. The wait in line at the Gornergrat station can be up to an hour and a half. Normally, however, when the line at Gornergrat is long, walk over to Sunnegga and head up the mountain. There's almost no wait. The Gornergrat area features wide-open skiing at the top back toward Riffelberg and on to Landtunnel. Exciting expert-only terrain is found on the side dropping to Gant from Stockhorn, Rote Nase and Hohtälli. A new cablecar links the Hohtälli with Rote Nase. This eliminates the 15-minute hike that until two years ago adventurous experts faced while their skis were being transported between peaks on a suspended trolley. This new lift is also important in that it now makes the connection possible between the Sunnegga area and Gornergrat without the need to make the abovementioned hike.

The Klein Matterhorn (Little Matterhorn) area is reached by a series of cablecars. The last one, which reaches the summit at 12,530 feet, is Europe's highest cablecar. It can easily take 45 minutes to an hour in order to reach the area's upper stations, but here you can ski throughout the summer on the glacier. New snowmaking facilities have been installed on the slopes above Furgg in order to keep the lower sections of the summer ski area open. Favorite runs on the Klein Matterhorn sector are to the far right side of the area, below Hörnli.

From the Klein Matterhorn, skiers shouldn't miss the opportunity for a special adventure involving skiing over to the Italian side of the mountain, visiting Cervinia and having a good Italian meal. Make sure to check weather conditions first, since excessive winds often close the cablecars. This can make the return trip impossible except by a four-hour bus ride. Change your money before you strike out for Italy—the rates are better on this side of the mountain if you plan on changing Swiss francs into Italian lire. Remember that your lift ticket is not good on the Cervinia lifts—a special lift pass must be purchased on the Zermatt side that will allow you to use the Cervinia lifts.

Mountain rating

Every level of skier will find thrills in Zermatt. Each area has runs that make beginners feel like experts, as well as runs that make experts wonder just how expert they really are.

Experts will enjoy the Kumme side of the Unterrothorn and

some of the steep drops back into the village from the Sunnegga area. There are a half-dozen steep, bumpy and exciting runs in the Gornergrat section from Stockhorn, Rote Nase and Hohtälli down to Gant into the valley between Sunnegga and Gornergrat. And although the Klein Matterhorn area is wide open with gentle slopes, the runs from Schwarzsee back into town can be testing. Experts also have almost unlimited opportunities for off-trail skiing. For example, skiing over to Saas-Fee is an option with proper equipment and the assistance of a guide or instructor.

Intermediate skiers can be happy in any area but should avoid many of the black runs, which are really for experts. If you take the cablecar over to the Stockhorn, Rote Nase and Hohtälli, be aware that there is no easy escape from the steep and bumpy.

Beginning skiers will find easy slopes on the Gornergrat and on the Klein Matterhorn glacier. Also, the Sunnegga area has a good, long beginner/lower intermediate trail network from Blauherd down into town.

Ski school

The Zermatt ski school (tel. 028-672451) has more than 175 qualified instructors and mountain guides who teach in the traditional Swiss ski school system.

Individual lessons

for one day	SFR 200
for each additional person	SFR 10
for half day	SFR 110
for each additional person	SFR 5

Group lessons (age 12 to adult)

for one day	SFR 50
for three days	SFR 105
for six days	SFR 155

Children between the ages of six and 12 get an additional discount from between 20 percent and 40 percent.

Zermatt also offers a special "Wedel-Ski Course" lasting a full week. The course includes a seven-day ski pass and an instructor for six full days (Sunday to Friday). The major difference between this program and standard group lessons is that the instructor stays with the group for the entire day instead of only three or four hours in the morning, and accompanies the group down almost every run within the skiers' abilities. The courses are conducted during the last weeks in November, the first weeks in December, the last three weeks in January and—a special spring skiing course—the last week in April. Cross-country classes are also available.

To enroll in one of the "Wedel Courses," write in advance to the tourist office and request enrollment forms. The price (including seven-day ski pass) is SFR 325.

"The Haute Route" is a classic ski adventure trek between Saas-Fee, Zermatt, Courmayeur and Chamonix. These treks are organized from mid-April through the end of May. These are tough, physical treks, and participants should be in good shape for high-altitude ski-climbing and must be able to ski in deep snow. The tour is normally conducted from early May to the first week in June. Cost is approximately SFR 820, which includes guides, acommodation in mountain huts, meals, hotel expenses during the tour and mountain railway and bus fares. Contact: Franz Schwery, mountain guide, 3920 Zermatt, tel. 028-672880.

Lift tickets

The Zermatt lift system has fairly complicated tariff formulas. You can buy ski passes for each of the areas separately or in any combination. You can also buy coupons, which may not be a good deal if you plan to do any serious skiing. This is because you have to purchase varying amounts of these depending on the area in which you'll be skiing. The coupons are designed for skiers who can spend only a limited time on the slopes. For those who will be skiing the entire day, the best deal is the full combination pass. The 1989/90 prices for it are listed below:

for one day	SFR 48
for two days	SFR 92
for six days	SFR 226
for seven days	SFR 240
for 14 days	SFR 412

Childern ski for half price.

NOTE: If you plan to ski to Cervinia, you must pay an additional surcharge in order to use Cervinia's uphill lift system. The surcharge for the combination ticket is SFR 48.

Accommodations

Zermatt may not be the sort of European resort that offers inexpensive hotels, but compared with U.S. resorts even Zermatt's best hotels are a bargain. Do yourself a favor when requesting a room and ask for one that doesn't face the main street. For some reason the disco denizens feel compelled to yell and sing at the top of their lungs as they stagger down main street after emerging from the music-filled cellars between one and three o'clock in the morning.

The prices noted are the middle-season prices effective during mid-January 1988 and from 10 April to 1 May 1988. Prices for February to 9 April 1988 are approximately 30 percent higher. Prices are based on double occupancy with half board.

For the best Zermatt has to offer, head for the Mont Cervin (tel. 661121, telex 472129) or the Zermatterhof (tel. 661101, telex 472145). Both cost SFR 178. The Hotel Alex (tel. 671726, telex 472112) and the Hotel Nicoletta (tel.661151, telex 472108) are considered the next best in town. The normal daily rate: SFR 162-210.

The hotels listed below feature lower rates and special packages, which are available during low season—early December, January after New Year's and the end of April.

Hotel Alpenhof (tel. 674333; telex 472139)—By all reports, one of the best hotels in town. A chalet-style hotel located just across from the main Sunnegga lift and only minutes from the center of town. SFR 119

Hotel Admiral (tel. 671555; telex 472155)—Shares the pool with the nearby Christiania. Friends who have stayed here have nothing but praise for the place. SFR 109-141.

Hotel Monte Rosa (tel. 661131; telex 472128)—One of the grand hotels in the center of Zermatt with access to one of the best pools in town. SFR 137.

Hotel Walliserhof (tel. 671174; telex 472123)—First-class rustic lodgings with an excellent restaurant. SFR 119.

Hotel Butterfly (tel. 673721; telex 472121)—Located in the center of Zermatt with whirlpool and fitness room. SFR 101-141.

Hotel Gornergrat (tel. 671027; telex 472122)—A fairly modern hotel located in the heart of Zermatt across the street from the train station and adjacent to the Gornergrat station. SFR 101-141.

Alphubel (tel. 673030)—A relatively small, two-star hotel located in the middle of Zermatt. SFR 74-96

Burgener Pensione (tel. 671020)—A small, traditionally rustic hotel. SFR 82.

Testa Grigia (tel. 672501; telex 472108)—This is a bed-and-breakfast attached to the Hotel Nicoletta. Through a passageway guests have access to Hotel Nicoletta's swimming pool—a good way to get some of the goodies of a big hotel at bed-and-breakfast prices. SFR 85-110.

Dining

In a resort as highly developed as Zermatt, your biggest dining out decision will be which of the numerous excellent restaurants to visit.

For gourmet, high-priced meals, try **Le Mazot**, where even normally taciturn Germans go out of their way to compliment the owner on great food and service. **Zamoura** in the Hotel de la Post (tel. 671932) has excellent seafood. Then try **Belle Epoque** in the Hotel Nicoletta (tel. 661151).

For the middle-of-the-budget crowd, try the fare at **Tony's Grotto** (tel. 674454) tucked into a tiny street between Hotel Pallux and Hotel Derby. For steaks, try **Victoria** (tel. 673871) opposite the railway station. **Cafe du Pont** has excellent fondue, raclette and wine. The **Walliserstubli** in the Wiesti section of town (tel.671151) is known for good steaks, stuffed pork chops and huge portions.

If you're trying to hold down spending but still want to get a great meal, head for **Averna**, the **Walliserkanne** or the **Bahnhof Buffet** in the railway station. **Northwall Bar** in the Steinmatte part of town under Hotel Rhodania makes the best pizza in town, according to many locals.

One of the other joys of a vacation in Zermatt is stopping in at one of the excellent mountainside restaurants that offer lunch and snacks during the day. Our favorites are the mountain restaurants at Findeln (especially **Enzo's**), just below Sunegga, the restaurant at the top of Unterrothorn and the restaurant at Furri, on the way back from skiing the Klein Matterhorn area.

Nightlife

The fun starts as the lifts close. For après-ski action from 4 p.m. to 6 p.m., stop at the **Olympia Stübli** on the way back to town from the Sunnegga area. In town, try the **Popular Pub** (younger crowd), **Old Zermatt** (slightly older and quieter) and **Elsie's Bar** (most pretentious crowd). **Zum See** is also a good after-ski watering hole.

The night action revolves around the discos in town. For the 18- to 27-year-old crowd, head for **The New Broken** or the **Village**— both located in the Hotel de la Poste complex. The Pollux also has an excellent disco. The 27- to 40-year-old group should go to the **Alex**, which is a beautiful disco with relatively subdued music allowing conversation. The crowd here is a very sophisticated international set. Check into the **Pink Elephant** in the Hotel de la Poste which has a café atmosphere and often features great jazz.

Child care

Kindergarten Theresia (tel. 672096) nurses take care of children up to eight years of age. A ski instructor gives lessons to those four year and older. Prices: Full day with lunch and snack—SFR 48-58; six full days—SFR 235-294; half day with lunch included— SFR 34.50-40; six half-days—SFR 175-210. Prices change based on the age of the child.

The ski school kindergarten costs SFR 30 per day; SFR 75 for three days; and SFR 120 for six days.

Apartments

Apartments are the best choice if you really want to save money in Zermatt. A well-organized rental system offers apartments for more than 10,000 people a night in town. Write to the tourist office and ask for a list of apartments that will be available during the time you will be in Zermatt. Be sure to include your requirements, such as the number of people in your party. The office will send a listing of available apartments in town, plus a map showing apartment locations. You then select the apartment you want and correspond either with the tourist board or directly with the apartment owner.

If you are fortunate enough to find an apartment in the Obere-Steinmatte section of town, you'll literally be able to put on your skis at your door and ski to the Sunnegga lifts or the Gornergrat when the snow is still on the streets.

The apartments normally include bed linen and kitchen utensils. You will be charged a visitor's tax, and there may be an extra charge for the electricity and heat you use during your stay.

Expect to pay between SFR 25 and SFR 40 per person a night, depending on the number of people sharing the apartment and its location.

Getting there

By train: From Zurich airport via Bern, Spiez, through the Lötschberg tunnel to Brig. At Brig you change to the special Brig-Zermatt train, which leaves from the front of the Brig station. Time: Zurich-Brig—about three and a half hours; Brig-Zermatt—an hour and 20 minutes.

From Geneva, trains run directly to Brig in two hours.

By car: Travel via Montreaux, then up the Valais pass through Sion to Visp where you turn south and follow signs to Zermatt.

If you are driving from Zurich or Basel, you can choose to take the Lötschberg tunnel from Kandersteg to Goppenstein, above Brig and Visp. This tunnel requires that you load your car onto a train. Trains transit the tunnel every half hour from 5:35 a.m. to 11:05 p.m. The trip takes only 15 minutes. Cost per car, including nine-seat vans, is SFR 15. From Goppenstein, continue your drive to Visp then on to Tasch outside Zermatt. The car park, just outside the village of Tasch, is about three miles from Zermatt. Buses and trains connect Tasch with Zermatt approximately every 20 minutes; the ride takes 11 minutes.

From the railway station in Zermatt, take a horse-drawn taxi to your hotel or apartment. It's a great way to start a vacation.

Other activities

Zermatt is up to handling non-skiers on vacation, although activities are much more limited due to its distance from other tourist destinations and its dedication to skiing. The town has 12 hotel indoor swimming pools; most can be used by non-guests with payment of a daily fee. Also available are 18 saunas, a salt-water swimming pool, two ice skating rinks, curling rinks, covered tennis and squash courts, miles of marked walking trails and cross-country ski circuits.

Tourist information

Tourist information, CH-3920 Zermatt, Switzerland; tel. (028) 661181; telex 472130.

France

France is moving to the forefront of European skiing due to the current focus on the 1992 Winter Olympics. Although those games are scheduled to be held in Albertville, the real scene will be the resorts of Courchevel, Méribel, Val d'Isere, Tignes, Les Arc and La Plagne. Albertville will be the largest town in the area—one without any skiing, ironically—that will anchor the events.

While 1992's games will no doubt focus world attention on French slopes, the French have skied for decades. Resorts like Chamonix, Megève and Val d'Isère shared in the initial development of alpine skiing. But many of the modern French resorts have only recently been "purpose-built" for skiing. This means entire villages, such as Avoriaz, Tignes, Courchevel and Les Arc, have been created with skiing uppermost in the designers' minds. The result has been thousands of low-priced apartments and hotels that combine the convenience of walking outside your door, stepping into your skis and starting to ski with some of the most extensive ski slopes in the world. In addition, the après-ski life is great, and the food and wine is France at its best.

A note on prices

The prices in this section are valid for the 1988/1989 winter season unless otherwise noted. You can expect prices to increase between 3 percent and 5 percent during the 1989/1990 winter season. Use the prices as a guide.

All prices are given in French francs (FFR). Information for the book was gathered when the franc was at an exchange rate of FFR 6 to $1. Any subsequent change in the exchange rate will be the biggest factor affecting the prices.

The seasons

High season—December 23, 1989, to January 6, 1990, February 3, 1990, to April 21.

Low season—January 6, 1990, to February 2, then after April 21.

Use these as general guidelines, because some resorts may have slightly adjusted seasons due to local school holidays. Check with your destination resort to get the exact dates if you are planning your trip on a season borderline.

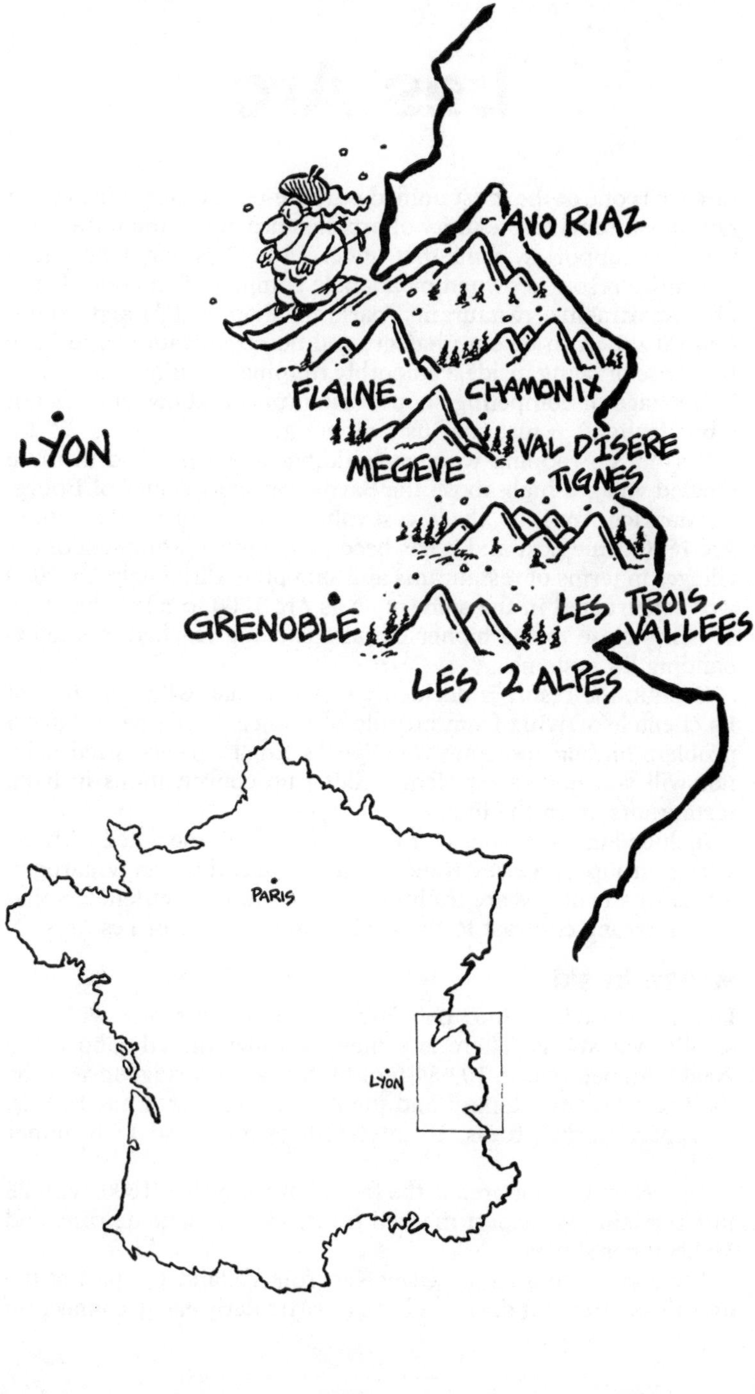
AVORIAZ
FLAINE
CHAMONIX
LYON
VAL D'ISERE
MEGEVE
TIGNES
GRENOBLE
LES TROIS VALLÉES
LES 2 ALPES
PARIS
LYON

Les Arc

Les Arc is one of the most unified purpose-built resorts, displaying not only a remarkable unity of architecture but of the infrastructure and support systems that underpin it. This may be because the entire resort is owned by a single company that controls the lifts, apartments, restaurants, parking, shop rentals and hotels. Centralization to be sure has created homogenization; you have the sense of being inside a smoothly running machine rather than in a village of competing shops, restaurants and owners. It's not a bad feeling . . . just curiously different.

Les Arc's swooping wooden buildings stand perched in three created villages high above the Savoy transport center of Bourg-St. Maurice. Arc 1600, the lowest village, was the original creation. Arc 1800 came next and it has become the most prominent of the villages in terms of restaurants and shopping. Ultimately Arc 2000 was constructed in the same style as Arc 1800 to take advantage of being close to the higher elevations being reached by the expanding lift systems.

Overall, the resort is decidedly international, with over half of its clientele arriving from outside of France. You'll never have a problem finding someone who speaks English if you need help, nor will you have a problem striking up conversations in bars, restaurants or on the lifts.

Included in the ski pass for the area are lifts associated with the village group of Peisey-Nancroix and Vallandry and Villaroger. These small villages are traditional, centuries-old settlements that offer a strong contrast to the stylized atmosphere of Les Arcs.

Where to ski

Les Arc is divided into two large sections for skiing with two smaller variations. There is a massive valley directly above Arc 2000 bounded by the 10,484-foot-high peak and ridge formed by the Col du Grand Renard and the Arpette. This area has 15 lifts, 10 expert marked trails, 10 intermediate trails and 11 beginner trails.

The second major area is the face above Arc 1800/1600, with 28 lifts servicing six expert marked trails, 15 intermediate runs and 19 beginner slopes.

The connected area of Peisey-Nancroix Vallandry is part of the overall ski area but does not have a particularly easily connection to the Arc 1800/1600 sector. This area has one expert trail, a baker's dozen of mellow, intermediate runs and 10 beginner runs.

Finally, another sector of the Les Arc ski pass is Villaroger, which effectively has only two long lifts carrying skiers who have completed the two long Aiguille Rouge runs back to the crest above Arc 2000. Another lift allows skiers who have skied below Arc 2000 to reach Villaroger without returning to the top of the Aiguille Rouge.

Mountain rating

This is one of the best compact areas featuring something for everyone from expert to beginner. There is great intermediate skiing all across the face above Arc 1800 dropping down from Arpette, Col des Frettes and Col du Grand Renard. Advanced intermediates will love the runs from the Aiguille Rouge across the glacier and down the Piste du Grand Col. Beginners and intermediates will have plenty of area at the bottom of the valley between the Aiguille Rouge and Arpette. Experts face some exhilarating runs down from the Aiguillle Rouge across the glacier, then dropping down the massive face immediately above Arc 2000.

The runs above the town of Peisey-Nancroix Vallandry are relatively gentle intermediate and beginner runs. And the drop along the ridge to Villaroger is for strong intermediates and experts.

Experts should sign up with a guide to tackle the off-trail tours circling behind the Aiguille Grive and the Aiguillle Rousse or for an itinerary off the backside of the Aiguille Rouge looping around to Villaroger.

Ski school

The Les Arc ski schools have a total of 180 instructors and are located at each of the three centers. Ski school offices are open from 9 a.m. until 12 noon and from 2-5:30 p.m. each day. Lessons are available morning or afternoon for two hours, for three hours or as part of a two-hour-by-two-hour formula.

Group lessons (1988/89 prices) The standard rate for two lessons of two hours a day for six days is FFR 530. A reduced rate of FFR 450 is available for most of January. The rate increases to FFR 570 for most of February.

The price for three hours of instruction a day for six days is FFR 450. The reduced rate in January is FFR 400, which goes up to FFR 490 in February.

A two-hour group lesson at any time will cost FFR 65.

Private lessons are offered based on the availability of instructors. The price per hour is FFR 140 during most of the season. January's reduced price is FFR 125 an hour. In February the rate goes up to FFR 150 an hour.

Special arrangements can be made with ski instructors or mountain guides for groups of skiers who want to go off trail or work on special techniques. The cost for instructors for a full day for up to four people is FFR 980; in January—FFR 850; and during most of February—FFR 1,100.

For beginning skiers, Les Arc is one of the few resorts in the world where a modified graduated length method of ski instruction is taught. Beginning packages include equipment, two hours of lessons twice a day and unlimited use of the lifts for FFR 1,390. In January there is a reduced price of FFR 1,050.

Other packages for improvement, which include two hours of lessons twice a day, plus equipment and lifts, are available for FFR 1,595 or in January for FFR 1,050. Ski Discovery packages with lifts, lessons and a chance to learn racing techniques, monoskiing and snowboarding are normally FFR 1,730 and in January FFR 1,225.

Lift tickets

Your ski pass is valid for the entire Les Arc, Peisey-Nancroix and Villaroger area; it also allows you to ski La Plagne, Val d'Isère/Tignes' "l'espace Killy" and the French/Italian area of La Rosiere/La Thuile for one day per resort during the period your pass is valid. For La Plagne, Val d'Isère and Tignes, present your pass at the resort's main ticket window. For La Rosiere/La Thuile, you must pick up your pass in Les Arc at a STAR ski pass office.

Normal lift ticket rates: half day—FFR 100; full day—FFR 148; three days—FFR 385; six days—FFR 710.

January lift ticket prices: half day—FFR 95; full day—FFR 130; three days—FFR 345; six days—FFR 640.

Parents staying at Les Arcs and buying a lift pass for themselves can obtain a free lift pass for each of their children under seven years of age. Identification is required.

Accommodations

Clone architecture has created a group of hotels that are very similar as far as size of rooms and layout are concerned. All hotels noted here are exceptionally good and are similar in quality. Two are located in Arc 1800 and the latter two are in Arc 2000. The prices given are for winter 1989 and are for January low season—January 2-28—and for the February high season—February 5-25.

Hotel du Golf (tel. 79074800) was the first constructed in Arc 1800 and is still the flagship hotel. The hotel features one of the best restaurants in the region. Rooms are simple, functional and comfortable with exceptional views from either side of the hotel. The hotel also has an extensive fitness/health center. Rates for a week with half board during January's low season in a room with a Mont Blanc view—FFR 2,142; during February's high season—FFR 3,689.

Hotel Latitudes (tel. 79074979) in Arc 1800 is located an easy 10-minute walk from the main commercial center of Le Charvet. The rooms are modern and sparsely decorated. The hotel offers rooms in combination with half board and lift tickets. There is a small fitness center. Evening meals include two theme dinners each week and an entertainment evening. Rates based on double occupancy with half board in room facing Mont Blanc (including seven-day lift ticket) during January's low season—FFR 2,825; same room during February high season—FFR 4,998.

Hotel Eldorador (tel. 70075050) is operated by the Jet Vacations/Air France/Meridian group. Here you won't have to worry whether the person next to you has a better room; they're all just alike. Watch out for the "solo rooms" sold to singles "with no supplement!" Signing up for this arrangement means that you will be sharing a toilet and bath with a stranger in another matching "solo room." Rooms based on double occupancy with half board in January low season cost FFR 1,925; same room in February high season—FFR 3,430.

Hotel de l'Aiguille Rouge (tel. 79073255) is only a two-star hotel, a notch below the Eldorador located across the skating rink, but our inspection showed it to be every bit as comfortable. Rooms here are offered in a special package with full board (drinks included), six-day lift tickets or child care for kids from three to six years. Rates per person in January low season are FFR 2,051; in February high season—FFR 3,465.

Apartments

Les Arc is oriented more toward apartment complexes resort than hotels, which is evident in the fact that there are literally thousands more apartments than hotel rooms. Apartments offer far better bargains for skiers willing to do without the amenities of hotels.

And despite the horror stories about the tiny French apartments there is plenty of room, unless you insist on fitting four people with their baggage into a studio apartment.

Again, as with the hotels, the prices given will be for the January low season and the February high season. There are two other price ranges between these two extremes.

In Arc 2000 a studio apartment for two during January low season will cost FFR 1,455 a week; the same apartment during February's high season is FFR 3,413 a week. A two-room apartment for four people during January low season will cost FFR 2,082 a week; in February high season expect to pay FFR 4,863 a week.

There are special packages that include apartment and lift pass in Arc 2000. These range from FFR 1,113 per person a week, based on two people sharing a studio apartment or four sharing a two-room apartment during January low season, to the February high-season rate of FFR 2,215 per person a week.

In Arc 1800 studio apartments cost FFR 1,809 a week during January low season; the same studio goes for FFR 4,675 during February high season. A two-room apartment for four will cost FFR 2,703 during January low season and FFR 6,856 during February high season.

NOTE:See the section on central reservations for phone contacts and addresses.

Dining

Les Arc doesn't seem to have the same passion for restaurants found in La Plagne just across the valley. Perhaps it is because more than 50 percent of the resort's guests are foreigners and these don't seem to place the same kinds of demands in terms of quality. Here the focus is on the functional—just like the architecture. When we asked locals about the restaurants the response was usually a puzzled look and a smile only after ponderous thought. Here are Les Arc's best, it seems:

Arc 1800

Le Green (tel. 79072517) in the Hotel du Golf is the best restaurant in Les Arc. Its chef is sous-chef to a Michelin two-star chef who plans the menus. The atmosphere is modern elegance and the menu can easily run to FFR 350 a person before considering wine. Come here to splurge.

Le Choucas (tel. 79074225) serves up local Savoyard specialties in two simple rooms with fake wooden beams and sparse country decor. Expect to spend between FFR 150-180 for a dinner with wine.

L'Equipe (tel. 79074176) is perhaps the most popular restaurant in Les Arc. Here heaping portions are served up under heavy rafters with a wide, picture-window view of the valley. Dinner costs between FFR 130-150, including wine.

Le Passing Shot (tel. 79074965) is the gourmet restaurant in the Les Villards section of Arc 1800. Its atmosphere is thin to nonexistent, its prices in the stratosphere without Michelin excuses. Meals can easily range between FFR 200-250.

L'Auberge Rouge (tel. 79074468) has the most character of any restaurant in Les Arc, exuding a happy spirit. It only serves light fare, such as crepes, pizzas and salads. The figure of a pirate pulling a sled with a cask of wine stands next to the stairs. Upstairs 10 red tables are tucked under the sloping roof. Crepes cost between FFR 10-25.

For pizza, try **Le J.O.** in Arc 1800 Le Charvet with its wood-fired oven. Pizza ranges from FFR 38-50. In Arc 1800 Les Villard, try the pizzeria **Gargantus**.

Arc 2000

Le St. Jacques (tel. 79073255) serves up excellent fondue and raclette, but little else can be heartily recommended.

Nightlife/après-ski

In Arc 1800 the ski instructors head to **Bar Le Gabotte** in the center of Le Charvet, as does the majority of the English-speaking crowd when the lifts shut down. The overflow congregates in **Bar le Thuria** only about 10 steps across the square.

In the Les Villard section of Arc 1800 the best après-ski is in **Bar Russel**, a very British-looking pub with dark wooden tables and bar and 40 different bottled beers. A price sampler: Heineken costs FFR 16, Whitbread is FFR 22 and Pilsner Urquel is FFR 28.

The best deal is the lounge of the Hotel Du Golf, which has live jazz before and after dinner in front of a flickering fire.

There are discos in both Arc 2000 and Arc 1800, and they all follow the French disco formula: Drinks in the FFR 90 range and opening times around midnight, with closing time about four in the morning. If you have insomnia, try **Le Fairway** in the basement of Hotel du Golf in Arc 1800. **Le Rock Hill** disco is packed with teenagers. **Le Carre Blanc** is the spot in the Arc 1800 Les Villard section.

Child care

In Les Arc children can have as much fun discovering winter sports as their parents have practicing them. All three villages—Arc 1600, 1800 and 2000—have nurseries and programs for children from one to six years of age. The nursery at Arc 1600 takes children from four months.

A special miniclub is organized by the ski school for children between the ages of four and eight to allow children time to play and learn the basics of skiing. Children who have the basics down can join a special children's ski school course that accepts kids from four to 11 years. Les Arc also has organized teenage courses for those from 14 to 18 years.

Lunch hours are from noon until 2 p.m. and can be spent with the parents or with the nursery/ski school depending on your plans.

The nursery for children one to three years for six full days costs FFR 700 during most of the season and only FFR 560 during January. Six half days, either mornings or afternoons, will cost FFR 415, or in January low season, FFR 335. Lunch for children costs FFR 275 a week.

Kindergarten for kids three to six costs FFR 685 a week for full days during normal season and only FFR 560 during January low season. Six half days, either mornings or afternoons, will cost FFR 355 during normal season and FFR 290 during January low season. Meals again cost FFR 275 a week.

The miniclub for a week costs FFR 1,120, plus FFR 240 extra if lunch is to be included.

Ski school with two two-hour lessons a day for six days will cost FFR 450. One three-hour lesson a day for six days will cost FFR 370.

Teenage classes for six days of training, with hours determined by activities chosen, will cost FFR 690.

Other activities

Three squash courts are available in Arc 1800 on the upper square of Les Villards. They are open daily from 2 p.m. to 10 p.m., Saturday from 5 p.m. to 8 p.m. Courts can be reserved for a half hour for FFR 30 a person. A package of six half-hour reservations can be purchased for FFR 150 a person. Half-hour private lessons are FFR 90 a person.

Skating rinks are located in all three Arc villages.

Hang-gliding lessons and accompanied flights can be arranged by calling 79074269 after 7 p.m.

Horseback riding is available at the La Cavale Equestrian Center at Arc 1600. Call 79077213 for more information.

Getting there

Les Arc is located directly above Bourg-St. Maurice, which during the past winter was linked to Paris by TGV speed train service.

The nearest, most convenient airport is Geneva Cointrin. The airport is connected with Les Arc by four scheduled buses each day.

By car, take the Chambery exit on the superhighway, then follow the signs to Bourg-St. Maurice.

Les Arc is linked with Bourg-St. Maurice by a funicular that runs approximately every 15 minutes from 7:40 a.m. until 6:30 p.m.

Tourist information

The tourist information offices of Les Arc are located in all three villages and in the separate sections of the villages as well. Four offices are open 24 hours a day to handle any emergency. The 24-hour offices are: Arc 1800—Les Belles Challes; Arc 1800—Les Villard, Les Arandelieres; Arc 1800—Charmettoger, l'Aiguille Grive; Arc 2000—L'Aiguille Rouge.

Central reservations are handled through Tourarc International, the management company for the resort. When making reservations, contact the Les Arc Office, 94, Boulevard Montparnasse, 75014 Paris, France; tel. 16143223610. In Britain, contact Les Arc Office, 197 B Brompton Road, London SW3 1LA; tel. (1) 5891918.

Avoriaz

Rather than just a lodge or restaurant above the cablecar, this is an entire town perched above steep rock cliffs at 5,400 feet, with a racy modern outline that the French call "integrated architecture." However described, this is a visual spectacular. Here, too, jazzy music fills the streets, and a casual, colorful atmosphere pervades. Sleighs whoosh through the streets and skiers nonchalantly model fashion at café tables.

Jean Vuarnet, the sunglass king, returned to France with a gold medal from the 1960 Olympics at Squaw Valley and persuaded a big real estate agency to invest up above. The original buildings of 1966 were joined by an expansion that today includes a cluster of 42 modern buildings made up of condos, a Club Med, two three-star hotels and 30 restaurants.

Vuarnet is still here, very busy running the tourist office and two ski shops while developing a line of clothing to go with his popular shades.

Avoriaz is well known for its **Festival of Fantastic Films**, which is held in mid-January, but it is also is gaining attention with its world professional snowboard championships, held in late February through early March. Its Childrens Village, managed by Olympic medalist Annie Famose and a staff of 120 instructors, is acclaimed for teaching youngsters ages three to 16 how to ski.

Avoriaz is at the center of Les Portes Du Soleil wheel, the link between France and Switzerland. The question becomes, Do you just go there to ski, for a meal, a drink and a look around, or do you stay? In the old days getting there meant climbing into a cablecar and then taking reindeer-drawn sled to your accommodations; today a road climbs up from Morzine, 14 kilometers and a half-hour drive away. The cable car to Les Prodains runs every 15 minutes, and that has a bus connection to Morzine. Ski runs also plunge down from Avoriaz to Les Prodains, although with light snow cover they can be treacherous.

Avoriaz can sleep 15,000 and has a great group following. Last Christmas, 5,000 Spaniards came in, although most groups are smaller, numbering in the hundreds. Maximum capacity at the Club Med is 600, the two hotels have a total of 78 rooms. Some complaints have been made about lack of space in the rooms.

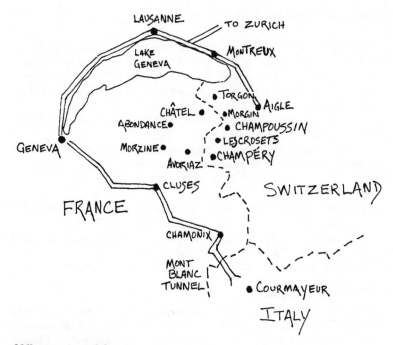

Where to ski

If you have come to really ski, Avoriaz is perhaps the best base
from which to explore the Portes du Soleil area. As well as easy
access to the Le Crosets/Champoussin sector reached over the
"Swiss wall of death," Avoriaz has easy access to Plaine Dranse
with perhaps the most enjoyable and varied skiing of the region.
The slopes directly above Avoriaz will challenge every level of skier
and the nearby section of Morzine and Les Gets offers another
full day of skiing. Any skier's plate will be overflowing for a one-
week stay here. (See also the Portes du Soleil description in the
Swiss Portes du Soleil section).

Mountain Rating

Avoriaz has some of the best beginner facilities in the Portes du
Soleil region. For experts—hold your hat. For intermediates—
you'll never have to ski the same run twice. (See Mountain rating
section in Swiss Portes du Soleil section.)

Ski school

The French Ski School office and meeting place is the Place du
Téléphérique. Lessons sign up can also be taken care of in the
Tourist Office and in the Cap-Neige building near the Fontaines
Blanches.

Group lessons: six days, from 10 a.m. to noon and from 2 p.m. to 5 p.m.—FF630 for adults (FF480 for children). One morning lesson from 10a.m. to noon—FF55 for adults (FF44 for children). One afternoon lesson from 2 p.m. to 5 p.m.—FF87 for adults (FF65 for children).

Private lessons: one hour—FF125; one day (7 hours)—FF990; half-day (3-1/2 hours)—FF505.

Monoski, surf and competition lessons cost FF125.

Ski passes are not included in the lesson prices.

Lift tickets

A ski pass for the entire Portes du Soleil costs: one day—FF135; three days—FF362; six days—FF680;13 days—FF1,130.

The pass for only the Avoriaz section of the Portes du Soleil costs: one day—FF105; two days—FF190.

Children under 12 receive about a 20 percent discount.

Accommodations

Avoriaz is primarily a resort of condos. The two hotels, with a total of 78 rooms between them, do not take groups. High season, when rooms are toughest to get and prices are highest, is Christmas, Easter, February and during the Fantastic Film Festival week in January. The ski season generally runs from December to mid-April.

Hotel les Dromonts (74110 Avoriaz; tel. 50740811) has 38 rooms. Rate with breakfast—FF385 to FF480; half pension, from FF550 to FF645; full pension, from FF665 to FF760. Large rooms, with breakfast, cost FF435 to FF545; half pension from FF600 to FF710; full pension, from FF715 to FF825.

Hotel les Hauts-Forts (74110 Avoriaz, tel. 50740911) has 40 rooms. Rate for a room facing north with breakfast, FF402 to FF506; half pension from FF586 to FF690; during film festival with half pension, FF874. For a room facing south with breakfast, from FF448 to FF563; half pension from FF632 to FF747; during film festival with half pension, FF937.

Apartments

This is what Avoriaz is all about. The tourist board will send you a list of agencies who will make reservations for you on request. Studios are one large room, while the phrase *deux pieces* means two rooms or one bedroom with a living room that can sleep another two people; *trois pieces* is three rooms, usually two bedrooms plus a living room.

Sample prices (one week) with the agency to contact:

Avoriaz Location (74110 Avoriaz; tel. 50740453), studio for four, FF1,900 to FF4,350; two-room for five, from FF2,300 to FF5,450.

Immobiliere Des Hauts-Forts (74110 Avoriaz; tel. 50741608), studio for four, from FF1,500 to FF4,200; two-room for five, from FF750 to FF5,350.

Pierre et Vacances (54, Avenue Marceau, 75008 Paris; tel. (1) 47233222), studio for four, from FF1,512 to FF4,130; two-room for four to five, from FF1,680 to FF4,550.

Maeva (30, Rue D'Orleans, 92200 Neuilly-Sur-Seine; tel. (1) 47451721), studio for four, from FF1,960 to FF5,180; two-room for four to five, from FF2,100 to FF5,320.

To contact the Office of Tourism in Haute-Savoie, write 74110 Avoriaz; or call 50740211. You can also telex the office at 385578.

Child care

Avoriaz child care services not only take care of children, but teach them how to ski as well. Located in the center of Avoriaz, the Childrens Village is open from 9 a.m. until 5:30 p.m., and accepts youngsters between the ages of three and 16. Tel. 50740446. Children who are not taking lessons can play in the snow playground. Half day (without lunch)—FF80; full day—FF184 (FF158 without lunch); six days—FF910 (FF765 without lunch).

Dining

Next to Courcheval, Avoriaz has perhaps the best collection of gourmet retaurants of any French resort. The four-star restaurant in **Hotel Dromonts** charges about FF350 for a meal; **La Grignotte**, at the bottom of the cablecar ranges between FF100 and FF120; **Crepy** runs from FF100 to FF150. Petit Vatel specializes in trout; **Bistrots** prepares mountain specialties that with a bottle of wine will cost FF150. Also recommended are **Marmottes, L'Eau Vive and Braize.**

On the Swiss side, try **Telecabine des Mossettes** restaurant in Les Closets, or try fondue **Chez Cocoz** at Planachaus above Champéry.

Late at night, head for **Mama's Pizza** or **Lapon** for cold fare.

Nightlife

Avoriaz has plenty of action, but as at all French resorts, the discos—in this case, **The Manhattan** and **Le Roc-Club**—begin filling up after midnight.

Other activities

Para-sailing; ultra-lights; squash courts; fitness center with exercise machines, weights, sauna and jacuzzis; two cinemas.

The tourist office also publishes a regular schedule of movies.

Getting there

The nearest airport is in Geneva. From the airport a special bus runs each Saturday and Sunday, leaving at 10:30 a.m. and arriving in Avoriaz at 12:50 p.m. The return trip leaves Avoriaz at 1:30 p.m. and arrives at the airport at 4:20 p.m.

Avoriaz can be reached by a train/bus combination. The train from Paris arrives at noon, then a bus makes the one-hour-and-fifteen-minute climb to the resort.

If you drive, take the Autopiste from Geneva to Mont Blanc and leave at the exit marked Morzine/Avoriaz. It is only 80 kilometers from Geneva.

Unfortunately, there is no free parking at the resort. Open-air parking costs FF150 for a week; covered parking for a week, FF400. Transfers, which are available 24 hours a day from the parking lots in the town center, cost FF38-FF60 for three to four people with luggage.

Parking in the lot at the bottom of the cablecar is free. Avoriaz is a 14-kilometer, or half-hour, drive from Morzine. The cablecar leaves every 15 minutes beginning at 7 a.m. until 9 p.m.; on Friday and Saturday it closes at until 1 a.m. Those with lift passes ride free from 9 a.m. until 5 p.m.; otherwise the charge is FF23.

Tourist Information

L'Office du tourisme d'Avoriaz, Place Centrale, 74110 Avoriaz-Morzine; tel. 50740211; telex: 385578.

Chamonix

Chamonix is the most famous ski town in France. It breaks every rule for a resort. None of the trails drop directly into town; instead, the ski areas are spread along a valley almost 10 miles long. None are interconnected. What's more, lift lines are long, as it sometimes takes skiers more than an hour to reach the summit of an area from the base station; shuttle buses are crowded and erratic; and the weather can change in a matter of hours from sunshine to a stormy whiteout. But what Chamonix does offer is perhaps the world's best expert and advanced skiing on spectacular mountains rising more than 12,500 feet above the town tucked deep in the valley. This combination of the world's best expert skiing and one of the world's most picturesque settings creates an experience that is hard to beat.

Chamonix itself is a large town with a strong alpine flair. You won't find any of the space-age structures that set the tone for so many of France's other resorts. Here, small-town coziness is the rule, with plenty of restaurants, narrow streets for shopping and good hotels. Such an atmosphere can make one forget about the logistics of getting to the slopes. But, remember, to fully enjoy Chamonix, you'll need a car to get to its slopes that are spread out for miles along the valley floor in the shadow of 15,767-foot-high Mont Blanc.

In Chamonix you can ski hard all day long, then sit at a café in a small square and sip a kir, wine or beer. The bars are crowded with an international group, and you are surrounded with other real skiers who are here not for the ritz and the glitz but for the challenge and the exhilaration of testing oneself against Europe's toughest slopes.

For years many critics charged Chamonix with living off its past and not improving the lifts or accommodations. Those critics will be happy to hear that Chamonix is no longer standing still. Recently, improvements have been made, and more are planned for the coming year. The lift capacity for the intermediate slopes in the popular Argentière sector has been doubled and there is now virtually no waiting, but the wait to ascend to the Grands Montets still can take an hour on sunny days. There are plans to increase the Grands Montets cablecar capacity for the 1990 season to alleviate the long wait. The Brevant section and the Flégère section will probably be linked next year if all ecological concerns are satisfied. That will create the first network of any future Chamonix ski areas. Some hotels in town currently provide private shuttles for their guests, a service that eliminates the shuttle bus hassles and makes starting out in the morning and returning much more pleasant.

Where to ski

Let's move on to the reasons Chamonix is fabulous for skiing. From the slopes of Les Houches to Chamonix and on to Argentière and finally La Tour, a string of lifts takes skiers up both sides of the valley. On the Mont Blanc side, you ascend above outcroppings and slopes of this magnificent peak, while on the opposite side you enjoy the Mont Blanc panorama as the lifts take you to outstanding runs.

There are six different ski areas. The first good one you'll encounter entering the valley is Les Houches. This is intermediate-level country, with a cablecar that takes you to Le Prarion at 6,453 feet. Les Houches links with the St. Gervais, another of the resorts served by the Mont Blanc ski pass.

The two-mile-long, blue-rated trail from Col de Voza below Le Prarion is ideal for a warmup. Our favorite trail in Les Houches is the shorter (about 1.5 miles long) red trail descending from the Bellevue summit (5,943 feet). You'll need advanced intermediate skills in order to get down comfortably.

In Chamonix, most skiers choose the challenges of Le Brévent at 8,288 feet. The cablecar rises from the town to Planpraz where the skiing really begins. The second section of the cablecar takes expert skiers and hearty intermediates to the top of Le Brévent, and a chairlift carries those of less than expert and advanced levels to the Les Vioz area. Try the black run from the back of Le Brévent in the company of another experienced skier. If after the first few hundred feet you're not confident of your turns, you can branch to the left and take an advanced intermediate trail down instead of the expert slope.

Intermediate skiers may prefer the midstation slopes at Planpraz, especially the chairlifts that reach the 6,560-foot level. In addition, work your way to the right and take the chair up to the Col Cornu's 7,488-foot-high level for a good intermediate run and off-trail possibilities.

Ten minutes away by car is Les Praz, ground station for the cablecar to the La Flégère midstation. From here, a gondola takes you to L'Index at 7,822 feet, where the skiing is outstanding for intermediates. There are off-trail challenges to the right and the left of the upper gondola.

The entire intermediate run from L'Index to Les Praz ground station will take 30 minutes, a challenging, advanced intermediate romp. However, during high season expect to wait as long as 45 minutes at the bottom in order to get back onto the cablecar. You'll probably want to stay on the upper mountain unless you're moving to another slope or making the last run of the day.

For our money, the best skiing in the valley is reached by driving 10 minutes up the valley from Les Grande Montets to Argentière. If you look across the valley from l'Index, the rocky finger of Aiguille du Dru juts straight up to the sky. Below it, to the left is Les Grande Montets, the 10,604-foot-high end station for the two-section cablecar from the valley.

The wait at the cablecar base station at Argentière should not be more than a half hour, even in high season. Then take the second stage of the cablecar up to Les Grands Montets. You'll have to pay an additional FFR 19 to take the second cablecar—it is not included on the Mont Blanc pass. The skiing is definitely worth the extra cost.

From the midstation there are only three main lifts. But these lifts open up excellent skiing. As one instructor observes, "Why ride lifts when you can ski?" Here, you can really ski. Don't plan on sitting at a café sipping hot chocolate or wine because none exists. A gondola and a chairlift offer excellent intermediate terrain and plenty of off-trail skiing for budding experts.

Advanced and expert skiers head up the second stage of the cablecar. At the top of Les Grande Montets take time to ascend the viewing platform from which you can see one of the most spectacular views in the Alps. When you are ready to ski you have two basic choices—both offer 4,200 feet of vertical and skiing as good as it gets. This part of the mountains has never seen a grooming machine. You can drop down a black trail across the Argentière glacier to Croix de Lognan, or drop around the other side of Les Grande Montets and ski under the cablecar. There are wide-open, off-trail opportunities for any skier willing to go for it. In fact, the "trails" really only offer a general direction to the midstation. The red-rated trail branches off from the glacier route and then drops beneath the cablecar to the midstation. It is often almost as much of a challenge as the expert-rated runs.

At La Tour there is a system comprised of one gondola and five other lifts at the valley's end, but after skiing Brévent and Les Grande Montets it will probably not interest you.

The most talked-about adventure—not necessarily the most challenging in terms of simple skiing—in Chamonix is the 13-mile-long glacier run from the Aiguille du Midi (12,601 feet) back into

Chamonix (m3,363 feet). The scenery is magnificent, and the memory of the run down the Vallée Blanche and over the Mer de Glace will remain forever.

The Vallée Blanche expedition could be more appropriately characterized as ski mountaineering rather than simple skiing. Go prepared for changing weather and changing terrain. The weather in town may be balmy, but at the top of the Aiguille du Midi the wind may be howling and visibility may be zero. Be ready for freezing, windy weather—goggles or mountaineering glasses, good gloves, a warm jacket with a hood if possible and your ski hat.

You start by climbing—roped to your guide and with your skis strapped together—down a narrow windy ridge. At the end of the ridge, you break the tether with the guide and, sheltered from the wind, step into your skis. For this trip ski straps are recommended because snow brakes often don't work on ice. Groups are separated from one another by several hundred meters. You may be skiing on trails for a time, then turn off for powder if your guide finds it. Sometimes the the trail simply ends, which means climbing over rocks with your skis over your shoulder or balancing over a snowbridge spanning a deep crevasse while roped together with your guide.

The mountains surrounding you are all famous in the annals of climbing. The Vallée Blanche is actually first part of the glacier; as it begins to break up and crevasses block the route, skiers sideslip down narrow chutes in a region called the Seracs. At the end of the Seracs and after almost two hours on skis, there is often a stop at the Refuge du Requin for a warm drink. From the refuge the run enters a wide-open area called the "Salle a Manger" or dining room.

The needlelike Aiguille de Dru with Europe's longest climbing vertical towers above the glacier. From this point the Mer de Glace begins its drop into the valley. Above and to the left the Hotel Montenvers stately stands guard over the glacier, and below the hotel workers dig a tunnel into the ice, which will be visited by hundreds of thousands of people during the coming summer. In late spring your guide may take you down to see the work in progress. As the glacier ends another refuge, Les Mottets, offers snacks and drinks. Then it's back into the town, the entire trip having taken about four hours.

The Vallée Blanche run is usually not open until February. Although guides are not required, it is strongly suggested that you have one. For if the clouds close in, the guides bring you down by compass. You're also assured of having someone to belay you when crossing over crevasses and during the initial climb down the ridge through howling winds. As an extra precaution each participant receives a beeper. Guides cost about FFR 890 for one to four persons. Add FFR 75 for each additional person. If traveling alone check in with the guides office in town to register for a small group.

What level of skier can handle the Vallée Blanche? A solid intermedite who can sideslip easily, make quick turns and is comfortable on skis can make the trip. You do need to be in good enough physical condition to tour for more than four hours at altitudes ranging from 12,000 to 3,000 feet.

An additional opportunity offered in Chamonix is the chance to travel through the Mont Blanc tunnel into Courmayeur, Italy, on the opposite side of the massif, where skiing is very good. There's often good weather here when Chamonix is clouded over. The toll charge is about 30,000 lire.

Mountain rating

Beginning skiers should look elsewhere for lots of easy slopes. This is not the most comfortable place to learn to ski, although thousands do each year.

Intermediates choose Chamonix year after year as an ideal area to increase their skills on challenging terrain.

Experts need never worry that there may not be a bigger challenge over the mountain. Because in Chamonix there always is.

Chamonix can best be enjoyed by skiers of all levels with a guide to take them to the best skiing for their level. Chamonix Ski Fun Tours has organized weekly packages that include a guide for small groups.

Ski school

Chamonix hosted the first Winter Olympic Games in 1924, and the French Ski School based its instruction manual on lessons given on these slopes. A total of 300 instructors offer courses in Chamonix (tel. 50532257) and Argentière (tel. 50540012).

Private lessons (one or two people) cost FFR 130 an hour. A day of private instruction runs approximately FFR 1,100 in high season and FFR 950 in low season.

Group lessons for a half day (two hours) cost FFR 58. A six-day course, consisting of daily morning and afternoon instruction (four hours a day), is FFR 475.

Out-of-bounds ski guides for groups of up to five skiers can be hired for FFR 940 (full day) or FFR 540 (half day).

Lift tickets

The Mont Blanc ski pass is valid for the entire Chamonix valley and Argentière, plus Megève, St. Gervais, Combloux, Cordon, Praz-sur-Arly, Passy, St. Nicolas de Véroce, Les Houches and Vallorcine, for a total of 300 miles of trails served by 180 lifts. There is one very notable exception—the upper cablecar to Les Grande Montets costs an additional FFR 19 for each trip.

Free ski shuttle bus services in the areas where they are provided are included, as well as a day of skiing in Courmayeur, Italy, with the purchase of a six- to 13-day pass. Children's rates (four to 12 years) are in noted in parentheses. These are winter 1990 prices.

two consecutive days	FFR 275 (225)
three consecutive days	FFR 400 (325)
six consecutive days	FFR 730 (600)
thirteen consecutive days	FFR 1,310 (1,080)

Day tickets are also available for the separate areas in the valley. For example, Les Houches lift tickets cost FFR 75 for a half day, FFR 99 for one day and FFR 475 a week. Day tickets at Brévent will cost FFR 94 a day and FFR 70 for a half day. The lifts at Argentière (excluding the upper part of Les Grande Montets cablecar) cost FFR 140 for a full day; FFR 130 from 11 a.m.; FFR 110 from 1 p.m. to closing time. A ride up the spectacular Aiguille du Midi cablecar will cost FFR 114 round trip, or FFR 86 if you're planning on skiing back down.

Accommodations

The Chamonix reservation service (which also has listings for Argentière and Les Houches) is provided by the tourist office, which you can contact at place de L'Eglise; tel. 50530024. Nearly 90 hotels provide a range of accommodation from luxury suites to dormitory-like rooms. Because of the many restaurants and snack bars, don't hesitate to book a hotel without a half-pension plan.

Mont Blanc (tel. 50530756) This is an aging, grand old hotel that is slowly being renovated by its owners. Most of the updated rooms are being recreated as suites, which offer roomy, upscale accommodations not found elsewhere in the town. The restaurant is considered to be one of the best in the region. High-season room rates, based on double occupancy with breakfast, are between FFR 485 and FFR 410; during low season, FFR 343-313. Half-board rates during high season are FFR 605-530; during low season, FFR 463-423.

Auberge du Bois-Prin (tel. 50533351) A Relais and Chateau Hotel, this is best in town in terms of quietness and coziness, but it is located a long walk uphill from the center of town. Rooms are decorated in heavy wood and fixtures are brass and gold. The views of Mont Blanc from most rooms are spectacular, with Chamonix town spread out below. A double room with breakfast during high season will run FFR 380 per person, during low season— FFR 340. With full pension during high season, add FFR 315; during low season, add FFR 295.

Le Prieuré (tel. 50532072) This is an excellent functional hotel with some alpine touches. It is large, short on quaintness but long on convenience. It also has a private shuttle to the ski areas, as well as covered parking should you be driving. The rates (double occupancy) with half board during high season are FFR 399-363; during low season—FFF 330-300.

Alpina (tel. 50534777) Thoroughly modern Alpina makes no attempt at alpine or regional decor. It could just as easily be a high-rise hotel next to Denver's Stapleton International Airport, but the views from the rooms of Mont Blanc are memorable. And its location in the center of town can't be beat. The rooms are among the largest in town. Rates per person based on double occupancy with half-board during high season—FFR 524-411; during low season—FFR 402-337.

Sapinière Montana (tel. 50530763) This hotel is located only a five-minute walk from the center of town. A shuttle bus takes skiers to the different ski areas. The rooms are basic and slightly aging. The rate (double occupancy) with half-board during high season—FFR 310; during low season—FFR 270.

Les Alpes (tel. 50530727) Another old hotel that is very much as it was in the 1960s. Rooms are spacious and the location is excellent. Rates per person for double occupancy (bed and breakfast only) during high season—FFR 234-214; during low season— FFR 189-169.

de la Croix Blanche (tel. 50530011) Centrally located, this aging property has decades-old interiors that are nonetheless well maintained and pleasant. Rates per person based on double occupancy (bed and breakfast only) during high season—FFR 234-214; during low season—FFR 189-169.

La Vallée Blanche (tel. 50530450) Just purchased by Patricia Byrne, a delightful Irish lady with big renovation plans, this small, two-star hotel is next to the river running through town and only steps from the center. The rooms feature beautiful, locally made and painted alpine furniture. Breakfasts are your basic Irish feast. Rates based on double occupancy (bed and breakfast only) during high season—FFR 195; during low season—FFR 145.

Dining

Chamonix's excellence in dining is augmented by the fact that because it's a real town and not a resort, prices are generally very reasonable. Still, it does have its share of excellent, top-quality restaurants.

Albert Ist et Milan (tel. 50530509) is Chamonix's best, where the chef mixes nouvelle cuisine with local mountain cooking. The giant dining room features expansive views of Mont Blanc. The cooking is praised equally by France's top critics and locals, who are most pleased by the size of the portions. The little menu is an exceptional value for FFR 150, with appetizer, main course, cheese and desert. If ordering a la carte, expect to pay about FFR 350.

Le Matafan (tel. 50530564) located in the Mont Blanc Hotel is laid out surrounding a large fireplace. The chef, Jean-Michel Morand, successfully blends tradition with menues of the day. Try the foie gras and the veal with figs. The wine cellar is one of the best in the region, with more than 14,000 bottles ranging in price from FFR 80 to FFR 4,400. The normal gourmet dinner menu is FFR 320, and a Savoyard dinner menu is FFR 200.

Auberge du Bois-Prin (tel. 50533351) is an intimate restaurant in an old home. Dinner is served by waitresses in local costume. The restaurant is noted for taking the normal and making it special. The menu ranges between FFR 150 and FFR 200, with a gourmet menu running about FFR 320.

Eden Restaurant (tel. 50530640) in the hotel of the same name is a bit out of the center of Chamonix in the subburb of La Praz. The views of Mont Blanc and the Drus are spectacular. Specialties are fish, including trout almondine and lobster au gratin. The menu here ranges from FFR 130 to FFR 300.

La Cabana (tel. 50532327) located next to the golf course, a few minutes' drive outside town, is a rustic chalet. The accent is regional, with plenty of meat and potatoes. Expect to pay about FFR 250 for a full dinner.

Le Bartavel (tel. 50532651), tucked in a small pedestrian side street off Rue du Paccard, serves up excellent food for modest prices. The restaurant has a quiet, traditional atmosphere. Fixed-price meals cost FFR 75 for lunch and FFR 120 for dinner.

Atmosphere (tel. 50559797) is a very elegant restaurant decorated in subdued tones. Try to get a table in the sunroom overlooking the river for a most romantic spot. The evening menu will cost FFR 130 without wine.

Le National (tel.50530223) is a very reasonable establishment serving dinners for less than FFR 100. Mountain decor with heavy stone walls, wood beams and painted, stuccoed arches.

Calèche (tel. 50559468) is an elegant regional restaurant with the traditional mountain wood on the walls, tastefully mixed with flowered fabrics and stuffed chairs. The restaurant serves up everything from fondue and raclette to full dinners. A very reasonable FFR 99 menu offers six choices of appetizer, main course and desert.

La Tartiffle is a tiny place on the Rue des Moulins with a bistro atmosphere and excellent food. Dinner's available for less than FFR 100, but there is also a gourmet side to the restaurant with the top-quality, fixed-price menu ranging upwards from FFR 190.

Chaudron (tel. 50534034), also located on Rue des Moulin, is very rustic. A heavy stone wall lines the small restaurant with wooden beams, and farm tools and a giant wagon wheel add a country flavor. Specialties are regional dishes, grilled meats and brochette. Fixed-price menu for dinner will run FFR 100.

Tortachu is the smallest and least expensive of the Rue des Moulin restaurants. The menu is simple, with only five specialties served each day, along with normal low-priced fare, such as spaghetti, crepes and omelettes. This is a good place to eat inexpensively with a bit of atmosphere. Expect to pay between FFR 75 and FFR 90.

L'M is a brasserie serving low-fare crepes, galletes and meals right in the middle of town. In the spring a large terrace opens, which makes snacking and nursing a long drink most enjoyable. Most selections with a drink will range between FFR 50 and FFR 75.

Grillandin, just off Rue Joseph Vallon, is the self-service cafeteria in town. The food is quite good and very reasonable. Anyone can enjoy a filling meal here for FFR 50.

Apartments

Better known as a hotel town, Chamonix does have some furnished chalets and apartments that are offered through several area agencies. Prices for a studio with sleeping arrangements for two to four—FFR 2610 during high season; FFR 1,390 during low season.

A two-room apartment housing four to five people will cost FFR 4,120 during high season; FFR 1,785 in low season. The tourist office offers a special brochure on how to rent. (*See address below*).

Nightlife/après-ski

The immediate après-ski usually consists of having drinks in one of the bars in the center of town. Try the **Chamouny, the Brasserie de Rond Point** and the **Irish Coffee**. In spring the outdoor tables fill up with skiers basking in the sun.

This is home to one of France's major casinos. Nightlife devotees have plenty of opportunity here besides gambling. There are seven discos, several nightclubs and several dozen hotel bars for the après-ski crowd. The **Blue Note Jazz Club** is excellent, with live acts throughout the winter season. **Le Pele** disco is large, loud and packed with teenagers. The **Scuderia** in the center of town is the best bet for those looking to get some dancing in after long days on the slopes. One of the main meeting spots for English-speakers is the **Choucas Video Bar**, which is normally packed, dark and smoky.

Child care

Argentière (tel. 50540476) offers a ski nursery for children two and older. Costs are FFR 105 for a half day; FFR 875 for six consecutive days, plus an additional FFR 200 for six days of lunch.

The Chamonix school (tel. 50531224) will take children from 18 months to six years. A half day for children costs FFR 76, and a full day costs FFR 99. Meals are not included.

The "Panda Club" in Chamonix (tel. 50558612) takes children from 18 months to 14 years. A full day of skiing and playing costs FFR 175, plus FFR 35 for lunch.

Child-care services are available at the larger hotels, and babysitting services are available for approximately FFR 65 (half day) or FFR 110 (full day). For more information on the services, contact the tourist office.

A kindergarten in Chamonix, "Maison Pour Tous" (tel. 5053012024), on Place du Mont Blanc, takes children between 18 months and six years. It is open from 8:15 a.m. to 6:15 p.m. Monday through Friday. Rates: full day, FFR 100; half day, FFR 75; one hour, FFR 30.

The "Panda Club" has kindergarten with ski instruction in both downtown Chamonix and in Argentière at the cablecar station (tel. 50540476). In Chamonix the "Panda Club" is on Clos du Savoy (tel. 50558612). Children between three months and 12 years are admitted to the downtown center, and from 18 months to 15 years at the Argentière cablecar station. These child care centers have games, crafts, ski lessons with videos and outdoor snow games. Rates: Infants between three and 18 months are accepted by the hour for FFR 35; half day—FFR 120; full day—FFR 230; six half days—FFR 600; six full days—FFR 1,150. Add FFR 35 a day for lunch. Older children up to 15 years can receive care and supervision for a FFR 105 for a half day; FFR 175 for a full day; FFR 525 for six half days; and FFR 875 for six full days. Add FFR 35 a day for lunch.

Getting there

Nearly everyone arrives via the autoroute or by train from Geneva. However, Chamonix—with Courmayeur on the other side of Mont Blanc—is ideal for visitors who have skied in Italy and who want to work their way up through Switzerland and France.

The TGV leaves Paris at around 8 a.m. and arrives in Sallaches at about 1 p.m. There is also a special train/bus combination, with the train departing from Paris a little after 7 a.m., with a change to bus in Annecy and arrival in Chamonix before 1 p.m.

Taxi from the Geneva airport will cost around FFR 600, and a bus from the airport to the resort costs around FFR 150.

Other activities

More than any other area you may visit, consider taking an aerial tour here. The Mont Blanc massif and the stunning series of surrounding peaks are best seen from the air. Choose from among four different trips ranging from FFR 100 to FFR 400 per person. Call Air Mont Blanc at 50581331.

The casino has long been a center of action, while the swimming center has three pools, all heated.

Tourist information

Tourist Office, place de l'Eglise, F-74400 Chamonix; tel. 50530024; telex 385022 OFITOUR CHAMX.
Office du Tourisme, F-74310 Les Houches; tel. 50555062.

La Clusaz

This village in the Haute Savoie of the northern French Alps had just over 1,000 non-skiing inhabitants back in the 16th century, but it counts some 1,700 downhillers among its visitors today. Although the first ski lift wa built here in 1935, La Clusaz was a village long before it became a ski destination, and it has kept its lived-in, workaday atmosphere.

Long known for its Reblochon cheese and tartiflette—potatoes with melted cheese (reblochon) on top—Clusaz has also become known for its access to five massifs connected by 56 lifts, providing 130 kilometers of prepared slopes.

The compactness of the village, its wraparound views of ski slopes, forests and peaks, its old, winding side streets and large snow play area flanked by restaurants and outdoor tables, make La Clusaz a winner for skiers who like to get away from cars and traffic.

Socializers tend to continue up the road to Megève. This is a nice family area, and the traditional French Alpine atmosphere makes it hard to believe Geneva is only a 35-minute drive away. On weekends, this is much easier to believe as city-dwellers stream in.

Where to ski

Beneath Massif de Manigod, just a tram ride above La Clusaz, intermediate and beginner territory allows for wide-open cruising. Here Beauregard Mountain rises to 5,070 feet. Moving across to Massif de L'Etale, the runs become both steeper and longer. Massif de L'Aiguille has excellent advanced terrain and a marvelous long plunge through Combe du Fernuy for strong skiers. Farther across on Massif de Balme, good bump skiing and usually the best snow in the area are found.

Mountain rating

Beginners and intermediates are going to have a swell time here. Experts who know the area, or who ski with guides, will find some toothy hideaways, but the mountain is more of a mild, far-flung adventure with patches of difficulty than an intense surprise.

Ski school

The school (tel. 50024083) is centrally located in the village and beneath the tram. **Private lessons:** A one-hour lesson for between one and three people costs FF126; for four to five people, FF157. A guide or instructor for the full day costs FF970; for 4-1/2 hours, FF635; for 3-1/2 hours, FF510.

Group lessons are available. One session for adults costs FF77; for children under 12 years, FF55. One week of morning or afternoon sessions costs FF346 for adults and FF242 for children; for a week of full-day sessions, FF578 for adults and FF452 for children.

Lift tickets

A full-day ski ticket costs FF11-FF110 for an adult; half-day after 11 a.m., FF95 to FF100; half-day after 12:30 p.m., FF84 to FF90.

For children under 13 and seniors over 60, tickets cost FF80 to FF85 for a full day, FF75 for half a day.

Four-day passes are available for between FF400 and FF370 for adults; seniors and children pay FF300-FF320.

For seven-day passes, adults pay FF590-FF630; seniors and children, FF480-FF520.

Accommodations

La Clusaz has five three-star hotels and 13 two-star lodgings. For information or reservations, contact La Clusaz Tour, tel. 50024078; telex 385125. For a brochure, write Maison du Tourisme, Place de L'Eglise, France 74220, La Clusaz.

Of the three-stars, the modern and well-designed Vitahotel, which has excellent views and is nearby to just about everything in town, has to be among the best. Half-pension rates run between FF295 and FF465 per person; with full pension it's FF375 to FF550 per person.

The two-star **Gai Soleil** runs FF211 to FF275 per person with half pension; FF238 to FF300 with full pension.

Hotels without pension run between FF160 and FF415 a night for two people in a room.

Apartments

La Clusaz has 1,250 chalets and apartments. Contact La Clusaz Tour (tel. 50024078; telex 385125) for information or reservations.

For groups of two to four people, you can expect to pay between FF1,210 and FF1,820 a week in January, between FF2,450 and

FF3,940 in February and between FF1,500 and FF3,000 in March or April.

For four to six people, rates run between FF1,560 and FF2,480 in January, FF3,690 to FF5,380 in February and FF2,030 to FF3,700 in March or April.

For six to eight people, you'll pay FF1,940 to FF3,465 in January, FF4,370 to FF6,250 in February and FF2,760 to FF4,370 in March or April.

Dining

The village has about 40 restaurants, but **La Vieux Chalet**, located about a kilometer from the center of town, is the best. It offers classic French and nouvelle cuisine.

Second best is **Le Foly**, which specializes in Savoie regional cooking.

Plan to eat inexpensively but well by having your big meal at lunch. At this time of the day many restaurants offer a daily special for about FF40. For a lunch menu with appetizer, soup or salad, entrée, cheese or desert, the price typically falls between FF50 and FF70. The entree may be ham, veal, steak or chicken.

Nightlife

Two attractive bars are **Montmarte,** which has pool, darts and videos, and **Le Pressoir**, which offers a big selection of beers, videos and a rugged atmosphere. Le Pressoir is popular with British skiers and locals.

An ice skating rink at the bottom of the ski area stays open until 11:30 p.m. Cost is FF16 for admission and FF10 for skate rental. Curling is offered at the rink, and there are organized ice hockey, curling and skating competitions. For information, call 50024845.

Even if you don't dance and hate discos, plan to visit **L'Ecluse,** a glass-bottomed disco that shows off the town's river flowing beneath it. A wide picture window also frames the frothy water. A FF70 admission charge includes one drink.

Le Birdy is a disco and piano bar where French songs are sung and dancing is done within close quarters. Admission is FF70, except Mondays when tourists are admitted free.

The cinema shows recent films, albeit dubbed in French.

Child care

Le Club Des Mouflets, located at the ski resort above the tourist office, takes children between 8 months and 4-1/2 years. Its rooms are adapted to the ages of the children. Kids are kept entertained by numerous indoor activities, including musical games, collage-making and crafts.

Le Club des Champions, in the ski resort center, accepts children between the ages of 3-1/2 and six years who can ski. One-hour ski lessons are given to children 3-1/2 years to four years old; 2-1/2-hour lessons are given to children five and above. There are other outdoor activities, as well, such as snow games, sledding and so on, plus indoor activities.

Rates for both clubs are as follows: half day, FF52; full day FF84; six half days, FF287; six full days, FF477. A lunchtime meal is included for an extra FF42 a day.

Getting there

From the Geneva airport, a daytime taxi ride costs FF400, FF500 at night. The bus to Annecy, with a change for Geneva, costs FF30.

The train from Paris TGV to Annecy, which takes 3-1/2 hours, costs about FF500. From there, a bus or taxi must be taken to La Clusaz. A taxi from Annecy costs about FF200.

Other activities

Three open-air swimming pools are open March 18-April 16. There's tennis in Thrones, about 10 kilometers away. Dance and gymnastics, two fitness centers, hang-gliding, ski parascending, all-terrain vehicle circuit on the road of Les Laquais, 1-1/2 kilometers away. Also, snowshoe walks, snowmobiling and horse-drawn cart drives.

Tourist information

Maison du Tourisme, Place de L'Eglise, 74220 La Clusaz; tel. 50026092; telex 385125. ort, a daytime taxi ride costs FF400, FF500 at niiht

Flaine

Flaine is an all-or-nothing proposition: Either you take to this "planned" concrete-and-steel French resort in the Haute Savoie region or you search deeper into the Alps for quaint chalets and sleighs to form the backdrop to your downhill adventures. You may dislike Flaine's soul, but its skiing, which is overwhelmingly intermediate, is bountiful and good.

Flaine was created on an empty mountain site a generation ago, another of the now-familiar "new" French high-rise resorts. The central complex, at 1,580 meters (5,182 feet), is linked to lifts above Samoens, Morillon and Les Carroz to form a ski circus of more than one hundred trails and a total length of 160 miles of downhill adventure. Snow is practically guaranteed from early December until April.

Where to ski

Head first to the 2,480-meter (8,134-foot) Les Grandes Platieres, which overlooks a treeless, snow-covered landscape dotted with lift stanchions.

For a quick reading of your ski skills, take the black-rated run from Platieres. Descending beneath the cablecar route, the run has been dubbed Black Diamond (*Diamant Noir*); you'll either enjoy it tremendously or hastily make your way over to the red-rated runs by the Chalet de Sales chairlift.

A favorite run lies on the other side of Platieres at Tete des Lindars (2,561 meters—8,406 feet), where there's a delightful intermediate trail all the way through the trees to Flaine.

We also liked the powder skiing down to the lift at Gers. Les Carroz, Morillon and the valley town, Samoens, are Flaine's supporting cast, but their attraction for thousands of skiers each year lies in their more traditional Alpine accommodation.

Of the runs above these towns we liked the blue-rated trail from Cupoire summit (1,880 meters—6,166 feet) to the bottom of the chair near the parking lot in Morillon. With easy turns, a few moguls and trees for orientation, it's a fine cruise. The runs on this side are almost invariably of the intermediate level. One exception to try is the black trail from Plateau des Saix summit to the Vercland lift station.

Mountain rating

Beginners will like Flaine because of its training slopes and the quality of the ski instruction.

Intermediate skiers are in the majority here and the slopes are laid out with that in mind. Les Grand Platieres is practically an intermediate's mountain, offering at least 15 different red-rated trail variations.

Expert skiers will find plenty of challenges, particularly if they enjoy off-trail skiing, which is permitted in most areas of Flaine.

Ski school

Flaine excels in ski instruction. There are two schools here: the French Ski School (*Ecole du Ski Français*, tel. 50908100) and the International Ski School (*Ski Ecole International*, tel. 50907441). Each has about 50 instructors.

Private lessons can be arranged for up to four people at one time. two hours will cost FFR 240 and a full day costs FFR 990.

Group lessons are a good bargain when class size is limited. The ESF guarantees a limit of not more than 10 people per group.

Group lesson prices for six half days of instruction are FFR 340 for adults and FFR 250 for children.

An extended ski school with four hours a day for 11 lessons costs FFR 480 for adults and FFR 340 for children.

Ski school prices are reduced during so-called "first-ski" times—periods outside the school holiday breaks when all facilities are jammed.

Prepared cross-country trails in the area total 20 miles and instruction is offered through the ski schools.

Cross-country lessons will cost for a full day—FFR 60 (adults) and FFR 55 (children); five days are FFR 285 (adults) and FFR 235 (children); and six days cost FFR 340 (adults) and FFR 250 (children).

Lift tickets

Flaine (includes 31 lifts) Children get approximately a 20 percent discount.

half day	FFR 80
one day	FFR 105
five days	FFR 455
six days	FFR 525
14 days	FFR 1050

Accommodations

Flaine primarily offers apartment accommodations, although you can choose from the following hotels near the Forum square. Hotel rates are generally: two-star hotels FFR 1,540-2,625 for full pension and FFR 910-1,855 for half pension per person based on double occupancy; three-star hotels are FFR 2,240-3,360 for full pension.

Le Totem (tel. 50908064)

Les Gradins Gris (tel. 50908110)

Les Lindars (tel. 50908166) This, like Le Totem and Les Gradins Gris, is a pensione hotel. Rooms come with bath.

The Aujon (tel. 50908010) This hotel offers half pension or bed-and-breakfast.

The least expensive week to stay in Flaine is the one after New Year's. The remainder of January and the first few days of February are also less pricy.

Dining

Your choice of where to eat is limited because most hotel guests are on the full-pension plan, taking meals in their hotels, and apartment guests cook in their apartments. We recommend the fixed-price menu at the Totem dining room.

The Aujon offers a less expensive menu.

In the mountains the lunchtime fare is pretty much standardized, although you'll pay less on the Samoens-Morillon side.

In Flaine, get a quick, tasty snack at **Trattoria**.

Apartments

Apartment complexes in Flaine have been built on three levels. Above the Forum on the hillside are the units of Flaine Foret. These are the better apartments, many privately owned. Apartment buildings are also clustered around the main Forum square and there are more below the Forum level at Front de Neige. The most convenient are those in the Forum area.

The least expensive studio apartment on the Forum level during middle season costs about FFR 1,555 a week. The same apartment during high season costs about FFR 3,110.

For rental bookings in all areas, call Agence Renand (tel. 50908140). In addition, the tourist office will mail a brochure and booking reservation information upon request. (*See address below*.)

Nightlife

Plan on staying in Flaine, because the road down the mountain can become treacherous, particularly after the sun goes down. Our ski instructor met with the class one evening in the lounge at the Hotel Aujon. And a friend from Liverpool took us to the very British (and nice) **White Grouse Pub. Quadrium** may seem like a disco to you.

Child care

A ski kindergarten is conducted daily from 9 a.m. until 6 p.m. The fee for a half day is FFR 70; six half days cost FFR 290. Full-day ski kindergarten runs FFR 130, or FFR 350 a week of half days and FFR 650 for a week of full days. Prices include instruction and a meal.

The baby-sitting services at Les Lindars Hotel are best. The hotel runs a nursery for children under two. Costs are FFR 140 for a full day; FFR 75, half day; and baby-sitting for hotel guests is FFR 28 an hour. A kindergarten without ski course from 9 a.m. until 6 p.m. for children from two to seven is also available.

The children's Rabbit Club ski school is another child-oriented program, which costs FFR 850 for six days with lunch (FFR 680 without lunch) and FFR 180 for one day with lunch (FFR 150 without lunch).

Getting there

Geneva airport, about 45 miles away by the Geneva-Chamonix autoroute, is the closest. Take the Cluses exit.

You can also take the train to Cluses and then a bus (for information on Transport Alpbus, call 50037009) to Flaine.

Tourist information

Office du Tourisme Flaine, F-74300; tel. 50908001; telex 385662 F.

Flaine-Information, 23 Rue Cambon, F-75001 Paris; tel. 12.61.55.17; telex: 670512 F.

Megève

Megève, France's most beautiful, quaintest ski resort, exudes small village charm. Huddled around the old church, a remnant tower and the town hall is a small village with narrow streets, small squares, trendy boutiques, quality antique shops, crowded bistros and dozens of small hotels. The upper crust of Europe and France make Megève their winter home when cold weather forces them to abandon the Riviera. Furs are the coats of choice for those strolling past shop windows, and the latest fashions are found on the slopes during day and in expensive gourmet restaurants and some of France's best discos and nightclubs during the night. You can spend your nights bouncing to the beat in packed jazz clubs or wandering through the town's romantic streets listening to the jingle of bells and the clip-clop of horses trotting through the town.

Together with Zermatt, Megève looks like what Walt Disney might have designed had he created a ski resort. Megève is quality and beauty from its quaint town buildings to its narrow streets, from its art deco deluxe hotels to its perfect French country inns, and from its gourmet restaurants to its pulsing late-night casinos and discos. Megève hits all the notes between hedonistic excess and traditional ski village delight.

For skiers, Megève's own ski area is relatively uninspiring, but the town has leveraged its small village ambience with the ski slopes of neighboring towns, creating a ski area with exceptional terrain variety. The skiing area links the slopes of neighboring Saint-Gervais-les Bains, Le Fayet, St. Nicolas de Véroce and Combloux, creating an overall skiing domain with more than 100 miles of trails that offer something for every level of skier.

Where to ski

Although Megève's slopes are not of the caliber of Val d'Isère or as extensive as the Trois Vallées, when the snow cooperates the region has some of the most varied skiing you can find in Europe. Megève does suffer from low elevation, which can be a serious drawback during low-snow winters, but its low altitude is also a blessing, because it also offers more comfortable skiing for the entire winter. Megève never experiences the chilling cold found in higher resorts.

Priority areas on an any expert's list should be Mont Joly and

Mont Joux. Both peaks are actually in the St. Gervais area, but the interconnection between the St. Gervais and the Megève ski runs is so well integrated that the areas are virtually seamless. The two peaks separating Megève from St. Gervais are lined with black- and red-rated runs, as well as excellent off-trail drops down toward Le Gouet in St. Nicolas de Véroce. A favorite from the top of Mont Joly is the chairlift run, which starts from the 7,637-foot-high summit of the Mont Joly chairlift and drops precipitously down to the base of the lift at 6,107 feet. You have one real choice coming down and it's black all the way. Nearby, a shorter run that descends from the Epaule lift is also rated black. To the right and left of both runs are wide-open steeps for plenty of off-trail action.

From atop the Mont Joux lift there are a half-dozen runs down to St. Nicolas that shift from steep to mellow, starting from the wide-open snowfields and ending through tree-lined trails. You can also drop down the other side of the Mont Joux and back into Megève.

The Mt. d'Arbois summit offers a mix of black, red and blue runs. The summit is served by four lifts on the Megève side and by another four lifts climbing up from the St. Gervais side. From this point long cruises for beginners or intermediates are the order of the day; they can drop back into Megève or down to Le Betex, or when the snow is good continue back into St. Gervais.

Across the plateau from Mt. d'Arbois rising above Megève are three peaks—Rochebrune, Alpette and Cote 2000. This series of peaks offers another varied system of runs. The best is a descent from the Rochebrune summit through the trees and back to the valley station. Experts can test themselves skiing from Cote 2000 down to the altiport on black and red runs. Beginners and basic intermediates can enjoy a field day with the swooping runs from the Arpette peak.

The third area served by the Megève pass is Le Jaillet. This lift system is half owned by the town of Combloux. It is best suited to beginners and basic intermediates who are gaining confidence or for experienced skiers who want to spend some time playing and cruising down mellow slopes. Advanced beginners and lower intermediate skiers will find Le Jaillet at 5,576 feet ideal. There are, however, four black-rated runs on this mountain; as skills (and courage) increase, you don't have to go far to try something new.

Most scenic of the black runs is the one-mile-long trail (6,133 feet) from Christomet. Our favorite on this side is the run through the woods along the Creve Coeur lifts just below Le Jaillet summit.

Mountain rating

Taken together, Megève's mountains offer several challenges and make the area an acceptable destination for the expert skier who realizes that this is no Chamonix or Val d'Isère. (If, however, you're skiing on a Mont Blanc ski pass, Chamonix is a possibility any day of the week.) Intermediate skiers and those trying to push to the advanced intermediate level should find this a great place to improve and test their skills.

Beginners should go to Megève without hesitation. There's enough good skiing at the lower ability level to keep them going until the improvements come. Then it's on up the mountain with the big boys.

Ski school

About 200 teachers are registered in the Megève area. Large ski classes are conducted by schools in Megève (tel. 50210097), St. Gervais (tel. 782100) and Combloux (tel. 586049). *NOTE: English-speaking instructors are a rare commodity—make sure you get a good one.*
Average price per person:

one hour (private instruction)	FFR 140
six days (half day)	FFR 400

Cross-country skiing instruction is available, and the amount of prepared trails—more than 60 kilometers—attests to the sport's popularity here.

Lift tickets

Mont Blanc's ski pass also includes the Megève area. It is by far the best lift-ticket bargain. In addition to Megève it covers Chamonix, St. Gervais, St. Nicolas, Les Contamines, plus eight other resorts around Mont Blanc. Comprised are 208 lifts and more than 370 miles of prepared runs. Prices for children under 12 are in parentheses.

four consecutive days	FFR 495 (420)
six consecutive days	FFR 700 (600)

Day tickets are available for all areas. A full day in Megève is FFR 132 (FFR 114), and six days will cost FFR 682 (FFR 600).

Accommodations

Megève has the best collection of upscale, beautiful and classy hotels of any ski resort in Europe . . . for that matter in the world. In style they range from avante garde and art deco palaces to gilt and velvet luxury to rustic French provincial.

Parc des Loges (tel. 50930503; fax 50930952; telex 385854) is Megève's newest four-star deluxe hotel. The art deco environment creates its own world. Halls are lined with chrome columns set against white walls on either side of black runners lined in royal blue and highlighted by modern art splashed across canvases. The rooms are dominated by the same black, white, royal blue, grey and chrome design. Each room comes with TV, VCR, glass-screened fireplace and anything else one could imagine.

Entrance to the bar and restaurants is through tall plants alternating with Cartier-style cabinets. The bar claims to have the best selection in the French Alps and serves them over a 1920s bar inlaid with mother of pearl. The main hotel restaurant, La Rotonde, serves gourmet dinners prepared by some of France's top chefs, who alternate daily throughout the year cooking their specialties. Rates at this ultimate luxury hotel: FFR 1,100 per person, based on double occupancy with half board. Suites run FFR 2,150-2,000 per person.

Hotel Mont Blanc (tel. 50212002; telex 385854) has long been on the fast track and at the end of the runway for the world's jet set. An opulent lobby and ornate rooms abound with gold trim, velvet and tassles. Megève's most upscale shopping arcade wraps around the Mont Blanc, and the infamous "Les Enfant Terribles" is one of France's top night venues. The rate is FFR 1,350 per person with half board. Limited weekly packages are available.

Chalet du Mont Arbois (tel. 50212503) is a small, super luxury chalet hotel owned by the Baron and Baroness Rothschild. Arrivals are treated like personal guests rather than hotel residents—an atmosphere that prevails during the entire stay. If you can imagine yourself moving into your own luxury mountain chalet, you'll enjoy the decor, which features a lot of mountain wood, giant fireplaces and priceless antiques. Rates for double occupancy and half board: FFR 440 to FFR 1,200, depending on the room you select.

Hotel le Fer à Cheval (tel. 50213039) will make you feel as if you're staying on a French country cottage movie set. The original hotel rooms have been termed "classic," and the new wing offers more modern and larger rooms with the same country touch.

Every highlight seems to be rendered in wood, the furniture is rustic, the rooms have walls covered in country patterned fabrics, stencils and hand-painted doors. The restaurant is almost overpowering French country. Rates based on double occupancy with half board: FFR 450 in the classic double; FFR 550 for a room with salon; and FFR 475 each for four sharing a two-bedroom suite.

Au Coin du Feu (tel. 50210494) is another country-perfect setting, owned in fact by the brother of the Fer à Cheval's owner, with all same French country touches. The restaurant, completed only a couple of years ago, is in the basement where wooden cupboards line the walls, alternating with stone arches around a fireplace. The hotel is small with only 25 rooms, but many have been converted into minisuite-type accommodations to add space. Rates for the normal double rooms with half board, based on double occupancy: FFR 490; for the minisuites, FFR 540; and for apartments, FFR 1,340 per day with half board.

At the next rung along the cost spectrum are the two-star hotels, which in Megève are very acceptable for anyone.

Hotel Alpina (tel. 50215477) in the center of town on Place du Casino is a two-star dream. The rooms are recently remodeled in the woodsy mountain style. All come with TV, and the hotel is only steps from Megève's excitement. Only bed and breakfast accomodations are offered, which will allow you to enjoy the many nearby restaurants. Rates based on double occupancy during high season—Christmas, February and Easter—FFR 215. During low season, January and most of March the rate is FFR 190.

Hotel La Prairie (tel. 50214855) is an excellent two-star hotel in Megève. The chalet-style building is bright and spacious, the rooms are simple with heavy wooden doors and pine highlights. Every room has a TV, and you are an easy, five-minute walk from the center of town. This hotel is bed and breakfast only, with a snack served from 7-8:30 p.m. Rates per person based on double occupancy: FFR 205 for a south-facing room with balcony, or as low as FFR 159 for a north-facing room.

Weekend Hotel (tel. 50212649) is located next door to Coin du Feu, about a five-minute walk up a relatively steep hill from the town center. The rooms have been recently redone and almost every room has an extra bed for a child or third person. Perhaps something as simple as getting rid of the chenille bedspreads would make the Weekend look more upscale, as it should be. The owner speaks excellent English. There are no TVs and the hotel offers bed and breakfast only. Rates per person based on double occupancy: FFR 240 during high season and FFR 220 during low season.

The tourist office offers an accommodation service (tel. 50212952) that will book a room, apartment or chalet for you. Altogether, there are 63 hotels and pensiones in town, although not all are open year round. The wealth of restaurants and the liveliness of Megève's night scene may cause you to opt for a hotel without half board. Accommodation is available starting at the weekly prices below. These are low-season prices available during most of January and late March. They include seven full consecutive days with full board, taxes and services (per person) in a double room occupied by two people, with bath or shower.

Four Star	FFR 4,760
Three Star	FFR 2,970
Two Star	FFR 1,550

During high season the rates are approximately 20 percent higher.

Dining

Megève is one town where you won't have any problem getting excellent food—there are four Michelin-rated and five Gault et Millau-rated restaurants.

La Rotonde (tel. 50210574) in the Hotel Parc des Loges is Megève's best, with a gourmet dinner prepared each night by one of five prize-winning chefs. Each renowned chef prepares his own specialty. Surrounded by glass, you'll be able to look outside into the woods for an effect that when augmented by the tiny ceiling lights and the candles is magical. Expect to pay between FFR 400 and FFR 700 for dinner, including wine, depending on the menu and the chef preparing the meal.

Les Enfants Terribles (tel. 50212002) in the Hotel Mont Blanc also serves exquisite meals in a fantasy atmosphere. Gold and velvet chairs trimmed with tassles and paintings by Jean Cocteau combine for a unique atmosphere. Meals cost at least FFR 280.

Chalet du Mont Arbois (tel. 50212503), located high on the plateau of Mont Arbois near the base of the lifts, is a chalet belonging to Baron Rothschild. The restaurant serves some of the area's best meals in a country chalet atmosphere created by heavy beams alternating with soaring, stuccoed arches. As you might expect, the chalet claims one of the best wine cellars in Megève. A meal will cost at least FFR 250.

Le Viking (tel. 50211155) is a restaurant with a strong personality. It seems that everything imaginable has been hung on the walls and ceilings, including a giant set of antlers that dominate the dining room. It's very rustic in an enjoyable way. Specialties are grilled meats. Expect to spend between FFR 200-250 for dinner with wine. Call for reservations. It opens at 7 p.m.

The second tier of restaurants in terms of price are still a formidable group.

Auberge Des Griottes (tel. 50930594) serves highly rated food in a chalet atmosphere that could be a little less sterile. But it's not the decor, rather the prices for this level of cooking in Megève that have created a stir among restaurant-goers. The food is simple, classic and excellently prepared. Expect to spend FFR 180 to FFR 200 for the dinner menu with a modest wine.

St. Nicolas (tel. 50210494) is a restaurant in the basement of the Hotel Coin du Feu. Its country atmosphere is set by giant wooden cupboards, armoirs and stone basement arches. The chef serves up basic Savoyard country specialties. Expect to pay between FFR 170 and FFR 230.

Fer à Cheval Restaurant (tel. 50213039) in the hotel of the same name also has a very rustic country feel. Country cooking with a Savoyard gourmet flair will cost about FFR 200-FFR 260 per person for dinner.

Auberge du Grenand (tel. 50213030), about three kilometers outside of town on the road to Leutaz Very, is worth the trip. This restaurant is set in a rustic chalet with plenty of mountain atmosphere and roaring fireplace. Meals will cost about FFR 200, including wine.

Le Tire Bouchon (tel. 50211473) across the street from the Parc des Loges is a simple restaurant with simple food and basic prices. This restaurant serves the best value, with a meal costing between FFR 90 and FFR 120, including wine. This may explain the frequent wait to get in the door.

Les Drets (tel. 50215178), better known as "Chez Loulou," gets a lot of repeat customers who claim they return because of the owners. Driving there is the easiest, as it is located on the road to Cote 2000 just before you get to the Altiport, but it can also be reached for a skier's lunch by short walk. Chez Loulou is open only for lunch, which can cost as little as FFR 100.

For local mountain specialties of fondue, raclette and pela, make sure to visit three small restaurants all within a one-minute walk of one another.

Le Chamois (tel. 50212501) located next to the church and old town tower, specializes in cheese fondue. A portion will cost FFR

80 per person. Unlike most restaurants, Le Chamois will serve a single guest who comes through the door wielding a fondue craving.

Les Marronniers (tel. 50212201) is a tiny rustic cafe at the opposite end of the same building that houses Le Chamois. The wooden walls are lined with hundreds of old, colorful pastel coffee pots. The specialty here is raclette served the old-fashion way—scraped off with a knife. You can also get crepes, galletes (like thick pancakes) and omelettes. Raclette per person costs FFR 90.

Le Savoyard (tel. 50214802) is located under the Hotel Alpina opposite the casino. Here they have revived the art of creating "pela." This is a regional country specialty in which pan-fried potatoes and bacon are covered with melted cheese and then served in the pan with a selection of mountain dried beef and sausages. A plateful of this rich and hearty fare costs FFR 80 per person. With the recommended local white wine and coffee you can walk away with paying just over FFR 200 for two.

Two notable pizzerias are **La Caponata** and **Pizzeria Madonna**. Both offer creative pizzas as well as a chance to eat on the cheap.

For eating on the mountain we recommend restaurants on each mountain. The best overall is **Le Relais des Communailles** between Le Bettex and St. Nicolas (tel. 50931015). **La Petite Coterie** in Le Bettex (tel. 50931174) is also excellent. Both will be crowded during high season, so you should make reservations. On the top of Mt. d'Arbois, try the **Igloo** self-service (tel. 50930584) located next to the upper station of the Princesse lift. On top of Mont Joux, the new **Espace Mt. Joux** has great views of Mont Blanc. The best mountain eatery on the Rochebrune sector of the resort is **La Cote 2000** (tel. 50213184) located near the Altiport. Across the valley in Le Jaillet, try **Le Jaillet Superior** (tel. 50210651) at the top of the gondola.

Apartments

Write to the Megève tourist office (tel. 50212592), which will contact the major rental organizations in town. You will hear from several agencies. Make your pick and let the agencies know your decision. In January expect to pay approximately FFR 1,800-2, 400 a week for a two-room apartment for four persons. In February the price will be between FFR 2,800-4,800 a week. During Christmas apartments are only rented for two-week periods and will cost between FFR 3,700 and FFR 7,500 for the 14 days. Linen will cost an additional FFR 110 a week.

Nightlife

La nuit, c'est Megève!, roughly translates as "the night belongs to Megève." Despite the rustic, chalet-style buildings and the old-atmosphere resort, Megève is modern in all aspects. Discos pulse and lights flash, keeping beat with the thumping music. The live entertainment ranges from France's top singers and entertainers to transvestite revues. It all continues until at least 4 a.m.

Don't plan to tackle Megève's nightlife after an eight o'clock dinner. There isn't any to speak of, not until later, much later. Discos don't get rolling until after midnight, and even then they seem deserted.

One veteran Frenchman offers this advice on handling Megève's nightlife: "Divide your day into four parts." He counsels that one should ski during the day from about 10 in the morning until four in the afternoon, making sure to enjoy a good lunch. Then have a cocktail with friends in a small bar and go home to sleep. Get up at 10 p.m. and go to eat. You finish at midnight or later, if you are lucky and the food is particularly wonderful, then begin to visit the nightclubs, the casino and the discos. At three or four in the morning, go back to bed and begin again the next day.

Megève sparkles for as long as you let it. For earlier action, try a drink in the **Brazil Bar** with its trendy Parisian decor—lots of mirrors and Brazilian crocodiles with strong cocktails. Later, about 10 p.m., head to the **Jazz Club Les 5 Rues** located in the tiny back streets of Megève and vibrating with great jazz in very rustic surroundings. The **Cave de l'Esquinade** also serves up jazz in a more modern club where music mixes easily with expensive drinks.

The casino actually opens at 5 p.m. but doesn't really get rolling until about midnight. **The Enfants Terrible** in the Mont Blanc has occasional shows. The discos are packed by 1:30 a.m. Squeeze into l'Esquinade in the basement of the casino, or visit **Le Glamour** downstairs from the Viking Restaurant. **Caberet Les Rol's** presents a transvestite spectacular at 1 a.m. each evening. At any of these disco and nightspots expect to pay between FFR 90-100 for a drink, or you can purchase a bottle of whiskey if you are planning to stay for FFR 900-1,000. You'll be amazed at how many people do just that.

Child care

Baby Club (tel. 50211776) kindergarten near the Jaillet runs is for children 12 months to six years and costs FFR 115 a day without lunch, or FFR 160 with lunch. Or pay an hourly rate, FFR 27. Chalet St. Michel, located on the road to Cret du Midi a bit outside of town, takes children from three to 12 years (tel. 50210477). Rates are FFR 150 for a full day or FFR 35 an hour.

Other daycare facilities are available for children from ages three to six and include beginning ski lessons. L'Alpage (tel. 50211097) is on Mont l'Arbois. Montjoie (tel. 50210156) on the Jaillet beginner runs has an English-speaking staff. Prices range from FFR 275 to FFR 170 for a full day and FFR 90-150 for a half day. Hourly rates are approximately FFR 40. For details, call the tourist office at 50212728.

The tourist office also maintains a list of multilingual babysitting services.

Getting there

Geneva is the main arrival airport; from there it is about an hour by car to Megève.

Trains run to Sallanches, 13 kilometers away, where bus and taxi services are available. The TGV makes the run to Salanches in only five hours. A bus from the train station to Megève will cost about FFR 125.

Other activities

Megève and the neighboring villages draw many non-skiers who as part of their entertainment walk throughout the area. To help them, the walkways are better kept than any you'll probably encounter at other alpine resorts. Megève's shops are outstanding for window shopping, and their prices are perfect for destroying your budget. Day outings to Chamonix and Geneva are popular.

Megève has an excellent sports center with skating, swimming with two covered pools, saunas, fitness rooms, covered tennis and golf practice ranges. Rates for the Sports Center are normally FFR 17 for skating or swimming. Tennis courts can be reserved by calling 50211571 and will cost FFR 140 per court-hour or FFR 700 for six coupons good for six hours of court time.

Tourist information

Office du Tourisme, rue de la Poste, F-74120 Megève; tel. 50212728; telex 385532.

Office du Tourisme, F-74920 Combloux; tel. 50586049; telex 385550.

Office du Tourisme, F-74190 Le Fayet; tel. 50470158; telex 385730.

Office du Tourisme de St. Gervais, F-74170 St. Gervais; tel. 50782243; telex 385607.

Morzine

Morzine is by far the largest settlement of Les Portes du Soleil, with 3,000 residents, 70 hotels, 45 restaurants and 20 ski shops. Although it's at a relatively low 3,000-foot elevation, a network of lifts reach the panoramic Chamossiere at 6,006 feet. And Avoriaz, at 7,080 feet, is a mere cablecar ride away.

The old part of town, going back to the 16th century, rises up to a 19th-century church and the tumbling Dranse River, with modern buildings and shops built higher beneath the ski slopes. Even if it doesn't appear to be as spectacular as Avoriaz, Morzine has more to offer in the long run. With the traditional chalets and small farms many people associate with the Alps, it's more like a town than a resort erected beside a lift system. Furthermore, Morzine attracts an English-speaking crowd so rudimentary English is widely spoken, a plus for Americans who don't want to grapple with French.

With its own gallic identity, the town is a pleasant place for walking and relaxing. Although nightlife lacks the glamour of Megeve or Courchevel—three discos, two cinemas, many bars and an ice skating arena that has hosted the world's top skaters—there is plenty to do. As for skiing, the restaurant-to-ski-shop ratio is more than 2-to-1, and locals say that if anything there are too many restaurants. This indicates very active slopes, and indeed there are many intermediate and beginner runs, some long and challenging black territory and easy access to the whole Portes du Soleil circus.

Where to ski

Beginners go to Le Pleney, which is a one-stop ascent by tram or cablecar. Nyon has a nice mix of black, red and blue descents, and Chamossiere has outstanding views, good long black runs and some fine cruising through the Col de Joux Plane. Some of the best tough skiing of the entire Portes du Soleil is nearby—from Pointes de Nyon to Col de Fornet in France and, in Switzerland, from Planachaux to Grand Paradis and Champery. Plan to go with a guide, however. The notorious Wall of Death between Avoriaz and Switzerland can be skied by an intermediate when the snow cover is good because there are broad segments for traverses and turns. Anyone who is fearful can take the chairlift down.

Mountain rating

A good mixed bag of skiing opportunities awaits, and most of them can be enjoyed by an intermediate skier. Morzine is also a very good place for beginners, relaxed and wide-open. The variety of lifts, terrain and passages makes sometimes less than challenging runs interesting.

Ski school

The ski school has 120 teachers and a following: fully one-quarter of Morzine's visitors take lessons. A lesson for up to 11 in a group costs FF75; for one or two people for an hour, FF120; for three or four people for an hour, FF150. Half-day skiing for up to six people in a group, FF400; for a day, FF950. For information contact, Ecole de Ski Francais, Avenue de Joux-Plane, 74110 Morzine; tel. 50791313.

Lift tickets

For the Pleney and Nyon areas, which are local to Morzine and include 27 lifts and 30 trails, a half-day ticket costs FF80 for adults and FF66 for children; full-day adult is FF105 or FF80 for children; two days costs FF193 and FF147, respectively; three days, FF278 and FF210; six days, FF525 and FF392; 14 days, FF1,008 and FF760.

For skiing Les Port du Soleil from Morzine, a half-day ticket costs FF87 for adults, FF70 for children; full-day adult is FF135 or FF107 for children; two days costs FF255 and FF181, respectively; three days, FF362 and FF255; six days, FF680 and FF478; 14 days, FF1,175 and FF825.

Accommodations

Because most hotels do not have what Americans consider to be standard rooms, you may want to ask for a larger room, or whatever you may require, when checking in.

Morzine has seven three-star hotels, which include:

Les Airelles (tel. 50791524; telex 385178F) is modern, well-designed and centrally located, with a big swimming pool, a toilet and phone in each its 45 rooms. Rates are FF380-FF540 with full pension; FF350 to FF495 with half pension.

Le Carlina (tel. 50790103; telex 385596F) runs between FF340 and FF440 with full pension; FF280-FF380 with half pension.

Le Tremplin (tel. 50791231; telex 385246F) has a friendly atmosphere, a pleasant sitting area and bar, and is located next to the slopes. Its rooms, irregular in size, cost between FF380 and

FF540 with full pension and between FF300 and FF460 with half pension.

Morzine has 18 two-star hotels, which include:
Le Samoyede (tel. 50790079) has 27 rooms ranging from FF285 to FF355 with full pension and from FF255 to FF325 with half pension.
Le Sporting (tel. 50791503) has 28 rooms and costs FF250-FF320 with full pension, FF220-FF290 with half pension.

The one-star hotels cost between FF190 and FF245.
La Bergerie is an attractive residence hotel. It doesn't have a dining room but has kitchen facilities in the rooms, telephone, television, a parking garage and sauna. Cost is between FF230 to FF550.

Dining

La Chamade's owner, Thierry Thorens, trained with celebrated chef Paul Bocuse near Lyons. Grilled food, local foods and traditional French cuisine are served in one area; in a larger room, gourmet service costs about FF300 minimum per person.

More typical of the regional and traditional food, with raclette and fondue, is **L'Egale**, where a meal will run FF80-FF110. There is a disco downstairs.

Les Sapins has an excellent view of Lake Montriond and is well-known for its home cooking. Roger Muffat, father of the restaurant owner, prepares the dried meats, ham and everything himself. A five-course meal costs between FF110 and FF180.

Nightlife

Generally low-keyed and relaxed, Morzine is no jet-set town crammed with sportscars. It is, however, good for pleasant wandering and window-shopping, with several opprtunities to stop for a hot chocolate or beer. The **Le Pacho** disco attracts locals and young people. **Le Pressoir** is a nicely decorated piano bar near the church. **Le Café Chaud** attracts young swingers.

Child care

Kindgergarten l'Outa welcomes children and infants from two months to four years. The chalet is located in the center of the resort, near the slopes and ski school. There is a large playroom for indoor activities, a nursery and a very large yard where instructors give first lessons to the youngest. Parents can bring a meal or take advantage of the special menu. Ski lessons are available for children over four years at the ski school. Instructors speak English.

Group ski lessons (tel. 50791313) for children cost FF60; six consecutive half days, FF280; seven consecutive half days, FF340; 11 days, FF450; 13 days, FF550.

The children's supervised play school and nursery (tel. 50792600) for ages two months to 12 years, may include skiing, costs FF70 for a half day, or four hours, FF120 a day. Six half days cost FF350; six consecutive days cost FF600.

For babysitting services, call 50790345.

Getting there

The nearest airport is in Geneva. From the airport a special bus runs each Saturday and Sunday, leaving at 10:30 a.m. and taking about an hour and a half to reach Morzine.

The resort can also be reached by a train and bus combination: The train from Paris arrives at Thonon, with a bus transfer of about 45 minutes.

For those driving, take the *autoroute* from Geneva to Mont Blanc and leave at the exit marked Morzine/Avoriaz. It is only 66 kilometers from Geneva.

Other activities

The arena complex at Morzine offers curling, skating, ice hockey, table tennis, a weight room, dancing, gymnastics and yoga. Painting exhibits, figure skating, ice dancing, hockey games and movies also are scheduled there. For information, call 50790843.

Tourist information

L'Office du Tourisme, Place Centrale, Morzine; tel. 50790345; telex 385620 F.

La Plagne

La Plagne is the largest single ski resort in Europe if you base such a superlative on the number of lifts and lift capacity. There are other ski areas that are larger but they are formed by combining several independent resorts, such as the Trois Vallées, the Dolomites or the Portes du Soleil, which link from three up to dozens of separate resorts.

La Plagne is also one of the highest resorts on the continent. Most of its skiing and accommodations are above 6,000 feet. For certainty of snow, La Plagne can't be beat. You can bet that there will be snow here, even in the middle of August, on the high glaciers of Bellecote and La Chiaupe.

La Plagne claims a vertical of 6,500 feet, but the lower 1,700 feet of that is through trees and consists for the most part of winding roads. But when the snow is good a skier can start out from Roche de Mio at 8,775 feet and drop down to Montchavin at 4,062 feet, which means more than 4,700 feet of maximum working vertical. The working vertical in the upper ranges of the resort is about 2,500 feet, more than any point in Aspen or Vail.

La Plagne started out as the basic purpose-built ski resort with modern high-rise buildings and continued in that mode as new building clusters were built through the area. Each village features apartments, with stores and ski shops all interconnected by a series of tunnels and walkways. La Plagne really revolves around apartment life, for it offers 25,000 beds in small apartments and only 2,000 beds in 16 hotels spread through the resort and in the region. Although the tourist brochures all speak of 10 villages the group includes four at low altitudes, which, although technically considered part of the resort, are really at the fringes. The real La Plagne comprises the six high-altitude building clusters.

Plagne Center at 6,463 feet is the original, built 25 years ago as one of France's first purpose-built complexes. What the buildings lack in charm they make up for in convenience—four hotels, dozens of restaurants, scores of shops, a cinema and apartment accommodations connected by underground passages. This is also one of the major lift centers, with no fewer than 20 lifts fanning out from the complex.

Plagne Village at 6,726 feet is a cluster of alpine-style buildings with wooden features and peaked roofs. There are no hotels, only apartments and several shops.

Aime La Plagne, also sometimes called La Plagne 2000, is another purpose-built complex above Plagne Center. Many consider this the most convenient of the complexes. Here are many of the best apartments in the resort, and the complex includes four covered tennis courts, two squash courts as well as a cinema and a good collection of shops and restaurants. A cablecar connects Aime la Plagne with Plagne Center.

Plagne 1800 is another Savoyard mountain village created with wooden chalets and peaked roofs. This complex includes squash courts and a good fitness center. Unfortunately, although many of the apartments are top quality, the village itself clings to a steep mountainside, making a walk from chalet to chalet difficult, especially in the snow.

Plagne Bellecote at 6,234 feet is a collection of what appears to be almost 50 connected 10-story, high-rise buildings. There are no hotels in this complex, but it has La Plagne's only heated outdoor swimming pool and is the starting point of the world's longest gondola reaching the glacier at 8,858 feet. The passages connecting these buildings are actually quite pleasant and spacious, allowing a bit of breathing space even in the midst of thousands of visitors.

Belle Plagne at 6,726 feet is the youngest of La Plagne's complexes. Here planners again chose the Savoyard village motif with wood-fronted chalet style and no traffic. An underground traffic system allows cars to reach each of the chalet compounds. A too-small shopping arcade in the village center provides a touch of alpine charm. Also, this winter a new fitness center, complete with sauna and jacuzzis, will open. Belle Plagne also has the resort's newest hotel, the Eldorador.

Where to ski

There are 107 trails, including seven black and 36 red trails, covering 200 kilometers of ski area.

There are 100 ski lifts, seven of which are gondolas and one that connects Bellecote and Belle Plagne with the glaciers. The remainder of the lift network comprises 23 chairlifts and 69 drag lifts.

Mountain rating

La Plagne is decidedly an intermediate and beginner mountain, at least as far as the prepared trails indicate.

Experts will have to work to find challenging skiing. As with any massive area there are plenty of spots for creative experts to go off-trail and find more than enough to keep them busy for a week.

But uncreative experts may end up yawning after only a day in this resort. Marked expert runs drop off the backside of the Biolley sector and down behind Aime La Plagne, or try the steeps dropping down the far left side of the glacier.

Intermediates will think they have died and gone to skiers heaven. The rolling mountains offer either acceptable steeps where intermediates can play or mellow off-trail areas in which to develop deep-snow skills.

Beginners and lower intermediates are in one of the best European resorts to learn how to ski. Here beginners can experience taking lifts to the highest points with all the thrill of the spectacular visuals and still be able to get back down the mountain safely.

Ski school

These prices are for the 1988/89 winter season.

The La Plagne ski school has 350 instructors available throughout the various village complexes. Each village offers the same series of courses.

Individual lessons are available for full days from 9:15 a.m. until 4:45 p.m. for FFR 990. Half-day private lessons cost FFR 605, except during high season when the morning lessons will cost FFR 670. A short two-and-a-half-hour lesson will cost FFR 465. Hourly lessons cost FFR 140 and FFR 160 on Sundays. All private lessons are limited to no more than five persons.

Group lessons are available on a weekly basis. Six full days cost FFR 600; six half days cost FFR 420. Off-trail skiing classes cost FFR 1,140 for six days. *Nouvelle glisse* courses, alternating between skiing monoskiing and snowboarding both on and off-trail, cost FFR 890 for six days; and competition courses will cost FFR 890 for six days of training.

Lift tickets

Half day (adults/children under 13 and seniors over 60)--FFR 100/ FFR 75; full day--FFR 148/FFR 111; three days--FFR 385/FFR 290; six days--FFR 710/FFR 530.

Lift tickets purchased for three days or more permit one day a week of skiing in Val d'Isère, Tignes or Les Arcs.

Accommodations

Hotel La France in Plagne Center (tel. 79092815) offers good if sterile accommodations. The decor is studied minimalist, but the rooms are sizable, especially for French standards, and the breakfasts include everything from eggs, ham, yogurt and cereals to the normal rolls, butter and jam. The piano bar actually employs a piano player, who makes sitting, chatting or reading a pleasure. The location is right on the slopes. Rates average about FFR 370 for half board, but call for special weekly package rates that include half board, lifts and lessons. Such packages run about FFR 4,000 during February and March and FFR 3,650 during January, based on double occupancy.

Hotel Eldorador (tel. 79091209) is La Plagne's newest hotel operated by Jet Vacations/Meridian/Air France. The rooms are virtually identical to those in Hotel La France in Plagne Center but with smaller bathrooms. Overall the atmosphere in Belle Plagne makes the Eldorador's location more desirable than Hotel La France, but what one gains in atmosphere in Belle Plagne one loses in choice of restaurants and shops. With the construction of the fitness center only steps away this will become the best choice for the resort. Rooms based on double occupancy with half board during January cost FFR 400; during February FFR 565; and during March FFR 450.

If you are a single and someone tells you that there will be no supplement, beware. These "half rooms" for singles with no supplement mean you will be sharing a shower and toilet with another unfortunate half-roomer.

Hotel Christina (tel. 79092820) is only steps from the main complex of Plagne Center. But it is also a step back in time, with old varnished wood walls and ceilings and early 1960s furniture. The owners are characters worthy of movie roles. All in all it seems that this would be an experience. Make sure to specify rooms with bath or shower. The rate for room with shower, based on double occupancy, with full board in January's low season is FFR 310-340; in high season, FFR 395-440.

Hotel Graciosa (tel. 79090018) is located high above Plagne Center, which makes reaching the shops of Plagne Center or Aime La Plagne above very inconvenient. The restaurant here is considered one of the best in the resort, so arranging for full pension is a good bet. The rooms are relatively small but have cable TV. Decor in the 10 rooms is strict 1960s, with rust-colored rugs and dark, varnished wood ceilings, walls and furniture. Low season rates with full pension, based on double occupancy, range from FFR 310-350; during high season rates are FFR 385-415.

Hotel Loup Blanc (tel. 79091102) is a small hotel will big expansion plans for the next couple of years. In the meantime its owners, Sylvie and Rene Eydieux, serve up pure mountain hospitality with bed-and-breakfast rates of FFR 173 a person, based on double occupancy during low season; during high season the rate goes up to FFR 263. The Loup Blanc restaurant only a few steps away offers hotel guests drastically reduced menu prices. A week in January with half board costs FFR 1,508-1,885, and in February costs FFR 2,200, based on double occupancy. The lifts depart from the hotel door.

Dining

Just as the resort is divided into separate villages, so are the restaurants. Most of these are located in Plagne Center. Since Plagne Center is connected with both Aime La Plagne and Plagne Villages by cablecar and telebus, it serves as a center for three of the complexes. The restaurants here prove that even in modern surroundings small, cozy eating spots can be created that have all the atmosphere and charm one might expect to find in a traditional town bistro. Although La Plagne is considered an economical resort by French standards, meals still can cost a bundle. Top restaurants here will run about FFR 200 for a full meal, excluding wine. The moderate restaurants serve up meals for about FF100-150, including wine, and the inexpensive will have a fixed-price menu costing about FFR 75 without wine. For those looking for less expensive meals, try one of the *creperies* or a pizzeria where a meal can end up costing as little as FFR 50, including a beer.

Plagne Center

The restaurant in the Hotel Le Graciosa, **L'Etoile d'Or** (tel. 79090018) is considered to be one of the best in La Plagne—the view is certainly one of the best. A meal here will cost between FFR 160-175 with wine.

Le Bec Fin (tel. 79091086) offers excellent French cooking for a fixed-price menu of FFR 160. The decor looks best in the dark by candlelight. English is spoken by almost the entire staff.

Le Chaudron (tel. 79092333) located in the open field in the center of the Plagne Center complex serves up excellent grilled specialties cooked over an open fire in the middle of the dining room. Currently the restaurant decor has questionable moonscape walls, but the owners promise a new interior for the 1989/90 season. Expect your meal to cost between FFR 100-150.

Le Refuge (tel. 79092513) is the oldest in the resort. Photographs of bobsled champions cover the walls in the very local, very French bar out front. In the dining room in the rear each table is centered under a telescoping copper hood, which is used to vent smoke while guests barbeque their own steaks at the table. It adds a bit a different atmosphere to the rustic setting. Expect to spend about FFR 100-125.

Restaurant l'Edelweiss (tel. 79092820) in the Hotel Christina serves up some of the best grilled meats in town. The owner/chef is a certified member of the Chaine des Rostisseur. His specialty is brochette or kabobs, with prices ranging from FFR 60-80, depending on what you want on your spit. Watching the chef at work in front of the fire is a big part of the show.

Creperie Bretonne, better known as "Le Crepe" (tel. 79090482), is the most popular creperie in the Plagne Center. On weekends and during holidays expect to wait in line for a seat. The restaurant has a maritime decor with fishnet and various fish plastered on the walls. Crepes cost between FFR 13 for a butter crepe to FFR 54 for a smoked salmon crepe with salad. The restaurant also serves raclette and fondue.

Across the hall from Le Crepe are four moderate to inexpensive restaurants: **L'Estiminet** (tel. 79091269), which serves Alsace specialties in huge portions; **Le Tire Bouchon** (tel. 79091179) with excellent fish fondue and a gourmet menu;**La Metairie** (tel. 79091108) serving Savoyard specialties on wooden tables with a fixed-priced menu of FFR 73; and **Le Bistroquet** (tel. 79092211) with great atmosphere, lace curtains, red tablecloths, looking like a bistro should.

For simple pizza and an exuberant welcome by the owner/cook, head to **Pizzaria Rolando** (tel. 79090536) where you can get away for as little as FFR 45 for a pizza and beer. Or walk to the end of the hall and pick up—would you believe, a pizza to go—at **Pizzeria Domino**.

Aime La Plagne

Here, our favorite is **Pizzeria 2000**(tel. 79090529) This cozy restaurant with an unfortunate name serves much more than pizza. After winding down a circular staircase you will have the chance to sample pizza if you insist, but with a difference. They make a pizza *quatro formaggio* with four French cheeses; its owners also have created a smoked salmon pizza. You've probably never tasted one unique creation, "tagliatelli fois gras." Try the normal raclette and fondue or the special rouergat, a duck fondue where the duck is cooked in liver oil. Or order the "royal stone," which is a superheated rock upon which you grill an assortment of mixed meat and fois gras. For the atmosphere, unique food and good service you'll end up spending between FFR 100-150 and leave stuffed.

La Soupe aux Schuss (tel. 79090644) is a tiny place with space for less than 30 diners. The atmosphere is pure French country, with wine stored in baskets, wooden tables covered with lace tablecloths and pine cupboards. The food is excellent but on the expensive side— expect to walk out spending at least FFR 200 without wine.

Belle Plagne

The most popular restaurant is **Le Matafan**(tel. 79090919), which normally seems packed. Tables fan out around an open fire, country cupboards stand against the wall and lace curtains drape the windows. A series of 11 different luncheon plates are offered, including mountain ham, paté and cheese for FFR 52, or an omelet with bacon, salad and fries for FFR 49. Dinner portions are mountain-sized.

Plagne 1800

La Bartavelle (tel. 79092563) is perhaps the best gourmet-type restaurant with the average meal in the FFR 200 range before you add in wine. The elegant dining room with open fireplace and beamed ceiling goes with the upscale meals and price.

Le Loup Blanc (tel. 79091102) at the base of Plagne 1800 is in an old chalet. Wooden tables are set under the roof rafters and regional specialties are served up with exuberance. **The Brazerade** where you grill your own meat will cost FFR 105 a person. Cheese fondue is FFR 65 and raclette is FFR 85. Also offered are two different menus each evening, for FFR 85 and FFR 125. If you call, Rene and Sylvie will send a van to pick you up and then get you back to your hotel or apartment.

Plagne Bellecote

The Piano Bar (tel. 79090307) presents an elegant atmosphere with black chairs and white, marble-topped tables. Each evening live music adds to the atmosphere. Lunch will run about FFR 70 and dinner ranges from FFR 150-200.

Bear Valley (tel. 79090143) is the biggest restaurant in the resort seating hundreds and serving up hundreds of steaks. The service is fast and impersonal. Prices for steaks average about FFR 65.

Plagne Village

Le Bon Coin (tel. 79092908) was recently rescued from mediocrity by Christopher Graham, the first British restaurateur in La Plagne. The menu is easy on your pocketbook and the food is good value. Figure on spending about FFR 100 a person for dinner.

On the slopes

There are 17 different mountain restaurants, not including the restaurants located in the complexes themselves, which offer excellent midday dining. Included are **Vega, La Galerne** and **Le Chaudron** in Plagne Center. Most of the mountain restaurants are of the self-service variety. Of these, **Le Biollet**, above Aime La Plagne gets the most sun and is reachable by only a short walk from the Aime La Plagne complex. For sitdown meals, try **Le Val Sante** at the far left edge of the resort area and be ready to ski home slowly, stuffed with lots of great food. **L'Arpette** just above Belle Plagne, recognizable by the motorbike hanging from the rafters, serves up good mountain food. **La Bergerie** above Plagne Bellecote has a very rustic atmosphere and pricy, mid-mountain dining. **La Grande Rochette** at the top of the gondola rising from Plagne Center offers spectacular views at lunch and dinner on Thursday nights. In Plagne 1800, **Loup Garrou** serves meals in rustic surroundings and each evening has a dinner complete with a horse-drawn sleigh ride to the restaurant.

Apartments

Apartments are by far the most popular form of accommodation in La Plagne. There are more than 10 times the number of beds in apartments than can be found in hotels. Accommodations range from tiny 17-square-meter rooms to spacious apartments. Two can make it without any trouble in a normal two-person French apartment but would be much more comfortable if they could afford to rent a place advertised for four. In Belle Plagne a studio apartment with plenty of room for two will run between FFR 1,500 and FFR 2,000 a week during January. There are bargain weekly rates of only FFR 995 per person during January, which includes ski lifts and half-day lessons. Such rates are hard to beat.

Nightlife/après-ski

The Piano Bar in Plagne Bellecote has live music every night. It serves up beer ranging in price from FFR 13 to FFR 25 a glass. Whiskey ranges from FFR 35-45, and mixed drinks start at FFR 45.

Club Video in Plagne Centre opens as a normal bar from 5 p.m. to 9 p.m. and becomes a disco from 10:30 p.m. on. Expect to find a normal French disco with a young crowd. Drinks are priced at FFR 80 each.

Challenger in Plagne Centre offers normal bar service from 5 p.m. to 9 p.m. and disco fare from 10:30 p.m. Prices are the standard FFR 80 per drink.

Tom's Bar and Disco at Plagne 1800 has bar service from 4 p.m. to 10 p.m. and disco from 10 p.m., when all drink prices increase. Tom's is run by a Brit, but the prices would make anyone back on the island turn pale. Free bus back to your accommodations after 2 a.m.

Rendez-vous . . . Cheers, Au Bon Coin, Plagne Village. Quaint building with atmosphere. Bar and restaurant upstairs, music bar and dancing downstairs. Also under British management. Bus services available.

Child care

Each complex in La Plagne has a nursery catering to children between the ages of three and six years. These facilities offer indoor activities, such as drawing, cartoons and games, as well as outdoor snowgarden play depending on the age of the child. Nursery Marie-Christine in Plagne Center (tel. 79091181) takes children above two years for FFR 160 a day, including meals, or FFR 60 for a half day. Plagne 1800 (tel. 79092250) provides services for babies from six months onward, and the Belle Plagne nursery (tel. 79090668) accepts children between three months and six years. Cost: Daily rates are FFR 155, plus FFR 30 for lunch; half days are FFR 100. Weekly rates: six full days with lessons but without lunch--FFR 530; six half days of lessons in the ski garden--FFR 420; six full days with lunch, lessons and nursery--FFR 910.

For older children, the ski school organizes special programs designed for young skiers. Absolute beginners can take a course that includes lifts and classes for six days for FFR 650 or seven days for FFR 760. Six normal lessons will cost FFR 500 for full days, and six half days cost FFR 350.

Advanced children skiers can get instruction in off-trail, monoski or snowboarding as well as competition training.

Getting there

A bus runs to Aime in the valley for FFR 37 each way, and trains connect Aime with Moutier or Bourg St. Maurice for FFR 11 each way.

Local transport

Plagne Centre to Aime La Plagne is served by a telemetro from 8 a.m.-1 a.m.

Plagne Center and Plagne Village are connected by a telebus from 8 a.m-1 a.m.

Plagne Center and Plagne 1800/Bellecote are connected by shuttlebus on the hour and half hour from 8:30 a.m.- 12:30 a.m.

Bellecote to Belle Plagne connection is by tele Belle Plagne from 8 a.m.-1a.m.

Bellecote to Plagne 1800 and Center is connected by a shuttlebus at quarter past and quarter to the hour from 8:45 a.m. until 12:45 a.m.

Your lift pass will cover you for this transport until 5:30 p.m. After that the telemetro and telebus cost FFR 12 for two trips.

Taxi
Christian Bouzon--tel. 79090341 or Taxi Silvestre--tel. 79097058.

Other activities

The heated pool in Plagne Bellecote is open from 3:30 p.m. to 7 pm.

The ice rink is open from 2:30 p.m. to 7 p.m.; on Wednesdays and Fridays it closes at 10:30 p.m. Adults pay FFR 30 and children pay FFR 25, including skates.

Tennis courts and squash courts are available in Aime La Plagne for FFR 70 a session. For reservations, call 79092504. Squash courts can be rented in Plagne 1800 for approximately the same prices. Call 79092630 for reservations.

Tourist information

Reservations for all La Plagne accommodations can be made by contacting the central booking office—tel. 79097979; telex 980 973 F; fax 79097010.

The tourist information office is located in Plagne Center. Send mail to Bureau de Tourisme de La Plagne, BP 36, 73210 Aime, France; tel. 79090201.

There are English-speaking doctors in the Plagne Centre medical center. It is open from 8:30 a.m. to 7 p.m. Visits to the doctor will cost FFR 125. For the doctors to make a house call you will pay FFR 190, more on Sundays and holidays.

Les Trois Vallées

Welcome to the largest ski area in the world. Well, maybe not *the* largest, but certainly one of the largest, depending on how one measures these things. Les Trois Vallées is the collective name for four separate villages in France's Savoie region that are connected by the most extensive lift system anywhere. The statistics are staggering: more than 200 lifts, almost 1,000 ski instructors, a 250-square-kilometer area boasting 350 miles of marked runs and a lift capacity of 150,000 skiers an hour.

The four villages comprising Les Trois Vallées are Courchevel, Méribel, Les Menuires and Val Thorens. All four are basically "purpose-built," as the French idiom translates, and that purpose is skiing. This is an area that has been constructed for skiers with skiing as its number-one priority. Let's deal with each of the villages separately.

Courchevel

This is perhaps the most cosmopolitan of the four resorts. It was France's first real upscale resort, created to cater to the upper crust and becoming the darling of those in the Riviera group who didn't flock to Megève. The town grew quickly and thus lacks traditional flavor. In fact, some factory towns probably display a cozier aspect than Courchevel. But the square, concrete buildings are now an endangered species—the town has decided on a facelift to be completed before the world's TV cameras are trained on it in 1992. The concrete flavor of Courchevel will be replaced by warm wood and peaked alpine roofs.

Courchevel itself is really a series of smaller villages whose names reflect their relative heights in meters; thus, Courchevel 1850, Courchevel 1650, Courchevel 1550 and so on. The most prestigious of the villages is the highest, Courchevel 1850. Here prices for everything are a bit higher than in the lower villages, but it's also where most trails run right outside the hotel or your apartment door. It is where the best restaurants are found and where the nightlife continues until the sky begins to lighten with coming day. Built for ski-in/ski-out, Courchevel 1850 really works. Its lift system covers both sides of the valley. The world's largest cablecar lift, heading up to La Saulire (8,885 feet), connects Courchevel to the rest of the Les Trois Vallées area.

Méribel

Méribel has been developed into a first-rate ski resort but has taken pains to retain a semblance of the traditional mountain architecture of the French Alps. The resort has two sections, Méribel les Allues—traditional and very popular with the British, and Mottaret—purpose-built and more French. Old Méribel was virtually founded by the British, still retains much of its British trappings and English seems to be spoken almost everywhere.

Méribel is located in the central valley of the Les Trois Vallées and is served by the smallest number of lifts. It makes up for this relative disadvantage, however, by providing the easiest connections to either of the other two valleys. Don't get the idea that you will have trouble finding a lift: there are 18 of them that originate in the village and link up with the other 175 lifts of the Les Trois Vallées system.

The lift to La Saulire provides the best access to the Courchevel valley and the lifts to either Roc des Trois Marches (8,868 feet) or Mont de la Challe (8,448 feet) provide the best connections To Val Thorens and Menuires.

Val Thorens

Val Thorens at 7,546 feet is the highest resort in the Les Trois Vallées area. It has been adopted by the Scandinavian skiers and a sprinkling of Dutch. Little more than a cluster of modern highrise apartment buildings and hotels, Val Thorens' real claim to fame is a cablecar that takes skiers to the summit of Cîme de Caron at 10,499 feet. From here, the skiing sweeps around the valley to the Thorens glacier and then to the west-facing slopes below Mont de la Chambre descending into Les Menuires. A new detachable four-seater chair and a high-speed button lift have opened a new Boismint area for skiing. In the summer this is one of the best places to ski in Europe.

Les Menuires

Les Menuires is also a modern resort with only a few hotels and lots of apartments. From a distance the original section of the resort looks like a misplaced spaceship resting on the snow. The newer sections have concentrated on smaller buildings built in community clusters, which seem cozy after walking through the massive original complexes. Here you will find skiers traveling with families and those looking for the steeps. The skiing is wide open on the west-facing slope with lifts running up toward Val Thorens. The east-facing side of the valley offers more challenging skiing from Pointe de la Masse (9,213 feet), which can be reached by riding a combination of two lifts. The off-trail skiing from this point and from Cîme de Caron are exceptional, especially during the spring when skiers can drop over the backside of the mountains with certified guides. Cîme de Caron, towering over Val Thorens, is also easily accessible and offers good runs.

The lifts taking skiers to the Roc des Trois Marches and to Mont de la Challe provide the best connections to Méribel and the rest of the Les Trois Vallées area.

Mountain rating

This area is so vast and varied that no skier should have trouble finding the perfect slope for his level of ability.

The best expert skiing is in the Val Thorens/Les Menuires valley. Here, on the Cîme de Caron and descending from Pointe de la Masse, experts can find the best steeps, the best powder and the smallest crowds. There are also good expert runs dropping from the ridge separating this valley from that of Méribel. Méribel has few expert runs, the only one of note being a straight shot from La Saulire into town. Courchevel is not known for expert terrain except for several chutes dropping from the Méribel ridge beside La Saulire. Otherwise, the best you can find in that region is under La Vizelle, running from Col de la Loze (7,480 feet) into Courchevel 1300, or try the runs dropping from Col de Chanrossa, which will test any expert.

Intermediates can ski almost anywhere because all expert trails have good escape routes. The area around Courchevel is wide open and good for intermediates.

Beginners will find plenty of trails for learning and will probably leave feeling that they have conquered the entire Les Trois Vallées area.

Ski school

All of the area's resorts have excellent instructors. There are more than 480 instructors in Courchevel (tel. 79080772), 150 instructors in Les Menuires (tel. 79006143), 80 in Val Thorens (tel. 79000286) and 200 in Méribel. The prices vary by resort—these are for Cour-chevel—Winter 1990.

Individual lessons

for two and a half hours (morning)	FFR 490
for two hours (afternoon)	FFR 315
full day	FFR 1,150

Group lessons

for six	FFR 660
consecutive lessons	
children's group	FFR 500

Méribel: six-day group lesson—FFR 600 (high season); private hour—FFR 210. **Val Thorens:** five-day group—FFR 620; private hour—FFR 140.

Special lessons for powder skiing, mono skiing, ski ballet and free-style skiing are offered. There are also racing clinics and a ski kindergarten. A special accompanied ski adventure through the Les Trois Vallées and another tour through the 12 valleys of the Tarentaise—including the resorts of Val Thorens, La Plagne, Les Arcs, Val d'Isère and Tignes—are also offered. For more ski school information, call 79000286; for special courses, call 79000808.

Lift tickets

Each area offers three lift-ticket combinations: one covers only the lifts in the resort area, the second covers lifts in the entire valley; and a third is a full Les Trois Vallées lift ticket. Skiers who are staying for a week or more will want to purchase the Les Trois Vallées combination ticket. The difference between a local pass and the combination pass for a seven-day period is less than FFR 130.

Winter 1990 prices for the Les Trois Vallées combination pass during high season are:

for one day	FFR 165
for six days	FFR 825
for seven days	FFR 903
for fourteen days	FFR 1,572
for each extra day	FFR 115

During low season prices drop by about 15 percent. For children under 13 and seniors over 60, day passes cost FFR 130 and low-season prices are in effect throughout the ski year.

Accommodations

Courchevel and Méribel are some of the most expensive areas in Europe. Accommodations in the Courchevel villages all fall within the same price range, except for Courchevel 1850, which is slightly higher. But even though its prices are between 15 percent and 20 percent higher than the other resorts, Courchevel 1850 still offers extremely reasonably priced accommodations in luxury surroundings, but you must be very careful about making arrangements during low season. This means coming to Courchevel from January 6 to February 2, 1990, if you are looking for any bargains.

The tourist office will send a complete list of hotels with information about "white week" periods and details of making reservations.

All rates are per person, based on double occupancy, with half board unless otherwise noted.

Val Thorens

Le Val Thorens (tel. 79000433) For American tastes this is perhaps the best hotel in town. The breakfast is not the usual croissant and coffee but a full buffet complete with eggs. Walk out your door and onto the slopes. Rates during high season—FFR 550; low season—FFR 410.

Fitz Roy (tel. 79000478) The most luxurious hotel in Val Thorens. Meals are a quantum leap above those of the Val Thorens. Rates during high season—FFR 950; during low season—FFR 600.

Hotel Bel Horizon (tel. 79000477) Right on the edge of the complex this hotel offers good-sized rooms but a very French atmosphere and limited English. The food is reportedly excellent. Rates during high season—FFR 540; low season—FFR 390.

Le Sherpa (tel. 79000070) This is considered the best two-star hotel in town. It is family-run and offers the best value for money with excellent food.

Les Menuires

This resort, formerly only a complex of apartments with hotels squeezed into what should have been more apartments, is now seeing real hotels. By this season there will be three with another three already in the works to be built during the next two seasons.

Hotel Le Menuire (tel. 79006033) This is a small, clean hotel on the road entering the complex. It resembles a good, upscale motel and is located close to the lifts. Rates during high season—FFR 360; low season—FFR 300.

Hotel Skilt (tel. 79006100) This hotel was completely renovated during summer of 1989. Prices have not been set but will be approximately FFR 450 during high season and FFR 380 during low season.

Hotel Althea (tel. 79007979) This will be Les Menuires' first real upscale hotel capable of supporting meetings. It was due to open during the summer of 1989 and should be in operation for winter 1990. Rates were not available.

Méribel

Le Grand Cour (tel. 79086003) The best Méribel has to offer, this hotel is filled with fine antiques, paintings and furnishings. There is normally a list of returning clientele, so make reservations early and hope there is room. The lounge built around a large stone fireplace and the dining room both have sweeping views of the town. Rates during high season—FFR 665-915; during low season FFR 590-700.

Allodis (tel. 79005600) This beautifully decorated hotel is new as of last winter. It features an interesting combination of modern color and design with tradition classical architecture featuring arches and columns. But while the hotel may be perfectly located for skiing, it is not close to town. Count on having a car available for this one. Rates during high season—FFR 800; low season— FFR 680.

l'Orée du Bois (tel. 79005030) This hotel provides good value, is on the slopes but is far out of the center of town for nightlife and restaurants. Rates during high season—FFR 490; low season— FFR 442.

Mont Vallon (tel. 79004400) Located in Mottaret, the Mont Vallon is the only real luxury hotel in the valley. You have everything here: pool, exercise room, jacuzzi, sauna, squash courts and spectacular rooms. Walk out the door and onto the lifts. Rates during high season—FFR 950; during low season—FFR 750.

Hotel La Tarentaise (tel. 79004243) Located in Mottaret right on the slopes with a big British clientele. Rates during high season— FFR 600; during low season—FFR 540.

Les Arolles (tel. 79004040) Also located in Mottaret, this hotel also enjoys a big group of British skiers, especially families. It is right on the slopes. Rates during high season are —FFR 550; during low season—FFR 450.

Courchevel

Bellecote (tel. 79081212) This hotel is more alpine, cozier and exclusive than the Byblos, which is described below. Its guests have had their fortunes for some time and are not interested in letting the world know their every activity. Much of the furniture was imported from the Himalayas; that which is in the lobby is leather and very soft. Heated swimming pool and a well-equipped exercise room. It all costs FFR 8,750 a week with full board during January low season. Expect to pay from FFR 980-1,300 per person a day with full board during high season.

Le Byblos (tel. 79081212) The mountain version of the world-famous San Tropez hotel, Le Byblos is conceived as an all-encompassing hotel. The soaring wooden archways, the heavy wooden columns in the bar, the secluded pool and the luxury rooms cater to hedonism at its best. This is where you rub shoulders with the jet-set elite during the winter. For the opportunity expect to pay FFR 1,150-1,800 a night with full board during high season. The special January low-season rate is FFR 8,750 a week with full board.

Hotel Trois Vallées (tel. 79080012) This is for our money the best of the four-star properties in Courchevel. The hotel itself is delightful with excellent light pine decor. Its designers paid special attention to the bathrooms, which are at the leading edge of design, featuring giant tubs—some marble, others black, brass fittings and every amenity. The hotel is also only steps away from the finest restaurants in town, as well as the wildest nightlife. Rates during high season—FFR 850-950; during low season—FFR 600-700. A special fixed U.S. dollar rate of $910 a week with half board is offered during January 1990.

Grand Hotel Rond-Point des Piste (tel. 79080269) One of the area's hotels to get face lift, this one has an exceptional location in the center of the resort action. The rooms were redone as the exterior was recreated. Everything is bright and cheerful. Rates during high season—FFR 745-845; low season—FFR 645-745. Special January week, US$ 910.

Les Ducs de Savoie (tel. 79080300) This is the best of the three-star lot with spacious rooms, a great swimming pool and lots of wood. The hotel is a bit out of town but right on the slopes and within easy reach of the gondola during normal operating hours. At night you'll have to walk 10 minutes to get home or take a cab. Rates during high season—FFR 600-710 full board; during low season—FFR 540-640. The guaranteed U.S. dollar rate for half board during January low season is $910.

New Solarium (tel. 79080201) This hotel has some of the best views over Courchevel. The dining room enjoys these views as well as the higher-priced rooms. This hotel is across the street from the Byblos and about a 10-minute walk from the town. Rates with full board during high season—FFR 670-550; low season—FFR 600-500.

L'Aiglon (tel. 79080266) This is perhaps the best two-star hotel in town, offering exceptional rooms for very low rates. Its location is excellent with only a short five-minute walk into town. People who stay seem to like it because they keep coming back year after year. Rates during high season—FFR 320-500; low season—FFR 300-390. Special U.S. dollar guaranteed rate for January low season is $560 a week with half board.

Chanrossa (tel. 79080658) In "1550," this hotel offers good access to 1850 for everything except nightlife. The hotel food is excellent. This is the best low-priced alternative to Courchevel prices. Rates in high season—FFR 390; in low season—FFR 340.

Apartments

Apartments are the French choice for accommodation. In fact, apartment beds outnumber hotel beds by at least 5-to-1. What you get is the ability to schedule off-slope life at your own pace. Apartment rates are slightly higher in Courchevel 1850. In general, for a one-week stay expect to pay:

	low season	high season
for two to three persons	FFR 1,000-2,000	FFR 1,740-3,090
for four to five persons	FFR 1,400-2,000	FFR 2,800-3,800
for five to six persons	FFR 1,800-2,500	FFR 3,500-4,900

Even at the high end of low-season prices, an apartment shared by four people costs less than FFR 75 a night per person.

During "white-week" periods, in Les Menuires, for example, apartments come with a six-day ski pass for the three valleys and cost FFR 1,200 per person a week when sharing a two-person apartment. For a four-person apartment the costs drop to FFR 1,010 per person. That's FFR 150 a day.

The tourist office will send more information and a registration card, and will help make reservations.

Dining

Courchevel

This resort is considered to have the best food of any French mountain resort. The **Chabichou** (tel. 79080055) maintains a friendly rivalry with the **La Bateau Ivre** (tel. 79080246) for the top restaurant in town. Both will end up costing about $70-100 per person. A meal in the **Bergerie** (tel. 79082470) shouldn't be missed. Henri Sauvanet has done an exceptional job of turning this century-old farmhouse into a cozy restaurant. If you can get there on Friday nights there is Russian night complete with rousing gypsy music and plenty of good times. Otherwise you have plenty of high-priced entrées and a chance to sample the most expensive raclette in the world. Expect to pay between $50 and $70 with wine.

Le Bistro du Praz (tel. 79084133)located in Courchevel 1300 serves up some of the best local specialties in the area. The atmosphere of the old farmhouse eatery adds a special flavor to the experience.

So much for high prices. For the more reasonable restaurants, try **Le Saulire** (tel. 79080652) with good local specialties and an owner who likes Americans due to years living in Canada. Expect to pay between FFR 220-350 per person for dinner. **Le Mangeoire** looks almost Western with cowhides, wagon wheels and lanterns. The food is simple but the crowds in the evening are great. Expect to pay between FFR 150 and FFR 200.

l'Arbe (tel. 79082603) is where the locals eat. It seems to always be crowded from lunchtime onwards, first with the lunch crowd and then with the après-skiers, then with the dinner folk.

Méribel

This town doesn't have anywhere the range of restaurants enjoyed by Courchevel. The best in town is **Le Grand Cour** (tel. 79086003) with a dining room overlooking the chalets of the town. The experience is hard to beat, with excellent fish as well as local specialties. Expect to spend FFR 250 per person.

La Petite Rosière between Méribel and Mottaret is small, with 15 tables set around a fireplace in a small chalet. You need a car to get here for the hearty meals. Expect to pay FFR 500 per person.

If you have a car, make the effort to dine at the **Hotel Allodis** (tel. 79005600). The restaurant, especially during lunch, is wonderful. The evening dining room offers meals in an interesting architectural harmony of modern and classic lines. Expect to pay FFR 200 per person.

Chez Kiki (tel. 79086668) is the Méribel version of Courchevel's original Bergerie. The atmosphere is not as lively but just as cozy. The food is comparable but half as expensive. You'll be able to get through the meal for only FFR 200 apiece.

Les Menuires

Where one would expect only mediocre meals with the emphasis on apartment living, Les Menuires is a pleasant surprise. **La Bouitte** (tel. 79006627) in St. Marcel is probably the best restaurant in the valley and the only real stand-out in the immediate area of Les Menuires.

La Marmite du Géant (tel. 79006101) serves excellent food in modern, rustic surroundings next to the pool and ice skating rink.

Auberge de Lanau (tel. 79006296) serves excellent grilled meats and fondue. It is located in the basement of the Hotel Oiseau.

La Mousse (tel. 79006906) has a wonderful stone-and-wood interior as well as the best fish in the valley.

Les Menuires also has several good restaurants on the slopes above the main village. Try **Chalet des Neiges** (tel. 79006055), where you'll get simple, good food for between FFR 80-100. In the evenings the restaurant sponsors fondue dinners, and a guide brings skiers into the lower village with torches.

Les Roches Blanches (tel. 79006022) on La Masse is a rustic chalet serving pizza and spaghetti. Just above Les Croisette and reached by a short walk is the **L'Etoile** (tel. 79006325) with tables huddled around a giant fireplace. It has one of the best chefs in the area. Staff pick up dinner guests in snowmobiles if they make prior reservations.

Val Thorens

The restaurant in the **Fitz Roy** is head and shoulders above the rest of the fare in Val Thorens. Then try the restaurant in Hotel Val Thorens, **Chalet de Glacier** for basic French and **Galoubet** for the best Savoyard specialties in town.

Nightlife

Courchevel is considered to have one of the best balances between nightlife and skiing of any European resort. It can be just as glitzy and upscale as Mégeve, Gstaad or St. Moritz. Après-ski entertainment here is varied and you will be sure to find a bar or disco to your taste, but expect everything to start late. Be prepared to fork over lots of money—this is some of the most expensive nightlife to be found in the Alps. Cover to get into a disco will run at least FFR 80 and every drink afterwards will cost the same.

The immediate après-ski centers in **Le Tremplin** at the base of the slopes, then seems to move to **L'Arbe** just before dinner. **Le Grange** offers earlier drinks until midnight, then everyone heads to a disco, such as **Caves du Roy** or **St. Nicolas** with its transvestite show.

If you are looking for wild nightlife, the rest of the three valleys is not the place to be. Méribel has one disco worth mentioning, **The St. Pere**. Nightlife consists of a few nightclubs, a piano bar, a jazz bar and whatever you can organize on your own. Try **The Pub**—it seems to be the best in town, or try **Le Capricorn, Le Refuge** and **Le Marquis**, all in the center of the village and a few steps from one another.

Les Menuires has four small discos, packed with the very young, tucked into the basement of the massive apartment buildings. The best is **Liberty** in the Roberty sector. In Val Thorens the nightlife is centered around the hotel bars, or try the **Malaysia Bar** or the **Calypso** for a slightly older crowd.

Child care

The tourist office, your hotel or apartment manager can put you in touch with qualified private babysitters who provide child-care services at any time of the day or night. Each resort also offers child-care programs. Here's a resort-by-resort rundown.

Val Thorens

The Val Thorens Ski School has a Mini Club (tel. 79000674). The "Mini-Club" kindergarten for children from three and a half to 12 years is at Le Roc de Péclet and features ski lessons for children over five and snow activities for younger kids. Ask about discounts for three children or more from the same family. The costs are FFR 98 for a half day, FFR 185 for a full day and FFR 890 for a six-day program without meals and FFR 1,070 with meals.

Marielle Goitschel, former world champion skier, has started a children's program in Val Thorens (tel. 79000047). Mornings cost FFR 95 without meals or FFR 125 with meal. A full day costs FFR 185 without meal and FFR 210 with meal.

Les Menuires has three possibilities for children. The "Schtroumpfs' Village" is divided into two sections: three months to two and a half years and two and a half to 10 years. An intro to skiing is provided for children from four years; different programs are offered to each group. Reservations are recommended (tel. 7906379). A second kindergarten, called "Scoubidou," is located in the "Les Bruyeres" area. It serves children between two and eight years (tel. 79006775).

The ski school also runs special programs for youngsters from five years. The lessons are coordinated with the "Schtroumpfs' Village" to allow children to spend the remaining time after and before lessons at the child-care facility.

Méribel has a highly respected child-care program. "Le Club Saturnin" accepts children between two and eight years. It is associated with the ski school and ski lessons are offered to children ready to ski (tel. 79086690). The second possibility for children is in Méribel-Mottaret. "Les Pingouins" accepts children between three and eight years (tel. 79004646).

Courchevel 1850 has a ski school for children from four years. Call 79080772. There are also two kindergartens, one in 1850 and another in 1650. Both take children between the ages of two and five years. Call (for "1850") 79083154 or (for "1650") 79080329.

Getting there

The closest airports are Geneva (152 kilometers), Lyons (190 kilometers) and Chambéry (110 kilometers). There are daily connections from the airport to the resorts. The rail service takes skiers as far as Moutiers, 36 kilometers away, a one-hour drive, from the resorts. Bus and taxi services are available from the station.

If driving, follow the signs to Chambéry, and then take route N90 to Moutiers and up to the Les Trois Vallées. Some distances: Paris, 657 kilometers; Brussels, 921 kilometers; and Strasbourg, 555 kilometers.

Other activities

Val Thorens —Facilities include an indoor swimming pool, whirlpool baths, saunas, squash courts, six indoor tennis courts, a gymnasium and an outdoor skating rink. Hang-gliding and aerobics are offered.

Les Menuires —There is a heated outdoor pool in Reberty as well as a fully equipped fitness center called "Espace Tonic" (tel. 79006551). Each activity costs FFR 50 or FFR 80 for two.

Méribel—Facilities include an indoor swimming pool, indoor golf practice range and an ice skating rink. Mountain flying lessons are offered.

Courchevel —Facilities include indoor swimming pools, saunas and an Olympic-sized skating rink. Hang-gliding, ski jumping, parachuting and mountain flying courses are taught. Special language courses are organized for foreigners, allowing participants to combine skiing with language lessons. On Wednesday there is a musical evening with concerts and recitals.

Tourist information

Courchevel—Office du Tourisme, La Croisette, 73120 Courchevel 1850, France; tel. 79080029; telex 980083

Méribel —Office du Tourisme, 73550 Méribel, France; tel. 79086001; telex 980001

Val Thorens —Office du Tourisme, 73440 Val Thorens, France; tel. 79000808; telex 980572
Central Reservations is handled by Val Thorens Tours; tel. 79000106; fax 79000649; telex 980573F

Les Menuires —Office du Tourisme, 73440 Les Menuires, France; tel. 79082012; telex 980084. For reservations only, call 79007979.

Tignes

Tignes, Val d'Isère's sister resort, appears to be nothing more than a group of concrete apartment buildings huddled at the foot of one of Europe's largest glaciers. Upon closer examination the large cluster is really a series of modern villages at altitudes that range from 4,900 feet to nearly 6,900 feet. The main village, Tignes Lac, lies at 6,890 feet. The highest village is Val Claret, and it is from here that the cablecar leaves for La Grande Motte glacier. The other villages are Lavachet, Le Rosset and Les Almes.

The entire area is modern, having been built after the original village was flooded in the early 1950s by the lake created when the Chevril dam was built. Tignes has been linked with Val d'Isère to form a massive ski area called "l'espace Killy." The combined network features 300 kilometers of runs linked by 120 lifts, with continuous vertical drops of over 5,000 feet. Snow and skiing are a certainty 365 days a year.

Where to ski

The skiing at Tignes is fantastic. The resort rates as one of the best in the world for intermediate cruisers, experts, beginners, sun worshipers, people who don't like to ski the same trail twice and people who travel with children. What more is there?

The lift system offers 24 different ways up starting from different parts of town. You'll never have to walk very far to start skiing. The area peaks at La Grande Motte at 11,995 feet, site of year-round glacier skiing.

The ski area can be broken into three main sectors. If La Grande Motte is directly in front of you, the Tovière Lavachet is on your left and the Palet/Aiguille Percée Palafour area rises on your right. There are also a few lifts rising from the village of Tignes-les-Brevières, 1,640 feet lower.

The skiing in the Tovière Lavachet area is a steep 1,950-foot vertical drop back into town. There are some great off-trail runs over the backside of Lavachet into Val d'Isère or around the cliffs back into Tignes.

Le Grande Motte is reached by a two-stage cablecar rising almost 6,000 feet from Val Claret. The skiing on the glacier is wide-open and relatively mellow. This sector offers the only lower intermediate terrain. The run under the cablecar is a good intermediate test of stamina, and experts can go off the trail over the Rocher de la Grande Balme into the Palet sector.

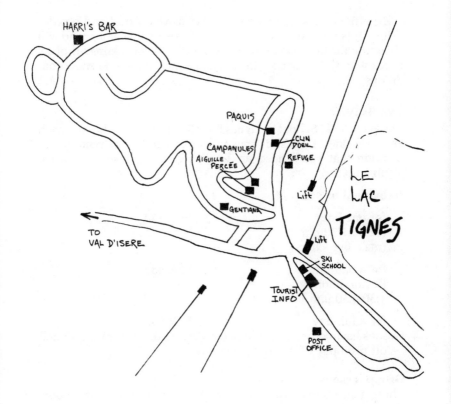

The Palet/l'Aiguille Percée offers relatively mellow terrain under the Col du Pallet, with relatively tough intermediate runs down from the l'Aiguille Percée. Experts have a wide swath of off-trail possibilities as well as itineraries over the Col du Palet or over the backside of the l'Aiguille Percée down the Vallon de la Sache to Tignes-les-Brevières.

Mountain rating

It's easy to see why the area has been rated as tops in every category. Just the snow expanse is mind-boggling. With a vertical drop of more than a mile and a third, coupled with 30,000 acres of terrain, you can be sure that there is something for everyone. Beginners and intermediates can cruise all over the resort's upper reaches.

Experts can test themselves on extensive off-trail and powder skiing. It is best, at least for a day, to take a guide along who will show you the best places to test your skills. Before skiing off-piste, check with the ski school for the latest information on snow conditions.

Ski school

The French Ski School in Tignes has 150 instructors who can teach any level skier. English is spoken by many of the instructors, but mention that you'll need an English-speaking instructor when signing up.

Individual lessons

for one hour (12:30-1:30 p.m.) (max. five skiers)	FFR 130
for a half day (9 a.m.-noon or 1:30-4:30 p.m.)	FFR 480
for a full day	FFR 950

Groups having the services of a certified guide for the powder and off-piste pay FFR 1,100 per full day.

Group lessons

Three-hour courses are conducted in the morning or afternoon. Prices are for one week.

	adults (with video)	children (4-12 yrs.)
for a half day	FFR 430	FFR 350
for a full day	FFR 780	FFR 625

Special courses in off-trail and powder skiing cost FFR 1,000 per person a week. A six-day slalom racing course is offered for FFR 930. More information is available from the tourist office.

The ski school has three offices: In Tignes Lac, call 79063028; in Val Claret, call 79063128; and in Lavachet, call 79065326.

Lift tickets

The prices below are for "l'espace Killy," which includes both Val d'Isère and Tignes areas. Prices in parentheses are for children 5-12 years of age and seniors over 60. (prices are for winter 1990)

for one day	FFR 153 (FFR 110)
for two days	FFR 285 (FFR 195)
for three days	FFR 400 (FFR 280)
for six days	FFR 730 (FFR 520)
for seven days	FFR 835 (FFR 590)
for 14 days	FFR 1,400 (FFR 985)

Incidentally, the company that runs the lift system in the Tignes sector of "l'espace Killy" is so confident in the efficiency of its lift system that it promises to refund a free coupon to any skier who can prove that he waited more than 17 minutes at the bottom of a lift. It's the only such guarantee in the world, and with a lift capacity of about 60,000 skiers an hour, the company has had very few complaints. There are some limitations to the guarantee, based on weather, but the point is well taken: They aim to see you skiing, not waiting in line.

Accommodations

A special low-season-only program has been organized by the tourist office and hoteliers. Low season normally runs from the end of September until Christmas, during most of January and during late April and May. Check with the office for exact dates.

The program's cost is based a two-star hotel with half board and type of package (with or without ski lessons) selected by the skier.

A hotel with lift tickets only will cost FFR 2,360. The same package with "super forme" added will cost FFR 2,660. If ski school is added, the package price comes to FFR 2,790.

For bookings, contact the tourist office's service, 73320 Tignes, France; tel. 79063560; telex 980030; Fax 79064544. The office will send more information, but you will be required to pay a 25 percent deposit to reserve your space.

Ski D'Or (tel. 79065160) is the best three-star hotel in town. Ask for room 23 if it's available. Each of the rooms is tastefully and uniquely decorated, and the restuarant is perhaps the best in the entire Val d'Isère area.

The Curling (tel. 79063434) across the street from the Ski d'Or is considered the next best, but it is far behind its classier counterpart. Rooms in the Curling are simple and functional, and the hotel has all such amenities as telephone, TV and dryer.

In the two-star range, which are the hotels associated with the tourist office special, we recommend **Paquis** (tel. 79063733); **Aiguille Percée** (tel. 79065222); **Campanules** (tel. 79063436) and **Gentiana** (tel. 79065246).

Apartments

When you learn that Tignes has only 1,200 hotel beds but almost 15,000 in apartments, you realize the importance of the rental system. The French have a very well organized apartment rental system. The tourist office acts as an information clearinghouse, providing an extensive listing of individuals and agencies who will rent apartments at extremely low rates.

In many cases, linen is not included but can be rented from the apartment owners or agencies. The normal linen fee is FFR 100 a week.

A typical sample of apartment rates in Tignes is provided below. The centrally located units are only about 100 meters from the lifts.

	high season	low season
studio: two to four persons	FFR 2,500	FFR 1,100
for four to five persons	FFR 3,550	FFR 1,700
for six to seven persons	FFR 4,200-5,800	FFR 2,200-2,500

Most agencies and individual owners offer apartments within similar price ranges. Note the differences between low and high season. But even during high season accommodation costs will only be $21 a day per person, based on four people sharing a two-bedroom apartment.

For more information and a complete listing of rental apartments, write to the tourist office.

Dining

Outside dining is limited, but the best in town is **Le Clin d'Oeil** (tel. 79065910). Make reservations as it is very small. The restaurant in the Refuge Hotel (tel. 79063664) and **Le Caveau** (tel. 79065232) in Val Claret are also excellent. There is a Japanese restaurant, **Myako** (tel. 79063479), which is fun for a change of pace.

Nightlife

Nightlife is almost non-existent because most people are either "there to ski" or are partying in their own apartments. Most English-speakers seem to hang out at **Harri's Bar** or the **American Bar**. But there are several other discos and pubs in town where true aprés-skiers gather. The most established discos are **Les**

Chandelles, the most popular in town, in Val Claret, and **Playboy,** also in Val Claret.

The best pubs are **Club 73** and **Pub 2000**, both in Val Claret.

Child care

This is a category in which Tignes excels. There are two kindergartens. The first, Les Marmottons in Tignes Lac (tel. 79065167), accepts children between two and a half and 10 years. Children over four are taught to ski. For six consecutive days, with lunch and skiing included, the cost is FFR 950. For children staying only a half day without lunch the weekly cost is FFR 400.

The other kindergarten, La Rotonde (tel. 79065098), is in Val Claret adjacent to the ski school. Children from three months to three years are accepted in its "Baby Club." A special first-steps-on-skis program is organized for children between three and five years. And children between six and 10 years take group lessons with the French Ski School. The costs are FFR 185 for a full day, including lunch, or FFR 950 for six consecutive days with all meals. Both kindergartens are normally open from 8:30 a.m. until 5 p.m.

The ski school children's program (tel. 79063028 or 79063128) accepts those from four to 12 years. Packages cost FFR 350 for six days of three-hour lessons.

Getting there

The closest international airports are in Lyons and Geneva. Geneva is about 140 kilometers (86 miles) and Lyons approximately 240 kilometers (150 miles) from the resort. A smaller airport that offers some domestic and international flights is Chambéry.

Rail transport is available to Tignes, but connections can become complicated. TVG trains run to Chambéry, then a normal train to Bourg St. Maurice, where a bus connections take you to Val d'Isère and to Tignes.

If you plan to drive, the best route from Geneva is autoroute A41 to Annecy and then N90 to Albertville. From there, follow the signs to Bourg St. Maurice and on to Val d'Isère or Col de l'Isèran. From Lyons, take autoroute A43 to Chambéry, then follow the signs to Albertville and on to Val d'Isère.

A daily regular bus service to Tignes from the Geneva, Lyons and Chambéry airports operates during the winter months.

Other activities

Tignes is relatively remote, so you will probably be content to keep your wanderings within the area's ski resorts, or try some of the activities in the town itself.

Areas that are close enough for a good day of skiing include Les Arcs, La Plagne and La Rosiere, among others.

Val d'Isère offers more shopping opportunities than Tignes and is only a short bus ride or drive away.

Hang-gliding lessons from the top of Toviere are offered for about FFR 400 a flight.

Special scuba diving courses, which are conducted beneath the ice in the lake, are organized in March and April.

There is the highest bowling alley in Europe with 12 lanes; FFR 30 a game.

Ice skating on the lake is on tap daily and at night twice a week, weather permitting.

Tignes also has one of France's best fitness clubs in the Lac du Tignes Sports Center (tel. 79065797) with weights, saunas, jacuzzis, steam baths, squash and indoor golf simulation. A fitness club is also established in Val Claret with more extensive body-building equipment. Costs are FFR 60 per activity.

Tourist information

Office du Tourisme, BP 51, 73320 Tignes, France; tel. 79061555; telex 980030 F.

For hotel and apartment booking, call 79063560; address and telex the same as above.

Val d'Isère

Val d'Isère has long been one of the true European meccas of skiing. But although the professional ski world knew about Val d'Isère, the average skier began to hear more about it after Jean-Claude Killy won his Olympic gold. The town was also home to three other Olympic champions, who won a total of nine gold medals. With many of the men's ski races during the coming 1992 Winter Olympics scheduled to be held in Val d'Isère, Olympic gold will again bring this resort to the world's front pages.

The town lies 6,012 feet and the ski area rises to 11,336 feet, with working verticals of more than 3,250 feet in all sectors of the resort. Skiers looking for the best on- and off-trail runs in the world need look no farther than Val d'Isère.

Unlike many French purpose-built resorts, Val d'Isère is actually a town. Unfortunately as the resort was initially being developed, architects opted for functionally square, flat-topped hotels. Recently, though, new buildings have been constructed in the Savoyard Alpine style of chalets, and many of the formerly ugly, square buildings are being dressed up with new facades to create a more mountain village atmosphere.

The ski area is linked with neighboring Tignes, creating "l'espace Killy," with 300 kilometers (186 miles) of marked runs for every level of skier, tried-and-true off-piste itineraries for serious experts and 120 lifts, including an underground subway with an uphill capacity of more than 100,000 skiers per hour.

Where to ski

An area as enormous as Val d'Isère/Tignes is virtually impossible to describe in words. Even the trail map printed in a relatively miniature size gives no feel of the immensity of the area. Your first clue will be when you exit from the funival or Bellevard cablecar and look out over the seemingly endless fields of snow.

The Val d'Isère share of the l'espace Killy is divided into four sectors corresponding with the three main ridges dropping into the town and the glacier area.

The Fornet sector is reached by Le Fornet cablecar, which rises the first 380 meters. From the top of the cablecar skiers can drop back down into the town on a steep and narrow expert run directly under the cables or loop to their right around an advanced beginner trail. There are also two choices of lifts farther up the moun-

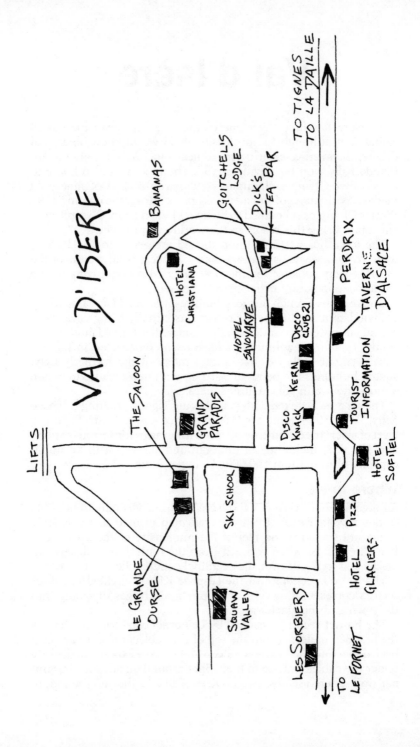

tain. The gondola leaving from the cablecar building reaches the Col de l'Isère area, which provides access to skiing on the Glacier de Pissaillas or allows skiers to take the connecting lift to the Solaise sector. The very long Signal drag lift will take you to just under the Signal peak at 10,633 feet. From there you can take a tough intermediate trail back to the cablecar or drop into the off-trail Le Vallon powder fields, which then drop more than 3,000 feet back to the base of the Fornet cablecar. This skiing is some of the most beautiful in the world.

The Solaise sector is reached by cablecar from the village center. This area is basically wide-open beginner and intermediate paradise. About 1,500 vertical feet wait for wide-open cruising. There are good off-piste itineraries from the Solaise that will keep any expert happy. The Danaides drops off the end of the ridge into town, and Les Marmottes offers precipitous drops into the valley separating the Solaise area from Bellevarde.

The Bellevarde sector has the best access with three methods of getting to the top of Rocher de Bellevarde and two additional lifts serving intermediate and beginner runs from La Daille. The funival, a high-speed subway, rises from La Daille through the rock to the top of Rocher de Bellevarde. A cablecar arrives from the village and a two chairlift combination can also bring skiers to the peak. Beginners have a series of runs at higher altitudes and a choice between two long runs with more a 2,900-foot vertical back to La Daille. Intermediates have their choice of two more challenging drops back to La Daille. Intermediates can drop down "The Face" or into the valley back to the town. There are also excellent off-piste itineraries from the top of the Bellevarde sector. Take Le Kern around the front side of the rock cliff and drop through powder back into town, or take the slalom drag lift to the side of the Charvet rock cluster and ski around the back side of the formation entering the valley eventually returning to town, or drop down to La Daille off-piste.

Mountain rating

There is something for everyone; the upper reaches of the mountains are excellent for any range of skier. Experts can test themselves on the steeps that drop into town and extensive off-trail and powder-skiing pockets. It's a good idea to take a guide along, at least for a day, so you can find the best places to test your limits. Also, if you plan to ski off-trail, check with the ski school before you leave for the latest information on snow conditions.

Ski school

Val d'Isère's French Ski School boasts having Jean-Claude Killy as its technical adviser. Its ski instructors are among the most qualified in the world: three former world champions and many members of the national ski team serve as instructors. In total, there are 150 instructors, 40 coaches and 19 mountain guides who can teach any level of skier, from the basic beginner to the absolute best racer. The school faculty includes former members of the French ski team. English is spoken by many of the instructors. Be sure to specify that you need an English-speaking instructor.

French Ski School offices are located in the tourist office, the Village Center (tel. 79060234) and in the La Daille shopping center (tel. 79060999).

Individual lessons (1988/89 prices)

Prices and session lengths differ between the December-January period and from February onward. Basically a lesson lasting an an hour and a half will cost FFR 190 and a one-hour lesson will cost FFR 130. Private lessons are limited to five students. Instructors or guides can be hired for the full day from 9:30 a.m. to 5 p.m. for FFR 1,050 for up to four people and FFR 1,150 for up to five. Morning lessons from 9:30 a.m. to 12:30 p.m. cost FFR 599; afternoon lessons from 2 p.m. to 5 p.m. are FFR 360.

Group lessons

February courses cost FFR 667 for six full days of lessons, which run from 9:30 a.m. to 12:30 p.m. and from 2:30 p.m. to 5 p.m. Six morning lessons cost FFR 441, and six afternoon lessons cost FFR 330. Lessons in December and January run approximately 10 percent less.

A new "Grand Ski" class that meets every morning from 9 a.m. to 1 p.m. allows skiers to ski in a group with an intructor on most of the off-trail itineraries. Six days will cost FFR 840, and a single day will cost FFR 168. At Val d'Isère, if you can afford it and you are a good skier this course is worth every franc.

There are also powder skiing lessons that cost FFR 950 for a six-day course and day trips to La Plagne, Les Arc and La Rosiere/La Thuile for expeditions.

There are several other ski schools and guide organizations in Val d'Isère. The largest of these is the École de Ski Val d'Isère whose brochure is titled *Snow Fun*. Prices are slightly less expensive than the French Ski School and all 30 instructors are bilingual in English and French. You can sign up with the English section of "Snow Fun" at the Solaise Gallery (tel. 79061979).

Patrick and Jean Zimmer also offer off-piste and normal resort skiing lessons for slightly more than the French Ski School. And the couple's interresort ski package allows skiers to take daily ski tours around Val d'Isère then to La Plagne, Les Arc, Courchevel, Bonneval and La Thuile for FFR 325 a person. Call Zimmer Top Ski at 79061480.

All ski schools are connected with off-piste guides by radio. Both the "Snow Fun" and the Top Ski programs outfit all off-trail skiers with beepers. The French Ski School does not.

Heliskiing is offered for FFR 1,000 for five mornings of skiing or FFR 750 for five afternoons. The helicopter drops you virtually anywhere, even in Italy for backcountry skiing. Call 79060553.

Europe is at the leading edge of snowboarding, which they call "Snow Surf" as well as monoskiing. Check with the tourist office and the ski school for a half-dozen opportunities to learn or improve on either technique.

Lift tickets

These prices are for the entire l'espace Killy, including the Val d'Isère/Tignes area pass. Reduced prices for children between five and years and seniors over 60 are in parentheses. (1989/90 prices)

for one day	FFR 153 (FFR 110)
for two days	FFR 285 (FFR 195)
for three days	FFR 400 (FFR 280)
for six days	FFR 730 (FFR 520)
for seven days	FFR 835 (FFR 590)
for 14 days	FFR 1,400 (FFR 985)

Children under five years go free. Photo is needed for all tickets two days and over. The ticket is valid for one day of your stay on La Plagne and Les Arcs ski lifts.

Accommodations

The tourist office and the hoteliers have organized special "blue/white/red week" programs covering the entire ski season. Costs for the program are based on the category of hotel chosen and the package being offered. Packages come in four categories, each with half board and breakfast-only options There are also full-board options for some of the programs. "F1-Free Ski" offers hotel, seven-day lift ticket (six days during red-zone periods), use of the swimming pool and holiday reconstitution insurance. The holiday insurance protects you in case an accident curtails your week-long program with a replacement program free of charge during the coming 1990/91 season.""F2-A la Carte" offers the F1 program, plus five hours of group lessons with the French Ski School or four hours of private lessons to be taken between 12:30 p.m. and 2 p.m. The "F3-Powder Snow Course" offers the F1 package, plus six days with an instructor skiing from 9:30 a.m. to 4:30 p.m. "F4-Cross-Country/Beginners" provides hotel, six days of cross-country or beginner skiing with an instructor and holiday insurance.

These prices are for Winter 1990 based on double occupancy with half board in the basic F1 and F3 programs. The F2 program costs fall between these two, and the F4-beginning/cross-country program costs about FFR 100 less than the F1 program.

Dates for the blue zone are December 16-24, 1989, and January 6-21, 1990.

Four-star hotel package: F1—FFR 4,610; F3—FFR 5,375.

Three-star-"C" package: F1—FFR 3,450; F3—FFR 4,215.

Normal three-star package: F1—FFR 2,935; F3—FFR 3,700.

Two-star packages: F1—FFR 2,595; F3—FFR 3,360.

White zone dates are January 11-20, 1990, and March 31-April 8, 1990.

Four-star hotel package: F1—FFR 5,220; F3—FFR 6,070.

Three-star-"C" package: F1—FFR 3,945; F3—FFR 4,795.

Normal three-star package: F1—FFR 3,470; F3—FFR 4,320.

Two-star package: F1—FFR 2,870; F3—FFR 3,720.

The red-zone periods (the most expensive) are December 23, 1989-January 7, 1990; February 10 to April 1, 1990; and April 7-22, 1990. Only the F1 and F2 programs are available during these high periods.

Four-star hotel package: F1—FFR 5,665.

Three-star-"C" package: F1—FFR 4,720.

Normal three-star package: F1—FFR 3,955.

two-star package: F1—FFR 3,390.

Hotels in the area are generally well-equipped to serve international skiers, who make up almost 50 percent of Val d'Isère's clientele.

Hotel Grand Paradis (tel. 79061173) enjoys perhaps the best location in the resort, downtown and just across the street from the lifts. It will be upgraded to a four-star hotel for this winter. The lobby has recently been redecorated in elegant dark wood, Tiffany lamps and mirrors. The hotel has its own underground parking. Rates: FFR 655 per person with half board, double occupancy.

Hotel Latitudes (tel. 79061888) is a new four-star built in the village center. The lobby/bar steps up several levels. Rooms are very businesslike with little of the alpine charm the exterior of the hotel promises. The rates during January's low season, double occupancy, is FFR 3,024; during high season—FFR 4,165. As of April 1989 this hotel was not part of the package program described above.

Sofitel (tel. 79060830) is a modern, four-star hotel located directly above the tourist office. It is very convenient and modern. The town's main fitness center is located in the hotel as well as one of the only heated hotel pools. Rates for high season with half board: FFR 705.

Hotel Christiania (tel. 79060825) is a chalet-style, older four-star hotel only two minutes from the lifts. The lobby is full of spongy overstuffed chairs, and the normal double rooms are disappointing with paneling and little warmth. On the other hand, the suites available on the hotel's top floor are among the best in the resort, with beautiful bathrooms, antique country furniture and rough-hewn appointments. Rates for double rooms with half board during high season—FFR 684. Suites cost FFR 1,354 per person with half board.

Hotel Mecure (tel. 79061293) is a three-star modern hotel located in the center of the village. Elsewhere this would be the perfect businessman's hotel, for it is clean, convenient and efficient. Rates during high season with half board—FFR 510-590.

Hotel Savoyard (tel. 79060155) is our favorite hotel in Val d'Isère. The three-star is chalet-style, has a cozy sauna and an excellent restaurant. It's best feature is being in the center of town, only steps away from the lifts. Rates during high season, with half board—FFR 580.

Hotel Samovar (tel. 79061351) is another three-star oozing with charm. The hotel is located out of the center of town at the base of the funival and the other La Daille lifts. Its restaurant is consistently rated as one of the best in town by locals, but its best section remains reserved for hotel guests or outsiders who often wait two weeks for reservations. The rooms are weathered, but comfortable. The owner says he wants to create the atmosphere of a chalet rather than a hotel. Room 10 is nice if you can get it. Breakfast is a sumptuous affair. Rates during high season with half board—FFR 395.

Hotel Sorbiers (tel. 79062377) is a beautiful three-star hotel built in modern chalet style. The interiors are rich with golden wood and rooms are cozy. The hotel offers only bed-and-breakfast arrangements. Rates during high season—FFR 290-330.

Hotel Altitude (tel. 79061255) has one of the coziest restaurants of any hotel in the village. The rooms need renovation, but the second- and third-floor rooms are some of the largest in town. The fourth-floor rooms are smaller but have a loft as well. All rooms rent for the same price—FFR 330-400 with half board during high season, depending on whether you select a north or south side room.

Chamois d'Or (tel. 79060044) is a two-star hotel filled with old alpine charm that greets you as soon as you enter the lobby and restaurant with its giant fireplace. The rooms vary in size but all have ample room. The hotel is only steps away from the cablecars up to the Solaise and the Bellevarde. If you want atmosphere, this is the place.

The central reservations system is run by Val Hotel, which can make arrangements in any of these hotels unless noted otherwise. The agency will also provide additional information on the packages. Contact: Val Hotel, BP 73, 73150 Val d'Isère, France; tel. 79061890; telex 980077.

Apartments

In the French apartment rental system, the tourist office acts as an information clearinghouse. It maintains an extensive list of individuals and agencies who will rent apartments in the resort area at extremely low rates.

In many cases, linen is not included but can be rented for the week from the apartment owners or agencies.

A typical sample of the apartment costs in Val d'Isère is provided below. These centrally located units are about 100 meters from the lifts.

The prices of apartments generally follow a similar season pattern as the hotels. The blue-zone prices will range between FFR 800-1,500 for a studio; and FFR 1,400-2,350 for a two-room condo. During the white zone prices will be between FFR 1,250-1,950 for studios and FFR 1,800-3,050 for two-room condos. During the red zone (high season) prices range from FFR 1,700-2,700 for a studio and FFR 2,650-4,440 for two-room apartments.

Most agencies and individual owners offer apartments within similar price ranges. Note the differences between various seasons or "zones." For more information and a complete list of rental apartments, write to the tourist office. It will send listings of both agencies and individual owners along with prices.

Dining

Surprisingly Val d'Isère has no nationally recognized restaurants. The smaller restaurants that have traditionally offered the top meals are being pressed by the hotel restaurants, which are filling the void by offering excellent meals at reasonable prices.

Le Grande Ourse (tel. 79060019) still reigns as the top restaurant in town after decades in that position. The interior is without a doubt the most beautiful of any restaurant in town. It's almost worth the prices just to eat in such surroundings. Meals here are as gourmet as they get in Val d'Isère. Expect to pay between FFR 200-250 for a meal with wine.

Hotel Savoyarde Restaurant (tel. 79060155) was consistently mentioned as the second-best spot in town. The dining room has a beautiful wooden ceiling, a warm Savoyard atmosphere and a menu that will allow you to walk out for FFR 150-200, including wine.

El Cortijo (tel. 79060325) is one of the pricier restaurants offering excellent fish in a very elegant atmosphere. Expect to spend at least FFR 200 for a meal with appetizer, main course, dessert and wine.

Bout de la Rue (tel. 79060327) serves up excellent food in a tiny, very rustic atmosphere. The walls are covered with wood and you sit on folding chairs, but folk across the town claim that the chef is one of the best in the resort.

The Hotel Bellier Restaurant (tel. 79060377) serves excellent fare. Menu prices are approximately FR 150 with wine. The dining room is an elegant and cozy alpine spot. Reservations are recommended unless you are a guest at the hotel.

All three of the following restaurants are located within a stone's throw of one another in La Daille, serving good meals in some of the most rustic settings in Val d'Isère.

The Samovar (tel. 79061351) in La Daille serves excellent wholesome meals. The real atmosphere is upstairs where the hotel guests normally eat and those lucky enough to have made reservations at one of the two tables reserved for outsiders.

Crech'Ouna (tel. 79060740) also in La Daille, serves regional cuisine around a giant fireplace under massive beams and stone walls.

La Vieille Maison (tel. 79061176) also in La Daille serves Savoyard specialties with the atmosphere of a flickering fire, whitewashed walls and flagstone floors.

The next group of restaurants serve up slightly less costly meals.

Restaurant La Corniche (tel. 79060205) tucked between the old stone buildings of the old part of the village is a new establishment with an atmospheric dining room. With large stone walls alternating with wood, this is what you'd expect a modern alpine restaurant to look like. Expect to spend between FFR 100-120.

Restaurant Le Kern (tel. 79060606) is located in a small two-star hotel and has real "old" alpine charm. Meals are excellent and reasonable. Prices will be about FFR 90-120.

Taverne d'Alsace (tel. 79060239) serves up German-Alsace cuisine, including a potent onion cake, in a very cozy bar setting.

Restaurant Florence across the street from the tourist office is a good, inexpensive restaurant where you can get away for less than FFR 100.

Pizza can be found at **Perdrix Blanche** and **Pacific Espace**.

Local specialties, such as cheese fondue (FFR 78), fondue bourgogne (FFR 120) and raclette (FFR 70), are best sampled in **La Raclette** in the Hotel Avancher (tel. 79060200) and **Restaurant Arolay** in Le Fornet (tel. 79061168).

On the slopes the best food is at **La Petite Folie** at the La Daille midstation. Other good lunches are at **Cabaret des Neiges**, the midstation at Solaise; **La Datcha** at Solaise; **Col de l'Iseran** with great views, a peaceful setting and fast food; **Le Crech'Ouna** at the bottom of La Daille for a real restaurant.

You can be sure that locals will promote their favorites, so ask them for other recommendations.

Nightlife

Until recently, Val d'Isère was not known for wild nightlife. In fact, the resort was best known for its lack of it. Times are changing. In this skier's resort, though many people come to ski and are in bed after a hard day on the slopes, the nightlife is beginning to pop. Whenever thousands of skiers gather, a good time can't be far behind.

For drinking and dancing, **Dick's Tea Bar** and **Playbach** are the two main English language hangouts. Dick's Tea Bar also has good immediate après-ski with happy hour, videos and then jazz before the disco scene cranks in. For real French discos, try **Club 21** or the **Knack** in the Blizzard Hotel. **Mephisto** in the Grand Paradis Hotel hosts an older crowd, mainly French.

Bananas is a good local spot with many English-speakers; **Perdrix Blanche** is normally packed with a young crowd immediately after skiing; and **Taverne d'Alsace** offers a very rustic bar for slightly older and quieter après-ski.

Child care

There are many alternatives for child care in Val d'Isère. The hotels and the tourist office can put you in touch with private babysitting services.

In addition, there are three organized daycare facilities. Kindergarten Les 3 Pommes (tel. 79061766) takes children between the ages of three months and three years. Cost is FFR 31 an hour, FFR 120 for a morning until 2 p.m. with meal and FFR 95 for the afternoon from 1-5:30 p.m. without meal.

Le Petit Poucet (tel. 79061397) is for children between three and 10 years. Costs are FFR 34 an hour, FFR 160 a day and FFR 980 for seven days. Both kindergartens are open from 9 a.m. until 5:30 p.m. and offer bus services that pick up the children from the hotels.

The third facility is the French Ski School, which has an extensive children's program for kids from four years all the way up to 12. There is the "Children's Corner" with 30 instructors and the Snow School Solaise (tel. 79061179), which conducts a 30-hour program of English-language lessons for FFR 420, including meals, ski lifts and equipment. Other ski school opportunities are the "Mini Champions," available for FFR 830 a week, including meals, or the "Enterlou Club" for more advanced child skiers. It costs FFR 905 a week without meals. Call the ski school at 79060234 for more information.

Getting there

The closest airports are in Lyons and Geneva. Geneva is about 140 kilometers (86 miles) and Lyons is approximately 240 kilometers (150 miles) from the resort. Rail transport via the TGV was inaugurated in December 1988, making access quick and easy by rail from Paris to Bourg St. Maurice, where a bus connection takes you on to Val d'Isère.

The best autoroute from Geneva is A41 to Annecy; then take N90 to Albertville, where you should follow the signs to Bourg St. Maurice and on to Val d'Isère or Col de l'Isèran. From Lyons, take autoroute A43 to Chambéry, then follow the signs to Albertville and on to Val d'Isère. There is a daily direct bus service from both airports to Val d'Isère during the winter months.

Other activities

Val d'Isère is at the end of a long mountain road and once you get there it is doubtful that you will be anxious to leave on day trips. The town offers good but limited activities for non-skiers.

There is a covered, heated swimming pool open from 3 p.m. to 8 p.m., with a daily entrance fee of FFR 20 for adults and FFR 12 for children (free to holders of seven-day ski passes). Cards for 10 entries can be purchased for FFR 160 (adult) and FFR 100 (children).

An outdoor natural ice rink is available for skaters from 10 a.m. to 7 p.m. Visitors interested in bubble-bath treatments, underwater seaweed massages, exercise rooms and regular massage can get the full treatment at Hotel Sofitel (tel. 79060830). The price for a six-day package relaxation package with massage, sauna, whirlpool and gymnastics is FFR 1,350. "The Fitness Cure" lasting six days and including more massages and ionizations will cost FFR 2,430.

An ice driving school is located near the La Daille section of the town. Lessons cost FFR 50 for the first trail and then FFR 200 per lesson. Contact the office at 79062140.

Paragliding courses are offered for FFR 550 per four-hour course, including all equipment and insurance. A flight with an instructor will cost FFR 250. Contact "Air Montagne Evasion" at 79060234.

Viking Snowmobile offers night smowmobile rides at the summit of Bellevarde on the Toviere plateau. Rides cost FFR 250 an hour. Contact Viking Snowmobiles at 79060527.

Tourist information

For more information, contact Office du Tourisme, BP 28, 73150 Val d'Isère, France; tel. 79061083; telex 980077 OFITOUR.

For accommodations, contact Val Hôtel, BP 73, 73150, Val d'Isère, France; tel. 79061890; telex 980077.

Italy

Italy has more of the Alps than any other country. Its high-altitude skiing means good snow. Mont Blanc, the highest mountain in Europe, straddles the France-Italy border, and the Matterhorn is right on Switzerland's border with Italy.

Italy also has the entire Dolomite mountain range, which many consider to be among the world's most spectacular mountains. Many Italian ski areas here are world-class, and the skiing is augmented by the Italian love of life and matchless cuisine and wines.

If the weather changes, there is always a beautiful city, such as Milan, Turin, Verona or Venice, just a few hours away from the slopes.

A note on prices

Most of these prices are from the 88/89 season. Where Winter 1990 prices are available they have been clearly noted.

Since prices do change, these should be used as a guide only.

All prices are given in Italian lire (L). The book was researched when the lira was at an exchange rate of L. 1,300 to $1. Any subsequent change in the exchange rate will be the biggest factor affecting the prices.

When are the seasons?

Some Italian resorts have adopted a rather complicated series of
mini-seasons. Basically, the seasons have remained intact with the
introduction of some in-between seasons. If you follow these season breakouts for planning you will not go too far wrong:

High season: 21 December to 7 January, and 5 February to 2
April.

Low season: 8 January to 4 February and 2-30 April.

Pre-season: 6 December to 20 December.

Cortina d'Ampezzo

Ever since hosting the 1956 Winter Olympic games, Cortina's wide, sunny valley in the eastern part of the Dolomites has come to qualify as one of the world's top ritzy ski resorts.

The town's picturesque square is framed by two massive mountain ridges: To the east lies the connected area formed by Cristallo (9,613 feet) and Faloria (7,690 feet); to the west, Tofana (9,317 feet) and Pocol (7,487 feet) form another connected area that is accessible from the town. Further to the west, approaching the Falzarego Pass (6,906 feet), the areas of Cinque Torri (8,438 feet) and Langazuoi (9,009 feet) beckon the adventurous skier.

These areas are loosely connected by a system of buses and taxis, none of which are very expensive.

Where to ski

One suggested approach to Cortina is to ski Faloria in the morning, then ski down to Tre Croce in the afternooon and take the lift up to Son Forca or Staunies in order to ski the rest of the day. Day two could be spent at Tofana or Pocol. Day three might be the Falzarego area, and subsequent days could offer repeats of the areas. Or, because Cortina is interconnected by use of Dolomiti Super Ski lift ticket, there is also the choice of skiing down the opposite side of the Lagazuoi, skiing the Corvara area and returning to Cortina by taxi or bus at an extra charge. Whatever your choice, there is plenty of skiing.

Mountain rating

This area is an advanced intermediate skier's paradise. With the exception of just a few slopes it is probably a bit too challenging for most beginners, and it will push most intermediate skiers.

The intermediate skier will find Tofana, Faloria and Cinque Torri enjoyable areas.

Beginners should stick to the Pocol area and the lower lifts on Cristallo, as well as several at Faloria.

Experts will enjoy shooting down the Lagazuoi; the cablecar ride to the peak is a thrill in itself. Other good expert areas are the Tofana and the last lifts of the Cristallo section. The off-trail skiing is exhilarating, although it should be done with a good guide and instructor along in order to get the most out of your day.

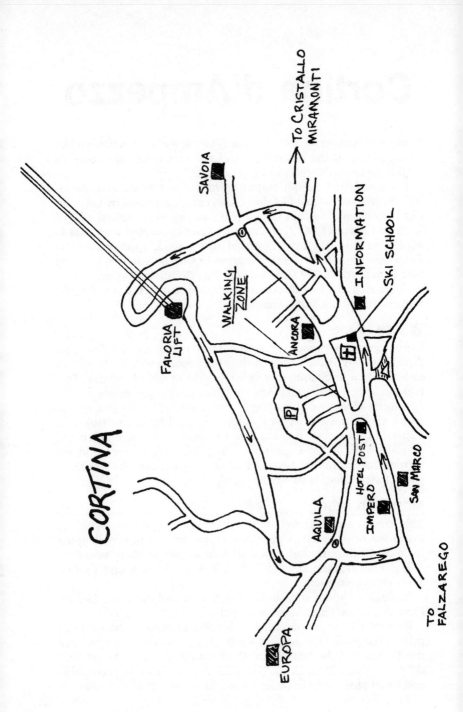

Ski school

Cortina has 140 instructors, and courses are offered covering all skill levels. The ski school is located at Piazza San Francesco, 2; tel. 2911 or 3495. Ask for an instructor who speaks English. Low season for lessons is from 8 January to 3 February. The 1989/90 costs are as follows:

Individual lessons

	low season	high season
one person	L. 30,000	L. 38,000
each additional person		L. 5,000

Group lessons (Six consecutive days)

	low season	high season
9:30 a.m.-12 noon	L. 130,000	L. 150,000
9:30 a.m.-4:30 p.m.		L. 320,000
12 noon-4 p.m.		L. 180,000

Lift passes

These lift prices are for the Cortina area only. For the Dolomite Super Ski prices, see the section covering Val Gardena.

	low season	high season
one day	L. 29,000	L. 35,000
two days	L. 57,700	L. 67,300
three days	L. 82,800	L. 99,600
six days	L. 145,000	L. 174,500
seven days	L. 153,700	L. 185,000

Children born after January 1, 1976, get a 30 percent discount; seniors born before December 31, l929, receive about a 20 percent discount. Bring proper IDs.

Accommodations

Cortina is a fairly mature resort so its hotels in some cases show their age. The quality is uneven in terms of room size and furnishings. When checking in, always make sure you see the room before accepting it. If you have already made a reservation, ask if it is possible to see several rooms from which to make a decision.

The following hotels are centrally located, offer good value and have been visited by a Ski Europe representative. Prices are for "white-week" packages, which include seven days at half pension in a room with bath; prices are per person, based on double occupancy. A seven-day ski pass costs L. 153,700 extra and ski school for six days is L. 130,000 additional. The low-season (7-20 Jan.) price is given first with high season (4 Feb.-18 March) in parentheses.

NOTE: The telephone prefix for Cortina is (0436).

Hotel Miramonti (tel. 4201; telex 440069) L. 1,120,000 (L. 1,470,000) This is the most luxurious and elegant hotel in town. A bit out of the center of the town.

Hotel Cristallo (tel. 4281; telex 440090) L. 1,260,000 (L. 1,470,000) A close second in luxury to the Miramonti.

Hotel Ancora (tel. 3261/3254; telex 440004) L. 735,000 (L. 1,260,000)—Our favorite hotel in Cortina is located directly on the famous central square. There are more luxurious hotels, but staying at the Ancora is an experience you will savor long after your vacation is over.

Make sure to meet the proprietress, Signora Flavia, who speaks good English and will make your stay memorable.

Europa (tel. 3221; telex 440004) L. 665,000 (not available) Corso Italia

San Marco (tel. 66941) L. 525,000 (L. 840,000) An absolutely beautiful hotel that was recently restored with fantastic woodwork. Don't let the price fool you.

Hotel Aquila (tel. 2618) L. 483,000 (L. 763,000)

Hotel Impero (tel. 4246) L. 238,000 (L. 385,000)—Bed-and-breakfast only; some rooms have kitchenettes.

Apartments

There are no rental apartments listed but some 18,000 rooms in private houses are available to rent. Prices for these rooms range from L.15,000 to L.25,000 in low season and from L.20,000 to L.35,000 during high season. For more information, contact the local tourist office.

Dining

The following restaurants, recommended by several local residents, offer good food for a relatively low cost; each offers a meal that costs between L.25,000 and L. 40,000, including house wine.

Tivoli Lacedel, 34; tel. 866400—Overlooking Cortina, Tivoli is rated as one of the best in town. It offers prize-winning, home-made pasta dishes. Call for reservations. Closed Mondays.

Baita Fraina Fraina; tel. 3634. Closed Mondays.

Da Beppe Sello Ronco, 68; tel. 3236. Closed Tuesday.

Lago Scin Lago Scin; tel. 2391. Closed Wednesday.

Bellavista Meloncino Gilardon; tel. 861043. Closed Tuesday.

Da Ferruccio Ronco, 115; tel. 866741. Closed Wednesday.

Nightlife

For all its glitzy reputation, Cortina is relatively quiet at night. An old wine bar, the **Enoteca**, is normally packed with merrymakers.

The disco at the Europa hotel, The VIP Club, seems to be the main action place. **Lub Club, Metro Club** and the **Bilbo Club** are discos that mainly cater to a young crowd earlier in the evening and an older group later on.

Child care

Child care in Cortina is not a school affair. There are scores of private babysitters and babysitting services available through the hotels or private homes where skiers may be staying. Child care services are relatively inexpensive, and children seem to get more than their share of affection from the Italians who take care of them. The ski school also runs a children's ski course for those old enough to begin skiing.

Getting there

We suggest going by car. The closest airport is in Venice (about a two-hour drive). The closest train station is in Calalzo, which is connected to Cortina by a regular bus service. Trains from Innsbruck and Munich arrive at Dobbiaco, a 50-minute bus ride from Cortina. A daily bus service connects Cortina with Venice and with Innsbruck. Both trips take about four hours. Check with your travel agent, because there are some packages that arrange for a special bus to meet incoming skiers at the Milan airport and bus them directly to Cortina.

Other activities

Regular tours to Venice and Verona are scheduled most days. There is also excellent ice skating, bobsledding, horseback riding in the snow, curling championships, World Cup ski races, ice hockey and more. The tourist office publishes a list of activities, and the local paper, *Il Notiziario di Cortina*, provides daily activity summaries in Italian.

Tourist information

The main office is located on Piazzetta S. Francesco, 8. A second, smaller information office is located on Piazza Posta. Call (0436) 3231 or 2711; telex 440004 AZIENT I.

Cervinia

Walt Disney's film, "Three Men on the Mountain," about the dangerous climb of the Matterhorn created an image of grandeur that characterizes the best of the Alps. That film added to the mystique of the Matterhorn and Zermatt, but there is another side to the mountain—the Italian side. Cervinia is a forerunner purpose-built resort in Europe. When Mussolini decreed that a ski resort should be developed where the town of Breuil stood, energetic Italians enthusiastically took up "Il Duce's" mandate. However, unlike other purpose-built resorts, which have a semblance of central architectural control, Cervinia is the product of a score of fathers. The architecture is the worst of the southern-Italian-square-apartment technique combined haphazardly with neo-modern circular and triangular buildings.

Despite being ravaged by architects and developers during its infancy, Cervinia manages to delight skiers year after year. The wide-open slopes, the certain snow and the chance to ski Zermatt on the cheap bring groups of Germans, British and Americans who zip across the slopes during the week until the weekend hordes from Milano and Torino arrive for their days in the snow.

One other important point to note at this juncture is the quantum improvement of the lifts from the village to Plan Maison. Once famous as one of the worst lifts in Europe, the parallel cablecars have been replaced by a sleek six-person gondola. The final stage of the present parallel cablecars should be opened this winter from Plan Maison to Plateau Rosa.

Where to ski

To the Italians the Matterhorn is *Il Cervino,* and the village at the base of the Italian side of the mountain is called Cervinia. Cervinia, without the old charm and beauty of Zermatt, has hotel and lift prices that are about 30 percent lower. Its lift system has been connected with Val Tournanche, a nearby village, so that, today, those who choose to ski the Italian side of the Matterhorn experience more than 100 kilometers of prepared ski runs, which are served by six cablecars, one gondola, five chairlifts and 23 ski lifts. The longest run covers more than 20 kilometers—from Plateau Rosa to Val Tournanche—with a vertical drop of about 1,500 meters.

One problem affecting where to ski is the poor guide map. There

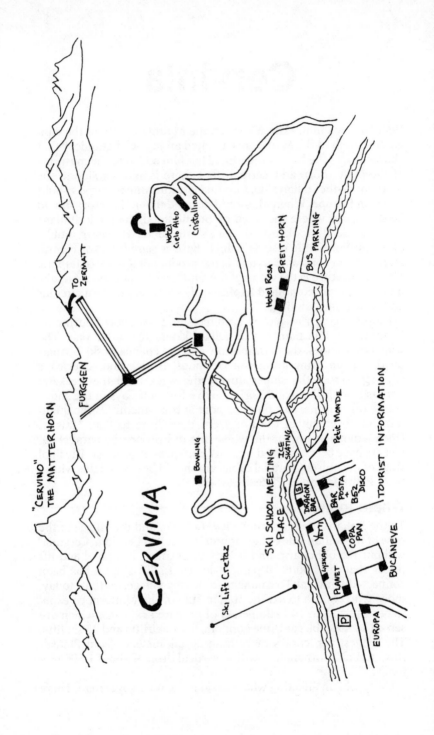

are at least two or three versions circulating around the resort, but none is useful except in the broadest sense. Don't expect to find well-marked trails either, but, fortunately, with relatively easy slopes and access to anything difficult requiring focused effort, anyone can eventually feel comfortable.

The descent to Zermatt starts from Plateau Rosa. Special lift tickets for use on the Swiss side of the mountain should be purchased before you go up the mountain; otherwise, expect to pay double to take the lifts back up the Swiss side. The Zermatt side has much steeper terrain and narrower trails. An expert skier can have a field day on the Swiss side, while the beginning and intermediate skier can find enough easy runs to make the trip enjoyable.

In the Cervinia area experts can perhaps find some challenges with good snow and an adventurous spirit off-piste. Try the Furggen if the cablecar is running (you have less than a 50 percent chance based on my efforts), do some off-piste dropping from Plateau Rosa, or try out the lifts above the Cristallo Hotel for a few bumps. Cervinia is really paradise for novice and lower intermediate skiers. The gentle, wide-open snow fields above Plan Maison build confidence.

Mountain rating

The Cervinia/Val Tournanche slopes support beginner and intermediate skiing skills. Wide-open and excellent for practicing, they offer an adequate number of challenging steeps.

Expert skiers may enjoy several great days of cruising the wide slopes but may also become bored. The Furggen (11,360 feet) offers excellent, albeit limited, expert-rated skiing. However, should a group of experts invest in the services of a ski instructor, they'll find the most challenging slopes. Experts will also have a great time on the Zermatt side, and this is the part of the allure of Cervinia as a resort: It lets you take advantage of the savings made possible by staying in Italy and skiing the wilder-and-woolier Swiss side.

Ski school

There is an excellent ski school at Via J. A. Carrel; tel. 949 034. Arrangements can be made at any hotel reception desk, or visit the school.

Ask for an English-speaking instructor.

Daily lessons are available at the approximate rates listed below:

Individual lessons

one person	L. 24,000 an hour
two people	L. 28,000 an hour
three people	L. 32,000 an hour
four people	L. 34,000 an hour

Group Lessons (includes three hours a day of instruction with about six to 10 skiers per group).

one day	L. 30,000
three days	L. 68,000 (low season)
six days	L. 103,000 (low season)

A ski instructor for an entire day costs approximately L. 180,000.

Lessons are also available for cross-country, ski competition (six-day course), off-piste skiing and summer skiing.

Lift tickets

half day	L. 22,500
one day	L. 29,000
three days	L. 79,000
six days	L. 130,000
seven days	L. 146,000
14 days	L. 224,000

The supplement added to the Cervinia ski pass to ski in Zermatt costs L. 20,000. If you do not have a Cervinia pass and want to ski to Zermatt you will have to pay L. 40,000 for an international lift. If you want to try to ski all of Zermatt in a day, forget it. But realize that the supplementary ticket you purchase in Cervinia is only good for the Klein Matterhorn section of Zermatt. It is possible to strike out for Gornergrat or Sunnegga. In that case, wait to get to Zermat to buy a day-pass.

Skiers with a weekly pass in Courmayeur can use it one day in Cervinia and vice versa, the Cervinia week pass is good for a day in Courmayeur.

Accommodations

These hotels and pensiones have been visited by a *Ski Europe* representative and offer good value for the money. Prices are per person and include seven days at half pension in a double room

with bath during low season (with the middle season—February/
March—price following in parenthesis). Where no telex number
is listed, reservations can be telexed (in English) through the Cervinia tourist office; telex: 211822 ASTCER I.

Hermitage (tel. 948918 or 948998) L. 710,000 (L. 910,000)—A
beautiful hotel that is the best choice in Cervinia. Everyone who
stays here loves it. Make reservations early because it is very popular.

Cristallo (tel. 948125; telex 210626) L. 770,000 (L. 980,000)—Located up the hill from the main part of town. A hotel shuttle bus
takes guests to the town and to the lifts in the morning. Ski directly
back to the hotel in the evening. This is a modern luxury hotel
that is comfortable but by no means cozy.

Europa (tel. 948-660 or 948-661) L. 420,000 (L. 595,000)—Located
in the center of town, just a few minutes' walk from the lifts; clean
and modern with parking.

Breithorn (tel. 949-042) L. 374,000 (L. 455,000)— Recently renovated, furnished with knotty-pine furniture, this hotel is about
200 meters from the lifts. Considered to have one of the better
restaurants in town.

Bucaneve (tel. 949-119) L. 490,000 (L. 595,000)—Center-of-town
location.

Planet (tel. 949-426) L. 455,000 (L. 560,000)—Plain and with little
atmosphere, this hotel is, however, relatively modern and very
convenient to the slopes.

Lyskamm (tel. 949-074) L. 364,000 (L. 448,000)— Small; perhaps
the closest to the slopes.

Mignon (tel. 949-344) L. 350,000 (L. 455,000)—Very small and
cozy, just minutes from the slopes. Its rooms have recently been
renovated and its restaurant has a good reputation.

Perruquet (tel. 949-043) L. 224,000 (L. 238,000)—Bed-and-breakfast only. In the center of town; clean and roomy.

Dining
Cervinia's best and most typical restaurants, such as the **Cime
Bianche** and **Les Clochards**, are located on the slopes just outside
town. Have your hotel call to arrange for a van or jeep to pick you
up free of charge. Both restaurants mentioned above serve excel-

lent food, so even if your hotel arrangement includes meals, make an effort to eat out at least one night in one of the two.

Try *bagna cauda*: vegetables covered with an anchovy sauce; *tomino*, a type of delicate riccota, normally covered with parsley or peppers; *brisaula*, cured ham from the mountain regions; *larde d'Arnaz*, lard that has been cured in a secret mountain concoction.

Other recommended restaurants: **Matterhorn, Serenella, Nuovo KL** and **Les Neiges d'Atan**, a bit out of town but with a menu well worth the taxi ride. **The Cave des Guides** and the Copa Pan were recommended by plenty of tourists but not by one Italian.

Nightlife

There is not a lot from which to choose; however, there is a growing English-speaking clientele at the few spots in town.

The town's disco is **La Chimera** with a younger crowd. **The Etoile** attracts an older crowd. The two most popular bars are the **Yetti** and the **Dragon Pub**. All the bars are within a five-minute walk of each other in the center of town.

Child care

Baby-sitting services and special ski classes for children are available. Contact the tourist office for more information; tel. 949-135 or 949-086.

Getting there

Drive to Cervinia easily from either the Geneva or Milano airport. From Geneva come through the Mont Blanc tunnel. From Milano and Torino, take the autostrada. Then take the Cervinia exit and drive the last 20 miles up to the resort. Buses make the trip between Aosta and Milan, but the connections with the local buses in the mountains to Cervinia are useless. Anyone attempting to catch a plane leaving at noon or even 1 p.m. will be forced to take a 6 a.m. bus to Chatillon, then a bus to the superhighway toll booth at Novara, then phone the radio taxi for the L. 60.000 ride to Malpensa airport. If you have any luggage or cannot speak Italian fluently enough to let the taxi dispatcher know where you are standing, forget this experience. I hate to think of the trip in the rain as well. There is no other way. The entire Val d'Aosta does not have any international car rental service, which would be wonderful.

Other activities

An Olympic-size pool is located in the Hotel Cristallo and is open to the public.

Cervinia has a bobsleigh run, an ice-skating rink and bowling alleys. Day-trips can be made to Geneva, Lausanne, Milano or Torino.

The ski trip over the Alps to Zermatt is a "must-do" side trip.

Fenis Castle and Issogne Palace are less than an hour away and well worth the trip.

The valley's capital city, Aosta, has several excellent Roman ruins. The valley also features Europe's most popular casino in St. Vincent, only 30 kilometers from Cervinia, where rubbing shoulders with the elegant upper crust is fun. Some tour packages offer an overnight at the Grand Hotel Billia adjacent to the casino for one last night of gambling and cabarets.

During the last weekend in January, the Feast of Sant'Orso, one of the largest craft fairs in Italy, takes place in Aosta. Fantastic woodcarvings and other crafts can be purchased at great savings.

During *Carnevale* the town of Ivrea is one of the wildest places to be in Italy. Costumed residents and a "Battle of the Oranges," in which a castle that's defended by "bad guys" is besieged by "good guys" hurling more than a ton of oranges, makes for pre-Lenten fun.

Tourist information

In Cervinia: Via J.A. Carrel, 11021 Cervinia; tel. (0166) 949136 or 949086; telex 211822 ASTCER I.

Courmayeur

Located at the Italian end of the Mont Blanc tunnel, Courmayeur enjoys one of the best ski resort locations in Europe, Mont Blanc, the highest mountain in Europe guarantees snow; the Alps in the region are among the most spectacular in Europe; and Courmayeur lies at the junction of Switzerland, France and Italy. If a skier tires of skiing the slopes of Courmayeur, Cervinia and La Thuile in Italy are within striking distance; Chamonix in France and Verbier in Switzerland can also be reached for a full day of skiing.

Where to ski

The major ski area is on the opposite side of the valley from Mont Blanc. This area is centered around the Plan Checrouit. The Plan Checrouit is a transfer point for the cablecars that carry skiers up to a ski area serviced by 24 lifts and covering terrain that will keep both the expert, intermediate and beginner happy.

The highest lift arrives at Cresta Arp at 8,954 feet. However, the skiing from that point is for experts only, and at that only with guides. The highest skiable point for the run-of-the-mill skier is the Cresta Youla at 8,528 feet. From here you can ski a good, tough, intermediate run, finishing at Zerotta at 4,940 feet.

The second major skiing area at Courmayeur is Mont Blanc itself. Here a cablecar carries skiers in two stages to almost 11,000 feet where they can ski back down toward Courmayeur over the mountain to Chamonix or take some time skiing on the glacier. This side of the mountain is connected to Chamonix by a cablecar, which makes getting back to Courmayeur fast and easy. If for some reason a skier manages to arrive at Chamonix after the lifts have closed, it is relatively inexpensive to take a taxi through the tunnel back to Courmayeur. Normally there are small groups of skiers with the same problem. Team up and save some francs.

Mountain rating

If you an absolute beginner this is probably a mountain you should avoid. Although there are some beginners' areas the terrain is steep enough to take the fun out of skiing if you are over your head. For the intermediate this is heaven. There are plenty of semi-steeps to make the intermediate feel like an expert and enough moguls to keep one's head from swelling. The expert can find some challenging slopes off-piste. The ski instructors can take expert skiers

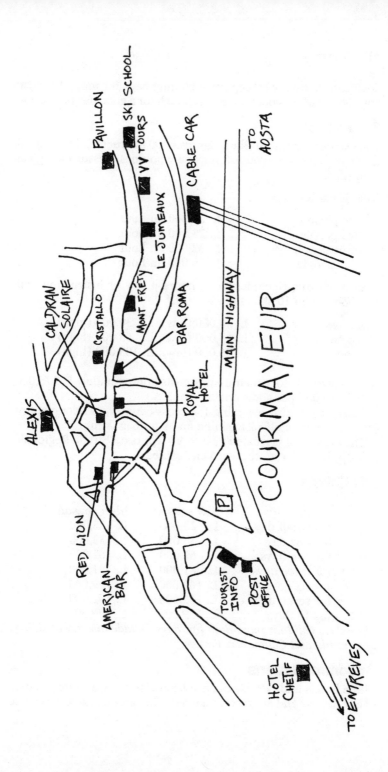

down slopes that will keep them coming back for more. Even the normally marked slopes are good enough for a good day of cruising.

Ski school

The ski school of Mont Blanc has over 100 instructors. Many speak English. Make sure you ask for one who does. Lessons are given every day.

Individual lessons

one person	L. 24,000 an hour
two people	L. 28,000 an hour
three people	L. 32,000 an hour
four people	L. 35,000 an hour

Group lessons (includes three hours a day of instruction with about six to 10 skiers per group).

one day	L. 28,000 (low); L. 30,000 (high)
three days	L. 64,000 (low); L. 68,000 (high)
six days	L. 96,000 (low); L. 103,000 (high)

A ski instructor for an entire day costs approximately L. 175,000, plus L. 15,000 per additional person.

Lessons are also available for cross-country, ski competition (six-day course), off-piste skiing and summer skiing.

The ski school is located next to VV Tours on Strada Regionale, just up the hill from the Val Veny cablecar.

Lift tickets

	low season	high season
for a half day	L. 23,000	L. 23,000
for one day	L. 33,000	L. 33,000
for two days	L. 62,000	L. 62,000
for three days	L. 81,000	L. 91,000
for six days	L. 142,000	L. 169,000
for seven days	L. 162,000	L. 192,000
for 14 days	L. 159,000	L. 300,000

Lift tickets valid for more than five days include one day of skiing in Cervinia and Chamonix, France.

Accommodations

These hotels and pensiones have been visited by a representative of *Ski Europe* and are recommended. The prices, unless otherwise noted, are for seven days/half pension, which means breakfast and one meal (normally dinner). High-season costs are in parenthesis. There is also a shoulder season between the lowest cost period and the high season with prices between these two ranges. This normally comes into effect for the week between low and high season, or for spring skiing.

Hotel Pavilion (telex 210541; tel. 842420) L. 805,000 (L. 1,015,000). The best in Courmayeur, with indoor pool, sauna, garage and TV. Only 100 yards to the lifts and the ski school.

Hotel Jumeaux (telex 214261; tel. 844040) L. 945.000 (L. 1,120,000). A first-category hotel, brand new and closest to the lifts. Sauna, TV and exercise room.

Hotel Palace Bron (tel. 842545) L. 665,000 (L. 875,000)

Hotel Cresta Duc (tel. 842585) L. 350,000 (L. 595,000)

Hotel Cristallo (tel. 842015) L. 364,000 (L. 560,000)

Hotel Lo Scoiattalo (tel. 842274) L. 330,000 (L. 385,000)
For bed and breakfast, try the **Bouton d'Or, Croux** or the **Vittoria**. Avoid the **Etoile des Neiges** about which I only heard complaints.

Dining
Most of the hotel restaurants are good. If you want to get out and explore the local restaurants, follow the rule: If it is crowded with locals then it must be good.

Special restaurants in town are the expensive **Cadran Solaire** on the main street (tel. 0165-844609). Reservations are suggested. Or try the very reasonable **Mont Fréty** at 21 Strada Regionale, just down from Hotel La Jumeaux (tel. 0165-841786). The Mont Fréty food is every bit as good as the Cadran Solaire, and it is perhaps the best place in town to try the regional specialties.

Outside of town is the famous **Maison de Filippo** (tel. 0165-89968) in Entrèves, where for a fixed price of Li. 35,000 you are served some 40 courses. The stream of food seems never to end, with servings of pasta, antipasti, sausages, contorni, salads, various meats and baskets of nuts and breads. Another enjoyable restaurant is next to the cross-country area "La Ferret," and known locally as **Da Floriana** (tel. 0165-89947). The owner rightfully prides himself on his local specialties of "Bouden"—blood sausage with beets, fontina cheese, marinated lard and excellent wines.

The local red wines are excellent. Try Donnaz—a strong heavy dry wine; and Enfer d'Arnier—lighter and fruitier. A good grappa or genepy finished off the meal in proper Val d'Aosta style.

Apartments

This is a relatively new development for Courmayeur. There are two areas where apartments can be rented for a week.

Residence Les Jumeaux includes two beds, TV/radio and maid service. Low-season price is approximately L. 850,000 a week. In high season the same room will cost L. 1450,000. Additional beds cost another 25 percent. These are located in the center of Courmayeur next to the main lift. (tel. 844040; telex 214261).

Residence Universo features several types of rooms, including a studio for two or three people and two-room apartments for up to five people. All are equipped with TV and complete kitchen equipment. A free shuttle bus takes guests to the ski lifts in the town. Low-season rates range from L. 350,000 a week for a two-person studio to L. 650,000 for a two room apartment for four or five people. In high season prices will be L. 440,000 for the two-person studio and L. 800,000 for the two-room apartment for up to five. Cleaning will cost a maximum of L. 60,000 for the week. Make reservations through VV Tours, Strada Regionale, 47, Courmayeur; tel. (0165) 842061, telex 210260.

Nightlife

The English-speaking crowd hangs outs in the **Bar Roma** on the main street. A few can be found in the **American Bar** and the Red Lion. The main street is the best place to wander. Keep an ear and eye alert for the sounds of a good bar and go on in. The most popular discos are **Le Abatjour** and **Le Trou**, which also has a good restaurant. The **Clochard**, a bit outside of town in Dolonne, is also an excellent disco.

Child care

The ski school runs an all-day ski course, which starts at 9 a.m. at the ski school and lasts until 4 p.m. The cost for one day is L. 36,00, and for six consecutive days is L. 170,000. These prices include lunch for the children.

Getting there

The closest airports are Geneva and Milan. Both are within a two-hour drive of Courmayeur. Train and bus service connects Milan with Courmayeur. Bus service connects Courmayeur with Geneva. Car rentals are available from both airports.

Other activities

Geneva, Milan and Torino offer excellent sightseeing and museums. The Val d'Aosta is spectacular in itself and features one of the best collections of castles in Italy, as well as excellent Roman ruins in Aosta, the capital city. During the last weekend in January the "Feast of St. Orso" is held in Aosta. It is one of the largest crafts fairs in Italy, featuring fantastic woodcarvings and other mountain crafts. During *carnevale* time, the town of Ivrea is one of the wildest places to be in Italy. The residents are decked out in costumes reminiscent of "Star Wars." They participate in the "Battle of the Oranges," which features a castle defended by the "bad guys" being assaulted by the "good guys" who hurl over a ton of oranges during the seige. The valley also boasts a casino in St. Vincent. Milan, in addition to its sights, features the La Scala opera house, the largest in Italy and one of the best opera companies in the world.

Tourist information

Courmayeur is as much as any place in the world a one-tourist agency town. In fact the tourist agency doubles in many cases as the tourist office. It also happens to own the lift system in Courmayeur. For any additional information, contact: Tourist Office (Azienda Autonoma Soggiorno E Turismo) P.lc Monte Bianco tel. 0165-842060 fax 8112072 – telex 215871. VV Tours, Strada Regionale, 47; tel. (0165) 842061 or 844161; or telex 210260.

Madonna di Campiglio

One of the jewels of the Brenta Dolomites in Trento is Madonna di Campiglio. The elegant resort is packed with hotels and is situated at 5,085 feet amid beautiful, easy-to-ski terrain. Long before Madonna di Campiglio became famous as a winter playground it was the favorite summer vacation spot of Austrian royalty, providing a stunning backdrop of brilliant mountain flowers and crystal-clear lakes.

Where to ski

The skiing areas surround the town. Start at one end of town and ski around the village—only a short walk is needed in order to complete the circle. Most of the hotels are at the base of the slopes, making them convenient for both lunch breaks and quitting time.

The immediate area is linked with two others, Folgarida and Marilleva. The area has 34 lifts and more than 100 kilometers of prepared runs. The Folgarida and Marilleva areas add another 20 lifts and 50 kilometers of prepared slopes.

The highest point accessible by lift is Groste at 8,235 feet.

Cross-country skiers will discover that this region is a mecca for the sport. Pinzolo, about 20 minutes away, hosts the 24-hour endurance race, and the Campo Carlo Magno boasts one of the world's best expert cross-country courses.

Mountain rating

The area is good for beginning and intermediate skiers. While the 3 Tre, Fortini and Spinale will give experts some good exercise, the area deserves an overall rating of "mellow." Experts can ski off-trail or try ski mountaineering.

Ski school

Check with your hotel or in town for recommendations for the best English-speaking ski instructors. There are a total of 150 instructors, that offer lessons.

Individual lessons (per hour)

for one person	L. 32,000
for two persons	L. 38,000

for three persons	L. 42,000
for four persons	L. 48,000
for five persons	L. 55,000

Group lessons are given two hours each day for six days. Prices below are per person:

| for six persons | L. 108,000 |
| for eight persons | L. 96,000 |

Children's lessons are given three hours each day for six days. There is a maximum limit of 10 per group. Cost: L.126,000

Lift tickets

Tickets for six or seven days are often included in "White-Week" packages. Six-day passes include one day of skiing in Folgarida and Marilleva and seven-day passes include two days. You can purchase the "Skirama" passes separately for L. 35,000 a day.

These prices are for high season. Low-season prices are approximately 10 percent less.

one day	L. 31,000
six days	L. 165,000
seven days	L. 187,000

NOTE: six- and seven-day tickets require a photograph.

Accommodations

Madonna's hotels are for the most part modern. Hotels listed here have been selected on the criterion of price and were visited by a Ski Europe representative. The prices listed below include seven days' stay during low season, full pension (breakfast, lunch and dinner).

A six-day ski pass, seven-day pass for the town's swimming pool, free Wednesday ice skating and free shuttle bus service to the lifts will cost L. 153,000 during low season and L. 165,000 in high season.

High-season prices are given in parentheses.

Hotel Des Alpes (tel. 40000) L. 1,015,000 (L. 1,400,000)—Perhaps the town's best hotel, built around the former hunting lodge of the Austrian emperors. The Grill restaurant is excellent.

Hotel Golf (tel. 41003) L. 735,000 (L. 987,000)—Excellent high quality, elegant hotels with all the amenities.

Hotel C. Magno Zeledria (tel. 41010) L. 504,000 (L. 728,000)

Hotel Cristallo (tel. 41132) L. 805,000 (L. 910,000)

Miramonti (tel. 41021) L. 625,000 (L. 890,000)

Hotel Palu (tel. 41280) L. 504,000 (L. 728,000)—Town's best value; a beautiful hotel.

Majestic (tel. 41080) L. 504,000 (L. 728,000)

Touring (tel. 41051) L. 441,000 (L. 595,000)

Ariston (tel. 41070) L. 441,000 (L. 595,000)

Gianna (tel. 41106) L. 343,000 (L. 504,000)

Apartments

Residence Roch has apartments for three, four or five people. During low season, expect to pay approximately L. 190,000 a week per person; during high season—L. 280,000. The price includes daily maid service (except kitchen cleanup). Rent garage space for L. 55,000. Both sauna and solarium are available.

The tourist board can provide additional listings of apartments in the same approximate price range and help with all arrangements.

Dining

The best restaurant in town in our view is **Grill**, which is located in the Des Alpes. The atmosphere is elegant and the service is excellent. You will pay a premium price, but this is a highly recommended splurge. For reservations, call 42877.

Other recommended restaurants are: **Artini** (tel. 40122), **Belvedere** (tel. 42712) and **Pappagallo** (tel. 42717). Perhaps the most typical restaurant in town is **Malga Montagnoli** (tel. 42670). Two good pizzerias are **Le Roi** (tel. 42670) and **Zodiaco** (tel. 41686).

Nightlife

The **Grand Hotel Des Alpes** has a pricy disco, as well as a very cozy piano bar, where you can nurse a drink for as long as you want. Each evening cabaret is presented in the restored Hapsburg ballroom. Less refined and more of a blast is the **Stork Club**, which features a country bar upstairs and both a pizzeria and full-blown disco downstairs. Find English-speaking tourists and Scandinavians here.

Child care

Both children's ski classes and a special skikindergarten are available. Contact the tourist office for details.

Getting there

By car, Madonna di Campiglio is two hours north of Verona. The closest airports are in Milan and Venice. Both offer rental car services. If driving from Milan, take the Brescia exit and follow the signs for Idro Lake, Tione, then Campiglio.

To reach Madonna di Campiglio by train, go to Trento and then transfer to a bus (the stop is about 50 yards from the Trento train station), which runs on a regular schedule during the day.

Other activities

Once you are in Madonna, it is not an easy task to get out. But if you insist on breaking away, Venice can be reached in about three and a half hours. Verona, with its giant Roman amphitheater and Romeo and Juliet legends, is about two hours away.

During *carnevale* just before Lent, Madonna di Campiglio hosts many costume balls and special events.

Tourist information

The tourist information office, or Azienda Autonoma di Soggiorno, in Madonna di Campiglio is located in the center of the resort in the Centro Rainalter. Its staff is well organized with information. Reservations for you at local hotels and pensiones can be made through Campiglio Holiday Travel Agency, Piazza Brenta Alta, 38084 Madonna di Campiglio, Trentino, Tel. 0465/42042.

Contact for Tourist Office, Centro Rainalter, 38084 Madonna di Campiglio (Trento); tel. (0465) 42000; fax. (0465) 40404; telex 400882 CARUPI.

Sauze d'Oulx

Sauze d'Oulx is part of the "Milky Way" system, which has undergone political maneuvers worthy of the most entangled bureaucracies. Sauze d'Oulx, Sestriere, Sansicario, Cesana and Claviere have linked their lifts and sell a single joint ticket. They make up the "galaxy" consortium of ski areas. Sauze d'Oulx is the best destination for English-speaking skiers and Sestrière is very Italian filled with upscale Italians packed into spanking new condos. One of the first purpose-built resorts in Europe, it today hosts a Club Med village. Chic and somewhat pretentious, it's not the type of resort an American or Englishman will feel comfortable in unless he is fluent in Italian.

Sauze d'Oulx, though, manages to combine good skiing with a fantastic, easy-going atmosphere. Curiously, the mix of tourists virtually guarantees that any English-speaking visitor will make friends and have a great time. Excellent pubs and inexpensive hotels will make Sauze d'Oulx your home base of choice.

Skiing Sauze d'Oulx and Sestrière

Sauze d'Oulx has more than 100 kilometers of prepared ski runs serviced by 26 lifts. However, the resort's ski pass is also valid for Sestrière, which lies just over the mountain and offers another 22 lifts and more than 100 kilometers of runs. Sestrière also boasts the largest and most modern snow-making equipment in Europe. Sauze d'Oulx' runs wind through deep forests, while those in Sestrière are mostly above the tree line. The Sauze d'Oulx runs are asprout with small restaurants and cafes where thirsty, hungry skiers can relax. Sestrière, on the other hand, has limited facilities on the slopes.

Mountain ratings

Elevations in Sauze d'Oulx that are accessible by lift range from 4,921 to 8,858 feet. Sestrière is a bit higher, with lifts running from 6,676 to 9,262 feet. Sauze, together with Sestrière, makes for a good, all-around resort. Experts will find few thrills in Sestrière, although it is perhaps a bit more difficult than Sauze.

Intermediate and advanced intermediate skiers will find plenty to do in both areas. The terrain is good for beginners and a cruiser's dream when the snow is good and the sun shines.

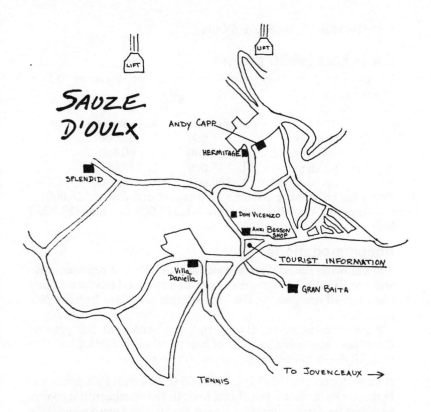

Ski schools

Sauze has two ski schools. The traditional "Sauze Sportina" school is located on the mountain and is the largest, with 85 instructors. The second, more non-traditional "Sauze d'Oulx" school has its headquarters in the town and employs only 20 instructors. Both schools offer a full range of classes for all classes of skiers, plus off-trail and helicopter skiing. "Sauze Sportina" has relatively fewer English-speaking instructors. "Sauze d'Oulx" staff tend to be younger, and its teaching methods more modern.

Individual lessons (per hour)

for one person	L. 25,000
for two to five persons	L. 30,000

Group lessons are given three hours each day for six days:

	low season	high season
	L. 90,000	L. 115,000

Lift tickets (89/90 prices)

The overall "Milky Way" pass is recommended. It covers 70 lifts, all interconnected.

	low season	high season
one day	L. 35,000	L. 35,000
two days	L. 60,000	L. 60,000
six days	L. 145,000	L. 155,000
seven days	L. 160,000	L. 175,000

Prices for only Sauze d'Oulx's 22 lifts are: one day—L. 26,000; two days—L. 45,000; and six days—l. 115,000 L.S. and 125,000 H.S.

Accommodations

The following hotels were visited by a Ski Europe representative and are listed in descending order of comfort. None are luxury class but all are good value, comfortable and have friendly proprietors.

Prices are for seven days during low season at full pension (breakfast, lunch and dinner) of half pension (breakfast and dinner). High-season prices are given in parentheses.

Il Capricorno (tel. 85273) L. 765,000 (L.870,000) Full pension—Perhaps one of the all-time hotel finds in Europe; beautiful rooms, excellent food and fantastic owners. One of our favorites in all the Alps. The kitchen rates a Michelin star, which means that a guest staying at full pension gets prize-winning meals three times a day. Take a ski lift to reach the hotel.

Villa Daniella (tel. 85196) L. 385,000 (L.420,000) Full pension—Its small rooms are well appointed and were recently renovated; has the second-best restaurant in town.

Hermitage (tel. 85385) L.315,000 (L.455,000) Half pension.

Gran Baita (tel. 85183) L.315,000 (L.455,000) Full pension

Splendid (tel.85172) L. 415,000 (L.450,000) Half pension

Dining

Be sure to visit **Il Capricorno** at least once. The lunch is fabulous and the restaurant's right on the slopes. **Villa Daniella** serves exceptional meat dishes. **Don Vicenzo** has great antipasti and atmosphere. **Old Inn** is good for steaks. **La Griglia** is the place for pizza.

Apartments

The tourist office's English-speaking staff can recommend apartments. Expect to pay between L.120,000 and L.180,000 per person a week, depending on the size of the apartment.

Nightlife

The town is not very big. Most discos were recently closed, but new ones are opening. Try **Babaiaga**, **Charlie Brown** and **VIP** for dancing. **Andy Capp** is the place to be when the lifts close.

Child care

A kindergarten ski school is available for children three years and older. Cost is L.225,00 for seven full days. For younger children, six to eight months, there is a full-service kindergarten that is staffed with nurses. Cost is about L.5,500 an hour.

Getting there

The closest airports are Turin (93 kms/one and a half hours), Milan (230 kms/three hours) and Geneva (190 kms/three hours). Rental cars are available at all three airports.

The main Rome-Paris train line stops in Oulx, just 15 minutes by bus from Sauze d'Oulx. Trains leave for Turin and Milan 12 times a day.

Other activities

Sauze has a public sauna and covered tennis courts. A ski shuttle bus runs through the town every 15 minutes and provides easy access to the lifts.

For a group of people, an organized evening at the Hotel Monte Triplex, complete with snow cats and torchlight skiing, is worth looking into.

Tourist information

The local tourist office has been organized to deal with English-speaking visitors. Call or write for information and reservations: Tourist Office, Piazza Assietta 18, 10050 Sauze d'Oulx (TO); tel. (0122) 85009; fax. (0122) 85497; telex 214321A ABI.

Garmisch-Partenkirchen West Germany

Garmisch-Partenkirchen, at the base of the Zugspitze (9,721 feet) the country's highest mountain, is less than an hour's drive from Munich. As Germany's most famous and best ski resort it attracts an international group of ski enthusiasts. The resort consists of the twin towns of Garmisch-Partenkirchen and ranks as one of Europe's friendliest and best-organized, with activities for visitors of every age. When considered along with neighboring slopes in Mittenwald and those across West Germany's border with Austria on the other side of the Zugspitze, Garmisch is an excellent ski-vacation destination. ($1.00 = DM 1.8)

Where to ski

Garmisch offers nearly 75 miles of runs, but the rugged Alpine landscape prevents any sort of continuous ski circuit between the seven different slopes. You'll ski in one of two large areas. One is on the high slopes of the Zugspitze plateau. You'll reach the top via cablecar from Lake Eibsee above Garmisch or from the Zugspitze cogwheel train; the cable is more scenic, the train more direct. Skiing here is at its best in early November and December, and in spring—April-May—when other resorts are closing. Best of the trails is the two-mile-long run from the Schneefernerkopf at 9,427 feet.

The Wank, at 5,835 feet, joins the adjacent, lower Eckbauer (4,062 feet) as the two most limited slopes in the area. We liked the Wank more, particularly after taking a deep-snow excursion with a guide on the trail from the summit down toward the Esterbergalm.

The Eckbauer is more popular for sentimental reasons. At its base is the Olympic Ski Stadium and the ski jumps where the greatest ski fliers in the world perform each year.

Garmisch hosted the Winter Olympic Games in 1936, and its facilities are well maintained. The World Cup runs on the Kreuzeck and the neighboring Hausberg provide several difficult turns but, overall, it's perfect terrain for intermediates.

Our favorite runs are from the Osterfelderkopf. From here you can make the only real skiing circuit runs in Garmisch, linking up with lifts from the Hausberg below.

For Zugspitze fans there is a new double-chair lift to the glacier at 9,186 feet. A new tunnel for the cogwheel train eliminates walking, and now allows direct access to the slopes.

One more suggestion: For interesting skiing and sometimes shorter lift lines, take the border highway past Grainau into Austria. Here, on the other side of the Zugspitze and less than a 30-minute drive away, try the slopes of Ehrwald. Occasionally, when Garmisch's weather is bad the sun will be shining in Ehrwald. Neighboring Lermoos and Biberwier, also in Austria, are popular with local skiers.

In the other direction, at Mittenwald, the Damkar run from the 7,822-foot-high Karwendel summit is interesting and the mountain panorama superb.

Mountain rating

Garmisch is intermediate country. Despite challenging parts of red runs that might be considered black and difficult World Cup sections on the Kreuzeck and Hausberg, the intermediate and advanced beginner will find it the place to be. Beginners could not come to a better place for outstanding ski instruction and a large number of lifts.

We gave Garmisch an excellent rating for its cross-country trails. There are 45 miles of maintained trails in the area.

Ski school

Garmisch's ski school program includes off-trail touring instruction and an outstanding climbing school. Eight schools offer instruction in the area. Rates for the various schools are within a few deutschemarks of one another.

Individual lessons

for one hour	DM 50
for each additional person	DM 10
for two hours	DM 95
for one day	DM 230
(four hours)	

Group lessons

for one day (three hours)	DM 45
for three days	DM 100
for five days	DM 115-140
for a five day tour (includes lessons in a different area each day)	DM 150

All schools have good reputations. However, their locations may play a role in your choice. The schools also offer cross-country instruction. For more information, contact:

Skischule Hohenleitner (tel. 50610) Located near the Zugspitze railway station.

Skischule Woerndle (tel. 58300) At the Hausberg cablecar station.

Olympia Skischule (tel. 4600) Near the Osterfelder station.

Skilanglaufschule (tel. 1516) Cross-country school at the Olympic stadium.

Skischule Garmisch-Partenkirchen (tel. 4931) At the Hausberg slope.

Bergsteigerschule Zugspitze (tel. 56361) Mountain climbing and ski touring instruction.

Cross-country

Garmisch, unlike many resorts, has a separate school for cross-country fans. The school at the Olympic stadium (tel. 1516) offers private and group lessons.

Individual lessons

for one hour	DM 40
for each additional hour	DM 10
for one day (four hours)	DM 200

Group lessons

for one day (two hours)	DM 25

for three days   DM 70
for five days   DM 100

Lift tickets

The least attractive aspect of Garmisch skiing is the mishmash of tickets you may need if you're moving around the area. The best general ticket to purchase is the Garmisch V ticket, good on lifts of the Wank, Eckbauer, Hausberg, Kreuzeck and Osterfelder areas.

for a half day   DM 27
(from noon)
for one day   DM 36

A day-ticket for the Wank area (*W Tageskarte*) costs DM 27; for the Eckbauer area (*E Tageskarte*) DM 21.

If you want to ski the Zugspitze, you need the *Z Tageskarte*, which costs DM 43 daily.

In addition, a special ticket for the V area offers a price reduction if you use it less than four hours.

The closest thing to a regional pass is the M card, good for a minimum of three days. It can be used at any of the area slopes, but you can't mix your skiing on any given day. For instance, if you choose the Zugspitze, then the ticket is good only there for the day. If you choose the V area, then the Zugspitze is out of bounds that day.

M card

for three days   DM 104
for four days   DM 135
for five days   DM 159
for six days   DM 183
for seven days   DM 204

Accommodations

Fortunately, the lift-ticket confusion is not carried over into accommodations. You can quickly find a place to stay, whether a farmhouse or an ultra luxurious hotel.

Garmisch has an outstanding selection of all-inclusive plans and especially caters to families or couples with one non-skier. There are at least a dozen other organized sports and free-time pursuits set up for non-skiers in week-long packages.

The best ski plan is SLI-1, a tourist-office special offered during middle season and priced from approximately DM 450 to DM 987. The price includes half-pension accommodation in several excellent hotels, including the famed Schneefernerhaus on the Zugspitze, plus five days of ski intruction and lift tickets for the Zugspitze.

The SLI-2 plan is even more outstanding for the budget-minded. Bed-and-breakfast in a private home, plus a week's ski course, starts at about DM 355.

Additional plans are: SLI-3 for cross-country, also beginning at approximately DM 264; EL for figure skating, beginning at about DM 364; and CL curling, from DM 294.

Listed below are the hotels and guesthouses that a Ski Europe representative found to provide comfortable, reasonably priced rooms. The prices are per person, based on double occupancy in high season, unless noted otherwise. *NOTE: Telephone prefix for Garmisch is (08821).*

Hotel Sonnenbichel (tel. 7020; telex 59632) DM 140-165 per person per night with half pension. This is considered by many to be the best hotel in the town.

Best Western Hotel Obermühle (tel. 7040; telex 59609) DM 125-165 per person per night with breakfast. It has what many feel is the best restaurant in town.

Hotel Boddenberg (tel. 51089) DM 65 per person per night (bed and breakfast).

Hotel Forsthaus Graseck (tel. 54006; telex 59653) DM 64-104 half pension per person per night.

Aschenbrenner (tel. 58029) DM 55-80 Bed and breakfast.

Hotel Hilleprandt (tel. 2861) DM 54-81—Quiet, family-run hotel within walking distance of the Hausberg ski school. Lower priced rooms begin at approximately DM 350 a week. A good choice for the budget plan.

Haus Hamburg (tel. 3003) DM 34-45—Small bed-and-breakfast guesthouse with 18 beds, located near the middle of town. Particularly quiet location.

Schneefernerhaus (tel. 58011) DM 99-117—On the Zugspitze slope, Germany's highest hotel at 8,692 feet. Unequalled for the skier; otherwise, extremely isolated.

Haus Schell (tel. 2989) DM 47-60—half board. No bath in rooms, go down the hall. Located very close to the station.

Apartments

The popularity of apartments has increased in Garmisch in recent years and many hotels now offer them. The Garmisch tourist office provides an 85-page accommodations booklet, which not only lists available apartments but also includes pictures of some of them. Most interesting of those we saw were the apartments in the Husar section (Alpina Hausbau, tel. 50084) with furnished apartments for two to six people. Prices begin at approximately DM 65-85 a day.

Child care

Larger hotels provide daycare services. In addition, check with the tourist office for a listing of babysitters in the area. Ski kindergarten and ski courses for youths are offered.

Ski kindergarten prices:

for a half day (9 a.m. until 12 or 1 until 4:30 p.m.)	DM 7.50
for one day (9 a.m. until 4:30 p.m.)	DM 19 (includes lunch)

A five-day children's ski course with four hours of instruction daily, including lunch, is approximately DM 95.

Dining

The **Obermühle** in the hotel of the same name is where you'll be served excellent Bavarian specialties and suprisingly good fish.

The **Post Hotel** in Partenkirchen on Ludwigstr. 49 also serves excellent fare.

We were partial to the bountiful, tasty dishes at another **Hotel Post** (tel. 08825-211) in Wallgau, about 12 miles from Garmisch. Traditional alpine decorations, massive wooden tables and chairs and extra-friendly service complement the food.

Of course, you need walk only as far as yet another Post Hotel (tel. 7090) in Garmisch's Marienplatz for excellent dining in the **Poststüberl**.

You can eat less expensively, surrounded by an international group, in **La Fattoria** (tel. 58445) or at the **Chapeau Claque** bistro (tel. 71300).

For a typical Bavarian evening, go to **Gasthof Fraundorfer** (tel. 2176) at Ludwigstrasse 24.

Nightlife

Young and old, continental rich and ski-bum poor—that's the usual mix of people at **Juergen's Pilsbar** on the Marienplatz.

Chapeau Claque, where the food is also good, is a popular meeting spot.

If you want to dance, we suggest the **Luge aus Karin** on Fürstenstr. 3. Try **Clausings Casino** in the former casino on Marienplatz for dancing, or try the **Peacock Bar** in the Sonnenbichel on Friday and Saturday nights.

Getting there

Riem airport on the outskirts of Munich is only an hour away via autobahn. Innsbruck is less than two hours away by car. Rail travelers will find connections to Garmisch excellent.

Other activities

Garmisch is ideal for the visitor who does not want to ski during his entire vacation. Within an hour's drive are world-famous attractions. Chief among them is Munich, the Bavarian capital and Germany's number-one museum city. Above all, visit the Deutsches Museum, the German technical museum that rivals the Smithsonian.

Central Munich, around the Marienplatz, should be included on any tour. Best view of the city is from the nearly 1,000-foot-high television tower on the 1972 Olympics grounds.

Oberammergau, site of the famed Passion Play, is about a half-hour away by bus or car. Here you can visit dozens of woodcarving shops displaying the work of artisans, many of them trained in Oberammergau's national woodcarving school.

Along the road to Oberammergau, take a side trip up the Graswang valley to Schloss Linderhof, the ornate palace built by Ludwig II, the Mad King of Bavaria.

Nearby Mittenwald is famous for its violin makers and Innsbruck, capital of the Austrian Tyrol, is one of the most culturally rich cities in Europe.

Also consider a full-day trip to Neuschwanstein, the most famous of Ludwig's castles (near Füssen) and to Berchtesgaden.

One of Garmisch's most exciting events is the international ski jumping competition at the Olympic stadium on New Year's Day.

Tourist information

Verkehrsamt Garmisch-Partenkirchen, D-8100
Garmisch-Partenkirchen; tel. 08821-1800 or 1806.

Sierra Nevada, Spain

Hard to believe, but there is skiing in southern Spain, less than an hour from Granada. The Sierra Nevada resort has skiing at an altitude of nearly 10,000 feet and brilliant sunshine most of the winter. The resort town itself is modern, basically a sparse cluster of hotels and apartments at the base of the first series of lifts. It is not a traditionally Spanish enclave, nor does it appear in any sense alpine. But if you want to find snow in southern Spain, this is the place to be. ($1.00 = Pts 125)

Where to ski

To be honest, it would be hard to get lost on this mountain unless faced with white-out conditions. The skiing range is not that extensive, but it is wide open, and the runs are long and gentle.

The resort is undergoing a major series of improvements that has added four new lifts. The first of these new lifts opens the upper reaches of the mountain, which previously required a change of lifts to reach. The other lifts add capacity to the slopes below the Veleta peak. Previously, the lifts went to the top of Veleta at 11,384 feet, but the wind was so strong that they rarely remained open.

Borreguiles is the hub of the mountain. Here at the mid-station of the cablecar rising from the town restaurants are grouped together with the ski school.

If you take the Veleta II lift and traverse a little to your right you will enter the Laguna Yeguas, a wide bowl offering more challenging intermediate terrain. When the snow is good, better skiers can drop down the Loma Dilar section of the resort and find some acceptable steeps.

Mountain rating

Don't even imagine that you will find anything to challenge the expert. There are some provocative sections to encounter when skiing off-trail, but for the most part this is a mellow beginning/intermediate paradise. You'll quickly discover that the object here is pure enjoyment, so relax and enjoy the sun.

High season in Spain occurs at Christmas and Easter. In addition, Saturdays, Sundays and holidays draw premium rates.

Ski school

There are few places that are this perfect for learning to ski. The Spanish temperament makes for great initial instruction. What's more, most of the mountain can be handled by beginners after three or four days of instruction. The Spanish Ski School (tel. 480168 or 480511) has 125 instructors and has offices in the main square of the town and at Borreguiles near the middle station of the cablecar. Approximately one-quarter of the instructors speak English.

Individual lessons During high season it cost Pts. 2,600 an hour for one or two students; Pts. 3,200 an hour for three or four students. During middle and low season, the prices are Pts. 2,200 for one or two students and Pts. 2,700 for three or four skiers.

Group lessons During high season you'll pay Pts. 11,000 for one week of three-hour classes each day. During low season the rates drop to Pts. 7,500 for the one-week class. Children's classes are Pts. 8,800 in high season and Pts. 6,000 during low season.

Lift tickets
These are the high-season prices. Low-season prices are about 12 percent lower. Children who were born in 1976 or later get about a 30 percent reduction.

One day	Pts. 2,000
Two days	Pts. 4,000
Six days	Pts. 11,000

Accommodations
All the hotels are relatively new. Add 12 percent value-added tax to each of these rates.

NOTE:The telephone prefix for the resort is 958 from Spain and 58 from outside Spain.

Hotel Melia(Sierra Nevada—tel. 480400; telex 78507)—Daily room rate is Pts. 12,650 for a double room with breakfast.

Hotel Melia (Solynieve—tel. 480300)—Daily rate for a double is Pts. 8,585.

Hotel Nevasur (tel. 480365)—Normal rate: Pts. 5,000 with breakfast.

Hotel Telecabina (tel. 480365)—Normal rate: Pts.4,400 (bed and breakfast).

Apartments
A typical apartment for two people for a week will cost Pts. 31,900 during the middle season. A four-person apartment will cost Pts. 53,500, and a six-person apartment will run Pts. 70,750.

Dining
This tiny village has plenty of restaurants. That's an indication of the importance the Spanish put on a good meal. **Pradollano, Antorcha, Carinvela, Alcazaba** and **Pepe Reyes** all serve traditional Spanish fare. For French food, try **Pourquoi Pas. Cunini** has excellent fish dishes, and **Mama Rosa** and **Fromagerie** serve up Italian cooking.

On the slopes, the best place to head for lunch is **Restaurant Nevasol** near the middle station at Borreguiles.

Nightlife

This is a small place, so you should be able to find out if anything is going on rather quickly. For checking out the scene after skiing, **McClarens** has a pub atmosphere and live music. Or try **Lemon, Don Paco** or **Crescendo**. The leading disco in town is **La Chimenea**—it usually has a good crowd every night.

Child care

The Hotel Melia has a kindergarten, and there is another on the mountain. The mountain kindergarten is open from 10 a.m. until 4 p.m. Rates are Pts. 650 an hour or Pts. 3,700 a day. The ski school will take children from six years to 12 for classes.

Getting there

From Granada there is only one road, and traveling by car is highly recommended. Buses leave Granada each morning at 9 a.m. and return at 5 p.m. The fare is Pts. 300. On Friday, Saturday and Sunday, visitors who want to see beautiful Granada can take buses to the city there from Sierra Nevada at 11 a.m.; return buses leave for the mountain at 4 p.m.

A taxi from Granada to the resort will cost about Pts. 3,500.

Other activities

The location is what makes this resort so special. Within an hour you can reach Granada and visit the fabulous Alhambra and the old center of the city. Malaga is only about two hours away, and the actual Costa del Sol—its chalk-white towns like Salobrena clutching small hilltops—is even closer. Excursions can be made to Jaen, with its massive cathedral and Moorish baths, or Gaudix and Purullena with their troglodyte villages. At nearby Lacalahorra castle you will have to find the gate-keeper in the town below the castle before heading up the hill.

Tourist information

The reservation center and information office has a 24-hour telephone line: (958) 480153.

The provincial tourist office in Granada has responsibility for the resort. Write Patronato Provincial de Turismo de Granada, Pl. Mariana Pineda, 8-3, 18009 Granada, Spain (tel. 958-223527).

In the USA, contact the National Tourist Office of Spain, 665 Fifth Avenue, New York, NY 10022; tel. (212) 759-8822.

For package tours to Sol y Nieve in the Sierra Nevada contact Petrabax, 97-45 Queens Blvd, Suite 505, Rego Park, NY 11374, tel. 800-367-6611 or 718-897-7272.

Andorra

The 1000-year-old principality of Andorra offers an awesome adventure of natural scenery set in a range of the fabled Pyrenees Mountains. A side benefit of the mountain landscape is good intermediate skiing which awaits the visitor with the time and the driving nerve to get to it.

Andorra is a first class excursion, a trip through the mountains which is nearly as exciting as the actual skiing you'll do once you get there. The country is about 90 square miles or 1.5 times larger than England's Isle of Wight. It is ringed by 65 peaks reaching to 10,000-feet. These snow-capped summits isolate the principality from France and Spain and from the pressing uncertainties of the 20th century. Andorra has no standing army and only a small police force.

Andorra is a long way from anywhere, about four hours drive from Barcelona and 15 hours (1,285 kilometers) from central Germany. Getting there is the rub although it's only the last three hours plus of driving which is difficult. Once you have negotiated the climb up into 3000 meter range, crossed Col de Puymont, at 2,400 meters, the highest pass in the Pyrenees and come down into Andorra La Vella, capital of the country, there is a feeling of accomplishment, as if you've reached a place where few travel in winter. Expectations are to see something unique, a blend of 1000 years of Spanish and Franch culture in a landlocked little place that time brushes only gently while elsewhere it rushes at a head-long pace.

Forget that thought. It disappears as soon as you get stuck in a traffic jam that would do Frankfurt or Madrid proud. Perhaps the drivers who never made it to La Vella, those whose crashed vehicles you passed in ravines, or over the side of hairpin curves and in rocky river bottoms, had a bit of good luck mixed with the bad. They didn't have to drive into the city expecting Pyrenees exotica, only to find the golden arches casting a dark shadow across the valley. Not only is there a Big Mac waiting for the traveler, but Best of Buck Owens cassettes and 30-minute A-Team segments of Mr. T and Murdoch swapping insults in Catalan, the local language.

There is a seemingly endless line of rather dirty looking shops, competing for the dollars of tourists, primarily Spanish, who fuel the economy of this mountain-rich, land-poor country. Skiing is the major winter sports activity and the five resorts are somewhere between average and good compared to the better Swiss, French or Austrian alpine stations. It's better skiing than Garmisch, inferior to St. Anton, hopelessly outclassed by Verbier.

Where to ski

The best skiing is at El Tarter/Soldeu and Pal. Both are within 25 minutes of downtown Andorra La Vella. El Tarter and Soldeu interconnect so park your car in the big lot at El Tarter and ride the chair up. In either place lock your car and keep valuables out of sight. Andorra seems to have a deserved reputation for sticky fingered thieves who prey on visitors.

El Tarter-Soldeu is intermediate with a touch of black. The finest runs are the linked mogul fields which seem to go on for miles down to the El Tartar chair.

Pal is the most picturesque of the three, situated above the tiny village of the same name. Everyone skis from the central station, a beautiful stone complex with chairs and poma lifts leading in. On top there are fine runs and two superior mogul fields from the Pic del Cubil summit.

A word of warning about the poma lifts, particularly those at Pal: They are brutal, literally snatching you off the ground when they startup. Take the chairlift when possible. Grau Roig/Pas de la Casa, is the most distant of the slopes, over half an hour by car. The runs are good and the lift system rivals Soldeu/El Tartar for number of ways up the mountain. All areas are subject to extremely high winds.

Mountain rating

Slopes are overwhelmingly intermediate. Soldeu has an excellent beginner area at the top of the first chair, but it is inconvenient to go up from Soldeu because there's a minimum 10-minute walk in ski boots before you reach the first chair.

Ski school

The school does a booming business with French, English and Spanish the three most popular languages for instruction. Pal is the best place for lessons because of the central station where all beginners start and where most of the lifts feed, thus ensuring that everyone in a group will come back together several times during the day.

Soldeu has over 75 instructors in high season and Pal and Grau Roig have about 50 each.

Individual lessons

for 1 hours 92 French francs FF
for each additonal person 20 FF
for 1 day 400 FF

Group lessons

for one day 96 FF
for three days 230 FF
for our days 275 FF
for five days 362 FF

Lift tickets

Despite the closeness of the resorts there is no combined lift ticket, a definite weakness for such a small skiing resort.

Prices at Soldeu are average for the region and are listed for high season. Low season is approximately 10 percent less. All weekend days are considered high season.

one-half day (from 1 p.m.) 62 FF
one day 86 FF
two days 156 FF
three days 234 FF
four days 296 FF

For each additional day add 74 FF. A passport-size photo is required for four or more days.

Accommodations

The city has good hotels but the streets are clogged with traffic, filled with stifling exhaust fumes and generally dirty. Look for a place out of the city on the way to the mountains. The Guillem, in Encamp, about 10 minutes from La Vella and 15 minutes from Soldeu, is modern and clean and quiet, one minute from the main road to the mountain. Daily rates are FF 188.The staff members speak almost no English. Tel. 32133.

To get on the mountain quickly, Parador Canaro at 1,700 meters in Soldeu, tel. 51046, will meet your needs. Daily rate is about 185 FF. For half pension add approximately 160 FF daily. The best mountain hotel we visited was Hostel St. Pere (tel. 51087), a superb little place across from the lifts in El Tartar. They only have half a dozen rooms from about 300 FF per day.

In La Vella the Andorra Palace (tel. 21072) and Andorra Center (tel. 24999) are full-service hotels with daily rates starting at 250

FF. The Eden Roc (tel. 21000), at FF425 for a double, is the most expensive of the group. The President (tel. 22922) has a less central location for shopping. Rates start at 240 FF. The annex to the President is not as well decorated but quieter, one block off the main street of Andorra.

The City Tourist Office, located one level below the main square, the Place of the People, will assist with directions and provide a map showing the location and telephone number of the local hotels. There is also a free guide to hotels and restaurants available from the Tourist Office.

Apartments

There are a substantial number of apartments available in the city and in towns near the slopes. The Tourist Office maintains a lot of apartments. In addition, the agencies listed below can book an apartment for you at a daily rate substantially below hotel prices.

Dining

Spanish customs apply with late meal hours in most places. To dine before 8 p.m. is boorish and around 10 p.m. is best. The best place to get true Catalan specialties is Hostel Calones (tel. 21312). They also have 26 rooms. The finest restaurant in the country is 1900, a deluxe establishment at the end of La Vella where the town meets Escaldes.

Nightlife

The best après-ski atmosphere is right on the slopes in the pubs that dot the ski towns. The biggest favorite with the English-speaking groups, especially the British, is El Duc, in Solde.

After the sun goes down, the action is in La Vella where Feelings, a disco adjacent to the President Hotel, is usually filled. Another is Pacha, near the Place of the People. Festa, nearer the river, is also a popular evening spot. But the best of the discos is Ambit, at Erts, about 20 minutes away near La Massala.

Because of the late closing and meal hours Andorra La Vella hardly springs into action before 10:30 or 11.

Child care

Both ski lessons and kindergarten are offered for children at the resorts. At Soldeu, for example, a five-day ski program for children under 10 is 331 FF. The kindergarten is 48 FF for one three-hour morning or afternoon session.

Five days of kindergarten care for 6 hours daily is 315 FF.

Getting There

Most convenient is to fly to Barcelona and take a special mountain taxi which will cost about $25 per person. If you are driving from Barcelona the trip is about 3 ½ hours. Coming in by car from Perpignan in France, the time is about the same through the other side of the Pyrenees. If you are squeamish about mountain driving on ice and snow, don't bring a car.

Other Activities

Andorra in winter is limited. Shopping is the chief attraction because of its customs free status. Prices on electronic items and clothing are often marked down substantially. But shop carefully because there's a lot of junk crowding the store windows.

The Pyrenees department store, associated with the Printemps stores in France, is a great place to start your shopping. It's near the center of town about a block from the tourist office.

Tourist Information

The Tourist Office (tel. 29345) is in the municipal center one level below the Place of the People. Coming in to town keep following the signs for Andorra La Vella city center.

Bulgaria Pamporovo and Borovets

In the far south of Eastern Europe, tucked between Romania, the Black Sea, Greece and Yugoslavia, lies Bulgaria. While for years it was considered the most secretive and xenophobic nation in Europe, Bulgaria has surprisingly pursued a steady increase in tourism, developing one of Eastern Europe's best tourism infrastructures. Although individual travel is still difficult and infrequent, the group business is well organized with improving hotels, excellent guides and efficient bus transfers.

Bulgaria has two well-developed ski centers—Borovets and Pamporovo. Although some might characterize Vitosha as a resort, it really is only a weekend ski mountain within a 20-minute drive of Sofia. If you're looking for skiing only—and lots of it—Bulgaria cannot really be recommended. Slopes are adequate for day or weekend skiing, but there is not enough to justify a week-long ski vacation for other than lower intermediates and beginners. But in terms of a total experience, Bulgaria offers a vacation that will not be soon forgotten. Besides the "experience," Bulgaria does have one of the best ski packages for beginners, with most instructors speaking excellent English. The country is also the absolute bargain capital of European skiing.

Bulgaria surprisingly draws a phenomenally international mix of cultures seldom found in Western Europe. In Borovets, you'll find groups from Britain, West Germany, Spain and Holland, not to mention Leningrad and Murmansk. There is no common language, but the dancing, laughter and smiles are contagious.

The Bulgarians will also keep you busy day and night. If you claim boredom on this vacation, it is only because you didn't take advantage of the opportunities. One night might be packed with Bulgarian folklore, the next spent sampling 50 or 60 Bulgarian specialties at a cuisine night. Then head out by horse-drawn sleigh to a hunter's lodge where lamb is roasted on a spit, or visit a family where tourists in small groups can enjoy real Bulgarian home-cooked meals. If the skiing is not overly demanding, break for a day and visit the famous Rila Monastery, Sofia or Plovdiv. These "extras" normally cost between $10 and $12.

Within Bulgaria the tourist trade seems to contrast boldly with everyday life styles. Here cities look like they're stuck in a mid-1960s time warp—car models haven't changed and clothing is functional. The resort hotels, however, are firmly planted in the 1980s—restaurants atop TV towers, guests splashing in indoor swimming pools and bright ski fashions can be seen everywhere—even on Soviet visitors. Whereas in the towns there may not be much person-to-person contact, at the resorts, where many Bulgarians speak English, the locals and tourists interact.

NOTE:Be careful about getting snared in the currency black market. Such markets for currency are widespread in Bulgarian resorts with rates up to four times better than the official exchange. You will be approached to exchange money by the chambermaids, elevator attendants, waiters, ski instructors, bus drivers and others. Although we've heard no recent horror stories about tourists being carried off to prison for illegal money exchange, the possiblity is real. If you do get caught, there is little that can be done.

The amount of money any tourist needs to exchange during a group tour is limited. The excursions and purchases at the "Corecom" stores must be paid for in sterling, dollars, travelers checks or any other convertible currency or credit cards. Changing money through Balkan-Tourist will allow an exchange bonus that is designed to limit the black market. When your money is exchanged you will receive a receipt. Keep it; you will need it to change your money back before you leave Bulgaria.

One other note: The duty-free store in the Sofia airport is perhaps the least expensive we have visited.

Passports and visas—Passports are necessary. Anyone ariving with a group of six or more, does not need a visa. If you plan to travel individually, contact the Bulgarian embassy in Washington, D.C., Toronto, Canada or London. Balkan-Tourist will also assist.

You will be given a white visa card, which you must keep with you during your travels through Bulgaria. This card is essentially an internal passport for Bulgaria and must be stamped by each hotel you visit. It then serves as your exit card when ready to leave the country.

Borovets

Borovets is only about 50 miles south of Sofia. The skiing in Borovets is split between the Sitnjakovo sector rising directly in front of the new Hotel Rila and the Jastrebets area, reached by a 20-minute ride on a gondola lift that stretches for more than three miles. Sitnjakovo's runs are for lower intermediates and beginners. Be prepared to do a bit of pushing to make it from one valley to the next. The last quarter of the run splits into four. The area is great for beginners looking for confidence or for lower intermediates who are practicing technique, but any expert will make two runs and probably have little interest in repeating the experience unless he's with a good-time group.

The Jastrebets sector provides the longest runs and is reached by a very long gondola. The distance is over three miles and the ride takes 20 minutes. The gondola is next to the Ela Hotel, about a three-minute walk from the Hotel Rila. The transfer to the five parallel lifts serving the slope behind Jastrebets requires a bit of a walk. These five parallel button lifts offer a series of short intermediate runs that have been cut through tough mountain brush.

The farthest lift is naturally the least crowded. The only way to reach it is by working across all lifts, but a skier can ski down the ridge past the five lifts to return to the gondola upper station. A climb over the peak is necessary before heading down the main slope into town. The long, three- and four-mile runs back into the resort are the highpoint of Borovets.

Accommodations The French-built Rila, Borovets' newest hotel, is close to the lifts but has no disco or pool. Hotel Breza, Hotel Bor and Hotel Ela all get good comments from guests. The Bor is the most desirable after the Rila; it is also the best for nightlife. The Hotel Sarnokov has just been completed by a Polish group and enjoys a spot in the center of the resort.

The major difference between Borovets and Pamporovo is that the former is much more spread out. This is true of the ski runs and the hotels. From the Rila to the Hotel Bor is a good 10-minute walk, while in Pamporovo all hotels are clustered together and connected by underground passageways. Pamporovo also has major resort-wide get-togethers, which are not duplicated in Borovets where the tour groups remain more autonomous.

Nightlife There are discos in the Hotel Mura and Hotel Mousala. You'll also find a live band playing everything from rock'n'roll to polka music in the basement of the Hotel Bor. After the discos close, head to the wine bar under the tourist information office across the parking lot from the Hotel Bor.

Pamporovo

Pamporovo is a more tightly knit resort than Borovets. Whereas Borovets has woods for walking between the hotels and spread-out skiing, in Pamporovo the hotels are clustered and the skiing area is compact. The hotels are about a 20-minute walk from the slopes. Shuttle buses run skiers back and forth between the hotels and lifts. There is also a ski storage area at the base of the lift system, which means you won't have to carry equipment back to the hotel.

Pamporovo is an excellent resort for an intermediate who wants to have time to practice and improve on more challenging steeps. It also has excellent nursery slopes for the beginners and plenty of slopes for the average skier to make major improvements during a week of lessons. There are some challenges for experts. As in Borovets, this is not a resort for advanced intermediates and experts who expect to cruise.

There is a beautiful view from the TV tower at the top of the mountain. The entrance fee is redeemable against purchases in the cafe.

Accommodations

The lead hotel, especially for English-speaking groups, is the Perelik. Pamporovo has more tourist facilities completed than Borovets, with an indoor pool in the Perelik and another in the nearby Hotel Smolyan, plus a bowling alley in the Perelik. The underground connections between the hotels also make the nightlife circuit more accessible.

Ski school, lift tickets, etc.

For beginners and lower level intermediates there is an excellent ski school. The instructors speak English, and the slopes lend themselves to beginners and lower intermediates. The prices for ski lessons are in the range of $35 or $24 a week, or $66 (£44) for two weeks. Children's lessons cost $22 (£15) a week and $45 (£29). **Lift tickets:** Six days—$27 (£18); 13 days—$48 (£35). For children, prices are $22 (£15) for six days and $44 (£29) for 13 days.

Equipment rentals

The equipment provided by the Bulgarian resorts is of good quality. But make sure the ski shop prepares your skis before you walk off with them. Getting to the top of the mountain and then discovering that the bottoms of you skis look as if they have been spread with a hair-growing elixer can make for a very unpleasant and difficult run down the mountain. We also suggest that you do a self-test to ensure that you can twist out of your binding—there is virtually no binding check unless you ask specifically for one.

Child care

Both resorts have excellent child care facilities. Check with your group leader for specifics.

Tourist information

All tours into Bulgaria are controlled through Balkan-Tourist. Even independent operators work in conjunction with Balkan-Tourist, which in Britain and the United States also acts as the national tourist office of Bulgaria.

In Britain, contact: Balkan Holidays Ltd., Sofia House, 19 Conduit Street, London W1R 9TD; administration telephone: (01) 491 4499; bookings telephone: (01) 493 8612; telex 262923.

In the United States: Balkan Holidays/USA/Ltd., 161 East 81st Street, New York, NY 10028; tel. (212) 722-1110 or 722-7626; telex 429767.

Yugoslavia

Yugoslavia has for years had a strong skiing tradition. But it was only with the 1984 Winter Olympics that the country became known as a real skier's destination.

It is in the north, where the Alps spill over from Italy and Austria, that skiing has come of age. Sarajevo, the site of the 1984 games, virtually did not exist as a ski resort before the games were held. Since then facilities have been developed at an accelerated pace. And three hours south of Belgrade, the Yugoslavs are developing a new resort, Kopaonik, virtually from scratch.

Ski Europe traveled to Yugoslavia to see what has developed in this budget holiday ski arena. We cover Kranjska Gora and the resorts of Sarajevo in detail and offer some observations on the still developing resort of Kopaonik.

Note: Prices are not consistently in Yugoslav dinars—Most are in West German marks (DM) or in dollars and sterling. This is because Yugoslavia's pricing for non-Yugoslavs has been formulated in foreign currencies.

Kopaonik

Accommodations

This resort, set in a natural forest in the rolling hills of southern Yugoslavia, has been created where once only pine trees stood watch. Five new hotels have been built. The Baciste and the Srebrnac are at either end of the area. Both are a long walk from the center of Kopaonik. Both have good facilities and self-contained evening entertainment with dancing and snacks. The "center" of Kopaonik is a group of new condominiums and three hotels. This tourist complex will feature an open market in the courtyard, and dozens of small stores will ring the courtyard as well. The Hotel Karavan is perhaps the best and most centrally located in the resort.

The skiing

Some 20 lifts open a lot of skiing area. The accent is on beginner and intermediate traffic, for although there is a section suitable for experts, the offerings are meager.

The verdict

A good resort for groups made up of people who get along well with one another. There is no life outside the hotels and apartment complex. Beginners will be happy, intermediates should leave smiling, and experts will wonder why they didn't spend the extra money and find a place where they could really ski.

Kranjska Gora

The largest ski resort in the northern Yugoslavian republic of Slovenija is tucked tightly against the Italian border to the west and the Austrian border to the north. Kranjska Gora is an alpine resort in every sense of the word.

The town, clustered around the old onion-shaped dome of the Cerkev church, is small—a 10-minute walk is all it takes to wander from one end to the other. Every year this resort hosts one of the first World Cup races of the circuit. Although its altitude is low (3,986-5,988 feet) and most of the runs relatively short, skiing can be enjoyable, demanding and far-ranging, thanks to an interconnected lift system stretching from the town center to nearby Podkoren and Planica.

Where to ski

Kranjska Gora's skiing embraces beginner, intermediate and expert sections. The only difficulty for those in the advanced beginner levels or who are lower intermediates is the shift from the mild, beginner slopes outside the Kranjska Gora hotels to the true intermediate slopes in the Planica section. Between these two sides of the ski area lie the FIS Slalom and Giant Slalom courses. Any traverse requires negotiating several steep drops, which will either offer a good test of skiing skills or of the waterproofing of your ski suits. Perhaps the best solution is to take the free shuttle bus from Kranjska Gora to the base of the Podkoren/Planica lifts.

For experts the trails are very limited but challenging. The slalom and giant slalom courses drop through the center of the area. For off-trail enthusiasts there is some very tight, steep skiing within the trees. The championship runs are served by a very slow single chairlift (which was to have been upgraded to a double-chair last season), another single chairlift linking central Kranjska Gora with the FIS and a button-lift. The lifts are slow, but with almost no waiting time in the area during weekdays, the total time to get up to the starting point of the slalom run is just over 10 minutes.

Mountain rating

Kranjska Gora has potential to become an excellent overall resort with some new lift construction. But for the moment, tour operators bill Kranjska Gora as one of the best places to learn to ski.

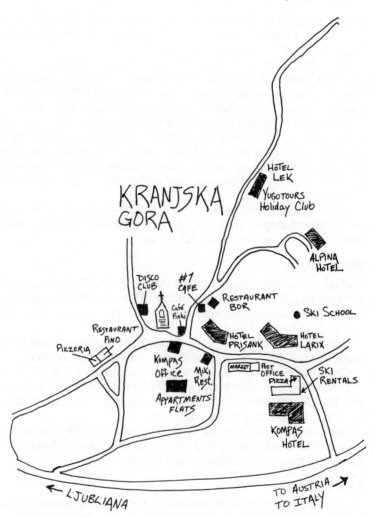

KRANJSKA GORA

The mild slopes are just outside most of the hotels. The ski school, according to reports from legions of beginners, is very good, with plenty of English-speaking instructors.

The beginner lifts are extensive and crowded with ski school students. Slopes reserved for "ski babies" are cordoned off to all except budding skiers learning the basics. Tourist officials estimate that more than 70 percent of the visitors here are beginners.

The most challenging sections of the mountain are empty. But, unfortunately, other than for the FIS slalom and giant slalom, it is poorly developed and poorly serviced by lifts. And while plans exist to extend the area and replace all single chairs with double or triple chairlifts, unless you hear differently, plan on the same slow lifts.

Experts may be tempted to stay in Podkoren within easy reach of the expert slopes. However, the nightlife there is non-existent and facilities relatively underdeveloped.

Ski school

The ski school specializes in teaching beginners. Experts wanting a lesson in off-trail or racing on the FIS runs virtually cause instructors to fight among one another for the opportunity to get out and ski hard.

Two ski schools in town have similar prices: Gorenjks and Kompas. Kompas seems to do more work with English-speakers.

Group lessons—for five days (two hours a day), DM 62.

Private lessons—for one hour, DM 25 per person; for two people, DM 20 per person; for three people, DM 15 per person; for four people, DM 10 per person.

Sign up in your hotel or with your tour guides. The school assembly area is located behind the Hotel Prisank and Hotel Larix. Currently there is no children's ski school.

Lift tickets

Group tour skiers obtain tickets through their group leaders. Some tickets require photos, some require payment in foreign currency, some you can only buy with a Yugoslav ID card. Current rates for non-Yugoslavs are: one day—Din. 6,000; three days—DM 54; six days—DM 106; seven days—DM 120; 13 days—DM 203; 14 days—DM 215.

If you come with a car, look into purchasing the special "Ski 3 Regions" international ski pass, which covers lifts in Italy and Austria, as well as Yugoslavia. The pass is only sold by the week for DM 140 per six skiing days out of seven, allowing a day for bad weather or rest. This ticket offers 76 drag lifts, 23 chairlifts and six cablecars in nine different resorts. It's only available from hotels in Yugoslavia.

The three-country pass sounds appealing and makes a good souvenir, but skiers are limited to only two days of skiing outside Yugoslavia. It may be less expensive to buy a four-day pass for Kranjska Gora, then purchase a day pass for the other resorts you visit. Buying your lift passes in this way offers more flexibility and insurance against bad weather.

Accommodations

Kranjska Gora does a remarkably good job of organizing its hotels and their staff. In almost all cases the least expensive lodging arrangements are made through a tour agency, such as Yugotours. These arrangements can be made for "ground only," eliminating the need to include airfare in the price.

The hotels are listed below with the current daily DM prices per person. The rates are for half board, based on double occupancy from early January to mid-March

Kompas—DM 69; **Larix**—DM 68; **Hotel Lek**—DM 68. These three hotels offer the best facilities in town, including pool, sauna, discos, bars and bowling alleys. Larix is a bit closer to the slopes, but Kompas has better après ski, and Lek has the Holiday Club.

Hotel Alpina—DM 57. Almost as good as Kompas and Larix, but Alpina is a bit of a walk from the town center.

Prisank—DM 53. Excellent rooms and food, also the closest hotel to the ski school. Its only limitations are no pool or sauna.

The **Kranjska Gora** and **Pensione Zrenjanin** are not in most tour programs. They offer good lodging for budget-conscious skiers who come into town on their own. Expect to pay around DM 50 a night.

If you arrive—or plan to arrive—without a group, call Kompas Agency (tel. 064- 88437) to make reservations.

Apartments

These constitute a new addition to Kranjska Gora. The best picks in town are the "Apartments Gorenjka,"which are centrally located. Each apartment sleeps from four to six very comfortably. Expect to pay DM 120 a day.

The tiny dorf of Podkoren is just two kilometers from Kranjska Gora. Here the Family Sedej has restored an old farmhouse and turned it into apartments. The house name is "Apartment Serc." Expect to pay about DM 21 per person a day. This small, family-run operation makes an extra effort to provide a traditional Slovenjan experience for their guests. Homemade "Ustek," a herbal schnapps, is served in the bar to fight the chills when the guests come back from the slopes. Reservations can be made by calling Andrej or Irena Sedej at (064) 88161. (Both speak excellent English.) Or call Kompas Agency (tel. 064-88437).

Dining

Even if you're locked into a half-board arrangement, make an effort to experience the Yugoslavian cuisine. Kranjska Gora offers a wide range of restaurants.

Restaurant Miki is best known for fish dishes. **Restaurant Milka**, about a 15-minute walk into the mountains, has good steaks. Next door on a tiny lake is **Restaurant Jasna**. **Restaurant Bor** offers traditional food and is located just behind Hotel Prisank.

For our money, the best pizza in town can be found at **Pizzeria Kompas**, adjacent to the hotel of the same name. Others rave about pizza from **Pizzeria Pino** in the center of town.

The restaurant at the top of Vitranc is not noted for its food, but does provide a beautiful view and great spring sunbathing when the weather is clear.

Nightlife

Kranjska Gora is not in the running for nightlife capital of Europe, but it does provide a healthy environment for night entertainment.

The main hotels all have discos or live bands that perform until at least 2 a.m. If people are still dancing then, the bars usually find a way to stay open a bit longer. The **Kompas Nightbar** can be fun. Only a few children hang out early in the evening. The disco in the Larix gets overrun with kids early in the night, and they seem to linger until midnight and often later.

The only independent disco is the **Club** in the center of town. It normally has the best action, beginning at about 11 p.m.

For an earlier rendezvous, try **Cafe No. 1** near the Prisank.

Yugotours has organized a **Holiday Club** in the basement of the Hotel Lek. It offers a good English-speaking crowd, relatively inexpensive beer, no cover charge and an English disk jockey, Anthony, who is responsible for making sure the guests have fun. Consequently, there are plenty of contests and games that force people to meet one another.

Child care

Kranjska Gora fails in providing good daycare. There is no organized children's kindergarten, nor is there an organized nursery.
If tourists are in a group of six or more, special arrangements will
be made for children.

Other activities

There are numerous organized tours to surrounding areas. Tours
to Nassfeld in Austria for a day of good intermediate and advanced
skiing are organized for DM 23; and into Italy to Sella Nevea for
DM 28. Ski passes are not included in these prices.

Venice is three and a half hours away, and day tours cost DM
83. Tarvisio tours, also in Italy, cost DM 20.

Visits to the Caves of Postojna and the city of Ljubljana take a
full day and cost DM 65.

Tourist information

There is an official tourist office (tel.064-88768) in the shopping
center across from the Larix Hotel.

The best bet is to inquire with the tour representatives, or check
the tourist information boards set up in the hotel lobbies.

Sarajevo

This city has long been at one of the major cultural crossroads—between Turkish and Austrian empires, between Eastern and Western Roman Empires and between Moslem, Jewish and Christian religions. But only since the 1984 Winter Olympics has it been considered a ski resort. Virtually all its resort facilities have been constructed in the last four years. The city itself is not a resort—the skiing is done at two centers both about 30 kilometers from the town. Jahorina, at an altitude of 5,478 feet, hosted the women's downhill 1984 Olympic events. Bjelasnica, 27 kilometers to the northwest and with an altitude of 4,134 feet, was the site of the men's downhill events.

Jahorina is better developed in terms of hotels and lifts than Bjelasnica. It has four excellent hotels and normally enjoys good weather.

Bjelasnica faces much more severe weather; in January and early February the resort is often partially closed due to storms and high winds. Plan any skiing here in late February or March. The one international-level hotel is located approximately four kilometers from the slopes. Frequent bus service shuttles skiers to the lifts.

Where to ski

Jahorina, with 11 lifts, offers about two dozen short runs. This is not a cruiser's paradise. With the main hotels at your back, the most challenging and the longest runs are to the far left.

Bjelasnica, which looks smaller on the few brochure lift maps, is actually a far more challenging mountain for intermediate and expert skiers. The runs are much longer and the vertical drop significantly greater than at Jahorina. If you enjoy a challenging cruise when the weather is good, this is a beautiful mountain.

Overall, however, Jahorina has the best support facilities and far better weather. Plan to stay in Jahorina and take a couple of day trips to Bjelasnica for more demanding skiing.

For cross-country fans, Mt. Igman, attached to the Bjelasnica area, has over 50 kilometers of prepared trails. Jahorina has none.

Mountain rating

Jahorina will keep any intermediate or beginner happy for a week. The expert can find some real challenges, but they are short-lived and limited. Beginners have no choice—head for Jahorina.

Bjelasnica is a great mountain, but aside from limited facilities, the major drawback is that it really isn't suitable for beginners or lower intermediates.

Ski school and lift tickets

Ski school for five days (two hours a day) will cost about $55, according to the U.S. brochure, and £22.50, according to the British brochure. Lift tickets good for both Jahorina and Bjelasnica for six days cost $30 or £21.

Accommodations

The best single hotel is the **Hotel Igman** in Bjelasnica. Its isolation forces it to be self-contained. In Jahorina, the three main hotels are close to one another. The **Bistrica** offers the most facilities, including a pool and bowling alley. The **Jahorina** and **Kosuta** are also nice, but neither has a pool. The Jahorina does boast the only after-midnight disco and a mediocre pizzeria. The **Hotel Vucko**, about three kilometers down the mountain, has only 24 beds and was the lodge of the King of Sweden during the Olympic Games. It offers a quiet, exclusive lodgings, with a great restaurant and lifts only a few steps from the lodge. All hotels in Jahorina are very convenient to the lifts.

Nightlife

After nine, music with a live band starts in the Hotel Bistrica. This is the place to be until midnight when the disco in the Hotel Jahorina revs up.

The Bistrica is a good time with dance contests and plenty of room to move. The disco is smoky and packed shoulder-to-shoulder most of the time ... but it is the only late-night game in the resort. The Jahorina also has a small casino where you may win or lose big money.

Child care

Jahorina has a children's ski school and a kindergarten. Bjelasnica has no facilities for child care.

Other activities

A bobsled run on the Olympic course is available for amateur riders. Your hotel can make arrangements.

There is a pool and bowling alley in the Hotel Bistrica.

The major non-skiing activity is a visit to Sarajevo. Buses depart both resorts four times a day for Sarajevo, and tour groups make the city tour regularly. A walk through the old town is a step into a Middle Eastern world. The dozens of mosques are leftovers from the days of Turkish rule when it was decreed that there should be one mosque for every 40 houses. Adjacent, the Turkish bazaar and the imperial buildings of the Austrians rise in stark contrast.

Visit the corner where the archduke was assassinated, making the start of World War I. Then head for the covered market, which has been restored with traditional stalls. Around the corner, visit the Gazi-Husrevbeg Mosque and then head down the street to Baśćarśija. Just off Marshall Tito street, be sure to visit the Old Serbian Orthodox church and see its priceless icons.

If you want a snack, try Cevapćići with drinkable yoghurt at "Cevapćiniza Ismet Kapitanović" on Prote Bakovića 12. For a more substantial meal, try "Morića-han" on Saraći 77, or "Daire" at Halsći 5. Both are in restored buildings in the center of the old town.

Tourist information

The tourist office is located on Marshall Tito street next to the Catholic church.

In the resorts, check the tour group information boards for all other information, or ask your group leader.

National Tourist Offices

Austria National Tourist Office

500 Fifth Ave.
New York, NY 10110
(212) 944-6880

500 N. Michigan Ave.
Chicago, IL 60611
(312) 644-5556

11601 Wilshire Blvd.
Los Angeles, CA 90025
(213) 477-3332

2 Bloor St. East, Suite 3330
Toronto, Canada
(416) 593-4717

30 St. George Street
London W1R 9FA
01-629-0461

Austrian snow reports in USA: From mid-December to early April, 24 hours per day: (212) 944-6917 and on West Coast: (213) 479-0940.

Swiss National Tourist Office

608 Fifth Ave.
New York, NY 10020
(212) 757-5944

104 S. Michigan Ave.
Chicago, IL 60603
(312) 641-0050

250 Stockton St.
San Francisco, CA 94108
(415) 362-2260

Commerce Court Postal Station
Suite 2015, Commerce Court West
Toronto, Canada
(416) 868-0584
Swiss Center, 1 New Coventry St.
London, W1V 8EE
01-734-1921

Italian Government Tourist Office (E.N.I.T.)

630 Fifth Avenue
New York, NY 10111
(212) 245-4822

360 Post St. #801
San Francisco, CA 94108
(415) 392-6206

3 Place Ville Marie
Montréal, Canada
(514) 866-7667

1 Princess Street
London W1R 7RA
01-408-1254

French Government Tourist Office

610 Fifth Avenue
New York, NY 10020
(212) 757-1125

9401 Wilshire Blvd. #840
Beverly Hills, CA 90212
(213) 271-6665

Box 8, 1 Dundas St. West
Toronto, Canada
(416) 593-4717

178 Picadilly
London W1V 0AL
01-491-7622

German National Tourist Office

747 Third Avenue
New York, NY 10017
(212) 308-3300

444 S. Flower St. #2230
Los Angeles, CA 90071
(213) 688-7332

61 Conduit Street
London W1R 0EN
01-734-2600

National Tourist Office of Spain

665 Fifth Avenue
New York, NY 10022
(212) 729-8822

57 St. James's Street
London SW1A 1LD
01-499-0901

Balkan Holidays

161 East 86th St.
New York, NY 10028
(212) 722-1110

Sofia House, 19 Conduit St.
London W1R 9TD
01-491-4499

Yugotours

350 Fifth Ave. Suite 2901
New York, NY 10118
(212) 563-2400

3440 Wilshire Blvd. Suite 206
Los Angeles, CA 90010
(213) 383-2438

150 Regent Street
London W1R 6BB
01-734-7321